Psychodynamic Perspectives on Working with Children, Families, and Schools

The New Imago: Series in Theoretical, Clinical, and Applied Psychoanalysis

Series Editor: Jon Mills, Canadian Psychological Association

The New Imago: Series in Theoretical, Clinical, and Applied Psychoanalysis is a scholarly and professional publishing imprint devoted to all aspects of psychoanalytic inquiry and research in theoretical, clinical, philosophical, and applied psychoanalysis. It is inclusive in focus, hence fostering a spirit of plurality, respect, and tolerance across the psychoanalytic domain. The series aspires to promote open and thoughtful dialogue across disciplinary and interdisciplinary fields in mental health, the humanities, and the social and behavioral sciences. It furthermore wishes to advance psychoanalytic thought and extend its applications to serve greater society, diverse cultures, and the public at large. The editorial board is comprised of the most noted and celebrated analysts, scholars, and academics in the English speaking world and is representative of every major school in the history of psychoanalytic thought.

Titles in Series:

Psychodynamic Perspectives on Working with Children, Families, and Schools, edited by Michael O'Loughlin

Working with Trauma: Lessons from Bion and Lacan, by Marilyn Charles

Desire, Self, Mind, and the Psychotherapies: Unifying Psychological Scienceand Psychoanalysis by R. Coleman Curtis

In Freud's Tracks: Conversations from the Journal of European Analysis, edited by Sergio Benvenuto and Anthony Molino

Searching for the Perfect Woman: The Story of a Complete Psychoanalysis, by Vamik D. Volkan with J. Christopher Fowler

Hypocrisy Unmasked: Dissociation, Shame, and the Ethics of Inauthenticity, by Ronald C. Naso

Psychodynamic Perspectives on Working with Children, Families, and Schools

Edited by
Michael O'Loughlin, PhD

JASON ARONSON
Lanham • Boulder • New York • Toronto • Plymouth, UK

Published by Jason Aronson
A wholly owned subsidiary of The Rowman & Littlefield Publishing Group, Inc.
4501 Forbes Boulevard, Suite 200, Lanham, Maryland 20706
www.rowman.com

10 Thornbury Road, Plymouth PL6 7PP, United Kingdom

British Library Cataloguing in Publication Information Available

Library of Congress Cataloging-in-Publication Data

Psychodynamic perspectives on working with children, families, and schools / edited by Michael O'Loughlin.
p. cm.
Includes bibliographical references and index.
ISBN 978-0-7657-0921-9 (cloth : alk. paper) -- ISBN 978-0-7657-0922-6 (electronic)
Psychoanalysis and education. 2. Educational psychology. 3. Psychodynamic psychotherapy. 4. Child development. 5. Child psychology. 6. School psychology. I. O'Loughlin, Michael.
LB1092.P84 2013
370.15--dc23
2012037061

The paper used in this publication meets the minimum requirements of American National Standard for Information Sciences Permanence of Paper for Printed Library Materials, ANSI/NISO Z39.48-1992.

Printed in the United States of America

Contents

Acknowledgments

The work in this book and its companion volume, *The Uses of Psychoanalysis in Working with Children's Emotional Lives,* represent a collaboration of more than fifty contributors. For each of those writers the work has been driven by a desire to share a vision of professional practice. Since the ideas in these two volumes are intimately tied in with the professional practices of the contributors, the writing is particularly intimate. I wish to thank all of the authors for their contributions and I particularly want to note the passing of Bertram Cohler in May 2012. The book that Bert edited with Kay Field and Glorye Wool in 1989, *Learning and Education: Psychoanalytic Perspectives,* served as inspiration for this book project. Happily, Bert had completed his chapter with his co-authors, and it appears in *The Uses of Psychoanalysis in Working with Children's Emotional Lives*. I wish to thank my friend and colleague Marilyn Charles of Austen Riggs Center for directing me to Jon Mills, and deep thanks to Jon for accepting both books in The New Imago series that he edits for Jason Aronson. My work on these books has been supported particularly by members of the *Schools Committee* of *The American Psychoanalytic Association*, and in particular I thank Daniel Frank, who graciously agreed to write a foreword for this book. Thanks also to colleagues in the *Association for the Psychoanalysis of Culture and Society* [APCS] and in *Reconceptualizing Research in Early Childhood Education* [RECE] who are tremendous sources of intellectual support and friendship. I wish to thank Cheryl Huber, Meredith Musgnug, Melodie Piciullo, and Raquel Castello for assistance with proofreading and index preparation. Thanks to my editor, Amy King, at Jason Aronson/Rowman & Littlefield for her professionalism and support of the work, and thanks, too, to production editor Lindsey Frederick. Finally, thanks to my wife, Margaret Healy, who has endured my preoccupation with this project with unwavering support.

Foreword

Daniel B. Frank

America desperately needs a renewed humanistic vision to inspire school principals and teachers to better educate our nation's children and adolescents. Current government policies mandate public school principals to require teachers to restrict themselves to teach only to the test. This policy is damaging to the intellectual and emotional development of young people, to the personal and professional spirits of their teachers, and, consequently, to the best interests of our country. While improving test scores is a measure to assess learning so skilled, talented, and confident Americans can compete in a tough global economy, it cannot be the primary goal of education in a democracy.

Instead, as Franz Alexander, the founding director of Chicago's Institute for Psychoanalysis, knew long ago, the future of democracy rests in the emotional maturity of its citizens to think critically, reflect thoroughly, and act empathically. John Dewey knew this too. In his 1934 essay, "*Educating for a Changing Social Order,*" Dewey argued that, in a democracy, schooling must promote "intelligent skepticism." This habit of mind in the lives of students is cultivated by classroom teachers who believe young people should be educated in a manner that teaches and encourages them to question the ways things are and imagine new possibilities.

This democratic vision for American education calls on us as educators, clinicians, and citizens to advocate for schools to have the resources to play a vital role in partnering with parents to educate each new generation of students to grow in character with a coherent sense of self and responsible citizenship. We must insist that schools become life-changing places. Young people grow in hope and confidence when their school experience makes them feel known, encouraged and affirmed in their efforts to master skills and knowledge through real, trusted relationships with teachers and classmates.

In this way, the future of American education rests less in the resources our nation devotes to improving standardized test scores, and far more in our public commitment to support the development of caring and trusted human relationships within school communities—among students, educators, and parents. This focus requires a radical shift in our national priorities and the allocation of resources. It is a commitment that must include creating smaller class sizes so empathic teachers can know their students and their growing interests and passions. Principals, too, must be freed to use their limited resources to pursue excellence by creating engaging and inspiring school cultures led by teachers who will educate the whole child—in mind, heart, body, and spirit through academics and the arts. And this commitment must also include supporting the growth and development of children in their earliest years, even before they are old enough to enter school, so that they can become ready to succeed in school.

Fortunately, a growing number of educators, clinicians, and organizational consultants are prepared to help develop this vision for American education. They understand the central role emotions play in the learning process and in the learning organization we call school. Informed with a range of psychoanalytic concepts, and with an understanding of psychoanalysis as a method of inquiry into human experience, these reflective practitioners have essential insights regarding how children, adolescents, and adults experience the normal idealizations, inevitable disillusionments, and acts of reparation that structure everyday school life.

This volume, *Psychodynamic Perspectives on Working with Children, Families, and Schools*, edited by Michael O'Loughlin, contains an impressive array of essays that bring interpretive depth and clarity to the ways adults in schools can attend with attuned care to the emotional and intellectual development of children, adolescents, and their parents, as well as to the inner lives of teachers and school administrators. This collection of papers is a compelling addition to the social scientific literature on applied psychoanalytic thinking in the field of education and schooling. Together, these essays improve our capacity to understand the ways emotions are embedded in how human beings, young and older, organize our subjective experience of learning and teaching in schools.

Learning is no simple matter. Its complexity involves reason and passion; and it takes strenuous emotional work. Learning is more than an individual experience that draws on rational processes of taking in new information. In school, learning is a social experience filled with emotions—excitement and terror, amusement and ambivalence, adventure and shame. Because of this, schools must become more than test-taking or test-failing factories. School leaders must be free to encourage teachers to exercise intimate attention and meaningful resonance in their working relationships with students and parents so they may inspire and engage those in their classrooms to find their own voices, to listen to the voices of others, to develop their own views as well as understand points of view other than their own, to pursue their own passions, and, as Dewey said long ago, to demonstrate the disposition and exercise the skills to "look into things, inquire and examine."

To conduct reasoned and thorough critical and creative inquiry without impulsivity are among the psychological and intellectual skills American schools must foster in the growing characters of its students. And, it is this set of skills that Franz Alexander understood as the emotional foundation for human potential in a democratic society.

With this insightful new volume of psychodynamic perspectives on schooling in hand to guide us, it's time we got busy.

Introduction

Michael O'Loughlin

As well as working with children therapeutically in my capacity as a psychoanalyst, I also work in the preparation of teachers, school psychologists, and clinical psychologists. I have long been struck by the absence of psychoanalytic ways of thinking in conventional professional discourses of schooling. With a few notable exceptions, for the most part the discourses of child development, classroom management, early childhood education, special education, school psychology, and school counseling have constructed notions of children and schooling that are often behaviorist, instrumental, and symptom focused. In the educational arena, curriculum too often focuses on rote acquisition of knowledge; discipline is conceptualized as compliance (Kohn, 1996) and symptoms such as anger, school resistance, oppositionality, etc. are pathologized and reacted to out of context. Children's special needs are often conceptualized instrumentally, and children with complex psychological symptoms or complex social backgrounds are delimited, depersonalized, or simply removed (Books, 1998; Polakow, 1998; Polakow-Suransky, 2000). While this has been true of North America for some time, the biologization and pathologization of psychic distress in children as behavior to be medicated and eliminated, is spreading across the world (O'Loughlin, 2012; Watters, 2011; Whittaker, 2010). The uncritical propagation of the trope of "evidence-based practice" has become a Trojan horse for the introduction of industrial and commercial accountability metrics for evaluating schooling, objectifying children, and reducing the vast possibilities of human development to one high-stakes test score based on dubious psychometrics and to the proffering of pills to those who willfully deviate or fail to measure up.

For a quarter century I have been teaching a course called "The emotional lives of children and the possibility of classroom as community" to teachers and psychologists. I also teach courses on child development, child therapy, and classroom management, all focusing on the emotional quality of children's lives, and on the complexities of transference relationships between children and the adults who care for them.[1] I have found students to be receptive to the person-centered and psychodynamic perspectives we study through fiction, memoir, film, and academic texts, and my students are invariably puzzled that these perspectives rarely form part of the core principles of their preparation. Why are so few psychologists, social workers, and teachers introduced, for example, to the writings of Donald Winnicott, Margaret Mahler, Maud Mannoni, Louise Kaplan, or Selma Fraiberg? Why does Vivian Paley (2004), after a lifetime in the field of early childhood education, have to formulate a plaintive plea for the preservation of the child's imagination in kindergarten? Is it because we are so out of touch with the exquisite vulnerability and beauty of children's minds that we need Joanna Lipper's (1996) beautifully filmed portraits of children to reminds us of the emotional sensitivity, adaptability, and vulnerability of children? What if, instead of manualized therapy and scripted pedagogy, we assisted professionals in using their talents and gifts to work *obliquely* with children (cf. O'Loughlin & Merchant, 2012) so that our services to children speak to desire and imagination instead of demanding rigid conformity and stifling uniformity?

This book, then, was born from the need described above as well as from my own awareness not only of a hallowed tradition of psychoanalytic writing that privileges children's capacities to make their own meanings, use their minds, and draw on resilience in the face of even the most daunting environmental privations, but also because of my knowledge that toiling among us, every day are deeply ethical, caring people who embody a wisdom of practice that includes all of these considerations. When I issued a call for chapters for a proposed volume that would speak to these issues in ways that were grounded, inviting, and practical, I received an overwhelming response and the result is the publication of this book and its companion volume, *The Uses of Psychoanalysis in Working with Children's Emotional Lives.*

In my first year as a teacher I patrolled the school yard, immersed all the while in Paulo Freire's (1970) *Pedagogy of the Pppressed,* which had been recently published. Freire's ideas caused me to elevate my gaze beyond the here-and-now to imagine possible lives for myself and the children in my care that transcended the scripted roles society had laid down both for me and for them. It is my hope that this book and its companion volume may serve that same purpose for early childhood workers, teachers, psychologists, and social workers who believe there must be more to our work than simple, prescriptive solutions that appear designed to prepare children to fit niches rather than to seek hopeful futures for themselves. We can indeed imagine things otherwise (cf. O'Loughlin & Johnson, 2010).

The specific purpose of these collections is to introduce readers to the power of psychodynamic ways of thinking about children and schools. Professionals who work with children psychodynamically draw on diverse frameworks including the work of Anna Freud, the long tradition of the Tavistock Clinic in London, the writings of Melanie Klein, Donald Winnicott and their colleagues, and French analysts in the Lacanian tradition such as Françoise Dolto, Maud Mannoni, and Catherine Mathelin. This work is valuable but often inaccessible to school professionals because the writing is somewhat specialized, and because there is no tradition of teaching such work in professional preparation in those fields. There is also a prejudice that psychoanalysis is neither social nor practical. I believe psychoanalysis is both eminently practical and has powerful things to say about children's social worlds, something this book and its companion volume illustrate persuasively. The purpose of these books, therefore, is to open the door to the possibility of introducing psychodynamic frameworks to early childhood and school professionals and clinicians, working with children so that they may elevate their professional gaze beyond the given to the possible.

For the appropriately skeptical reader, let me note that while psychoanalysis has had a long tradition of social activism, particularly in its earliest days, but continuing into the present (Altman, 1995; Danto, 2005; Moskowitz, 1996; Watkins & Shulman, 2008), the view that the field as a whole has slipped into bourgeois, self-interested complacency is not entirely misplaced. As I noted in a recent paper:

> From a pragmatic perspective, American psychoanalysis ultimately made a grievous miscalculation by hitching its wagon exclusively to psychiatry in the early days. While psychoanalysis had unprecedented influence in psychiatry through the 1950s, the invention of psychopharmacological treatments for psychosis and schizophrenia, and later for depression, anxiety and other supposed disorders, eventually brought American psychoanalysis to the brink of extinction. Robert Whitaker's (2001, 2010) history of the opportunistic shift of psychiatry away from psychoanalysis and toward psychopharmacology documents how institutional psychiatry has virtually abandoned psychoanalysis in favor of more profitable brief medical consultation and a decidedly deterministic and biologized view of mental disturbance as neurochemical in origin. Ethan Watters' (2010) recent book, *Crazy like us: The globalization of the American psyche* underlines how this "victory" is leading to a world-wide colonization of mental health by reductionist biological and psychopharmacological discursive practices.
>
> Academic psychoanalysis appears to still have theoretical vigor, particularly in cultural studies, literary theory, and postcolonial studies, largely thanks to the influence of Lacanian theory. Mainstream American psychoanalysis, however, seems increasingly to be holding a conversation with itself—often a fretful conversation about economic survival. I should add as a side-note here, following Stepansky, that while I freely use the term "American psychoanalysis," there really is no such thing, since, lacking a central vision and strong leadership, the field is highly fractionated with more energy going into battling internal feuds and splitting hairs, than into addressing the potential power and

> relevance of psychoanalysis to understanding and addressing society's problems. I should also add that while Michael Moskowitz (1996), a critical psychoanalyst, would share much of my perspective, he is decidedly more optimistic about the vibrancy and social relevance of American psychoanalysis, particularly the relational branch located at New York University and ideologically similar institutes. However, he and I are in agreement on the radical and liberatory potential of psychoanalysis both as a means of treatment and as a tool of social analysis, or perhaps, more precisely, as a means of treatment *through* social analysis. (O'Loughlin, 2010, ms.)

In keeping with Paul Stepansky's (2009) conclusion in *Psychoanalysis at the Margins*, I believe that psychoanalysis has as much to gain as to give by engaging critically in collaborative work across interdisciplinary boundaries and with professionals in applied fields such as education, child care, social work, and community psychology. I believe the work reported in these two volumes points toward the mutual benefits to be gained from such collaboration and applications.

PSYCHODYNAMIC PERSPECTIVES ON WORKING WITH CHILDREN, FAMILIES, AND SCHOOLS

Authors in this book focus on core themes in the application of psychoanalysis to education; on key psychoanalytic concepts relevant to understanding children; and on understanding and working with children in the contexts of families, cultures, societies, and schooling. The first four chapters deal with conceptual issues in applying psychoanalysis to work with children and school. The next five chapters focus on contextual issues, particularly ancestral, cultural, and familial considerations in understanding and working with children and families. These chapters explicitly address the usefulness of psychoanalytic thinking in addressing the sociohistorical contexts of suffering in the lives of children and families. The remaining chapters focus specifically on schooling as a context, and the chapter authors bring a rich variety of lenses to bear on analyzing schooling.

The book opens with Jonathan Cohen's survey of historical and contemporary relationships between educators and psychoanalysts. For readers interested in understanding either the historic relationship between psychoanalysts and educators, or readers who are interested in knowing about current psychoanalytically based programmatic efforts to work with children in schools, this chapter is an essential resource. In the chapter Jonathan notes that because of their shared mission, psychoanalysts and educators ought to be natural allies. Jonathan analyzes in great detail the many ways psychoanalysts have sough to contribute to improving education including the creation of psychoanalytically informed schools; psychoanalyst serving as consultants to teachers and school systems; the development of systematic programs of services and research that are built around core psychoanalytic and socio-emotional educational principles; and the role of psychoanalysts in teacher education. In his capacity as director of the National School Climate Center, Jonathan explains the mission of that organization, details its programmatic and research efforts, and, while successfully navigating the treacherous waters of "evidence-based" mandates for "reliable, replicable research," Jonathan also demonstrates an acute self-reflexivity about the limitations of such approaches when it comes to constructing humane learning communities for children and teachers. As Jonathan notes, when parents are asked what they most wish for from schooling, "Their answers have been very consistent: they want their children/students to be life long learners, to be responsible, caring members of the community who can work and love and participate in a democracy. Although they do occasionally mention wanting their child to get into a "good college" this is always secondary to the social, emotional, and ethical goals that are in the forefront of the adults' dreams and wishes for their children." Echoing my comments earlier, Jonathan concludes with a plea for psychoanalysts to abandon the snobbery and myopia that have for long characterized the field, and view the applications of psychoanalysis to pedagogical problems not as inferior or lesser, but as of great importance to our world.

Patrick Lewis, writing with a deep sensibility for children's lives, and locating his work beautifully in his own teaching life, begins by exploring how early education and child development has shifted from a foundation of *description* to a core principle of *prescription*, of the kind embedded, for example, in the core instructional principles of Developmentally Appropriate Practice, as expounded by the National Association for the Education of Young Children. Patrick speaks of a troubling "biomedical" approach to literacy, again with the emphasis on prescription rather than on an approach that might build upon the natural narrative capabilities of children. Following Dwayne Huebner, Patrick beautifully captures the image of the pedagogical project with children as "a journey into story . . . where child, teacher, and family share a page, a passage, a chapter in each other's lives in a reciprocal journey of becoming." Patrick is not a psychoanalyst. He is a professor of early education. His work, joining these two important disciplines with its emphasis on heremeneutics, meaning making, and the power of narrative, is highly synchronous with the philosophy underlying analytic work and provides a powerful illustration of the dynamic that results at the nexus of psychoanalysis and education.

Karen Lombardi draws on her extensive knowledge of Melanie Klein's work to explore what must be, for educators, one of the core concepts of psychoanalysis, namely the capacity to be curious about knowing, what Klein termed "the epistemophilic instinct." Karen addresses the risk of children ventriloquating adult demand rather than seeking to come to ask their own questions and pursue their own answers. Her chapter is an antidote to the all-pervasive educational discourse that reduces thinking to either regurgitation or to trudging down paths well-trod by others. Karen moves on to explore Bion's theory of thinking and particularly the form of thought disorder that occurs in what Bion calls *minus K* and *no K* states of mind. Karen poses the question, "How may the child be unburdened from the care of the parental unconscious?" and argues, both theoretically, and in two richly illustrative case studies, for the replacement of "driven curiosity" with what she calls "creative curiosity."

In chapter 4, Derek Bunyard brings his formidable theoretical and historical understanding of psychoanalysis to bear in describing the work of renowned French analyst Françoise Dolto. "Renowned" may be a tricky term here, as, while Dolto was a household name in her native France, very few of her works have been translated into English and she is a comparative unknown in English-speaking countries. Dolto became famous in France in part for radio broadcasts in which she took questions from parents, and in part because of her development of *Maison Verte* ("Green Rooms"), which rapidly spread throughout France as drop-in storefront resource centers for parents and their young children. As Derek deftly illustrates, Dolto's work defies simple classification. Although she worked alongside Lacan for many more years than any other co-worker, being actively involved in each of the radical institutional changes he brought about, she never directly cited his work in her writing, and she hewed to an independent line of thinking. In addition, as an avowedly devoted Roman Catholic, Dolto had to reconcile the principles of her faith with the iconoclasm and challenges of being an orthodox psychoanalyst. I do hope that Derek's well-situated exposition of Dolto's thinking will add to a nuanced understanding of her work and an increased demand for her work to be published in English.

My chapter on "ghostly presences in children's lives" builds upon the implicit emphasis on the social in Derek's discussion of Dolto's writings, and places a psychoanalysis of the social front and center. I locate children explicitly in communities of meaning and I argue for "the sociohistorical and ancestral/familial constitutedness of children's coming-to-be." Beginning with a personal ghost story I move on to explore ghosts, specters, and unconsciously transmitted memories in the formation of who we are becoming. While this kind of work occupies a relatively narrow place in orthodox psychoanalysis, it occupies a larger place in studies of intergenerational trauma, and in writings that seek to understand mass trauma, as well as writings that seek to embrace indigenous epistemologies and other non-Western worldviews, as the chapters below by Karen Lupe and Norma Tracey clearly illustrate. I conclude my chapter with psychodynamic implications of this work for adults who are charged to work with children in either educational or therapeutic settings. Echoing Patrick Lewis's chapter on the importance of narrative, I conclude the following:

> If indeed we can acknowledge subjectivity as sociohistorically constituted and spectrally located, then an engaging, revivifying, and ancestrally anchored curriculum process would seem to be indicated if we aspire to recreate social links and give children of a particular community a possibility of moving forward with a sense of history, pride, and belonging. Children who have been rendered *loreless,* to use Judy Atkinson's (2002) term, need opportunities to re-inscribe themselves in their history in order to heal soul wounds and fully experience their own subjective possibilities.

In chapter 6, Karen Lupe narrows the lens from the larger sociohisorical constitutedness of subjectivity to an exploration of the family unconscious. Karen's work is influenced by Jungian studies, by her own *Pasifika* origins, and by her deep respect for indigenous epistemologies. Describing the family unconscious, Karen says "This 'common or shared field' is an intimate web connecting our parents and children, spouses and lovers, friends, and the wider community. The family unconscious is a field with energies that transmit images, feelings, and thoughts among families' members and beyond." Key to Karen's thinking is an acknowledgement of dreamtime and the inherent presence of ancestors among us. This soothing notion of ancestor presence and ancestor communication is so valuable, and yet it is notably dissonant from the pejorative notion of ghosts and haunting that are so endemic in Western cultures. Karen explores *morphic resonance* as a form of communication, and underlines the importance of narrative as a way to understand our inheritance. Much as I have elsewhere lauded oral history as a means to tap into ancestral inheritance (O'Loughlin, 2009), Karen speaks here of the importance of genograms as a means for opening up inquiry into the familial legacies that constitute our coming to be. Karen concludes: "Exploration of the mythic themes of a client's family patterns–the deeper stories that are enacted and often disguised by personal experience–can facilitate the healing process within the counselling relationship. Rather than deny our family roots, it is vital that we counsellors and clients understand, live with, and address them as creatively as possible."

Norma Tracey has devoted her entire professional career to working with children and families, and a substantial portion of it assisting indigenous Australian families in working through the catastrophic traumas that have been visited upon them by colonial and post-colonial Australian governments, and working respectfully to assist them in stitching narratives from the tattered remnants of lives fragmented by intergenerationally inherited trauma and by the catastrophic effects of cultural genocide. For people whose lives were built around connection to land, connection to ancestors, and the honoring of lore, the damage is incalculable. Describing the Gunawirra project in chapter 7, Norma notes, "I was challenged to use my 46 years of working with infants, young children and mothers to seek a method of healing from within a culture steeped in ancient art, ritual and myth; programs that would give our Aboriginal children a better start in living experience and in learning. My professional colleagues at Gunawirra and I felt supported by the knowledge that the responsiveness of the psyche at this tender age allows growth which may never again be available in their lifetime." Norma then goes on to lay out the key principles governing the formation of Gunawirra. Most important of these are an acknowledgement of dreamtime: "The Dreaming imbues the world around us with meaning. This meaning is born out of our internal imagining; it becomes a wisdom transposed through generations by Aboriginal elders in oral and cave art form. An ancient spirituality, it gives historic continuity to the inner self, giving links to ancestors and elders in the past and in the present living community." Second, there is Dadirri: "Dadirri is the ancient name given to restoration in dealing with trauma. It is a ritualised form of 'deep listening,' not an ordinary witnessing, but an empathic psychic action. A version of this is known to the modern world as psychotherapy." Norma explores both of these concepts in detail, shows the ways in which they link with psychoanalytic principles of deep listening, and illustrates her chapter with deeply moving clinical material illustrating the courageous ways in which people assist each other in moving from "zones of non-existence" to spaces of mutual healing and hope.

In chapter 8, Donna Wolf-Palacio, a community therapist in Philadelphia, presents two detailed case studies of her work in assisting two young children in crisis in containing their trauma, and the ways in which she sought to invite their mothers into the therapeutic process. Donna draws upon family systems theory and psychoanalytic theory, and she shows how one approach proved more effective therapeutically with one dyad, while the other proved to be the treatment of choice for the other mother and child. Her work is testimony to the resilience of children, the necessary resilience of therapists, and the importance of therapist as "meaning broker" who can facilitate communication between parent and child. For therapists or teachers seeking reassurance of the importance of an attachment-sensitive approach to working with a troubled child and family, or indeed for anyone who doubts the importance of the creation of safe play spaces for young children and their mothers, Donna's chapter is essential reading.

In a world where parents are often demonized, Carola Chase's discussion of parents as collaborators (chapter 9) offers a welcome change of perspective. Carola is sympathetic to the difficulties of managing a classroom full of children, but she is committed to the notion of "children as having complicated emotional lives." Her chapter is rich in illustrative clinical material showing how, beneath the typical symptoms children express in school, are complex emotional difficulties. Teachers who gain insight into the psychodynamic search for what lies beneath overt behavior, not only respond more empathically and usefully to children, but, as Carola illustrates, they are in a much better position to elicit a similar empathically attuned response from parents. Carola's chapter reads like an encyclopedic clinical resource of appropriate psychodynamic responses to fear, guilt, shame, anger, anxiety, and depression in children. Carola summarizes the essence of psychodynamic thinking about children this way:

> Children are not miniature grownups, able to recognize their own feelings, be aware of ways in which emotions affect them, and adapt accordingly. While adults can learn to contain and manage their feelings to the extent that they do not impinge on work or relationships, children— when worried, angry, sad, or agitated— are often unable, even if attuned to these feelings, to express them. Their emotions at times feel confusing, unwanted, and frightening, but this does not protect the child from having these feelings. Emotions continue to affect behavior, mood, interpersonal relationships, and self-esteem. It is therefore the job of the adults in a child's life to help sort out and translate these perplexing parts of a child's inner world.

It should be noted that Carola does not see the world through rose-colored glasses and her chapter concludes with an exploration of problematic collaborations between teachers and parents.

In chapter 10, Ana Archangelo and Fabio Camargo Bandeira Villela explore parent school collaboration using an analytic framework that is highly innovative. Using a conceptual framework from group dynamic theory and psychoanalysis they analyze the interaction between parents and the institution of school using core concepts such as projection and transference. Ana and Fabio explore the separation that is inherent in the child's separation from her or his parents, and examine the ways in which parental fantasies around separation contrive to build up a transferential relationship between the parent and the school. The authors play out a variety of these scenarios, illustrating how particular transferential stances that fail to be recognized or understood by willfully misunderstanding schools, can lead to a toxic breakdown in communication: "But it is always necessary to highlight certain points that the school must not forget if it is aiming to build a relationship with the family for the benefit of the student/child. First, the task of educating is grounded in the fantasies, and fears already mentioned. Second, these impressions, these fantasies, and these fears, produce different requests and demands that the family brings to the school. In the end, the way the school listens to such requests and demands cannot be just administrative or prescriptive. It is not enough to listen to parental requests and to merely try to decide what can or cannot be done, or worse, whether this is the school's job or the responsibility of the parents." Ana and Fabio explore these dynamics in exquisite detail, ultimately arguing that schools ought to practice a form of *social reverie*, akin to the kind of reverie advocated by Bion as a core feature of psychoanalytic practice. If the kind of analysis exemplified here gains currency it promises to offer a new set of tools to school and community agency administrators who seek to build genuine partnership with parents, who, with inevitable trepidation, entrust their children to an institution's care.

Leon Hoffman, Carrie Catapano, and Katy Meyer use chapter 11 to give an overview of the core principles underlying the operation of West End Day School in New York City, a school that serves as a model of the integration of psychodynamic principles, developmental principles, and a progressive educational philosophy to provide comprehensive, tailored education to children with emotional challenges. Leon and his colleagues describe dynamic diagnosis, explain the principles of mentalization underlying the school's philosophy, and show how behavioral, cognitive, and psychodynamic principles can be deployed to articulate a tailored psychoeducational plan for each child. The authors describe how the school cultivates a "psychoanalytic atmosphere," one which "conveys a tone of respect and acceptance where one allows both parents and children to communicate their story in their own way and at their own pace." Integral to the approach described is an emphasis on the internal experience of the child, a foundation of respect and empathy, and a commitment to interdisciplinary collaboration between psychiatrist, social workers, speech-language pathologists, and classroom teachers, described here under the rubric of "therapeutic education."

In chapter 12, Robbie Lloyd takes us to the Northern Territory of Australia to offer a solution to the disconcerting alienation that conventional schools seem to produce. Robbie tells us that "schools have swung from chalk-encrusted Victorian era discipline factories, through seventies child-centred free-schooling environments, to contemporary electronic white-boarded, dog-eat-dog meritocratic, web-published, competition-tabled, measurement-obsessed, sausage machines of 'knowledge'. "Robbie's solution is to revise the notion of schools as caring communities, evocatively described by Robbie as "great good places." Robbie has pioneered Social Emotional Wellbeing Teams to create spaces of liveliness, love, and nurturance in schools that, mirroring shopping malls and airports, are rapidly becoming non-places in which children wither. He describes one of his restorative concepts the following way:

> The Gathering Place is a regular ritual ceremony, where students, staff, parents and community come together to share rhythmical occasions of celebrating belonging and identity. This is especially crucial for those who may have been vulnerable to not fitting into the mainstream flow of classroom relations. Which is what I have come to call "having a scratchy life"—i.e., when things for any person (student, teacher, parent) are rubbing up against "normal" expectations of how to behave in groups, usually due to serious exhaustion, trauma at home, or in the overall family and community environment: i.e.,

> things that require compassion and empathy, rather than judgment about someone "being badly behaved," or "not cutting it."
>
> By creating special moments and spaces where these individuals can come back into the circle, and receive a witnessing and testimony of their contributions in a setting of communal acknowledgement, schools are doing a full job of "growing up everyone" about "how life goes round, round, round."

Echoing Ana and Fabio's articulation of *social reverie* (chapter 10), Robbie explores a notion of *social poetics* that could underline the creation of schools as communities of respect and dialog—a notion that, again ties in with the notion of narrative articulated in many of the chapters of this book.

Howard Covitz, a psychoanalyst, offers a cautionary tale (chapter 13) of the misadventures and successes of his attempt to run a school on psychodynamic principles, early in his career, in spite of the forces of darkness that tried to discipline him and his students and put them back in a box. Howard took on the struggle against objectifying acronyms and stultifying policies and did his best to champion the possibility of creating a genuine Gathering Place for his staff and students. Howard offers a sophisticated discourse on the notion of resistance in psychoanalysis and the power of a pedagogy that goes with the grain of the resistance rather than against it. Howard cites the old maxim: "Never fight the resistance, You will lose!" He also addresses the issue of transference, and he offers poignant examples from the lives of his students of the power of humane, insightful, psychodynamically informed pedagogy in opening up possible lives for children whose futures already appeared foreclosed. As I noted, Howard's is a cautionary tale and thereby begs the question whether society as a whole will ever throw its weight behind this kind of attentive education for more than an elite group of children.

Devin Thornburg (chapter 14) has worked for all of his life in seeking to reform the practice of schooling. In this chapter, after beginning with a historical overview of attempts by psychoanalysts to influence school reform, Devin offers a personal account of the problematic of his own countertansference as he worked as a school consultant with teachers whose attitudes toward children he found hard to stomach. Wisely, however, he discovered that change needed to begin with self-analysis rather than prescriptive bromides for apparently recalcitrant teachers: "Mostly what these questions led to is not answers but a type of thinking that made myself the focus of inquiry. As a result, my communication and my relationship with this teacher began to change. A psychoanalytic "stance" has the capacity to engender a shift in role for a teacher. This thought has been a continuous one for me and has encouraged me to examine other views of learning and teaching in the hopes of deepening my understanding of the mechanisms of change that a psychoanalytic position can bring." Devin also goes on to explore points of convergence between psychoanalysis and the writings of Piaget and Vygotsky, and he offers a critique of mechanistic approaches that purport to teach socio-emotional education. Devin concludes that the kind of self-reflectivity so intrinsic to psychoanalysis is a vital characteristic for teachers.

In chapter 15 Al Galves offers a utopian vision of what he terms a Psychoanalytically Informed School. Drawing on notable child analysts as well as on the long tradition of radical school experiments, epitomized in A.S. Neill's *Summerhill*, Al lays out the tenets of a school that will counteract the numbing conformity and authoritarianism of conventional American public schooling. After a robust polemical critique of the shortcomings of schooling, Al articulates a radical vision of what Paulo Freire would undoubtedly call schooling as the practice of freedom. In Al's Psychoanalytically Informed School there is no patronizing agenda, no attempt at offering pseudo-choice. Students are expected to think and act in ethical, thoughtful, and responsible ways. Following George Counts (1932), Al's chapter invites us to ask indeed whether schools might dare to build a new social order. Al concludes his chapter with a discussion of Richard Hopkins's notion of "root metaphor of narrative," concluding, in synchrony with many authors in this book, that self-reflective narrative is a key to education that has the promise to initiate a reflective and agentic life-journey.

The book concludes with a meditation by Daniel Frank on the close relationship between the progressive tradition in American education and psychoanalysis. Drawing on Freud's notion of *family romance* Daniel frames his vision of schooling as *school romance.* Key to this understanding, as Daniel explains, is the Deweyan notion of *learning from experience*, a notion that holds great resonance for psychoanalysts. Daniel speaks of teachable moments, and illustrates the potential of learning from experience when educators pose large questions about goodness in life: "What is the relationship between narcissism and citizenship? How can connectedness, openness, and freedom develop in students a sense of self-confidence that can be applied to the task of forwarding creativity and social progress for all? How can reflective teaching and learning connect personal passions, interests, and talents with the ideals articulated in a progressive school's mission statement?" The scope of Daniel's vision pushes psychoanalysts and educators to engage not just with personal fulfillment but with social responsibility and social activism as core elements of a fully lived life. As principal of the Francis W. Parker School in Chicago it is fitting that Daniel draws his core inspiration from the ideals of Col. Parker in his articulation of the paradigm of the subjective experience of school life, "a dimension of human experience that is informed by the interplay between the personal and the public, between self and citizen, between fantasy and reality, between teaching and learning." Daniel devotes much of his chapter to articulating this vision and to showing how both the progressive tradition in education and the core principles of psychoanalytic practice can support the development of moral, creative, activist human beings who view their individual achievement as integrally connected with the propagation of social and collective goodness. At the conclusion of his chapter Daniel, too, turns to the development and refinement of narrative—in this case through *hidden questions*—as a key force in developing the kinds of citizens he hopes a democratic society would wish to produce.

For readers with an appetite for more after completing this book, I hope you will also consider consulting the companion volume, *The Uses of Psychoanalysis in Working with Children's Emotional Lives*, also published by Jason Aronson.

NOTE

1. To view syllabi for these and other courses I teach, please visit my website: michaeloloughlinphd.com

REFERENCES

Altman, N. (1995). *The analyst in the inner city: Race, class and color through a psychoanalytic lens.* Hillsdale, N. J. : Analytic Press.

Books, S. (1998). Speaking of and against youth. In S. Books (Ed.), *Invisible children in the society and its schools.* Hillsdale, NJ: Erlbaum.

Counts, G. (1932). *Dare the school build a new social order?* New York: John Day Company.

Danto, E, (2002). *Freud's free clinics: Psychoanalysis and social justice, 191–1938.* New York: Columbia University Press.

Freire, P. (1970). *Pedagogy of the oppressed.* New York: Continuum.

Kohn, A. (1996). *Beyond discipline: From compliance to community.* Alexandria, VA: ASCD.

Lipper, J. (1996). *Inside Out: Portraits of Children.* Available from http://joannalipper.com/video_IO.html.

O'Loughlin, M. (2012). Countering the rush to medication: Psychodynamic, intergenerational, and cultural considerations in understanding children's distress. In U.S. Nayar (Ed.). *International Handbook on Mental Health of Children and Adolescents: Culture, Policy & Practices.* Delhi, India: Sage.

O'Loughlin, M. (2010, October). Reclaiming a liberatory vision for psychoanalysis. In symposium *The Psychologies of Liberation: Clinical, Critical and Pedagogical Perspectives* presented at *Annual Meeting of Association of Psychoanalysis, Culture & Society,* Rutgers University, New Jersey.

O'Loughlin, M. (2009). *The subject of childhood.* New York: Peter Lang Publishing.

O'Loughlin, M. & Johnson, R. (Eds.). (2010). *Imagining children otherwise: Theoretical and critical perspectives on childhood subjectivity.* New York: Peter Lang Publishing.

O'Loughlin, M. & Merchant, A. (2012, June). Working obliquely with children. *Journal of Infant, Child & Adolescent Psychotherapy, 11,* 149–159.

Polakow, V. (1998). Homeless children and their families: The discards of the postmodern 1990s. In S. Books (Ed.), *Invisible children in the society and its schools.* Mahwah, N. J. : Erlbaum.

Paley, V. (2004). *A child's work: The importance of play.* Chicago: University of Chicago Press. Univ. of Chicago

Polakow-Suransky, S. (2000). America's least wanted: Zero-tolerance policies and the fate of expelled students. In V. Polakow (Ed.), *The public assault on America's children: Poverty, violence and injustice.* New York: Teachers College Press.

Stepansky. P. (2009). *Psychoanalysis at the margins.* New York: Other Press.

Watkins, M. & Shulman, H. (2008). *Toward psychologies of liberation.* New York: Palgrave Macmillan.

Watters, E. (2010). *Crazy like us? The globalization of the American psyche.* New York: Free Press.

Whitaker, R. (2010). *Anatomy of an epidemic: Magic bullets, psychiatric drugs, and the astonishing rise of mental illness in America.* New York: Crown.

Chapter One

Promoting Children's Healthy Development and Ability to Learn

Past and Current Partnerships between Educators and Psychoanalytically Informed Mental Health Practitioners

Jonathan Cohen

Psychoanalytically informed child clinicians and K-12 educators of young children are potentially natural allies. Both are primarily concerned with promoting children's healthy development and capacity to learn. These mutual interests were apparent from the first hours of psychoanalysis as Sigmund Freud and his "Wednesday night" colleagues wondered how they could apply analytic ideas to the education of children, including their own. These meetings opened an evolving dialogue about the application of psychoanalytically informed thinking and work to the education of young children (Midgley, 2008). Freud came to consider such an application as "perhaps the most important activity of psychoanalysis" (Freud, 1933, p. 146).

In this chapter, I will review the multi-generational history of how psychoanalysts[1] and pre-Kindergarten through twelfth grade[2] educators have worked and learned together. Building on this history, I will consider current psychoanalytic-educator partnerships. Finally, I will comment on the growing recognition within psychoanalysis that we can and need to consider how to build on this history of multi-disciplinary work.

ANALYSTS AND EDUCATORS LEARNING AND WORKING TOGETHER: HISTORICAL AND CURRENT DEVELOPMENTS

Hermine Hug-Hellmuth was the first of many child analysts to recognize how mental health professionals need to work collaboratively with educators—as well as parents—to promote children's learning and development (Hug-Hellmuth, 1914). Anna Freud, building—in part—on Hug-Hellmuth's work, created a framework for educators and child analysts to learn and teach together. Beginning her professional life as a teacher, Anna Freud came to psychoanalysis not only as the Sigmund Freud's daughter but also as someone deeply involved with teaching and learning with young children. From her early study group meetings with Bernfeld, Hoffer, and Aichhorn in the 1920s, Anna Freud sought to systematically discover how analytic understanding might illuminate the developmental experience of children and promote psychosocial capacities in and outside of the classroom (Young-Bruehl, 1988).

Drawing on earlier and contemporary experiences of psychoanalysts' involvement in the world of childhood education, I propose that there are four major modes of work or, ways in which educators and psychoanalysts have worked together. First, analysts and educators have worked together to organize and direct psychoanalytically informed schools. Second, there is another long-standing tradition of analysts providing consultative assistance to educators about a given child, school, and/or larger educational system. Third, they have worked together to develop replicable analytically informed programmatic school-based efforts. And, finally, analysts and educators have worked together with Departments and Colleges of Education and/or continuing education for practicing school personnel.

In this chapter, I will summarize these four overlapping areas or approaches to collaborative work. I will then address the following three questions: What it is about this applied analytic work that makes it "psychoanalytic"? To what extent does the work actually produce the desired results? And, is the work described "generalizable" and/or is it largely a function of the one individual who is practicing it?

PSYCHOANALYTICALLY INFORMED SCHOOLS FOR NORMAL AND/OR TROUBLED STUDENTS

The longest standing analytic-educational tradition involves psychoanalysts organizing and directing psychoanalytically informed schools for normal and/or troubled children. Willie Hoffer and Siegfried Bernfeld's educational programs in the Baumgarten Institute in Vienna initiated this work during the early 1920s to provide care for war orphans and abandoned Jewish children

(Geissmann and Geissmann, 1998). August Aichhorn also developed the Oberhollabrünn Institute for delinquent adolescents around the same time. He detailed how an analytically informed understanding of the developmental experience of the child, parent-child experiences, transference-counter transference dynamics and the internalization of a "new" relationship with the teacher fostered learning and healthy development (Aichorn, 1935).

At roughly the same time, a Children's School affiliated with the Psychoanalytic Institute of the Soviet Union was established for children, age 1 through 5, who were cared for by specially trained educators. In the late 1920s the school was closed by Stalin (Miller, 1998).

Anna Freud helped to form a school that was directed by Eva Rosenfeld (for one year) in the late 1920s. This work created the foundation for the Vienna Jackson Nursery for deprived infants that Miss Freud co-founded with Dorothy Burlingham in 1937. When they moved to England, they founded the Hampstead Nurseries in 1940 that included three nurseries for vulnerable children and one home for older children displaced and in need of institutional care as a result of the war (Freud & Burlingham, 1973). Each of these early opportunities was based on naturally occurring opportunities and settings for educators and analysts to learn and work together. This work became the first sustained child psychoanalytic center for observational research as well as teaching and learning for young children. The work of the Hampstead Clinic (now the Anna Freud Centre) was one of the first to not only initiate an analytically informed school, but to work in the three other areas of analytic-educational collaboration: consultation; developing analytically informed programmatic school-based efforts, and teacher education. Virtually all of Anna Freud's and her colleagues' work was grounded in naturalistic in-depth observation and anchored in a collaborative approach to child rearing and education.

In the United States, there have been wide ranges of ways that analysts applied psychoanalytically informed thinking including hospital care, working with delinquent youth, legal work, law enforcement, and considerations about what is in the best interest of the child. Educator-analysts partnerships were one important part of interdisciplinary and applied work. Anny Katan founded the first psychoanalytic early childhood program in America, which later became a part of the Hanna Perkins Center (Furman and Katan 1969). This work as well as an evolving dialogue between Anna Freud, Peter Neubauer, and Albert Solnit and their colleagues in London, New York, and New Haven spawned a number of additional psychoanalytically informed school programs. Most of the early educational work focused on early childhood. Bruno Bettelheim's work at the Orthogenic School—a coeducational residential treatment program for children and adolescents in need of support for behavioral or emotional issues—was another important example of analytic schoolwork. Over the years, many of these schools closed or moved away from an analytically informed set of understandings, goals, and methods/strategies used to actualize these goals.

Today, there are a number of vital, analytically informed early childhood schools: The Allen Creek Preschool, Ann Arbor, Michigan; the Hanna Perkins Center, Cleveland, Ohio (Furman and Katan, 1969), Harris School, Houston/Galveston, Texas (Farley, & Manning, 2002); The Cornerstone Project in San Francisco (Kliman, 1975; 1979), and Lucy Daniels Center for Early Childhood, Cary, North Carolina (Rosenblitt, 2004). In fact, these schools are founding members of the recently formed Alliance of Psychoanalytic Schools (Rosenblitt, 2003). There are two on which I would like to comment.

The Cornerstone method provides interdisciplinary education and treatment for emotionally disturbed or developmentally disordered children ages three to six years. Within a therapeutic or special education classroom group setting (Kliman, 1975; Lopez and Kliman, 1979), a therapist works six or more hours per week. During that time the therapist provides psychotherapy individually right in the classroom to each of the five to eight children in the group, each child for fifteen to twenty minutes a day. During each child's in-classroom psychotherapy session a full range of play therapy and analytic techniques are often used, including interpretations of transference, dynamic and genetic interpretations. The interpersonal and educational setting allows a "here and now" focus on resistance to successful socializing and learning. Since sessions occur almost daily and occur in a real life space, there is little need to delay talking to a child whose attention span might not allow discussion of an event a few days later.

Two early childhood educators are in charge of the classroom educational activities, which proceed with all the other children throughout any one child's in-classroom psychotherapy sessions. Teachers and therapist brief each other with the child's help before and after each child's classroom psychotherapy session. The team meets weekly to share communications from parents, as well as to view videotapes and hear the material gathered during treatment that may not have been overheard in the class session. Parents are interviewed and guided by the teacher each week and by the therapist once a month. Most of the children have existing emotional disturbances, but are also accepted for preventive reasons such as death of a parent, or placement in foster care. Kliman's, Zelman's, and Hope's data (summarized in Kliman, 2006) show considerable rapid emotional growth measured by Children's Global Assessment Scale (DSM IV, Axis V) scores and intellectual growth measured by Wechsler Preschool Scale of Intelligence (revised version) "IQ" scores.

Kliman and his colleagues were the first group of analysts to operationalize, manualize, and make both retrospective and prospective psychoeducational studies of their efforts. Statistically significant findings include educationally and clinically impressive results of the interdisciplinary treatment (Hope, 1999; Zelman, 1985 & 1996; Kliman 2006). IQ gains average one to two standard deviations among fifty-two twice-studied children, while sixty comparison and control children show no such gains. Among foster children an additional measure has been used for Cornerstone patients: transfer rates among homes. In a study of thirty foster children in the program transfer rates were reduced to zero over the course of a year, compared to 25 percent a year in comparison populations (Kliman, 2006; Kliman & Schaeffer, 1984). Replication and training for others to carry out the method is now occurring in two sites (Cornerstone Buenos Aires and The Ann Martin Center, Piedmont, CA). A manual and illustrative videos are available without charge from Kliman at gil.kliman@cphc-sf.org. Another important example of a psychoanalytically informed educational setting is The Lucy Daniels Center program. This program resembles the Cornerstone Project with one exception: the former works clinically with children outside the classroom, while Cornerstone treats children clinically within the classroom. Like Cornerstone, the Lucy Daniels Center for Early Childhood Intervention Program (EIP) is an intervention program for children at high risk for emotional and social difficulties. Extensive clinical evaluations, for example, revealed that all of the children were significantly "off" their appropriate developmental course and the vast majority met criteria for DSM diagnoses (Rosenblitt, 2006). In a ten-year follow-up study, the parents of thirty-two out of the forty-seven graduates of the program (68 percent) reported the EIP approach positively changed the school course of children who were at the highest risk of school failure. The vast majority of these children was able to remain in standard (non special education) classrooms and were promoted at each grade. Ten years later, parent satisfaction is reportedly extremely high (Rosenblitt, 2001).

The application of psychoanalytic thinking to the creation of schools is one of the most common forms of applied analytic work in education. Historically and to a great extent currently, most of these efforts have focused on early childhood. These programmatic efforts are psychoanalytically informed in four major ways: (1) each tends to emphasize the intra-psychic meanings of behavior; (2) they are each profoundly focused on the mother-child dyad (e.g., the fundamental importance of the real as well as the internalized maternal figure as protector, nurturer, and facilitator of development); (3) each pays close attention to and fosters the child's attempts to master both internal and external demands while increasing adaptive functioning over the course of development; and, (5) each program appreciates how relationships (interpersonal and intrapsychic) shape learning and development (Rosenblitt, 2004).

The vast majority of information or data that we have about these educational efforts are anecdotal reports: the literature is filled with ethnographic and case study reports about how successful these schools are. However, it is rare that analysts and/or educators in these schools have delineated goals and methods in a way that allow us to evaluate to what extent these goals are reached, and which components of their programs are actually helpful. The Cornerstone and the Lucy Daniels Programs are the only two that have begun to systematically evaluate these efforts. With these two exceptions, it is difficult to know to what extent reported positive gains have been the function of one or more individuals and/or whether this work can be generalized. In fact, the lack of systematic study has also—inadvertently—undermined analysts' ability to be learners in general.

Most psychoanalytic school efforts are not grounded in any kind of ongoing systematic research. This, in turn, has dramatically reduced the interest of educators, school systems, and philanthropic foundations in these projects. Echoing the evolution and debate within the clinical world (e.g., Kernberg, 2006) there has been a major shift in education over the last twenty-five years to systematically study goals, methods and outcomes (Cohen, 2006). Public schools systems and foundations are now encouraged, if not mandated, to *only* consider programmatic efforts—psychoanalytic or otherwise—that have been empirically evaluated (U.S. Department of Education, 2005).

Psychoanalytic approaches to research have generally been clinically based, with almost exclusive attention to the details of individual experience. Case studies and anecdotal reports certainly provide rich data from which we can learn and generate hypotheses. The Cornerstone and the Lucy Daniels Centers projects have gone a step further and have translated these clinically generated hypotheses into systematic efforts of research and evaluation. These efforts have also created a model that others may use to further empirical study of process and outcome of programmatic efforts. This has the potential for broader application and dissemination of psychoanalytically informed observations and innovations that benefit the health, education, and well-being of children.

CONSULTATIONS WITH EDUCATORS, SCHOOLS, AND/OR LARGER EDUCATIONAL SYSTEMS

Consulting with educators, schools, and occasionally larger educational systems is another common way that analysts have worked with educators to further children's learning and development. There are countless instances of psychoanalytically informed clinicians—around the world—who consult to schools about given children and, sometimes the school as a system.

There are scores of reports describing this kind of work stemming from Anna Freud's early consultative work. Growing out of the Committee on Psychoanalytic Education (COPE) group[3] that developing a *Curriculum to*

Teach Courses on Psychoanalytic Thinking Applied to Community and Social Problems, Wilkinson (2004) has summarized and annotated these reports. The vast majority are case studies that focus on the *inner* lives of children over time: the historically dominant psychoanalytic focus.

One of the many ways that Anna Freud was such an extraordinary leader and learner was her exploration and writings about how the culture and climate of the environment that children live within powerfully shapes social-emotional growth (Freud & Dann, 1951). In the 2001 volume of the *Psychoanalytic Study of the Child* a series of papers re-examine this important and neglected topic. This work was a precursor to current educational research and practice focusing on how the "climate" of the school as well as the home creates—or undermines—a climate for learning and how internal and external reality are always shaping one another. Although this is a truism, it has not been a consistent focus for applied—or clinical—analytic work in the education and/or treatment of young children until recent years (Cohen, 1997a).

There has been little psychoanalytic consultation work with larger K-12 systems: school districts, state, and/or national Departments of Education or educational ministries. Interestingly, this has not been the case with younger children (zero to four). As described in more detail below, The *National Center for Infants, Children and Families/Zero to Three* was founded by a group of analysts and non-analysts. Their work has shaped American and to some extent, international research, as well as practice and policy in programs that involve infants, toddlers, and their families.

There have been some analysts consulting to larger educational systems. Berkovitz (1999) for example, has been involved with and contributed to an important movement within American education to make the school a community center: a base for a range of health and mental health services (Blank & Berg, 2006; Dryfoos & Quinn, 2005). James Comer's early thinking and work with schools was shaped—in part—by Anna Freud and Al Solnit's analytically informed narratives about child development (Comer, 1988; 1995). His important consultative work with two inner-city low-income elementary schools became the foundation for the *School Development Program*, which has been utilized in more than 600 schools (Comer, Edward T. Joyner, and Michael Ben-Avie, 2004). Twemlow and colleagues have worked with the Jamaican government to further analytically informed violence prevention efforts (Twemlow & Sacco, 1996).

Over the last decade, a number of my colleagues at the National School Climate Center (NSCC) and I have worked with a growing number of school districts, State Departments of Education (Iowa, New York, New Jersey, Ohio, Rhode Island, Tennessee) and foreign educational ministries (Australia, China, France, Israel, Switzerland, Singapore, Sweden, Norway) and the UN Children's Fund. This work has ranged from developing social emotional educational/violence prevention/school safety guidelines for a State (Fuchs-Nadeau, et al., 2002) to working directly with school leaders about how they can and need to become reflective social emotional learners themselves to educate students most effectively and create coordinated and effective educational-mental health partnerships (Cohen, 1999a; Marans & Cohen, 1999) to developing data driven school improvement models that support students and adults (educators and parents) learning and working together to create even safer, more supportive, engaging, and joyful schools (Cohen, Pickeral, Cohen, Pickeral & Levine, 2010). All of our work is grounded in two processes: educating and supporting parents and educators to intentionally promote K-12 students' social, emotional, civic and cognitive competencies and ethical dispositions as well as working to create safe, caring, participatory, and responsive schools and homes (Cohen, 2001, 2006; Cohen, Pickeral, & Levine, 2010).

In each consultation the following ingredients have been central psychoanalytically informed elements: (1) promoting reflective capacities and deeper understandings of intrapsychic meanings attributed to learning, teaching, youth development, and the purpose of K-12 education; (2) appreciating unrecognized or unconscious aspects of school life; (3) being keenly attuned to children's developmental experience; and, (4) appreciating how inherently anxiety provoking learning, teaching, and school life can be on the one hand and how (adaptive or maladaptive) defensive strategies color the process of development and learning on the other hand (Cohen, 1999a; 2006). In an overlapping manner, our consultation work with schools builds on a longstanding analytic tradition of listening, observing, collaboratively identifying realistic and helpful goals and working on them together.

Our appreciation of empirical and systematic research—its strengths as well as limitations—has been an additional factor contributing to invitations to confer with these larger educational systems. Interestingly, after research-related findings are established, I have consistently discovered a paradoxical response to empirical research findings as they are introduced into our consultation work. As much as educational leaders want and need to believe that our work is "research based," most educators also recognize that the process of teaching and learning can never be reduced to measurable or simply observable, operationally defined variables. These leaders and other educators have a deep appreciation that teaching and learning is "grounded' in human relationships. Like many clinicians and clinical researchers, these education professionals also recognize that fundamentally important aspects of relationships, often those unconscious and pre-conscious contributing elements, are extraordinarily challenging to measure and study empirically.

Educational systems request our assistance because we have expertise that they imagine they don't. And, typically this is the case. But, just as it is unhelpful to simply tell a patient what they need to do, the history of school reform is filled with unsuccessful instances where "outside experts" told school leaders what to do. It never works. We position ourselves as "co-discoverers" with educational leaders. What is working and not working? What are the meanings that they attribute to their strengths, challenges, and problems? What is clear and not about how accurate these narratives are? To what extent do other school staff, parents, and students share these perceptions? How ready is the system to embark on a process of substantive learning, goal setting, and the hard work that is virtually always an integral part of change? Establishing an alliance or a trusting relationship is an essential part of this initial process of co-discovery, community building, and goal setting. This is a process that typically entails months of work to establish.

There are now almost three hundred empirical studies from school-based mental health, risk prevention, health promotion, character and social emotional education programs that support the notion that when we purposively teach students to become more socially and emotionally competent and simultaneously work systemically to create a safe, caring, participatory and responsive school, academic achievement increases and school violence decreases (Durlak, Weissberg, Dymnicki, Taylor, & Schellinger, 2011; Weissberg, Kumpfer, & Seligman, 2003; Zins, Weissberg, Wang, & Walberg, 2004).[4]

We help schools to develop goals that are aligned with research and best practices. I have asked educators and parents across America and abroad what they hope their sons, daughters, and/or students will have learned and "be" when they graduate from high school. Their answers have been very consistent: they want their children/students to be life long learners, to be responsible, caring members of the community who can work and love and participate in a democracy. Although they do occasionally mention wanting their child to get into a "good college" this is always secondary to the social, emotional, and ethical goals that are in the forefront of the adults' dreams and wishes for their children. What I have described above begins to outline the first and to some extent a second "stage" in a five-stage school climate improvement process that I will describe below. Transforming a school—like working with an individual—is necessarily a process that occurs over years. We have begun to systematically study schools that are using this model (Cohen, Shapiro, & Fisher, 2006; Cohen, Pickeral, & Levine, 2010).

There are scores of anecdotal reports about analytic consultative work. My impression is that there is a much larger number of works in this area that have not been documented. And, virtually none of it has been studied in systematic manner: ethnographically, experimentally, or otherwise. Hence, it is difficult to make thoughtful generalizations about work in this area. Based on my review of the literature (Wilkinson, 2004), as well as talking with clinicians and educators in America and Europe, and to a much lesser extent, Scandinavia and Japan, my impression is that there are two overlapping themes that make this kind of consultative work psychoanalytic in nature: a focus on developmentally informed unconscious as well as conscious experience and the meanings attributed to experience.

We know little about whether this work actually produces desired results. More often than not, goals are so general (e.g., "conferring to be helpful") that it is not possible to understand what has and has not been helpful on the one hand and to what extent positive results are due to a gifted clinician and/or are grounded in analytic insight that is larger than one clinician's gifts.

There is another trend that has colored too much of our consultation work with educators that is worth noting. Psychoanalysts and educators could be natural partners. However, too often analysts have often positioned themselves as the "expert" in ways that inadvertently undermine collaboration and learning. In a penetrating analysis of three analytic efforts in schools by Sklarew, Manning, and Farley, and Kusche (see Cohen 2002), Shepherd (2002) describes how the analytic interventions, "at least as described in the articles, are either imposed on the work of teachers and students or isolated from that work. Either circumstance ultimately limits the impact of the intervention. I claim that analysts and teachers are natural allies despite lack of evidence for alliance in these articles." More often than not, educators expect that analysts will assume a somewhat imperious and uncollaborative stance. Unfortunately, this—in conjunction with analysts' historically unhelpful anti-research stance (Cohen, 1997a)—has undermined educators' interest in learning from and with analysts and about analytically informed thinking.

DEVELOPING ANALYTICALLY INFORMED REPLICABLE EDUCATIONAL PROGRAMMATIC EFFORTS

Creating analytically informed replicable programmatic efforts overlaps with the development of schools as well as the Cornerstone and the Lucy Daniels Center programs described above. Many of these school efforts, for example, have included programmatic efforts to work with children and sometimes parents. There are scores of reports describing short term and, typically, short-lived analytic-educational programmatic efforts (Wilkenson, 2004).

Here I will focus on another—less common—analytic-educational tradition: the development of programs that create replicable guidelines, curriculum, and/or learning activities. In the United States, there has been a dramatic educational movement to ground educational and psychoeducational programmatic efforts in behaviorally based terms that can be operationally defined and evaluated. This is trend is also growing in Europe, Scandinavia, South America, and Asia (e.g., China, Japan, Malaysia, and Singapore).

Perhaps the largest and most validated programmatic effort is the *Life Space Crisis Intervention* (LSCI) model for working with children in crisis

(Long, Wood, & Fecser, 2001). The LSCI model grew out of Aichhorn's work (1935). One of Aichhorn's students was Fritz Redl. Trained by Anna Freud and committed to working with delinquent youth Redl moved to America in the late 1930s. The boys he worked with had extremely poor self-regulatory capacities and their lives were a series of crises. Redl and his colleagues described how adults can and need to focus on creating an emotionally healthy milieu as well as the importance of a positive peer group as an essential foundation for healthy development. He created the notion of the "Life Space Interview" that focuses on how adults can engage the youngster in crisis (Redl & Wineman, 1957). They detailed how analytic principles need to shape understanding and the management of the youngster's crisis as it is occurring to maximize social and emotional learning and therapeutic work. For example, the overlapping notion that students usually are "doing their best" (an appreciative attitude), as well as the idea that behavior typically signals unrecognized internal experience, are simple, but profound examples of analytically informed thinking—and this program—that many educators have not really considered. When Redl became the chief of the Child Research Branch of the NIMH he continued his systematic studies of LSI, group process, psychotherapy, and remedial interventions. One of Redl's younger colleagues—Nicholas Long—added to this work in important ways.

In a series of studies and linked manuals, Long and his colleagues translated, concretized, and added to Redl's work in developing a series of specific, operationally based steps (Long & Newman, 1963). They delineated, for example, the specific skills, knowledge, and conceptual frameworks adults need to understand what various "crises" may be signaling. Explicitly building on Aichhorn's and Redl's work, the goal is to transform problems into opportunities for social emotional learning. The emphasis is to discover the underlying causes and patterns of self-defeating behaviors. They specified a series of intervention strategies in the actual milieu that clinical and research work had shown to support adults making a student crisis an opportunity to learn (Long, Wood, & Fecser, 2001). This work has been independently evaluated in a series of studies–nationally and internationally—and is now recognized as a powerful framework and strategy for professional staff to teach youngsters engaged in destructive behavior to act more responsibly. It is now an integral facet of many special education school systems, some regular education systems, and is taught in a growing number of colleges of education.

Another project that focuses on troubled children is the School-Based Mourning Project. This program has been designed to help high-risk inner-city elementary school children deal with multiple losses and trauma. This model is based—in part—on the notion that grieving is especially difficult for inner city children living in a chaotic environment of poverty and often traumatized by violence. The program is designed to enable these children to deal with the feelings of hopelessness, the pain of grief, violent fantasies, and guilt. Preliminary clinical pre and post testing indicate the effectiveness of the intervention (Sklarew, et al., 2002).

The PATHS Curriculum (**P**romoting **A**lternative **TH**inking **S**trategies) is an analytically informed social emotional learning program that can be taught to K-5 children (Kusché & Greenberg, 2001). Initially developed for special education students, it is now being used within a growing number of regular education settings as well. In a series of controlled studies with randomized control versus experimental groups, psychoanalyst Carol Kusché and developmental psychologist Mark Greenberg have demonstrated that this program increases children's ability to recognize emotions, understand social problems, develop effective alternative solutions to problems, and, decreases the frequency of aggressive/violent solutions. Teachers reported significant improvements in a variety of student prosocial behaviors. This work also had a positive effect on children's cognitive testing. One-year teacher follow-up study indicated impressive reductions in behavioral difficulties (Kusché & Greenberg, 2001). The PATHS curriculum is included in most national registries of "research-based" and "approved" programs, a designation that is increasingly required if American school systems are to receive state and/or federal funding to support educational, risk prevention, and/or health promotion efforts.

Since 1969 Henri Parens and his colleagues have been involved in parenting education (Parens, 1988; 2011). They have developed a Curriculum for Students in Grades K through 12, as well as Workshops for child caregivers (Parens et al. 1997; Parens & Rose-Itkoff, 1997). These parenting materials and strategies grew out of their Early Child Development Program, a longitudinal observation project that lasted seven years the effects of which, based on a nineteen-year follow-up study, revealed significantly improved adaptive functioning in the areas of legal difficulties, drug and alcohol use, and education), improved aggression profiles in the children, and a dramatic positive change in self esteem and parenting style in the mothers (Parens 1993 & 2011; Parens et al, 2006). The thrust of the Curriculum for Students in Grades K through 12 is that children have shown that they can be taught how to optimize the development of children many of whom will have them within years of graduating from high school. Parens's work has been used in a number of American sites as well as in Israel. It has also provided the foundation for *Educating Children for Parenting* (ECP), an effort that has educated more than 125,000 young people (P–12) helping them to understand and develop skills linked to parenting. ECP provides a school based parenting education curriculum and trains teachers to integrate that curriculum across all academic subjects. ECP has conducted several independent evaluations that show it helps young people to alter defensive strategies, and that itfosters learning and interpersonal problem solving (Puriefoy-Brinkley, et al., 2004).

Twemlow, Sacco, Fonagy, and their colleagues have a programmatic effort that is organized around the bully-victim-bystander cycle that has two aims: to reduce bully-victim behavior and to promote responsible, caring communities. This effort teaches students—and school personnel—skills and linked sets of understanding about the toxicity of being a passive by-stander and sets in motion a community-wide effort to promote "upstander" behavior. (Twemlow, et al., 2001; Twemlow & Sacco, 2012). This is an important and ongoing educational and research effort that has experimentally demonstrated that it reduces violence in schools and increases academic achievement (Fonagy, et al., 2005). In addition, this group of analysts and educators are looking at a variety of individual student as well as teacher characteristics. For example, a recent study of educators showed that teachers who experienced bullying themselves when young are more likely to both bully students and experience bullying by students both in and outside the classroom (Twemlow, Fonagy, Sacco, & Brethour, 2006; Twemlow, 2012). Although this finding will not surprise analytically informed clinicians, it is important in two ways. Bullying by teachers has been an overlooked—but common—problem. It also applies a psychoanalytically informed perspective about personality development to a fundamentally important school problem. Twemlow, Fonagy, and their colleagues have developed the notion of "mentalizing communities" and are studying it application to three arenas: (1) reducing bullying and creating a peaceful climate in schools; (2) promoting compassion in cities by a focus on end-of-life care; and (3) a mentalization-based intervention to modify the parenting styles of borderline and substance abusing parents (Twemlow, Fonagy, & Sacco, 2005).

As noted above, the National School Climate Center has developed a five-stage school improvement process that builds on our Comprehensive School Climate Inventory (CSCI) that recognizes how K-12 students, parents, and school personnel experience the school. School climate reflects the individuals' perception of school life. Although no two people perceive school in the same way, school climate trends are very strongly associated with students' self-concept, absenteeism, high school graduation rates, behavioral problems, effective risk prevention, and academic achievement as well as teacher satisfaction and retention (Cohen, 2006; Freiberg, 1999). The CSCI is garnering a great deal of attention from U.S. State Departments of Education and several foreign educational ministries. Although there are literally hundreds of school climate measures, the CSCI is the only measure that has been recommended in the three independent evaluations of school climate measures (www.schoolclimate.org/climate/practice.php). Surveys are—necessarily—thin: they reveal conscious and delimited accounts of experience. Nonetheless, they are potentially very meaningful in education because what is measured "counts." Today, what is measured and what counts are two dimensions of student life: reading and math achievement. In America and abroad, there is a growing awareness that this represents only "one leg" of the proverbial elephant and that we need to recognize and promote the social, emotional and ethical capacities of K-12 students. To the extent that school systems and State Departments of Education use comprehensive school climate measures, we will influence educational policy and practice.

"Test results" are often not understood and fail to be used as a springboard for learning and change. This is true for an individual child's comprehensive psychoeducational test findings (Cohen, 1997b) as well as school climate measures. As a result, our Center has developed a "road map" that helps school leaders appreciate that the CSCI is simply a springboard for community wide learning, goal setting, and implementation efforts.

We have developed a series of detailed guidelines, resources and, web-based learning communities in the *School Climate Resource Center* (http://scrc.schoolclimate.org/) to support the following five phases of school climate improvement: (1) Recognizing past efforts and planning for evaluation and change; (2) Evaluating the social, emotional, and ethical as well as academic aspects of school life; (3) Understanding and "digging deeper" into evaluation findings and creating an action plan; (4) implementation; and, (5) reevaluation and planning for the next phase of school improvement. In a number of ways, the third stage is particularly important and analytically relevant. To begin with, school personnel are too often in a continually "reactive mode" and anything but reflective. This third stage of "unpacking evaluation findings and creating an action plan" provides a wealth of opportunities to support school leaders—as well as the whole community—to become more reflective. For example, parents and educators in a recent twelve school study reported that bullying was a "minor" or "moderately severe" problem. On the other hand, students in all of the schools report bullying to be a "severe" problem (Cohen, 2006). From an analytic large-group perspective, this student-based experience has been "split off." Recognizing that all or a given sub group of students are experiencing a significant problem presents opportunities to not only think together about why this is and what can be done. It also raises larger questions about why this experience has been unrecognized.

Although there have been many school-based analytically informed programmatic efforts, it is only in recent years that analysts have developed programmatic efforts that include replicable guidelines, curricula, and/or learning activities. These efforts are important as they are garnering attention—for good reason—outside of the analytic community. Too often in clinical and applied analytic work we have just talked to each other and not created a platform for an inter-disciplinary dialogue and scientific discovery.

Echoing what I have described above, there is no single answer to the question of what makes these applied analytic programs psychoanalytic. Their work is analytically grounded in appreciating (1) unconscious life; (2) the central role of emotional development; (3) the importance of understanding the inter-relatedness of social, emotional, and cognitive growth; and, (4) the essential importance of creating safe, caring, and responsive environments for children to grow up within.

For many years in America and abroad, risk prevention and health promotion efforts were characteristically "stand alone" programmatic efforts split off from the rest of school life. The vast majority of school-based bully prevention efforts are examples of this as are Sklarew's and Parens's programs (described above): they are added on to the students' schedule and not integrated into the life of the classroom and/or school. A series of meta-analytic studies have revealed that risk prevention and health promotion efforts for children in general and disadvantaged and/or troubled children in particular are dramatically more effective when they are a part of a wide, coordinated, and comprehensive school effort (Catalano, et al., 2002). Long's work with special education students, and Kusché's, Twemlow's, and our Center's work with special as well as general education students, are examples of programmatic efforts that have been successfully integrated into the day-to-day fabric of student life. It is not surprising that they have garnered national and international attention. In fact, comprehensive school climate reform efforts have been officially supported by the Centers for Disease Control and Prevention (2009) as an essential improvement strategy that supports students feeling and being connected (school connectedness) to schools; The Institute for Educational Sciences and the *What Works* Clearinghouse suggests that there is "moderate" support for school climate improvement efforts as a dropout prevention strategy (Dynarski, Clarke, Cobb, Finn, Rumberger, & Smink, 2008); and, the U.S. Department of Education has invested in the *Safe and Supportive Schools* (S3) grant program that supports State Departments of Education (1) developing state-wide school climate measurement systems and (2) studying of school climate improvement process with small groups of low performing high schools.

EDUCATING EDUCATORS

Another significant area of work has to do with educating educators. When analysts teach and learn with educators during their formative training, we potentially shape how they understand and work with generations of colleagues, students, and their parents. Psychoanalysts have lectured and/or led workshops at Colleges of Education on many occasions. However, there have been few sustained efforts that have focused on the education of teachers. Most of these efforts have focused on early childhood educators (Furman, 1987 & 1995; Manning, et al., 1996; Cath, 2004) who have, historically, been most appreciative of an analytically informed perspective.

Anna Freud initiated the tradition of educating educators in an ongoing manner when her study group contributed to a psychoanalytic pedagogy magazine and developed the first course on the application of psychoanalytically informed thinking to teaching young children in the early 1920s. This work gave rise to her 1920/1930s lectures to teachers (Freud, 1930; 1974). There have been a number of other individual efforts to influence teacher education (Ekstein & Motto, 1969; Shane & Shane, 1974), but that these efforts have not become an ongoing facet of teacher education in America or abroad.

The Bank Street College of Education is the first and one of the very few examples of a psychoanalytic/educational partnership that shaped the curriculum and educational process within a College of Education. A group of European analysts and American educators constituted the College's original leadership team. From its inception in 1931, Bank Street has been committed to promoting children's developing social and emotional as well as traditionally "academic" competences and underscoring the fundamental importance of being a *reflective* educator. Promoting reflective capacities has always been *the* organizing center for this teacher education program (Lewis, 1991).

In the 1960s a teacher education program began under the auspices of the Chicago Institute for Psychoanalysis and evolved into the Human Development and Learning Program when a partnership was formed with DePaul University's School of Education. This program operated for thirty-four years and created a forum to bridge educational-mental health-analytic perspectives. Case studies and the role of children's developing emotional as well as cognitive life were an organizing focus for teaching and learning (Cox, 1980).

The single most important analytic-educational/multidisciplinary effort affecting teacher education is the *National Center for Infants, Children and Families: Zero to Three*. Although their primary emphasis is on the first three years of life, their inclusion of four and even five year olds warrants including the group in the four to eighteen year old scope of this paper. From its inception, the founders created an interdisciplinary forum where research and practice informed one another in an ongoing manner. This effort has dramatically influenced the education of early childhood teachers as well as having a major impact on diagnostic, educational practice, treatment, and policy.

The National School Climate Center has also been involved with teacher education in a number of ways. Our Teachers College Press *Social Emotional Learning* series, has become an award winning series of edited and authored volumes for academics as well as practicing school personnel. Several books in the series (Cohen, 1999b; 2001; Devine & Cohen, 2007) have been organized around cases written by analysts. These narratives of students' lives over time are a "red thread" that runs through each volume. There have also been a number of chapters written by analysts about analytically informed efforts. In 2004, in response to a request from the City University of New York, our Center developed a new four course, graduate level sequence in *Social, Emotional and Academic Education* (for details see, www.schoolclimate.org/programs/higherEd.php); we are hopeful that this certificate bearing sequence will be recognized by the New York State Department of Education as a new area of teacher expertise in the near future.

Although there have been very few examples of sustained efforts at teacher education, several common denominators make this applied work "psychoanalytic." These efforts have all included the explicit goal of promoting the adults' reflective capacity in general and an appreciation that conscious and unrecognized emotional, social, and cognitive life are inter-related and shape mental life and behavior. Case based learning tends to be a core method used to achieve these goals.

Unfortunately, we know very little as to whether this work is significantly more helpful than non-analytically informed efforts that have been carried out along similar lines. With the exception of *Zero to Three*, there have been few attempts to systematically study the impact of these efforts over time. As a result it is difficult to know to what extent the work is "generalizable" and/or is largely a function of the one individual who is implementing it.

CLINICAL AND INTERDISCIPLINARY WORK

Clinical work and applied work with an educational system differ in many important ways. The intimacy and depth of clinical work is, naturally, unique. Before I suggest three steps that will further interdisciplinary work, I want to briefly note several interesting similarities as well as differences in the theory, goals, and methods that define clinical and applied or interdisciplinary work. Our theory always—consciously and not—shapes our goals, which in turn, ideally suggest particular methods designed to actualize given goals.

Many levels of theory guide our work (e.g., about psychosocial functioning and development; therapeutic action; role definition; and more). There is not one psychoanalytic theory of mental functioning that clinicians adhere to. Although some clinicians think systemically, more commonly analysts who work with educators also use systems theory to understand how facets of school life color and shape behavior. Another critical theoretical dimension is related to how we conceptualize modes of therapeutic action and our role. Most analysts consider transference analysis or the process of discovering unrecognized meanings and structures to be an essential mode of therapeutic action in child and adult analysis. Over the last two decades, I suggest that there has been a growing appreciation within the analytic community that there are many modes of therapeutic action: many of them not unique to a psychoanalytically informed clinical process (e.g., promoting a climate of safety; internalizing the therapist; enhancing reflective capacities; facilitating greater affect tolerance; and more). Unlike clinical work, this framework is typically in the background rather than the foreground of our interdisciplinary conversations.

In the clinical situation, we conceptualize and position ourselves as the expert and "provider" of treatment. As I described above this stance has deleteriously colored and inadvertently undermined analytically informed clinicians consultative work with educators. I suggest that a more helpful applied/interdisciplinary role definition is that we are and need to be true "learners as well as teachers." We are not "healers" in our work with educators. However, this distinction is not a neat one. I believe many, if not most, clinicians would say that they are co-discoverers or learners as well as having expertise that leads us to provide or create a "platform" for co-discovery.

Clinical and applied goals are similar and importantly different. Both have an overall goal of "improving functioning." Clinically, our goal is to understand and help an individual child and to a greater or typically lesser extent, the family. In applied consultative work our goals are often broader. Even if we are in the role of consultant focusing on a given child, we tend to necessarily be attuned to peers in the classroom, the family, and the overall climate of the school. And, often, our goals are to influence larger groups of students, parents, or school personnel. Often our goal is to promote learning rather than to heal or address conflict and the range of ways that children's development has become stymied. Methodologically, there are few similarities between clinical and our applied interdisciplinary work with educators. Although we may think in very similar ways (e.g., about unrecognized experience and developmentally informed psychosocial functioning) and work towards similar goals (e.g., discovering together what is and is not working as well as learning together how this came to be) few analysts today work with educators in the way we work with patients.

FUTURE DIRECTIONS IN INTERDISCIPLINARY PSYCHOANALYTIC WORK

Applied and interdisciplinary psychoanalysis has been a subject for discussion within the field from its inception. It has been an area of sustained work and learning for child analysts since its inauguration. In recent years, there has been a growing appreciation that the future of analysis will to an important extent rest on this type of work. There is growing interest in this work in national and international psychoanalytic organizations (Ramzy, Twemlow, & Maher, 2004; Twemlow, & Ramzy, 2012). At the same time, there continues to be another analytic tradition that defines anything save intrapsychically focused clinical work as "not analysis." Applied analysis tends to be devalued by many analytically informed clinicians. I have been surprised and at times, disheartened to discover how few analysts are interested in work outside of the consulting room.

To further effective applied analytic work in the educational arena, there are three important areas to consider. First, we need to include courses on applied analytic work in the curriculum of our institutes. The fact that it is not an integral facet of training is but one manifestation that this work is institutionally devalued. In fact, there is a growing range of creative applied analytic work in schools and the community (e.g., Rosenblitt, 2004; Sklarew, Twemlow & Wilkinson, 2004). As noted above, a COPE group has developed curricular guidelines for institutes that want to consider adding this course of study (Twemlow & Parens, 2006).

Secondly, I suggest that we need to create more forums where analysts and non-analysts learn from one another. Too often our efforts have been focused on "applying" analytic ideas to education, rather than being part of an interdisciplinary process of being learners as well as teachers together. To the extent that we position ourselves as "the experts" who are not also "learners," we undermine our capacity to be effective teachers as well as learners. The American Psychoanalytic Association's *Committee on Schools*, The International Association for Child and Adolescent Psychiatry and Allied Professions (IACAPAP), The International Society for Adolescent Psychiatry and Psychology, and the International Association for Applied Psychoanalytic Studies as well as the *Zero to Three* are committed to these efforts.

Finally, we need to support the systematic study of applied analytic efforts. How can we operationally define what is psychoanalytic about a given form of applied work? How can we discover what the power and limitations of these factors are? It is well known that clinical psychoanalytic work has suffered because we only recently begun to systematically study process and outcome. The same is true for applied analytic work in schools and the larger community. Encouraging the systematic study (serial case study, ethnographic, empirical, or otherwise) of these efforts is the single most important step we can now take. Unfortunately, the current "gold standard" of federally (and to a great extent, internationally) supported "approved research" is experimental studies that focus on one or a very limited number of "forces" (variables). In a terribly important paper Wachtel (2010) brilliantly critiques the assumptions and limitations of this mode of discovery/research. In fact, every mode of systematic discovery—research—has limitations as well as strengths. I suggest that the most helpful and sophisticated modes of discovery/research are a combination of ethnographic research and case studies on the one hand and experimental methods that recognize that human development and life are always shaped by a multitude of "forces" that we can systemically track, study, and learn from through the utilization of hierarchical linear modeling (Raudenbush & Bryk, 2001).

Research efforts can and should overlap with policy-related considerations. Too often, in our applied efforts— like our clinical—we have operated in splendid isolation. In fact, state and national policy powerfully shapes funding, dissemination efforts, and educational practice.

Freud's original vision was that psychoanalysis had the potential to be a healing force in society generally and in the education of young children in particular. We have ample opportunities and a responsibility to continue and deepen this tradition.

ACKNOWLEDGMENTS

This paper is a revised and updated version of my 2007 paper: Interdisciplinary psychoanalysis and the education of children: Psychoanalytic and educational partnerships. *Psychoanalytic Study of the Child.* Volume 62. Edited by R. A. King, P. B. Neubauer, S. I. Abrams & A. S. Dowling. (pp. 180–207). New Haven: Yale University Press. It is re-printed with permission from Yale University Press.

NOTES

1. In this chapter, I will use the terms "psychoanalytically informed child clinicians" and "psychoanalysts" interchangeably.
2. In this chapter, I will focus on 4 to 18 year old children and adolescents or Kindergarten through 12th grade in the American educational system.
3. Group members include: Phyllis Jean Cath, M.D., Jonathan Cohen, Ph.D., Nancy Kulish, Ph.D. (co-chair), Steven Marans, Ph.D., Henri Parens, M.D., Moisy Shopper, M.D., Bruce H. Sklarew, M.D., Stuart W. Twemlow, M.D. (co-chair), and Sallye M. Wilkinson, Ph.D.
4. Although none of these studies are psychoanalytic in nature, many of them grew out of early psychoanalytic work and writings (Cohen, 2006). These researchers have, for the most part, been cognitive-behavioral/primary prevention specialists who, in important ways, built on analytic ideas and practices, empirically studying those ideas, simplifying them, but rarely honoring or crediting the analytic roots of their findings. This is another instance where the psychoanalytic "anti-research" culture has inadvertently undermined credibility and reputation and retarded learning within the analytic community (Cohen, 1997a).

REFERENCES

Aichhorn, A. (1925). *Wayward youth.* NY: Viking Press.

Berkovitz, I. H. (1999). School-based mental health services: the future of child and adolescent psychiatry. *Adolescent psychiatry: Developmental and clinical studies,* 1999, 24, Hillsdale, NJ: The Analytic Press.

Blank, M. J. & Berg, A. (2006). *All Together Now: Sharing Responsibility for the Whole Child.* Alexandra, VA: Association for Supervision and Curriculum Development.

Cath, P. (2004). Personal communication, December 15, 2004.

Catalano, R. F., Berglund, M. L., Ryan, J. A. M., Lonczak, H. S., & Hawkins, J. D. (2002). Positive youth development in the United States: Research findings on evaluations of positive youth development programs. *Prevention & Treatment, 5*, Article 15. Centers for Disease Control and Prevention. (2009). School connectedness: Strategies for increasing protective factors among youth. Atlanta, GA: Author. Retrieved January 30, 2012, from www.cdc.gov/healthyyouth/adolescenthealth/pdf/connectedness.pdf.

Cohen, J. (1997a). Child and Adolescent Psychoanalysis: Research, Practice and Theory. *International Journal of Psychoanalysis, 78*, 3, 499–520.

Cohen, J. (1997b). On the uses and misuses of psychoeducational evaluations. *Adolescent Psychiatry: Developmental and Clinical Studies, 21*, 253–268.

Cohen, J. (1999a). The first "R": Reflective capacities. *Educational Leadership, 57, 1*, 70–75.

Cohen, J. (ed.) (1999b). *Educating minds and hearts: Social emotional learning and the passage into adolescence.* New York: Teachers College Press.

Cohen, J. (2001). Social emotional education: Core principals and practices. In J. Cohen (Ed.). *Caring classrooms /intelligent Schools: The social emotional education of young children.* NY: Teachers College Press.

Cohen, J. (2002). Guest Editor: *Psychoanalysis and Education* published in the *Journal of Applied Psychoanalytic Studies, (Special Issue) 4*, 3.

Cohen, J. (2006, Summer). Social, emotional, ethical and academic education: Creating a climate for learning, participation in democracy and well-being. *Harvard Educational Review. 76, 2*, 201–237.

Cohen, J., Shapiro, L., & Fisher, M. (2006). Finding the Heart of Your School: Using School Climate Data to Create a Climate for Learning. *Principal Leadership* (The journal of the National Association of Secondary School Principals) *7, 4*, 26–32.

Cohen, J., Pickeral, T., & Levine, P. (2010). The Foundation for Democracy: Social, emotional, ethical, cognitive skills and dispositions in K-12 schools. *Inter-American Journal of Education for Democracy, 3, 1*, 73–94. Available at: http://scholarworks.iu.edu/journals/index.php/ried/index.

Comer, J. P. (1988). *Maggie's American Dream: The Life and Times of a Black Family.* Penguin Books

Comer, J. P. (1995). *School Power*. Free Press.

Comer, J. P. (2005). *Leave no child behind.* Yale University Press.

Comer, J. P., Joyner, E.T., & Ben-Avie, M. (2004). *Six Pathways to Healthy Child Development and Academic Success: The Field Guide to Comer Schools in Action* (Comer Schools in Action). Corwin Press.

Cox, C. H. (1980). Between Teacher and Child: An Interview with Kay Field. *Curriculum-Review, 19, 5*, 390–94

Devine, J. & Cohen, J. (2007). *Making your school safe: Strategies to Protect Children and Promote Learning.* NY: Teachers College Press.

Dryfoos, J. & Quinn, J. (2005). *Community Schools: A Strategy for Integrating Youth Development and School Reform: New Directions for Youth Development.* San Francisco: Jossey-Bass

Durlak, J. A., Weissberg, R. P., Dymnicki, A. B., Taylor, R. D., & Schellinger, K. B. (2011). The impact of enhancing students' social and emotional learning: a meta-analysis of school-based universal interventions. *Child Development, 82, 1*, 405–32.

Dynarski, M., Clarke, L., Cobb, B., Finn, J., Rumberger, R., and Smink, J. (2008). *Dropout Prevention: A Practice Guide* (NCEE 2008–4025). Washington, DC: National Center for Education Evaluation and Regional Assistance, Institute of Education Sciences, U.S. Department of Education. Retrieved from http://ies.ed.gov/ncee/wwc.

Ekstein, R. & Motto, R. L. (1969). *From learning for love to love of learning: Essays on psychoanalysis and education.* New York: Brunner Mazel.

Erikson, E. H. (1979). *Identify: Youth and crisis.* New York: W.W. Norton.

Farley, A. J. & Manning, D. (2002) A three-tiered, applied psychoanalytic intervention to support young children's emotional development. *Journal of Applied Psychoanalytic Studies, 4, 3.*

Freiberg, H. J. (Ed.). (1999). *School climate: Measuring, improving and sustaining healthy learning environments*. Philadelphia, PA: Falmer Press.

Fonagy, P., Twemlow, S. W., Vernberg, E., Sacco, F. C. & Little, T. (2005). Creating a Peaceful School Learning Environment: The Impact of an Anti-Bullying Program on Educational Attainment in Elementary schools. *Medical Science Monitor*, 2005, *11, 7*, 317–325.

Fuchs-Nadeau, D. LaRue, C. M., Allen, J., Cohen, J., Hyman, L., (2002). The New York State *Interpersonal Violence Prevention Resource Guide: Stopping Youth Violence Before it Begins*. New York State Center for School Safety, The New York State Office of the Governor and the New York State Education Department, Albany, New York.

Furman, E. (1987). *The teacher's guide to helping young children grow*. Madison, CT: International Universities Press.

Furman, E. (ed.) (1995). *Psychoanalytic consultations with parents, teachers, and caregivers*. Madison, CT: International Universities Press.

Furman, R. A., & Katan, A. (1969). *The therapeutic nursery school*. NY: International Universities Press.

Freud, A. (1974). 1922–1935 Lectures on psychoanalysis for teachers and parents. In *The Writings of Anna Freud*, 1, pp. 73–136. New York: International University Press. (Original work published 1930).

Freud, A. & Dann, S. (1951). An experiment in group upbringing. *Psychoanalytic Study of the Child*, *6*, 127–168.

Freud, A. & Burlingham, D. (1973). *Infants without families. Reports on the Hampstead nurseries 1939–1949.* New York: International Universities Press.

Freud, S. (1933) (1964). *New introductory lectures on psychoanalysis*. SE. *22*, 146.

Geissmann, C., & Geissmann, P. (1998). *A history of child psychoanalysis*. London and NY: Routledge.

Hope, M. (1999). Outcomes of Cornerstone treatment: A controlled assessment. Doctoral dissertation, Wright Institute, Berkeley, CA.

Hug-Hellmuth, H. (1914). Kinderpsychologie, Padadogik, *Jahrbuch fur Psycho-analytische und psychopathologische Forschungen*, *6*, 393–404.

Kernberg, O. (2006). The pressing need to increase research in and on psychoanalysis. *International Journal of Psychoanalysis*, *87, 4*.

Kliman, G. (1975). Analyst in the Nursery: Application of Child Analytic Techniques in a Therapeutic Nursery, *Psychoanalytic Study of the Child*, *30*. Kliman, G. (1997) The Cornerstone Project: Analysis in Special Ed Classes, *The Am Psychoanalyst*, *31, 2*, 27–28.

Kliman, G (2006) Methods for maximizing the good outcomes of foster care: Evidence-based strategies for reducing transfers among homes and raising I.Q.'s. *International Journal of Applied Psychoanal*ysis, *3* , *1*, 4–16.

Kusché, C.A. & Greenberg, M.T. (2001). PATHS in Your Classroom: Promoting Emotional Literacy and Alleviating Emotional Distress. In Cohen, J. ed. (2001). *Caring classrooms/ intelligent schools: The social emotional education of young children*. New York: Teachers College Press.

Lewis, C. (1991). The early years of the advisement program at Bank Street College. *Thought and Practice, 3, 1*, 29–32.

Long, M. L. & Newman, R. G. (1963). The teacher's handling of children in conflict. *Bulletin of the School of Education, Indiana University, 37, 4.*

Long, N. L., Wood, M. M. & Fecser, F. A. (2001). *Life space crisis intervention: Talking with students in crisis*. (Second edition). Austin, TX: Pro-ed.

Lopez, T. and Kliman, G. (1979). The Cornerstone treatment of a preschool boy from an extremely impoverished environment. *Psychoanalytic Study of the Child*, *35*, NY Times Press.

Manning, D., Rubin, S. E., Gunther, P., Gonzales, R. G., & Schindler, P. (1996). A "worry doctor" for preschool directors and teachers: a collaborative model. *Young Children*, July, 68–73.

Marans, S. & Cohen, J. (1999). Social-emotional learning: A psychoanalytically informed perspective. (Chapter 7) In J. Cohen (Editor) (1999). *Educating Minds and Hearts: Social Emotional Learning and the Passage into Adolescence*. New York: Teachers College Press and the Association for Supervision and Curriculum Development.

Midgley, N. (2008). The 'Matchbox School' (1927–1932): Anna Freud and the idea of a 'psychoanalytically informed education. *Journal of Child Psychotherapy, 34, 1*, 23–42.

Miller, M. A. (1998). *Freud and the Bolsheviks*. New Haven & London: Yale University Press.

Parens, H. (1988). "A Psychoanalytic Contribution Toward Rearing Emotionally Healthy Children: Education for Parenting." In: *New concepts in psychoanalytic psychotherapy*, J. M. Ross & W. A. Myers (eds.) pp. 120–138. Washington, DC: American Psychiatric Press.

Parens, H. (1993). "Toward preventing experience-derived emotional disorders: Education for Parenting." In: *Prevention in Mental Health*, H. Parens & S. Kramer, eds., pp. 121–148. Northvale, NJ: Jason Aronson, Inc.

Parens, H. (2011). *Taming Aggression in Your Child: How to Avoid Raising Bullies, Delinquents, or Trouble-Makers*. New York: Jason Aronson.

Parens, H., Scattergood, E., Duff, S., & Singletary, W. (1997). *Parenting for Emotional Growth: A Curriculum for Students in Grades K Thru 12. Vol. 1, The Textbook; Vol. 2, The Lesson Plans*. Philadelphia: Parenting for Emotional Growth, Inc. © TXu 680–613.

Parens, H. and Rose-Itkoff, C. (1997). *Parenting for Emotional Growth: The Workshops Series. (1) On The Development of Self & Human Relationships*; *(2) On Aggression; (3) Conscience Formation; (4) Sexual Development in Children*. Philadelphia: Parenting for Emotional Growth, Inc. © TXu 842—316 & 317.

Parens, H., Rose-Itkoff, C., Pearlman, M., Reid, K., Turrini, P., Fallon, T., Singletary, W., & Scattergood, E. (2006). "Into our 4th decade of prevention via parenting education: Where we have been—where we are going." *International Journal of Applied Psychoanalytic Studies, 3, 1*, 17–38.

Puriefoy-Brinkley, J. & Bardige, B. (2004). Learning from babies: Vital lessons for school children. *Journal of Zero to Three: National Center for Infants, Toddles and Families, 24, 3*, 22–287.

Ramzy, N., Twemlow, S. W. & Maher, A. (2004). Psychoanalysis in the larger world: The International Association for Applied Psychoanalytic Studies, *The American Psychoanalyst, 38, 2*, 12–13.

Raudenbush, S. W. & Bryk, A. S. (second edition) (2001). Hierarchical Linear Models: Applications and Data Analysis Methods. Thousand Oaks CA: Sage Publications, Inc.

Redl, F. & Wineman, D. (1957). *The aggressive child*. Glencoe, Ill: The Free Press.

Rosenblitt, D. L. (2001). Lucy Daniels Center for Early Childhood Early Intervention Program 10 year Follow-up Study Interim Data. Unpublished paper.

Rosenblitt, D. L. (2003). The Alliance of Psychoanalytic Schools, Association *for Child Psychoanalytic Newsletter*, Winter, p. 11.

Rosenblitt, D. L. (2004). Translating Psychoanalysis from the Playroom to the Classroom: Opportunities and Choices. *Journal of American Psychoanalytic Association, 53, 1*, 181–211.

Rosenblitt, D. L. (2006). Personal communication, September 25, 2006.

Shane, E. & Shane, M. (1974). An Exceptional Child in the Normal Classroom: A Psychoanalytic-Developmental Approach to Teacher Education. *California Journal of Teacher Education*; *2, 2*, 86–101.

Shepherd, M. J. (2002). Consultant or Comrade: Comments about Analysts' Working Relationships in Schools. *J Applied Psychoanal Studies, 4, 3*. 331–337.

Sklarew, B. Krupnick J.; Ward-Wimmer D.; Napoli C. (2002). The School-Based Mourning Project: A Preventive Intervention in the Cycle of Inner-City Violence. *J Applied Psychoanal Studies 4, 3*. 317–330.

Sklarew, B. Twemlow, S. W. & Wilkinson, S. M. (2004). *Analysts in the trenches: Streets, Schools, War Zones*. Mahwah, NJ: Analytic Press.

Twemlow, S. (2012). Adult bullying. *School Climate Matters*, Vol. 6, 1, page 3 (Available on: http://www.schoolclimate.org/about/newsletter.php).

Twemlow, S., Sacco, F. (1996). Peacekeeping and Peacemaking: The Conceptual Foundations of a Plan to Reduce Violence and Improve the Quality of Life in a Midsized Community in Jamaica. *Psychiatry*: 59, 156–174.

Twemlow, S., Fonagy, P., Sacco, F. C., Gies, M. & Hess, D. (2001). Improving the social and intellectual climate in elementary schools by addressing bully-victim-bystander relationship power struggles. In Cohen, J. ed. (2001), *Caring classrooms / intelligent schools: The social emotional education of young children*. New York: Teachers College Press.

Twemlow, S. W., Fonagy, P., Sacco, F. C. (2005). A developmental approach to mentalizing communities: I. A model for social change. *Bulletin of the Menninger Clinic, 69, 4*, 265–81.

Twemlow, S. W., Fonagy, P., Sacco, F. C. & Brethour, J.R. (2006).

Teachers Who Bully Students: A Hidden Trauma. *International Journal of Social Psychiatry, 52, 3*, 187–198

Twemlow, S. W. & Parens, H. (2006). Might Freud's legacy lie beyond the couch? *Psychoanalytic Psychology, 23, 2*, 430–451.

Twemlow, S. W. & Ramzy, N. (2012). Editorial. *International Journal of Applied Psychoanalytic Studies, 9, 1*, pp. 1–3,

Twemlow, S. W. & Sacco, F. C. (2012). *Preventing bullying and school violence*. Washington, DC: American Psychiatric Association Press.

U.S. Department of Education (2005). *No Child Left Behind Act of 2001*. Retrieved November 25, 2005, from www.ed.gov/nclb/.

Wachtel, P. L. (2010). Beyond "EST's: Problematic Assumptions in the Pursuit of Evidence-Based Practice. *Psychoanalytic Psychology, 27, 3*, 251–272.

Wilkinson, S. (2004). COPE: *Curriculum for applied psychoanalysis in the community* Bibliography—With Some Annotation. Unpublished manuscript.

Weissberg, R. P., Kumpfer, K. L., & Seligman, M. E. P. (2003). Prevention that works for children and youth: An introduction. *American Psychologist, 58 , 6-7*, 425–432.

Young-Bruehl, E. (1988). *Anna Freud: A biography*. New York: Norton & Company.

Zelman, A., Samuels, S., and Abrams, D. (1985) IQ changes of young children following intensive long-term psychotherapy. *Journal of Psychology, 34*, 215–217.

Zelman, A. and Samuels, S. (1996) Children's IQ changes and long-term psychotherapy: A follow up study. Chapter in Zelman, A. (Ed.) *Early Intervention with High-Risk Children: Freeing Prisoners of Circumstance*. Northvale, NJ: Jason Aronson.

Zins, J., Weissberg, R. W., Wang, M. C. & Walberg, H. W. (2004). *Building school success on social emotional learning: What does the research say?* NY: Teachers College Press.

Chapter Two

The Child, Childhood, and School

Patrick Lewis

I wanted a loneliness unfettered by a need for belonging, an integrity integral to the cosmos but independent from its whims, and a wholeness that allows me to realize myself and who I am supposed to be.

—Lewis, 1995, p. 74

The construction of childhood development and early learning is not a new phenomenon. In fact it is a process that began in earnest at the beginning of the twentieth century with the advent of the field of psychology, and in particular the psychology of human development, and has evolved from a process of description of childhood to a prescription of childhood. The National Association for the Education of Young Children (NAEYC), through its notion of Developmentally Appropriate Practice (DAP, 2009 version) embodied in the same titled document is demonstrative of the historical process of psychology's influence on early childhood education. From the first and second editions of DAP (1987, 1997) to the most recent iteration (2009), the historical (un)changing theoretical influence of developmental psychology discourse(s) manifest themselves through recommended praxis in early childhood education. Today, when critics of the dominant discourse of early learning turn their gaze upon current policy, curricula, and teaching practices they are in fact critically analyzing over a century of work. This is not to say that all things (in)formed by educational psychology are in need of critical analysis, rather it would be more accurate to say that "the bewitching language of psychology and the behavioral sciences has skewed our view of education" (Huebner, 1999, p. 404) and consequently, how we as teachers might live alongside children and families. Through the creation of state sanctioned curricular documents delineating the desired goals and objectives for learners in the form of discrete learning outcomes, developmental psychology, as taken up by policy makers and educators, has facilitated the creation of a prescribed childhood and adolescence. We find ourselves in a world that strongly delineates accepted and valued ideas of what it means to be normal; that is to say,

> the ideal individual is predetermined in the eye of psychology and education, and the role of both these disciplines is to assist, support, and guide the individual to progress along the road to toward this ideal. Young children are viewed as immature and primitive forms of the ideal; education is assigned the function of creating the universal, ideal human being. Consequently, someone who does not meet this idea . . . is not considered desirable and is viewed by society as a failure. (Johnson, Christie, & Wardle, 2005, p. 5)

A pervasive and unquestioned pedagogical paradigm like this has far reaching implications for not just a few individual children and youth, but for large populations of culturally and linguistically diverse children and youth.

Over the past two decades or more a sense of urgency about literacy and numeracy learning has emerged in regional and national governments that utilize assessment and evaluation processes from such international organizations as the Organisation for Economic Cooperation and Development (OECD) or locally through state and/or provincial standardized assessments. It is a narrative that is supported through a political-economic discourse of employment, competiveness, and sustainability. The result is that the public discourse about education has been reduced to math and reading and to a Euro-American middle-class model of the expected behaviors that all learners should possess if they are to be successful in school and subsequently in life. A biomedical approach to literacy and numeracy learning is beginning to inform most early learning (Pre-K to Grade 3). It is an approach to literacy that "is a reworking of psychological reading with its insistence on behavioral, prescriptive curricula, and literacy as perceptually based decoding" (Heydon&Iannacci, 2009, p. 37) with the addition of emphasizing the new phonics, and the blend of phonemic awareness with direct phonics and decoding instruction (p. 37). Furthermore, the approach views learning difficulties with reading as a neurological glitch most probably related to genetics and offers "scientific research" for developing curricula for enhancing brain development to solve the problems. However, such an approach ignores "the affective and discursive elements of literacy" (p. 37) and creates a system "operating from a deficit-perspective, [which] pathologizes and disables entire schools" (p. 37).

When a child does not measure up, a prescriptive lens is brought to bear; the learner failed to try hard enough and did not embrace the appropriate behaviors; the teacher is not equipped to teach the appropriate skills and behaviors; the learner has some brain glitch that is preventing her from correctly processing and integrating the phonological and phonemic data when engaged in reading; and the child's family literacy learning behaviors are not congruent with the school culture. Literacy is always and everywhere socio-political; it is not simply a technical process of decoding symbols, it is a socially and politically mediated process integral to a child's becoming. School literacies not only give something to children, they construct them along particular epistemic and ontologic lines that may not be in their best interest culturally, emotionally, or cognitively; in that pedagogical process something is often taken away from the child. Developmental theory as manifested in school "privileges a particular model of normality, to the extent that it is certain children, who are "Othered," who become the object of pathologisation discourses" (Walkerdine, 1999, p. 3). As Luke and Luke (2001) noted, this narrative is an "insidious ideology of early childhood" (p. 113) that has manufactured a belief that children and families are deficient if they do not measure up to the norms embodied in the literacy and numeracy standards set out by the curriculum guides of departments and ministries of education or provide the appropriately "enriching environments" (p. 113) necessary to realize the desired behaviors. School literacies are where children apprehend and are included, or miss and are excluded from the perceptual participation in the language zones, where context always takes primacy over text (Bakhtin, 1981). Within any single language approach there occurs an "internal stratification" into

> social dialects, characteristic group behavior, professional jargons, generic languages, languages of generations and age groups, tendentions languages, languages of authorities, of various circles and of passing fashions, languages that serve the specific sociopolitical purposes of the day, even of the hour. (Bakhtin, 1981, pp. 262–263)

In the United States children, youth, teachers, and families continue to negotiate the uneven, and at times treacherous landscape created and evolved by the No Child Left Behind (NCLB) legislation. In Canada several provinces utilizing standardized assessment and evaluation continue to narrow the notion of learning (British Columbia, Ontario, Alberta), but more importantly teaching practices in both countries and elsewhere continue to be shaped and formed by such legislation and the ongoing development of dominant discourses about learning as technical process informed by scientific evidence based research. Yet, in all of the rhetoric about early learning, improving education, standards, and practice where is the notion of the child as a person, a subject, a self in relationality with her family and the teacher?

> Over time the idea of developmental norms have shifted from "description to prescription: from a mythic norm (mythic because no one actually 'fits' it) to statements of how people should be" (Dahlberg & Moss, 2005, p. 7). When we

> can stand outside the very discourse(s) that have (in)formed us as students and as teachers marching toward a prescribed future based upon "secur[ing] both social order and economic success" (p. 5), perhaps then we can begin to speak more clearly and loudly *with* children and youth and live not "objectives," "learning outcomes" and a place in a prescribed future, but the wonder and uncertainty of life's journey together. (Lewis, 2009, p. 14)

The pedagogical project of schooling needs to realign itself with the notion of pedagogy; from Greek, *paidagogia* "attendance on children," from *pedo*, "child" and *agogos,* to "lead," the leading out of the child. Pedagogy must return to the notion of a "journey into story" (Huebner, 1999, p. 381–382) where child, teacher, and family share a page, a passage, a chapter in each other's lives in a reciprocal journey of becoming. The "teacher, to participate in a young person's emerging or unfolding story, must be an able listener, one who 'listens' the young person into an articulate consciousness, and a narrator who has the necessary language to fit an episode into the young person's story line" (p. 383). As teacher I must not only be a storyteller, I must be a story listener and listen, really listen a child's story into *being*.

THE LANGUAGE AND PRACTICE OF SCHOOL

The lexicon of the pre-service and in-service teacher is full of revealing terms: objectives, goals, planning, lesson plan, classroom management, observation, records, check list, standards, rubrics, assessment, evaluation, performance standards, on task, student engagement, outcomes, to name but a few. These terms and many more similar ones dominate the discourse of school and education in day-to-day practice. They are not new ideas and many have been around for a long time; however, they all spring from a notion of a technical turn in education that began a long time ago. In the early twentieth century ideas such as scientific management, social efficiency, and psychology, newly armed with IQ testing, began to influence and shape education to an extent not previously seen.

> However, it was the work of Franklin Bobbitt, through his scientific approach to curriculum making that set the course for Counts, Tyler, Bloom and numerous other educators in the evolution of the technical approach to teaching. Bobbitt's curriculum making method has had a profound and lasting influence upon teaching, schooling, and the curriculum, and still lies at the core of curriculum development. (Lewis, 2009, p. 15)

"Objectives," "classroom management," "observation," "on-task," and "standards" are terms that carry with them a certain philosophical perspective and practice that tends to dehumanize the activity we call teaching. Ideas like classroom management betray the dehumanizing effect when a group of twenty-five six- or seven-year-old children, each possessed with her own identity and story, become something to manage, direct, and control under the "surveillance" of the watchful teacher. "Large, complex and contestable concepts such as 'the child, 'education' and 'evaluation' are reduced to a small, simplified and technical discourse of classifications, norms and criteria."(Dahlberg & Moss, 2005, p. 2) Goals, objectives, indicators, targets, and learning outcomes— some of the many euphemisms employed in curricular documents—become the means, if not authority, to manage, observe, assess and evaluate "the class." The child is absorbed into a curricular prescription of what she will learn, do, and know. The individual child becomes the denominator; the objectives are the numerator eclipsing the needs of each child. In the calculus of schooling there is an absence of attending to each child's pains, joys, and desires. Life, the child's life story, continuously recedes to the background, like the countryside out the window of a moving train as she is propelled down the curriculum track.

It is important to remember that it was in the beginning of the twentieth century that childhood conduct disorders first appeared in learned journals. It was the site of schools which provided and inspired the bio-medical lifting of how a child should be as constructed through schools and the early days of developmental psychology (Laurence & McCallum, 2009, p. xix).

> The schoolroom . . . emerges as an institutional site that provided the psy-sciences with the necessary means of "visualising" children's conduct . . . the problem of disorderly conduct was lifted out of the social and administrative context of educational aims to do with managing the student body as a whole and translocated onto the body of the individual. . . . We do not suggest, however, that the schoolroom is the single generative site of childhood conduct disorders. Its origins, we argue, are more rhizomatic than that. (Laurence & McCallum, 2009, p. xix)

Michael O'Loughlin (2010) asks, what is the subjective experience of the child who finds herself outside the prescribed norm? Is her experience "*invalid*" because it is perceived to deviate from the normative? (p. 57) Is it possible to "develop notions of subjectivity that are sufficiently displaced from the bourgeois-centre to include subaltern and contrarian experiences" (p. 57)? The Diagnostic and Statistical Manual of Mental Disorders (DSM) clearly states that a disorder must originate in the individual; it "must currently be considered a manifestation of a behavioral, psychological, or biological dysfunction in the individual. Neither deviant behavior nor conflicts that are primarily between the individual and society [school] are mental disorders." (DSM, 2000, p. xxi–xxii) Nevertheless, the increasing number of school age children being diagnosed with disorders has been on the rise over the past two decades; one can't help but wonder if the caution from the authors of the DSM has been overlooked or simply ignored. With this in mind I ask some questions to provoke our thinking: Can schools become places that create spaces "where diverse identities can be imagined, inscribed, and invented"? (O'Loughlin, 2010, p. 57) Can schools become sites of resistance to how things are and places to imagine how things might be? Can school notions of assessment and evaluation be reimagined? Assessment is derived from the Latin *assessus* "a sitting by," *assidre* "to sit beside," and "assist in the office of judge"; can schools become sites of reciprocity in and through an assessment of care?

The Red Ones are Best

"Mr. Lewis! Mr. Lewis!"

"What is it, Christopher?" replied Mr. Lewis a little anxiously.

"He's done it again!" said Christopher.

"Who?"

"Kody!"

"What has he done, Christopher?"

"He's eaten all my crayons, again while I was at the Listening Center."

"How do you know, Christopher?"

"Cuz I saw him! I came runnin' over and grabbed the rest from him. He ate the reds and the blues!"

Mr. Lewis turned around slowly and faced Kody thinking he was a strange little guy. Kody was extremely small and all the other Grade 1 and 2 students towered over him. He had a slight, frail-looking build that belied his toughness, which he had demonstrated several times by falling off the top of the playground equipment without complaint or tears.

Mr. Lewis looked down at him. Kody had a look of defiance set upon his face, with the bottom lip sticking out ever so slightly. He was holding his little hands in front of himself, twisting them nervously against each other like he was coiling up the string of an imaginary kite. They were delicate-looking little hands that were very wrinkled, almost wizened. His curly dark hair was cut short and his ears had perceptible points to the top of them. The thought crossed Mr. Lewis's mind that maybe little Kody was an elf and didn't really belong in this world. That would explain why he was having such a hard time getting along in this alien land. Perhaps he was a changeling substituted in the crib of the real Kody. No. He was just a little boy banging up against the ways of the world in his own particular and sometimes peculiar way. Kody continued to stand there trying to look defiant, but realizing that because of his position and the circumstances it wasn't looking too promising. Mr. Lewis told Christopher to return to the Listening Centre and that he would deal with Kody.

This wasn't the first time Kody had eaten crayons. A few weeks earlier Mr. Lewis had to remove the can of crayons from the Art Centre and keep them in his desk. Kody had been found eating from the can like it was a bowl of pretzels. Not long after that the glue sticks and the paint tablets were locked up because Kody had found that they caressed his palette in a most enjoyable way. It was not for want of food that Kody's epicurean tastes went for such things. He always had a large lunch, which he handily walloped into himself. Shortly after the glue sticks had been eaten, Mr. Lewis had invited Kody's parents in to discuss his classroom tastes. During the discussion it was discovered that he also ate a number of things at home that were not on the menu. Mr. Lewis suggested that they take Kody to see a pediatrician and perhaps the doctor could suggest some reasons why Kody ate all these things and might even be able to offer some ideas of how to have him eat like the rest of the population.

Mr. Lewis knelt down so he had his face level with Kody's. "Well?" began Mr. Lewis, "did you eat Christopher's crayons?"

Kody stood firm, making no reply. He lowered his gaze while still twisting his hands nervously together and coiling in that imaginary kite string. Mr. Lewis was trying to think what he should do. He did not know what to do. Kody's mom and dad had been in earlier and announced that the doctor determined that he had pica, a lack of iron that causes one to eat dirt. However, Kody, like many children with pica these days, ate very little dirt but all kinds of other things.

"Well?" inquired Mr. Lewis again. He was trying to think of what he should say to Kody and couldn't get past this word. Kody fidgeted his feet a little and kept looking down at the floor.

"Which colour is your favourite?"

Kody stopped fidgeting and slowly raised his gaze to meet Mr. Lewis's.

"Which colour is your most favourite to eat?"

Kody's forced expression of defiance had drained away from his face. He was examining Mr. Lewis's face to determine his sincerity in what he was asking.

"If I were to eat a crayon, I think I would begin with red and follow it with a blue and maybe a nice yellow one to top it off. Yes, that sounds pretty good to me," Mr. Lewis declared.

Kody began to open his mouth and then said, "Yeah, the red ones are best. And the blues are good. But the yellow's kinda bad!" He made a face to demonstrate his distaste for the yellow crayons.

Mr. Lewis smiled, "Well, I guess we have something in common. We both like red and blue."

Kody's face opened up into a smile and in his gravelly little voice he confessed, "Green's pretty good, too!"

Mr. Lewis smiled at Kody, whose broad grin was filled with bits of chewed up red and blue crayons, "I think you'd better go to the water fountain and have a nice, long drink, Kody."

The next week Kody began coming to school with a long thin piece of leather around his neck with an odd-shaped object attached to the end of it. Apparently this was modern medicine's way of dealing with his unique culinary tastes. He was to suck the object on the leather necklace whenever he felt the urge to eat crayons or glue sticks.

Mr. Lewis approached him one afternoon at the Math Centre and knelt down beside him where he was working on a problem with his partner.

"How you making out, Kody?"

"Oh, not bad," Kody rasped.

"How's the necklace thing working out?"

"Oh, it's okay," he sighed. "But sometimes I feel like I'd do anything for a red crayon! Wouldn't you?"

"Yes, Kody. I know what you mean."

Kody looked pensively out the window toward the forest of fir and cedar trees that hemmed the playground. In his very quiet and gravelly sounding voice, to no one in particular, he sighed, "Even a yellow one would be good now." (Lewis, 2007, pp. 114–116)[1]

BEING HUMAN / HUMAN BEING

Story, narrative, imagining is at the heart of being human, it is the central tenet of the human mind (Bruner, 1996; Boyd, 2009; Cavarero, 2000; Lewis, 2007; Turner, 1996). Children are born with the mental capacity of basic story structure, which then quickly develops into the more sophisticated narrative imagining of pretend play and the accompanying complexity of story-play generation between the ages of two and five years. By the age of four or five years we tend to consolidate our sense of identity, thinking that from that time forward the self does not change. However, the self does change through our lived experience and our narrative understanding of that experience is what often makes it feel like we are still the same person we were when we were five. The notion of a unified self is formed and informed narratively throughout a life; it is our playing at being. If humans are in a continual process of becoming, and narrative has a significant and central role in that becoming, shouldn't there be more emphasis on the role of story both in and out of school? Prescriptive curricula do not allow for deviation from the curricular objectives, outcomes, or indicators. How can we possibly know what each child will need before we even meet them in our classrooms, begin to build relationships with them, learn their present story and listen next to their passage into being? I didn't know why Kody ate crayons and glue-sticks and I don't think the pediatrician knew either. Nor did I know what I should have tried to do to help him; I did not draw upon some previous teaching experience or theory and apply it. I "came to" Kody and the crayons and I tried to be present and listen, really listen to his story. Perhaps being present and authentic in "listening" the child into being is akin to the psychoanalyst urging that we "rely on an absolute receptivity to the child's being, patient to move at the child's pace" (O'Loughlin, 2010, p. 67).

Story, narrative imagining, and play are central to "cognitive, affective and emotional development of children. They support and aid a child's development of identity and meaning making through an intricate engagement that is both somatic and cognitive blending together to integrate the ontological and epistemological nature of narrative" (Lewis, 2007, p. 14). As Michael O'Loughlin (2010) has noted, the process of play and pretend play in particular is also a therapeutic space created through the enactment of story, initiated by the child creating a "freeing space" where "the child's desire is likely to be released" (p. 55) and her ability to *be* is unhindered by adult prescriptions of childhood. It is from play (pretend play in particular) that narrative imagining is nurtured and grows. A child is that which she has been, is what she is now, and is what she is becoming. The child is what she does, but she becomes more through the creation and acquisition of her own story. "We are not taught narrative. Rather narrative reflects our mode of understanding events, which appears . . . to be a generally mammalian mode of understanding" (Boyd, 2009, p. 131). Through her day-to-day inter/intra-personal endeavors she narrates a self. It is not a question of an essential self of phenomenology or a discursive self of poststructualism. The self *is*—it exists in our actions and is (re)defined through them, and the self exists narratively through the ongoing process of becoming. Consequently, "narrative identity is then at once subjective and intersubjective, and entails answerability and responsibility and the capacity for negotiation" (Whitebrook, 2001, p. 10). We come to know our self through the world and its stories; we come to know the stories and the world through an other.

Kody is only one of a host of children whom I lived alongside over my twenty-five years of teaching, and was a witness of my struggle to be present in the day-to-day life of the classroom. I don't know if I helped Kody that day and I probably won't ever know, but I do know I tried to listen. Although I did not understand him, I appreciated him and just listened. It was in that act of authentic listening that *care* is born. When we care, *really* care, and we combine that care with love, what Max van Manen (1991) called "pedagogical love," we come to see that "love and care provide not certainty but hope. Hope makes possible patience and peaceful waiting in the midst of turmoil and unsettledness. With openness, love, and hope, new creation is possible" (Huebner, 1985/1999, p. 350). To be with another is to care, what NelNoddings called an ethical caring or rather a *care for*—"a state of being in relation, characterized by receptivity, relatedness and engrossment" (Flinders, 2001, p. 211). Perhaps I provided some hope for Kody because I cared, and this provided a possibility for him to be who he was at that moment even as he bumped up against the world in all its wonder and strangeness. One should consider Jackie Seidel's (2006) notion of teaching as a contemplative practice so that "contemplative teaching turns our work into a form of love, memory and intimacy, reminding us of our deep life relations through time and place, and possibly having incalculable implications for our curriculum interpretation and classroom practices" (p. 1901).

The world as created by adults is fraught with mystification from a young child's standpoint. Adults often forget or never think about how a five- or six year-old entering Kindergarten or Grade 1 is beginning a puzzling and at times perplexing journey into an adult-literate landscape where everything and everyone is not only new, but often unfamiliar and novel in terms of the young child's schema and/or reference points. She meets with adults who often wish to interrupt her learning and meaning-making of the world by imposing print literacy and textual frameworks of how to construe the world; disrupting her experience with their adult literate prescriptions rooted in adult-literate school-centric notions of learning and becoming. Yet, "this same child has already developed language, a narrative way of knowing and a sophisticated ability to negotiate meaning and further develop her understanding of experience and the world through play and oracy—no small feat"

(Lewis, 2007, p. 110). Too often as teachers we fail to recognize that children come to school with experience and understanding of the world that is often decidedly different than our own and different too from what the school teaches. But that does not make it any less valuable, only different, and isn't it that very diversity that embodies the richness that is human being? Schools and educators need to transform their traditional praxis from one rooted in a deficit-oriented approach to that of an ethical praxis founded upon an *asset-oriented* approach to teaching and learning (Heydon & Iannacci, 2009). We need to recognize and acknowledge each child, who she is, and the story she has lived and is living as she tries to negotiate the landscape of school, the customs and traditions of the institution, and the ideas it has been built upon. In welcoming children through an asset-oriented approach we might enter education as "a constellation of encounters, both planned and unplanned, that promote growth through the acquisition of knowledge, skills, understanding and appreciation" (Noddings, 2002, p. 283).

As teachers we need to acknowledge and accept our own limits of knowing and being in the pedagogical landscape of school and schooling, while at the same time recognizing the limits of the institution itself and all that it entails. We must be conscious of the limits of knowledge and understanding of others and take up what Heydon and Iannacci call an ethical praxis: "An ethical praxis does not claim to privilege one theory or practice over another; it asks us educators to assess our ways of knowing, being, and doing in order to reflect upon the conditions of these structures to oneself and others" (p. 97). Accompanying that ethical praxis must be the ethic of care proposed by Nel Noddings (1984, 1992, 2002), with its emphasis on reciprocity, but also an acknowledgement of its inherent complexity as lived out in the unequal relationships of care (i.e. student—teacher; parent—child; adult—child); relationships that must be lived through together beside each other. Clifford Mayes (2002) reminds us that care

> must involve caring not only *for someone* but also *about something*. Without some sort of orienting purpose regarding what the Other may become or do, care may *feel good*, but one may well question whether it will always *do good*. Care that is not contained and directed by some salutary purpose tends to become diffuse and sometimes even destructively permissive—and in this sense, is not ultimately *care-full* at all. This is why it is so easy to caricature care as a fuzzy-headed indulgence of self and other. However, care as "ultimate concern" is different. It is "concern" for the other in the light of the "ultimate" [italics in original]. (p. 703)

In that process we may then be able to take up the ontological care of each child. But that will require us to transcend current practices and knowledge with respect to children, teaching, learning, and schooling. If our ultimate concern truly is for the well being and well becoming of each child, we need to imagine children and schooling otherwise so that in that transcendence teachers become attuned with not just the literacy learning needs of each child but their psycho-emotional and existential needs that flow deep and wide through all their learning and being. After all it is children who remind us of the awe and wonder in the quotidian, which as adults we tend to have fewer experiences with because we immerse ourselves in the moments just ahead and behind us. However, we can intuit that awe and wonder that pervades the everydayness in moments with children if we allow ourselves to attend to and hold the space for the newness that children bring to the classroom each day; all things are new again. But that requires us to welcome and embrace that which is given afresh through the daily wonderment of the young.

ACKNOWLEDGMENTS

One thousand words from "Red Ones are Best" were reprinted from *How We Think but not in School* (2007). Permission courtesy of Sense Publishers.

NOTE

1. It is important to note that Kody replaced the crayons he had eaten that belonged to Christopher, just as he had done in previous incidents. In our class at the time we were using a philosophy of the three R's, restitution, resolution, and reconciliation.

REFERENCES

Bakhtin, M. . (1981). *The dialogic imagination four essays by M. M. Bakhtin*. Trans. C. Emerson & M. Holquist. Edited by M. Holquist. Austin, TX: University of Texas Press.

Boyd, B. (2009). *On the Origin of Stories: Evolution, Cognition and Fiction*. Cambridge, MA: Harvard University Press.

Cavarero, A. (2000). *Relating narratives: Storytelling and selfhood*. NY: Routledge.

Dahlberg, G. & Moss, P. (2005). *Ethics and politics in early childhood education*. New York, NY: Routledge/Falmer.

DSM (2000). *Diagnostic and Statistical Manual of Mental Disorders IV-R* (4th Edition), Washington D. C.: American Psychiatric Association.

Flinders, D. J. (2001) 'Nel Noddings' in Joy A. Palmer (ed.) *Fifty Modern Thinkers on Education. From Piaget to the present*, London: Routledge.

Heydon, R. M. &Iannacci, L. (2009). *Early childhood curricula and the de-pathologizing of childhood*. Toronto, ON: University of Toronto Press.

Huebner, D. (1999). Education and spirituality. (1993). In V. Hillis (Ed.), *The lure of the transcendent, collected essays by Dwayne E. Huebner* (pp. 401–416). Mahwah, NJ: Lawrence Erlbaum Associates.

Huebner, D. (1999). Teaching as vocation. (1987). In V. Hillis (Ed.), *The lure of the transcendent, collected essays by Dwayne E. Huebner* (pp. 379–387). Mahwah, NJ: Lawrence Erlbaum Associates.

Huebner, D. (1999). Spirituality and knowing. (1985). In V. Hillis (Ed.), *The lure of the transcendent, collected essays by Dwayne E. Huebner* (pp. 340–352). Mahwah, NJ: Lawrence Erlbaum Associates.

Johnson, J., Christie, J., & Wardle, F. (2005). *Play, development, and early education.* New York: Pearson.
Laurence, J. & McCallum, D. (2009). *Inside the child's head: Histories of childhood behavioral disorders*. Rotterdam, NL: Sense Publishers.
Lewis, P. J. (1995). *The stories we tell: The search for meaning through stories*. Unpublished master's thesis, University of Victoria, Victoria, B. C.
Lewis, P. J. (2007). *How we think, but not in school: A storied approach to teaching*. Rotterdam, NL: Sense Publishers.
Lewis, P. J. (2009). Who in this culture speaks for children and youth? In P. Lewis & J. Tupper (Eds.), *Challenges Bequeathed: Taking up the Challenges of Dwayne Huebner* (pp. 13–24). Rotterdam, NL: Sense Publishers.
Luke, A. & Luke, C. (2001). Adolescence lost/childhood regained: On early intervention and the emergence of the techno-subject. *Journal of Early Childhood Literacy, 1*(1), 91–120.
Mayes, C. (2002). The teacher as an archetype of spirit, *Journal of Curriculum Studies, 34*(6), 699–718.
Noddings, N. (1984). *Caring: A feminine approach to ethics and moral education.* Berkeley, CA: University of California Press.
Noddings, N. (1992). *The challenge to care in schools: An alternative approach to education.* New York, NY: Teachers College Press.
Noddings, N. (2002). *Starting at home. Caring and social policy.* Berkeley, CA: University of California Press.
O'Loughlin, M. (2010). Ghostly presences in children's lives: Toward a psychoanalysis of the social. In M. O'Loughlin & R. Johnson (Eds.), *Imagining Children Otherwise: Theoretical And Critical Perspectives On Childhood Subjectivity* (pp. 49–74). New York, NY: Peter Lang Publishing Inc.
Seidel, J. (2006). Some thoughts on teaching as contemplative practice.*Teachers College Record, 108*(9), 1901–1914.
Turner, M. (1996). *The literary mind: The origins of thought and language.* New York, NY: Oxford University Press.
Van Manen, M. (1991). *The tact of teaching: The meaning of pedagogical thoughtfulness.* London, Ont: Althouse Press.
Walkerdine, V. (1999). Violent boys and precocious girls: regulating childhood at the end of the millennium. *Contemporary Issues in Early Childhood 1*(1), 3–23.
Whitebrook, M. (2001). *Identity, narrative and politics.* New York, NY: Routledge.

Chapter Three

Subjection and Subjectivity

The Child and A Mind of One's Own

Karen Lombardi

The curiously paradoxical meaning of subjectivity—that which refers both to personal interior experience and to a divided or alienated identity that is imposed on us from exterior forces—continues to pose problems in the defining qualities of subjectivity. Is our subjective experience created by us in our encounters with the outside world, and can we claim that subjectivity as something personal and meaningful? Or are we marked by powers that exist outside of us, subject to the insistences of parents and of culture, increasingly alienated from ourselves the more we enter that social order? This interrogation might seem more suited to the discipline of philosophy, but it is my experience as a psychologist and a psychoanalytic clinician that our views of subjectivity place claims on our children's rights to their own thoughts and feelings, and that these claims affect children's lives in direct ways.

I have found in my practice that too often, in the schools, in the courts, in academia, and in the consulting room, children tend to be disqualified from knowing. They are seen as blank slates on which to be written, or as pawns in the brainwashing games of their parents, the products of family systems that create and direct the pattern of their thoughts. Less often, they are given due credit for having the capacity to think their own thoughts, to have feelings and perceptions and ideas that are regarded as legitimately based in real personal experience. In this way, children tend to be treated more as objects than as subjects in their own right.

THE LAW

Before second wave feminism, the court system was seen to take a protective stance towards children (and secondarily towards mothers, who with rare exceptions were the primary custodians of their children), often ruling, at least in principle, that paternal responsibility for mother and child must continue until the child was grown. Divorcing fathers were expected to maintain their children in the family home, and to take financial responsibility that would allow their children's lives to continue uninterrupted in their homes, their neighborhoods, and their schools until the children graduated from school and were no longer dependents. In the last thirty years or so, the ethos of the court has shifted to a Solomonic one, without the wisdom. Divorcing mothers and fathers are seen as having equal rights and responsibilities toward their children, which on the surface seems like a progressive and just position. However, the unfortunate reality is that the children are often split in two between warring parents who are often unable to come together for the good of their children. Joint custody is regarded not only as the ideal position but also the default position, despite research that indicates the efficacy of joint custody only under circumstances where parents manage to remain friends with each other, or at the very least are on good terms (e.g., Wallerstein and Kelly, 1996). When parents fail to be on good terms, it is sometimes the father, but most often the mother, who is viewed as poisoning the children's minds against the other parent. Parental Alienation Syndrome (Gardner, 1998), a diagnosis often used in court proceedings to reestablish parental authority in cases of divorce, states that one parent (usually the mother) exercises undue influence over the child. The child is seen as a blank slate whose mind, in these cases, has been highjacked by the mother. This position effectively disempowers the child, who has no legitimate voice in the decisions that are presumably made in his/her best interests.

Court appointed law guardians, lawyers who commonly have little or no training in child psychology or child development, interview children under the age of sixteen (the age at which children are usually considered by the courts to be entitled to their own opinions and to make their own decisions). These interviews are conducted not through the methods of child psychotherapy, which are guided by the child's natural interests, through play and through indirect inquiry, and with as little direct questioning as possible, but through a more lawyerly interrogatory method. Such adult-style interrogations are unlikely to yield useful or reliable information. When reliable information is obtained, it is often discounted as invalid, as the child is seen as having an adultified voice, speaking his/her parent's words rather than speaking in an authentic or personal voice. In this way, such interviews are often perfunctory and self-negating. If the child offers a direct opinion, he/she is seen as parroting his parent's desires; if the child is unable to offer a coherent, cogently organized adult response, he/she is seen as failing to provide a useful perspective.

Case 1: Sebastian

Sebastian, a boy of seven, lives with his mother in the New York area. His father lives in Colorado. His parents lived together for a brief time when he was an infant; by the time he was nine months old, the father had left for Colorado. When Sebastian was two, the father returned to the area to visit, desiring to see his child. Supervised visitation was instituted, and Sebastian saw his father for a few hours twice a month. All seemed to go well until visitation was changed to unsupervised visitation with overnights. Sebastian, still under three, was distressed by the separation from his mother, and cried bitterly when his father arrived to pick him up. Returning from visitations, he would shadow his mother, not letting her out of her sight, would wet the bed after having previously been successfully toilet-trained, began to demand the breast even though he had been weaned, would wake up with nightmares, and would bite his mother and then apologize and kiss her hand. Children of this age speak through their symptoms; this child was saying that something was wrong. After a week or so the symptoms would disappear, only to reappear after the next visitation with the father.

Over the next several years, the parents were in and out of court, with various rulings that included court-ordered couples' therapy for the parents and reduced visitation. The couples' therapist eventually "fired" the parents, as he could make no progress with them. As the child grew older, weekend overnights were reinstituted, after which the child again became symptomatic. Around the age of five, Sebastian began to develop his own voice, and to verbally protest the visitations. He stated, both to his therapist and to the law guardian, that his father put him in diapers overnight, that he refused to let him speak to his mother on the telephone, that he called his mother "a bitch" and "a psychopath," which made him cry. Upon examination by the court, it was determined that Sebastian was being influenced by the mother's negative attitude toward the father, and that visitations should continue without therapeutic intervention for the child and his father. At last report, Sebastian ran to neighbor's house and hid when the father attempted to pick him up for visitation. The battle continues to rage.

There is little doubt that children are most certainly affected by the negativity of both parents; in this case, by the mother's fear and anxiety as well as the father's hatred toward the mother. The question remains, however, as to whether the child has desires which should be legitimately acknowledged and taken into account, or whether those desires should be overridden by parental rights.

THE EPISTEMOPHILIC INSTINCT

Do children have minds of their own and voices which should be heard? As early as 1928, the psychoanalyst Melanie Klein added the desire for knowledge as a primary human motivation. Rooted, for Klein, in the discovery of sexual difference, the desire to know, provoked by the originary problem of "Where do I come from?," precedes and exceeds the capacity to articulate and understand in words and speech. "The infant, still undeveloped intellectually, is exposed to an onrush of problems and questions . . . these many overwhelming questions, which are apparently only partly conscious and even when conscious cannot yet be expressed in words, remain unanswered . . . [The child's] first questions go back beyond the beginnings of his understanding of speech" (1928, p. 188).

Bion (1967), influenced by Klein, extends the epistemophilic instinct to a theory of thinking, based in affects and bodily experience and serving as a fundamental link between human beings. The first form of thinking strives to know psychic qualities, and is the outcome of the early relationship between the infant and its (m)other.[1] For Klein and for Bion, thinking is not simply some abstract cognitive process, but is the "endeavor to understand, comprehend the reality of, get insight into the nature of, etc., oneself or another. It is an emotional experience of trying to know oneself or someone else (O'Shaughnessy, 1981, p. 178). Amending the Freudian instincts of sex and aggression, Bion, following Klein, posits three human instincts, L (love), H (hate), and K (knowing). The desire for knowledge, the desire to know oneself and the other, are as central to human functioning as are love and hate.[2] O'Shaughnessy elaborates K in terms of clinical practice with children. *K* functions when the child is trying to know, even when anxiety may be interfering with his ability to think. *Minus K* operates as a link of misunderstanding between the child and internal or external objects; here, the child is misunderstanding or denuding his experience. *No K* is the situation where the links between self and other are broken, and the child is operating without the capacity to think. This latter situation is equivalent to psychotic thinking. Children (and people in general) move from K to minus K, depending on circumstance and the emotion that is being evoked. The desire to know, however, remains central, with minus K occurring as a defensive operation (K is known but is split off, as in "I know it but I can't bear to think (admit) it") and no K occurring under conditions of disordered psychotic thinking, where the mind itself is attacked.

As clinicians, as parents, and as teachers, we often recognize that the child has more to say for himself than is actually said. While the child may have endless questions in a search for personal knowledge (e.g., "Where did I come from?" "Where was I before I was born?" "Is there a God? Where does he live?" "How do things grow?"), he/she is not always so adept at answering the questions posed by adults. In clinical supervision of work with children, one of the first things I suggest (as do most child therapists) is to avoid direct questioning, and to obtain "information" through play and indirect questioning. "Why," a supervisee asked me, "does my child patient always shut down when I ask him questions?" This, I thought, was a very good question in itself. Pontalis (1977) suggests that Anna Freud and the ego psychologists would most commonly respond to my supervisee's question by addressing the course of cognitive development, seeing the lack of speech as a developmental deficiency. Not so Klein, who turns things around and instead "submits[s] psychoanalytical theory and methods to the disconcerting test of the *child's speech* (1977, p. 83, italics mine)."We are left with two different sets of ethics. For Anna Freud, it is a question of imposing the adult's alleged autonomy on the child, both assuming that the child is not sufficiently cognitively developed to speak for himself and demanding that speech meet adult requirements. For Melanie Klein, it is "a matter of coming to meet the child's psychic reality and measuring adult knowledge against it in the spirit of free and unprejudiced research (1977, p. 83)."We are left with the possibility that the questions of adults miss the mark, and are experienced by the child as impositional and demanding of an adult response. The child's speech is never entirely split off from the body, emotion, play, and phantasy, and requires the pursuit of understanding in those terms.

Case 2: Mommy, Why Did You Pack My Suitcase?

At four months old, Corinna's father literally disappeared from the family residence. When he did not return home at the end of the day, the mother became worried and called the local hospitals and police stations, to no avail. Looking for clues, she found that while his belongings remained behind, his toothbrush was missing. Three days later, the father called to say that he was feeling undue pressure and needed to get away for a bit. At nine months, when Corinna was hospitalized for emergency surgery, the father showed up at the hospital to make sure she was all right, and promptly disappeared again. When Corinna was five, the father called, asking to see his child. He had remarried by then, and intended to arrive with his new wife, whom Corinna had never met. The mother, wanting to do the right thing and even more, fearing to do the wrong thing, had been advised by her lawyer and the courts to allow this visitation, which was scheduled to be an overnight. Approaching the date of the visit, the mother had a dream that the father took her daughter out to the playground, never to return (a repetition of the experience of her husband's disappearance). Not wanting to make trouble despite her anxiety, she packed a suitcase for her daughter and prepared her for the father's visit. When the father arrived with the new wife in tow, Corinna was walked onto the porch with her suitcase. She began down the driveway where her father waited, turning back to look at her mother, who was standing behind her. As her father approached, she began to cry and protest the visit. After an emotional scene, where Corinna's protests increased in strength and the father was heard to yell at her "You're coming with me, whether you want to or not," the father picked her up and carried her like a bundle under one arm, picked up the suitcase with the other and began to head for the car. Corinna was now in acute distress, crying and kicking in desperation. A family friend went to restrain the father, the police were called, and the visit was aborted. Once back inside her house, Corinna looked into her mother's eyes and tearfully said, "Mommy, why did you pack my suitcase?"

Some weeks later, Corinna and her mother went to a child psychologist to manage the trauma of this aborted visitation, and her disappearance behind the mother's pseudo-betrayal and the father's aggressive insistence. In the therapist's office, she was reticent and refused to speak. The therapist handed her some paper and crayons and told her she could draw whatever she wanted to say. She then said, "Could you do me a favor?" Corinna looked into the therapist's eyes expectantly. The therapist said, "I will speak to Mommy. If there is anything we say that is true, will you nod your head yes, and if there is anything we say that is not true, will you shake your head no?" Corinna agreed by nodding her head. Some time into the session, she handed the therapist a picture she had drawn, with the words "My name is Corinna."

What is the significance of Corinna's question:" Mommy, why did you pack my suitcase?" Did Corinna "read" her mother's anxiety about the visitation, even though the mother was careful not to say anything negative about Corinna's father? We can assume this is so, as children are especially sensitive to the moods and emotions of their parents; emotions are a primary mode of communication, and a major source of children knowing much more than their parents actually say to them in words. Corinna might have read this anxiety as her mother's fear of the father, and also as the mother's fear for Corinna herself. Corinna might have assumed that her mother knew of her own desire not to go for an overnight with her father, who was essentially a stranger to her. Perhaps she thought that her mother should have known that Corinna's father would be aggressive toward her and frighten her when she should have been protected. Why then, did her mother pack her suitcase? Corinna might be said to feel this action as an act of bad faith, a betrayal of her truth and of her mother's truth. To refer back to Bion, both mother and child were operating in minus K mode, until Corinna's question brought them back to the psychic reality of each of their subjectivities. The therapist, with her paper and crayons and invitation to participate through head-nodding and head-shaking indications of truth and falsehood, made space for Corinna's subjectivity, both in union with her mother and apart from her mother.

EMPATHIC LINKAGE AND SYMBOLIZATION

In *The Origin of Signs* (1999), Mary Jacobus examines Klein's account of the unconscious phantasies of children and their relation to the language, play, drawings, stories, and other symbol-making activities of childhood. She states that Klein's "insistence on infant phantasies as coterminous with the earliest instinctual experience" serves as "an alternative to the Freudian Oedipus complex [and] the Lacanian Law of the Father" (1999, p. 25). The literalness with which Klein treats children's speech is contained within, and simultaneously reveals, the metaphor. The bodily experience through which the child speaks, linked to the object world of the child, is what develops the symbol. So what begins as literal develops as a link between subject and object, allowing for the development of meaning.

Klein (1930) presents a perspective on the formation of the symbol through the case of Dick, a four year-old boy with simultaneous failures in language development and object relations.[3] Klein capitalizes on Dick's few interests in trains and stations, and in door handles and the opening and shutting of doors. Her interpretations, which she offers to give words to his experience, are framed in terms of his body in relation to his mother's body. In Klein's words:

> I took a big train and put it beside a smaller one and called them "Daddy-train" and "Dick-train." Thereupon he picked up the train I called "Dick" and made it roll to the window and said "Station." I explained, "The station is mummy; Dick is going into mummy." He left the train, ran into the space between the outer and inner doors of the room, shut himself in, saying "dark" and ran out again, directly. He went through this performance several times. I explained to him, "It is dark inside mummy. Dick is inside dark mummy." (1930, p. 225)

Klein's words link Dick's few interests in the outside world back to his original objects, and even more specifically link his body with the mother's body. Klein's characteristic literalness is meant to serve a specific purpose: to name Dick's experience in a way that concretely grounds it in relation to the body of the object. These literal and concrete originations express the link between subject and object, providing the basis for the making of meaning and metaphor. Dick's use of language a few months into his treatment with Klein demonstrates his own employment of this symbolic equation.[4] Observing some pencil shavings in her lap, Dick commented empathically, "Poor Mrs. Klein." As Segal (1957) points out, "To him the shavings were Mrs. Klein cut into bits" (p. 54).

The Kleinian notion of the symbol does not refer to cognitive mastery or abstract thinking, but to the creation of personal meaning that allows for a productive relationship with the world. The interplay between the symbol as a concrete experience equated with the original object and the symbol as something created by the self may be seen not simply as a developmental trajectory, but as a dialectical process wherein the evocative and creative power of the symbol relates to the more sensory experiences out of which meaning originally arises. In the Kleinian canon, the less persecutory the internal (and external) situation, the more symbols come to serve creative, enlivening, and enriching functions.

Klein views Dick as a child with an excess of empathy, in the form of an over-identification with an internally deadened mother. When the internalized mother is threatened or attacked, premature empathy develops to ward off anxieties around destructiveness. Dick became internally frozen, losing his speech and inhibiting his interests in the world around him, so as not to disturb his fragile universe. Under more ordinary circumstances, for the rest of us, our empathy tends to increase for the objects that we experience as attacked, whether internal (our unconscious identifications) or external (our intimate relationships). Sebastian, in case 1, experienced an increase in empathy for his mother and became anxiously attached to her in response to his father's verbal attacks on his mother. More integrated and healthier than Dick, he was also free to express his anger and aggression at his mother by biting her, and then repairing the damage by kissing the bitten hand. This is an internal subjective experience that belongs personally to Sebastian. It is not, as the courts and law guardian maintained, a case of Parental Alienation impressed upon him by his mother. Although he was certainly affected by his mother's anxiety, his father's hateful words destabilized him and actually increased his devotion to his mother. When one parent attacks the other parent, and the child is blamed for the increase in empathy for the attacked parent, alienation is increased. Corinna, in case 2, was additionally attacked directly by her father, when he shouted at her "You're coming with me!" and grabbed her. This aggressive attempt to install parental authority backfires on itself, causing the child to lose the very respect that was sought by the parent.

DRIVEN CURIOSITY AND CREATIVE CURIOSITY

In cases of divorce, children often know the seriousness of the situation before the parents themselves do. Tension and anxiety in the household, no matter how carefully the parents attempt to protect children and to insure they are not put in the middle, are nevertheless often felt by children; the emotional atmosphere is transmitted, even as the parents are unconscious of it themselves. I relate two cases where preadolescent girls discovered their fathers' infidelities before the mothers themselves were consciously aware of it. In one case, the daughter went into her father's drawer in the parental bedroom, and read the text messages on his phone, sent to him by his lover. In another case, the daughter found a discarded cell phone in a kitchen drawer that the father had carelessly left behind, and listened to several messages left by a girlfriend. Both of these girls harbored their discoveries for many months, telling no one, fearing that if they spoke the truth that they would destroy the fragile balance of the family. These are cases of driven curiosity. The children, already knowing that something is not right, search for clues to what is not being said. The disturbed balance of safety and security impels the search for the underlying truth.

Driven curiosity is the desire to know the truth in the midst of conflict, evasion, refusal, or silence. This conflictual curiosity is driven by the desire to know the mind of the other when one's own subjectivity has been displaced. "What's going on?" "Where am I in this?" "Have I been lost?," the child wants to know. The contradiction between the state of one's own subjectivity and the relation to knowledge appears through the unconscious transmission by the parents of what they may believe are their own closely guarded secrets; parents then become not only the natural object of desire but also the agent of prohibition. Adults impose their own desires and prohibitions on the child, attempting to repress the child's search for truth and unwittingly making her the bearer and messenger of the parental unconscious.

Where do the child's unconscious and the parental unconscious intersect and separate from one another? How may the child be unburdened from the care of the parental unconscious? The answer is not a simple one. Phantasy and knowledge have a deep and interpenetrating relationship. What we can say is that this interpenetration is positively fostered through tenderness and love, and corrupted by denigration, evasiveness, and hate.

Both Klein and Jacobus suggest that the epistemophilic instinct is simultaneously aimed at the object and is without an object. That is, the pleasure of inquiry serves as an end in itself. Curiosity may take the form of the quest for forbidden knowledge, in the search to put together a reasonable story to explain, frame, and hold the anxiety in the family. But it may also take the form of knowing for pleasure's sake. The child is a truth-seeker, a *petit philosophe,* who seeks to create his own personal meaning, This is the natural state of creative curiosity.

THE SCHOOLS

At Mt. Holyoke College, where my daughter is currently a philosophy major, Dr. Thomas Wartenberg teaches a course called Philosophy for Children. Starting from the belief that young children can think reflectively and abstractly, his students learn to apply methods of philosophical inquiry appropriate for eight year-olds, using children's books as a platform. An essential part of their classwork is to go into second grade classrooms of local public schools with books of their choice to lead reading and discussion groups. The New York Times (2010) ran a story on Wartenberg's course after observing discussion groups led by Mt. Holyoke students in a charter school in Springfield, Massachusetts. The Mt. Holyoke students ask questions based on the texts they read to the children, suggesting lines of inquiry and, most importantly, following the lines of inquiry developed by the children themselves. *Alexander and the Terrible Horrible No Good Very Bad Day* (Viorst, 1972)is used to inquire about emotions: Have you ever woken up in a bad mood? How do you know you are in a bad mood? Is it possible to be in a bad mood and not show it on the outside? A story from *Frog and Toad* (Lobel, 1972) is used to inquire about the nature of courage: Can you be brave and scared at the same time? My daughter used one of her favorite childhood books, *The Lion and the Little Red Bird* (Kleven, 1992), to inquire about the relationship between nature and creativity and the nature of friendship. The Times reporter observed a discussion of Silverstein's (1964) *The Giving Tree,* where the line of inquiry focused on how we should treat natural objects. I quote from that article to give a sense of the children's thinking:

> Most of the young philosophers had no problem with the boy using the tree's shade, but they were divided on the apples, which the boy sold, the branches, which he used to build his house, and the trunk, which he carved into a boat.
>
> "It's only a tree," Justin said with a shrug.
>
> "The tree has feelings!" Keyshawn replied.
>
> "If they take the tree's trunk, um, the tree's not going to live," said Nyasia.
>
> Isaiah was among only a few pupils who said they would treat an inanimate object differently from a human friend.
>
> "Say me and a rock was a friend," he said. "It would be different, because a rock can't move. It can't look around."
>
> That gave his classmates pause.

Isaiah is the abstract thinker, correct in his observation that inanimate objects are insensate, and perhaps also correct in his inference that at least most of us treat trees and rocks differently than we do human friends. But so are Keyshawn and Nyasia correct, as they read the story metaphorically from the perspective of empathic relatedness. I read the story as they do, and perhaps go a step further in seeing the giving tree as a metaphor for the maternal relationship. Silverstein genders the tree from his first line": Once there was tree . . . and she loved a little boy," the story begins. She offers him shade, food, and play when he is a youngster, apples to make a living when he is an adolescent, branches to make a house, and her trunk to make a boat and travel when he is an adult. When the boy has grown up and used all her resources, he returns to rest next to her trunk, providing companionship and acknowledgement in old age." And the tree was happy," the story ends, as perhaps, idealized giving mothers are meant to be in the eyes of their children.

The epistemophilic instinct begins as a quest to know our origins, and to apprehend the psychic qualities of oneself and the other. The development of the epistemophilic instinct gives rise to metaphor and symbolization, widening our interests and our capacity for vital and creative living in the world. Like Silverstein's story, no matter how far we travel, we circle back to our origins.

NOTES

1. Although Bion specifies the mother, who has a privileged bodily relationship to the infant through gestation, birth, and breast-feeding, I suggest that the other may also be the father, the grandparents, or other primary caretakers of the infant and young child.
2. The Freudian instincts of sex and aggression were posited within the framework of a one-person psychology of energic theory, where these instincts were thought to originate in an internal closed system, without reference to others within the interpersonal world. Klein and those after her in the school of British Object Relations view these instincts as always occurring in reference to the experience of an object, in infancy specifically the mother; thus the transformation of sex or libido into the human feeling of love, and aggression into the human feeling of hate, which may be directed at experiences of the self as well as experiences of the other.
3. For a fuller discussion of the case of Dick, see Lombardi (2006).
4. The symbolic equation is a forerunner of symbolism proper, wherein the young child rediscovers, through an interest in the external world, a part of his internal and personal bodily experience. The symbolic equation is an early form of linkage between inside and outside, or self and other.

REFERENCES

Bion, W. (1967). *Second Thoughts: Selected Papers on Psychoanalysis.* NY: Jason Aronson.

Gardner, R. (1998). *The Parental Alienation Sydrome: A Guide for Mental Health and Legal Professionals.* NJ: Creative Therapeutics.

Goodnough,A. (2010). The Examined Life, Age 8.*New York Times,* April 18.

Jacobus, M. (1999). The Origin of Signs. *Journal of Melanie Klein and Object Relations.* 17(1), 23–93.

Klein, M. (1928). Early Stages of the Oedipus Complex. In *Love Guilt and Reparation.* London: Hogarth Press, 1975.

Klein, M. (1930). The Importance of Symbol Formation in the Development of the Ego. In *Love Guilt and Reparation.* London: Hogarth Press, 1975.

Kleven, E. (1992). *The Lion and the Little Red Bird.* NY: Dutton.

Lobel, A. (1972). *Frog and Toad Together.* NY: Harper Collins.

Lombardi, K. (2006). When a Body Meets a Body: A Neo-Kleinian View of Language and Bodily Experience. *Psychoanalytic Review,* 93(3), 377-390.

O'Shaughnessy, E. (1981). W. R. Bion's Theory of Thinking and New Techniques in Child Analysis. In Elizabeth Bott Spillius (ed.).*Melanie Klein Today: Developments in Theory and Practice, v.2.* London and New York: Routledge, 1988.

Pontalis, J.-B. (1977). The Question Child. In John Phillips and Lyndsey Stonebridge (eds.). *Reading Melanie Klein.* London and New York: Routledge, 1988.
Segal, H. (1957). Notes on Symbol Formation. *International Journal of Psychoanalysis,* 38, 391–397.
Silverstein, S. (1964). *The Giving Tree.* NY: Harper and Row.
Viorst, J. (1972). *Alexander and the Terrible Horrible No Good Very Bad Day.* NY: Athenaeum.
Wallerstein, J. and Kelly, J. (1996). *Surviving the Breakup: How Children and Parents Cope with Divorce.* NY: Basic Books.

Chapter Four

Françoise Dolto

Someone to Watch over Me

Derek Bunyard

As for every chapter in this volume, it is a reasonable for the reader to ask what is at stake in the psychoanalytic tradition being featured, in terms of education. In the case of Françoise Dolto, the short answer is the nature of the child's self, but this should be extended to include the nature of the interactions stimulated by an analyst working with a child. By implication, such a study extends to a consideration of the forms of pedagogical response that are appropriate in the light of these findings.

Dolto was a French psychoanalyst who was born in 1908, before the Great War and the many social, political, and economic changes that followed its final armistice. She died in 1988, and by then had established a national reputation—one largely built up through many radio and television appearances in which she advocated the earliest possible recognition of a child's identity within the social world. Subsequently, through the diffuse agencies of the European Union, she has become one of the named early childhood theorists featured in most courses for intending practitioners—although this is not true for Great Britain, despite its geographical proximity to France. It remains to be seen if the global perspectives on economics, politics, and culture now prevailing will eventually encompass a general acceptance of the continued relevance of psychoanalytic study itself in an era of social and scientific change even greater than those which followed both of the World Wars.

The plan for this chapter has changed as I have wrestled with the problem of how best to represent the relevant aspects of Dolto's work. In the end, I have decided that in the interests of making comparison easier her work needs to be located relative to the three principal traditions of psychoanalysis dominant during her working life—roughly, between the 1930s and the 1970s. I describe these through the differences that existed then between each tradition's understanding of the ego, or sense of self within consciousness. What I have left out of this first section is much discussion of the nature of the unconscious, the significance of the Oedipus complex, and the role of transference in therapy. These are addressed in the second section largely by reference to Dolto's own practice and the scientific claims of psychoanalysis itself. The third and last section reviews her ideas about the contribution psychoanalysis can make to what might be called the pre-institutionalization of early childhood.

DOLTO AND THE TRADITIONS OF PSYCHOANALYSIS—PARALLELS AND DIFFERENCES

Dolto was associated with the various centers for psychoanalytic study, therapy, and education that Jacques Lacan created throughout his professional life, working alongside him for far longer than anyone else, and yet very little of her work has been translated into English. This may seem surprising, but much followed from being "associated" with Lacan. His reception in England was delayed, not so much by the barrier of language, as by the ambivalence of its own psychoanalytic practitioners towards Lacan's re-reading of Freudian theory and practice. After Freud died in London, before the onset of the Second World War, those of his followers who remained in England began to develop a distinct interpretation of his teachings that today is usually referred to as the School of Object Relations. Although this label is one that is commonly applied, as with most large-scale groupings factions soon developed. The three most prominent in the 1950s were those who sided with Melanie Klein's conclusions deriving from her work with very young children; those who decided to follow a more authorized form of Freudianism as sponsored by Ernest Jones and developed in relation, again, to child study—this time by Anna Freud—Sigmund Freud's daughter; and those who refused to take sides in the frequently acrimonious debates that followed from this split—the so-called "independent" or "middle" group, amongst whom was Donald Winnicott, the analyst most often cited in comparisons with Dolto.[1] Freud had not conducted any direct studies of children himself, so this later focus was entirely appropriate, as well as being revelatory. The School had its base in what became the Tavistock Institute in London, and by the early 1950s, a set of therapeutic assumptions had developed there that was distinct, not only from the interpretations being developed by Lacan, Dolto, and others within his sphere of influence, but also from the general direction that North American psychoanalytic work had taken, which at least until the 1970s was particularly influenced by the work of Anna Freud.[2] Although both Lacan and Dolto were already publishing in France at this time, and Dolto had begun to participate in a first series of national radio broadcasts, their work remained almost completely unknown within the English-speaking world outside of a small circle of psychoanalytic practitioners. Within this group, the work of Lacan and his colleagues gathered notoriety rather than support, particularly in relation to Lacan's introduction of much greater flexibility in the duration and frequency of analytic meetings with patients. From the perspective of the Tavistock analysts, the clinical advances they had made—by adapting aspects of the existing British and German work in ethology so as to extend the theorization of meaning in social environments—were now challenged by a new, upstart tradition.[3] In this, meaning-making was apparently stripped away from its biological foundations so as to become instead a linguistic descriptor within a formal system that eschewed direct commentary on the nature of any language's referents, i.e., the work of Ferdinand de Saussure (Saussure, 2006).

But by the 1970s, Lacan's various Saussure-inspired studies were being translated and enthusiastically featured in a growing number of courses within and outside of psychoanalysis: Dolto's work, meanwhile, continued to be largely unknown outside of France, and the work of the British Object Relations School was itself becoming eclipsed by the "Lacan phenomenon." Just what was going on in the Seventies—on either side of the Atlantic and later, the Pacific, to have brought about this unexpected reversal? There are, of course, a number of possible answers to this question. Outside of psychoanalysis, two developments seem particularly pertinent—both involving the social acceptance of a form of relativism where before there was, effectively, none. In terms of pragmatics, there was a growing public and scientific acceptance of the power of pharmacological products to directly influence brain and sensory function; and in terms of academic theory, there was a related and growing readiness to recognize the creative possibilities released by embracing cultural relativity. Courses in Cultural Studies began to spring up across the English-speaking world for the first time, along with media studies and film studies—all fascinated by the potential that Lacanian theory offered for fruitful analogies within their own developing disciplines.[4] Both of these developments were corrosive of the social project of psychoanalysis. With regards to the former, the validity of psychoanalytic therapy was thrown into question by the increasingly powerful means by which brain physiology (and hence, perception and mood) could be manipulated.[5] With respect to the latter, the traditional fixities of family life in the West, and therefore the "given" structure of the Freudian psyche, began to seem less secure, particularly in relation to gender and sexuality. In general, then, wherever the need arose, the theorization of culture demanded a body of theory that could tackle the description of the subject and its objects in such a way as to avoid any reference to fixed points of attachment—to specific matters of Western biology, or to equivalent assumptions of social formation and function, such as patriarchy.[6] "Structural" anthropologies, such as those of Claude Lévi-Strauss, were initially used by many, but soon Lacanian theorizing seemed to answer these needs more fully—at least for a time; and yet still Dolto's work did not find favor, even when it was recognized, and even when its potential scope of application was restricted to education. What continued to be "wrong" with her brand of psychoanalysis in this new cultural climate? In terms of education, the immediate answer was straightforward. In nearly all British courses of teacher preparation in the 1960s, a simplified version of Piaget's "genetic epistemology" was taught. In particular, and consistent with a general cultural focus of the time, the child was thought of as a "little scientist"—one, moreover, who acted largely autonomously in its task of self-creation. By the 1970s, this was being questioned, but when a new theorist did finally emerge to replace Piaget's influence, it was Lev Vygotsky's version of interactive learning through discourse with a skilled "other" that was adopted; Françoise Dolto never did enter the frame. In fact, apart from a few experiments by enthusiasts in the 1930s, psychoanalysis never was, and never has been, endorsed as an essential part of these State-inspected courses. Today, symptomatic of a prevailing tendency to opt for the reproducible rather than the individual, Cognitive Behavior Therapy is assumed to be nearly always an appropriate form of intervention.

Therefore, in the absence of any direct evidence of Dolto's influence on British education, evaluating what her contribution might have been, and perhaps still could be, requires an understanding of the fundamental splits in psychoanalytic theorizing itself—at least to a level of detail where her therapeutic divergences become intelligible in educational terms. The first of many such splits that occurred relates to the experience of "instinct." Freud had begun his own authorship at a time when the basic architecture of the human mind was still conceived in relatively simple terms. The observed regularities of all animal life—their specific patterns of survival behavior—were attributed to inherited instincts since it was assumed that animals had little or no capacity for learning. It was also assumed that the "animal" part of the human was essentially the same. However, setting us apart from the rest of the animal kingdom was our consciousness, our sense of self, our will, and our capacity for ethical judgment. To be truly human, then, was to have the capacity to exercise control over instinct in the interests of the public good: to be less than human was to be subject to instinctive life—to be without morals, weak-minded, sub-human, or simply bestial. Freud seems largely to have accepted this account—one which not only pre-existed the Enlightenment, but which was remarkably similar to Plato's metaphor of the driver of a chariot harnessed to wild horses. As a result, Freud's notion of the psychic experience of these instinctive patterns of behavior was as separate forces that wrestled for control over the Self's agency.[7] These were the "drives," and each sought particular categories of "object" which might allow a specific aspect of the animal/physiological to aid the human individual's survival. Freud's notion of a drive is most simply defined as the psychic experience of a biological instinct, but by the 1930s, a debate over the reality, or otherwise, of human instincts had begun. Freud's own writing on this subject predates this by a long way, and it therefore became a fruitful ground for later study in all three of the traditions being tracked here. For Lacan in particular, great significance was attached to the distinction between physiological need, and the semantics of desire. Whereas the former typically had a well-defined object as its source of immediate gratification, the latter replaced the concrete object of need with a linguistic expression of desire that entailed a permanent lack. Biologically I might need some water, but my request for "a glass of water," is only the start—I "want" a lot other things as well, as a continuing aspect of a social life entirely mediated through language.

But for Freud, within a mental organization under "pressure" from the drives, the concrete "objects" of each drive was perceived both as source of relief and pleasure, and he coined the term libido to designate what he imagined to be a psychic field of competing, and sometimes "blocked" flows of psychic potential seeking discharge. This characteriztic of the drives was assumed in most of his subsequent theorizing. However, he revised this explanation in relation to the sex drive itself. At its simplest, his theoretical difficulty was that the sex drive was not essential for individual survival in the way that gaining food and drink were. But at a deeper level, the etiology of narcissism indicated the need for an explanation that differed from that of autoeroticism. Whereas the fact of autoeroticism suggested a general capacity of the Self to view a part of its "body" as an object, the existence of Narcissism indicated a paradoxical capacity for it to accept itself in its totality as its own object. Freud's response was to produce a different theory of the libido. Rather than it being likened to a river with tributaries (the individual drives), he now credited it with a capacity to "project" parts of itself onto external objects, such as a child's personified toy, an adult's prized possession, or an idealized image of the person one wanted to be. Equally, such projections could be withdrawn, producing a sense of isolation and loss. From these notions of projection and introjection, and the two consequent accounts of the libido, much was to follow after Freud's death. For instance, once the idea of projection was entertained, the notion of privileging the fixed boundary of the body as a sub-division within the larger and more fluid boundaries of this second ego-type became problematic for theory. On what basis were the processes of projection and introjection of ego-affect able to recognize such a distinction? One answer was supplied by Melanie Klein's introduction of the idea that there were recognizable "positions," i.e., configurations of the psyche relative to the outside world, the so-called depressive, and paranoid-schizoid positions, but these were themselves underpinned by two distinctive and entirely human instincts: the life instinct (Eros) and the death instinct (Thanatos) which competed against each other for dominance in a syncopated beat throughout the individual's life.

The problem also existed for Lacan and Dolto, and both developed different theoretical responses—Lacan through an exploration of semiotic and topological analogies, while Dolto developed the notion of there being unconscious "images" of the body which did not correspond directly to "normal" anatomical reference points.[8] But despite these splits in theory over the nature of the drives and the ego, the basic Freudian vocabulary survived these battles. Freud had declared once that the aim of psychoanalysis was a modest one: "to turn neurotic misery into common unhappiness." And yet this "modest" approach had resulted in Western culture, particularly from the 1920s onward, gaining a number of terms with which it could critically examine its own assumptions about the integrity of the rational self, i.e., precisely the assumptions that even today lie at the heart of nearly all judicial, penal, and educational programmes. While Marx had given society the means to distrust the experience of capitalist exchange, Freud gave it the means to analyze the purity of willed action.[9] He summarized his ideas in a little essay written shortly before his death entitled "Some Elementary Lessons in Psychoanalysis," and these can usefully be extended by reference to another late publication of his, *An Outline of Psychoanalysis* (Freud, 1938, 1940). Taken together, these works offer a list of therapeutic assumptions that can be sub-divided into those which imply something about the structure and the organization of the mind, and those that reflect Freud's conception of our species—being as one in which individuals have an ontology that starts by being biological, and only secondarily becomes social.

Of the first set, something like the following should be noted. Our experience of consciousness is not all that there is to say about mental life—unconscious mental processes are a part of this experience and, in fact, collectively they constitute the major part of psychic life. Additionally, in each of us this mental life has a unique history in which, nevertheless, it is always the case that the child is father to the man, no matter how extraordinary subsequent adult experience might be. This is not to deny the significance and scope of adult adaptation to new social settings, but from the perspective of neuroses this inversion becomes of paramount consideration in therapy. At various points Freud uses an archaeological metaphor to explain this feature of our psychic lives—the layered persistence within the mind of past forms of tactical, psychic configuration which were once found to be appropriate responses to our changing personal and social worlds.[10] Crucially, for Freud, neurotic regression reveals past configurations to be intact, rather than in a ruinous state.

As for the second set of therapeutic assumptions, two further conclusions dominate Freudian thought: our understanding of reality in all its forms never escapes the influence of our desires, fears, affections, and dislikes—each can, and regularly does, distort our perception of the world; and, secondly, psychic conflict is an inevitable part of our lives. In a sense, this is Freud's earliest and most profound conclusion since it is understood to be a direct consequence of our species being; its resonance with Klein's life and death instincts is also clear. As sketched above, then, the Freudian individual is equipped with a set of instincts that have primarily evolved to enhance individual survival, but as a species-type such individuals are too weak to sustain themselves for long in any natural setting. As a result of this inherent, biological contradiction—we survive biologically by acting socially—one might conclude that all the calculative powers of rationality are needed to maintain an enlightened self-interest in the preservation of those actions which enhance the stability and survival of the social group, even when this is opposed to the survival of the individual. But for Freud, the Enlightenment oppositions between reason and the irrational, between the logical and the pre-logical, and even between the intellect and the emotions, are to be replaced by another opposition entirely—the meaningful and the meaningless—the meaningful being rationality experienced in its highest form through human agency.[11]

Within this overall framework, the three broad traditions of psychoanalytic practice mentioned so far can be understood as dividing amongst themselves on the basis of ego definition. As we have seen, Freud came to produce two theorizations of the libido, and corresponding to this, he offered two different accounts of the ego. The earliest one assumed that this central feature of psychic life existed as an entity that was functionally equivalent to a bodily organ, i.e., its functionality was relatively fixed. Its primary task was to always seek out some rational compromise between the immediate gratification of the competing individual drives, interests, and desires, and the objective demands and expectations of our social settings—demands that were frequently hostile to any immediacy of expression and to the potential variety of their outcomes. In its role as rational arbitrator, Freud saw this "realist" ego as the major agency by which drive-experience could eventually obtain acceptable socialised forms of satisfaction, i.e., the individual's response to these experiences could be "sublimated"—the immediate objects of their needs transformed into distanced goals, their gratification deferred, i.e., the normal experience generated by most systems of education. Broadly speaking, the North American tradition of psychoanalysis, at least until about the 1970s, accepted this account of mental life, and developed its own patterns of therapeutic interventions on this basis—often referred to collectively as "ego psychology." This drew the conclusion that since psychic conflict was an inevitable consequence of social life, neuroses developed in those cases where the mental "organ" mediating between the social world and the embodied and drive-conflicted individual—the ego—had for one reason or another failed in its efforts to maintain mental equilibrium. Therapy therefore entailed procedures aimed at strengthening the ego so that it could regain its capacity to achieve its self-preserving function within inter-subjective relationships.[12] It cannot be stressed too much that there was one major clinical consequence of this outlook. Since the source of these neuroses would always have their origin in a relatively stable, biological foundation, for which there was an equally stable psychic "organ," it became possible for therapeutic study to advance alongside other forms of medical intervention and palliative care on an equal footing, and the same held true for pediatrics.

To American readers it will not be a surprise to hear that the British "Object Relations" tradition, in the main, took a different line of interpretation, but one that swung uneasily between this version of the ego and Freud's second definition—the one more fully embraced and extended by the French "renegades"—Lacan and Dolto. Freud's revised notion of the libido entailed an account of the ego in which, rather than it being restricted to a fairly predictable range of tactical responses aimed at curbing the excesses of drive expression, it was now conceived in less prescriptive terms—one allowing it to engage in larger, more creative—even playful—strategic changes to its relationships with others and the world. No longer thought of as equivalent to a bodily organ, it was now posited as a fluid boundary between the Self and the not-Self, open and capable of making spontaneous responses to a changing world, relying initially on an existing stock of past psychic templates or psychic images—meaningful figurations of its own agency and the agency of others—in order to reach its accommodations with social reality.[13]

This, of course, entailed a changed understanding of neuroses and regression. To the degree that the analyst in question accepted some version of the Kleinian "positions," it becomes possible to say relatively simply what this understanding comprised. The ideal adult state—and therefore the disposition that the developing child should be nurtured towards—was the Depressive Position. In this state the fluid boundary of the Self could creatively extend into a world that offered it possibilities for new becomings.[14] However, it could also respond non-Self destructively to a world turned hostile to such endeavors—while the Self might draw back its boundaries, it could do so without losing its integrity and its readiness to look outward to new opportunities for turning aspects of the world into meaning-for-Self. But to do full justice to Klein, one needs to understand that the Depressive Position is essentially a dynamic balance point between the forces of life and creation (Eros), and those of death and destruction (Thanatos). Neurosis and regression within this same perspective were theorized in Klein's account of the Paranoid-Schizoid Position, which she considered to be the initial mental configuration at birth, i.e., one incapable of perceiving complex unities (e.g., Klein, 1961). In this position, the libido of the neurotic responded to a world judged to be devoid of hope by drawing itself into the smallest possible form so as to offer less of a target to the persecutory forces now filling the individual's world. Klein also indicated that these persecutory forces came to exist within the boundaries of the Self through a process of splitting and introjection. The individual, in a regressive attempt to maintain an earlier, "ideal" psychic configuration in which a kind world turned its face towards the individual, transposed real, hostile forces—events and other individuals existing within, or threatening to breach, its ego-boundary—onto a split component of the ego/libido that was now considered to be "bad"—justifying various forms of Self-punishment and Self-correction.

This kind of explanation, and the extended therapies associated with such diagnoses, sat increasingly uneasily alongside the run of medical theorizing and intervention being developed in the 1950s, and 1960s, i.e., the beginnings of cell-level physiological understanding and the deployment of early psychotropic drugs. Nevertheless, for the British Object Relations group, there were a number of propositions that did become generally accepted and which became a source of inspiration for Lacan when he visited London immediately after the Second World War.[15] (I think the same, albeit more indirectly, is perhaps true of Dolto, although there are very few references to other analysts in any of her published works.) Rather than accepting the essential directionality of Freud's conclusions—from a pre-existing biological self to the Self as agent of social compromise—the Object Relations theorists modified this. Greater emphasis was placed on the child's interactions in early social settings—typically within a family—and the child's search for meaning within these, i.e., the processes of social projection and introjection, were seen as "shaping" mechanisms by which the Freudian drives were progressively brought into ever more efficient connections with reality. For the British Object Relations School, then, what was significant about early childhood was the readiness of the child to look for meaning in the outside world, and to progressively construct from these experiences a set of meaning-for-Self patterns of instinctive life which, in turn, and ideally, could form the basis for the discovery of the more complicated forms of social meaning leading to the child's eventual entry into adult life.[16] Child neuroses, therefore, became largely seen as a failure in the ability to constructively shape felt/instinctive meaning-for-Self out of social relationships, and the source of such problems was sought in the particular nature of the "reality-testing" that the child had been able to conduct in meaningful social settings.[17] In contrast to this, the "Freudian" child of his first characterization of the ego—that of Anna Freud's, and by implication, the child posited by many North American psychoanalysts—was one in which the instincts (and hence drives), and their development, were progressively mediated by the regulatory ego as its functionality developed and matured to cope with the physiological, anatomical, and social changes, generating a familiar and recognizable sequence of developmental "pressure points."

Granting the existence of factions within the Object Relations School, beyond these basic "architectural assumptions," it is perilous to offer much more in the way of generalization, but the following do strike me as having been widely held during the 1950s and 1960s. First of all, and to re-state the major difference between the traditions, in terms of functionality this ego was no longer thought of as being a separate entity or agency within the subject—consciousness itself and its boundaries become fluid, strategic, autopoietic, and fundamentally social in nature through the phenomenon of projection. This natural outward impetus to the Self's survival strategy would always attempt to proceed initially by employing a selection from the pre-existing stock of psychic images or templates—past figurations of agency—that would allow it to perceive the present social setting through a familiar lens, i.e., in a way that would supply a clear initial location for the Self and its activities in relation to a present but self-conceived "object-world." This "narcissistic" ego was, in other words, predominantly inter-subjective and prone to fantasy as a consequence of its projective identifications (and retractions), but much hung on the spelling of the word "fantasy." For Melanie Klein, and those who followed her, the word was spelt as "phantasy" so as to distinguish it from the normal meaning of fantasy, i.e., wishful imagining. The experiences associated with Kleinian phantasy were very much like those Freud attributed to the drives, but in Klein's own work these emerge more as *figurations* of desiring relationship that are susceptible to modification by experience; indeed, Klein sees this process of "reality testing" as the primary generator of thought itself.[18] However, for many others in the school the word remained "fantasy," which of course lessened the implication of it being driven so directly by an underlying, instinctive pre-figuration. But, equally, the strategic boundary of consciousness was often said to be amenable to the "desires" of the inter-subjective other, and in this respect many in the group were close to the position Lacan reached in his own theorizing, although by a different route.

Lacan, Dolto, and others while they worked alongside him, developed a further interpretation of Freud's narcissistic version of the ego. As has been suggested, these analysts started from a position that was to some degree influenced by that of the British Object Relations School; but Lacan introduced a more radical interpretation based on his re-reading of early Freudian theorizing. Essentially this difference in the understanding of the ego arose from a much more intellectualized appreciation of the structure of communication needed to establish, maintain, halt, destroy, or simply avoid social relations. Principal amongst the various social media employed was language; and since social life was almost entirely mediated by language, a study of its nature became an essential prerequisite to any re-conceptualization of the Freudian drives, or the Kleinian phantasies. Dolto shared this perspective, but her own work was built upon a rather different understanding of language. In the first place, it seems certain that Dolto had reached an appreciation of the central significance of language as *the* medium of inter-subjective reality by independent means. Not only was her own childhood full of instances where language, or silence, had wrought dramatic changes to her family and social circumstances, her subsequent clinical practice had also provided many vivid confirmations of its significance to any study of psychic life. Apart from the two autobiographical accounts of her family life—one of which also details her early professional life (Dolto, 1986, 1989), Dolto's various pedagogical seminars and published case studies are remarkably consistent when compared, for instance, with the many publications of Freud and Lacan, in which theory seems often to evolve almost independently of clinical observation. Certainly, most of Dolto's professional publications demonstrate the therapeutic efficacy of the use of direct language as a means to resolve problems in family settings of long standing. Time and again, these were shown to be caused by the persistent use—on the part of principal carers—of evasive accounts of a child's domestic circumstances, or by a parent's forgetfulness or embarrassment caused by the circumstances of their child's birth or some other intimate social relationship, e.g., the appearances and disappearance of "uncles" and "aunts." Another aspect of this same personal history is one that emerges more by the absence of direct evidence to the contrary. My own sense is that Dolto arrived at her conclusions about the significance of language largely by being drawn to the religious significance of language as *testimony*—as a means to bear witness—rather than as an abstract system of signifiers, or as a model for psychic structure.[19]

DOLTO AND THE SCIENCE OF PSYCHOANALYSIS

In the following sections attention shifts to the three, principal features of psychoanalytic work: the nature of the unconscious itself, the significance of the Oedipus complex in the life of the individual, and the implications of transference within therapeutic settings. Of the three, the only one considered here in any detail is the unconscious—and largely by reference to Dolto's own practice.[20]

From the start, then, any study of Dolto has to tackle the re-conceptualization of psychoanalysis that her Christian faith demands. Eric Binet, for instance, writing under the auspices of UNESCO in 1999, chose to title the first section of his appreciation thus: "A Christian educator out of the ordinary" (Binet, 1999). Given Freud's antipathy towards religion, e.g., his book of 1927 entitled *The Future of an Illusion*, and the disgust with which he responded to Jung's "mystical religiosity," this seems a remarkable way to reference Lacan's longest-serving co-worker, since Lacan continued to call himself a Freudian—as did Dolto. Yet within this contradictory professional frame one must place Dolto's intense and passionate advocacy of the seriousness with which children and their lives within families must be taken: babies were people. In the two autobiographical texts already referenced, as well as in the conduct of her professional life, Dolto was always at pains to point out how deep-seated were her interests and her efforts to understand and improve the lot of children. And when Dolto affirms the necessity—in every family and personal circumstance—of speaking, she thinks it essential that such speech should always be truthful and articulated as one person to another; this being as much a necessity of faith as a clinical conclusion.[21] From this perspective, the intelligibility of the world in the mind of a creator, and the glimpses of order and pattern afforded to human intelligence, are to be connected by a language that must continually strive to be as supple and as complex as the realities that it attempts to contain and convey to others. And, since it is impossible to separate this "truthful" speaking from desire and the life of the emotions, a radical interpretation of the significance of the Christ figure follows in Dolto's own theorizing (Dolto, 1996, 2000).[22] Jesus Christ becomes an emblem of the possibilities of desire, as Guy Hall, in a recent collection, summarizes:

> The unconscious use of the body takes on a unique paradigm when Francoise Dolto considers the birth, death, resurrection, and divine incarnation of Jesus. The life of Jesus becomes a psychodrama, and he becomes the master of desire. He is the one who reveals the perverse desires in others and offers them the possibility of finding their true desires. The humanity of Jesus is emphasized, while a spark of the divine is found in every human being. (Hall, in Hall et al., 2009, p. 205)

This position, however honorable and sincere, risked professional ostracism, and yet Dolto persisted to the point where she likened the task of the analyst to that of Christ. With this fundamental cast to her thought, she experienced many difficulties with the institutional aspects of Catholic interpretation, but once introduced to the more egalitarian and libertarian practices of the Russian Orthodox Church by her husband, Boris Dolto, she began to feel confident enough to argue in public for a professional position relative to religious belief, in broadcasts, television interviews, essays, and books—eventually producing eight of these, all of which had the reality of religious experience at their core. Given the specific form of primacy Dolto accorded to language, and the parallel emphasis on inter-generational social structure, one is now in a better position to move towards more general comments that follow from what is, in effect, a religious foundation. In relation to Dolto's understanding of the unconscious, it seems to me inescapable that one has to turn towards a concept of genesis, implying both a site of origin *and* a process of reproduction. At one and the same time this relies on a genealogy—an understanding of the individual child's familial, biological inheritance, but also on its symbolic equivalent—its existence even before birth as a unique center for meaning-generation within the overall warp and weft of family discourse.

For Freud, this process of coming to be started *at* birth and effectively terminated with the Oedipus complex, since this last transition left the child with a functionally distinct unconscious operating alongside the ego and superego. For Dolto, however, the child's genesis extended back before its birth, while the nature of its unique psychic configuration was one, ideally, of continual dynamic change, both before and after the time of the Oedipus complex, since for her individual growth involved a process of multiple "symbolic" castrations as I discuss below. Similarly, the child's social location also extended to earlier, inter-generational structures, and to later semi-adult public arenas. As a thought-in-discourse, therefore, the child's coming-to-be preceded its physical genesis; this view was also shared with Lacan, although without the added implication of the family entering into a state of blessedness and extended obligation to a wider community.[23]

At this point one searches for some hint of what Dolto considered the kernel of these discourses—the nature of the unconscious itself—which according to other theorists could act as a conductor extra-ordinary, as a field of spontaneous creation, and as a rubbish pit of unspeakable filth, etc. Short of reproducing her case studies of children, what follows must remain a generalization, but it is significant, I think, that in her key text, *The Unconscious Image of the Body*, she builds each analysis of the twelve children featured there around the central role that desire plays in the child's psychic "economy" (Dolto, 1984). In a sense, this is not so very different from the Object Relations School in its prioritizing of social meaning as centered on affect, but one senses that Dolto wants to go beyond even the modified ego/libido of the Object Relations School, particularly in relation to the focusing of desire. My suggestion is that one should think of the unconscious for Dolto as being an origin of a far more integrated genesis of desire; an integration, moreover, that is from the start biased towards the expression of each desiring being through language, rather than through a "scopic" drive within an ego searching for its primary figuration, as Lacan describes. What emerges, then, is a notion of there being a continual, self-renewing, autopoietic Self-figuring through language within the life of each child and in the life of the adult that they will become. Central to this is the sociality of education, in its broadest sense; since it is through education that an encounter with the Divine will first becomes "thinkable"—through language and the mediations of the ego/libido.[24] Through this encounter the child's intrinsic creativity begins to turn its basic needs into a field of playful desire, but one which is usually constrained by gender, by family, by society, and by the representations of institutionalized religion. However, over and above these constraints, Dolto sees the force of this creativity always working outward towards the fulfillment of the child's potential for an ever greater degree of complexity and refinement in living—towards an ever sharper focus on Self-being that is both religious and social at the same time. In the end, then, I think, one is forced towards the identification of an underlying belief on Dolto's part that there is a sense of time, and of an event, structuring the entire psychic existence of humanity, as much as the life of a single child. The unconscious becomes, finally, a means by which the Divine order expresses our original and ultimate obligation to that time and that event, and the play of our desires in reality corresponds to the infinity of ways in which this obligation might be discharged. At the same time, consciousness becomes the sometimes joyful, sometimes painful, travail of the soul towards its unique vocation.

This interpretation seems so far removed from Freud's insistence on the scientific credentials of psychoanalysis that one may wonder how Dolto managed to stay in professional practice, even allowing for the fact that she followed Lacan when the International Psychoanalytic Association rejected their claim for re-affiliation.[25] However, this rejection was not what it might seem. The problem posed by Lacan's insistence on the variable length of therapeutic sessions went to the heart of the entire edifice that Freud had constructed, and that Ernest Jones had fought so strenuously to preserve after Freud's death. Freud had always insisted that psychoanalysis was a science, but coming to judge the validity of this claim from a contemporary perspective demands an understanding of the leeway in definition existing in the late nineteenth century—one which allowed Wilhelm Wundt to be later dubbed "the father of psychology," as well as Freud being identified as "the father of psychoanalysis."[26] A consideration of this issue now allows a better estimation of the social value of Dolto's unique professional position.

The starting point for such arguments is the definition of the principal "object," or class of "objects," that the discipline attempts to address through theory. In the case of psychoanalysis, this is the unconscious, Freud's "Copernican" insight into the nature of mind. Freud's theory object—the unconscious—had, ideally, to be apprehended in such a way as to indicate its limits, its extension, its conditions of functionality (and therefore its forms of existence and their effects), and the requirements that had to be met in order to observe and act upon it. So much seems clear today and probably was clear in large part to Freud at the time, but so much also was not available. Faced with a domain of phenomena largely left unrecognized by the science of his time, convinced that Charcot's own explanations of hysteria were inadequate, and yet feeling unwilling or incapable of offering public demonstrations as Charcot had, Freud fell back on the assumptions of private medical practice as *the* means to develop his therapeutic interventions *and* further identify the phenomena of the unconscious. The natural insistence on patient anonymity in all published case studies, and the restriction of access to the observed phenomena *via* his own reports in the first instance, and subsequently only to other professionals within a tutorial relationship, resulted in a form of verification that today would be unacceptable in the physical sciences, and ethically questionable in the social ones. If the patient's presentation of symptoms was always to be shrouded in the analyst's own language, even when observation was shared through training, the notion of the independent repeatability of observation became difficult to sustain. Hence, Freud's obsession with the use of consistent terminologies and aetiologies within the small group of psychoanalysts he gathered around him: without an agreed discourse there could not even be grudging acceptance by the outside world that authoritative professional discourse was possible in this new domain of scientific study.

But even in Freud's time there was an alternative explanation of what psychoanalytic work and study might entail. A relatively recent characterization of this was provided by Adam Phillips:

> Psychoanalysis, at its inception, had no texts, no institutions, and no rhetoric; all it had to see itself with were analogies with other forms of practice. The first practitioners of psychoanalysis were making it up as they went along . . . Psychoanalysis, that is to say, was improvised; but improvised, despite the medical training of the early analysts.
> . . . Psychoanalysis began, then, as a kind of virtuoso improvization within the science of medicine; and free association—the heart of psychoanalytic treatment—is itself ritualized improvization. (Phillips, 1993, pp. xiv–xv—my ellipses)

Phillips's sketch makes clear the weak points in the transmission of psychoanalytic knowledge from the perspective of the scientific paradigms that psychology itself aspires to today. Without close adherence to a prescribed induction into the profession, and an equally prescribed notion of professional conduct, the project as a whole was threatened by continual schism, as one charismatic practitioner succeeded another; it was also threatened by dissolution, as each practitioner responded to the vagaries of inter-subjective therapeutic interpretation and wrote up variant case histories. And yet, of course, charismatic individuals continued to be attracted to the project of psychoanalysis, and continued to break away from Freud's "dogmatism"—an approach to dissent that he thought essential for the survival of psychoanalysis as a cultural as well as scientific project.

In relation to Dolto's practice, then, Phillips might be understood to argue that what is at issue is not her supposed waywardness, or even her individuality, but rather her relevance to patients, and perhaps to the cultural life of France during a period dating, roughly, from the 1950s to the 1980s. In terms of the radio broadcasts where she welcomed calls from the public on issues of child-care, and offered immediate commentary on the problems expressed, Phillips's sketch meets that explanatory need: these "shows" had the effect of alerting a public to a novel way of seeing family life. But in relation to the many successes of her clinical work, one needs a more penetrating analysis. This is answered particularly well by one of Paul Ricoeur's papers (Ricoeur, 1977), which is in English. Ricoeur focuses on the nature of psychoanalytic facts, or more properly, on the criteria for "facts" in psychoanalysis, "Even when we are not dealing with a narrow empiricism which does not require a theory to be directly validated by observables, we nevertheless continue to ask the same questions we would put to any observational science" (Ricoeur, 1977, p. 836). Ricoeur then argues that psychoanalytic theory codifies what takes place in the analytic relationship, since it is there "that something happens which merits being called the *analytic experience*" (Ricoeur, 1977, p. 836; Ricoeur's italics). For Ricoeur, then, the analytic situation is the source of "observables." He argues that there are four criteria used by psychoanalysis as the means by which its facts are identified, describing each of these as a "formative vicissitude" of the analytic situation. The first is that the facts are such as are capable of being said, and he comments immediately that this restriction is the "particular context of un-involvement with reality belonging to the analytic situation that forces desire to speak, to pass through the defile of words, excluding substitute satisfactions as well as any regression towards acting out" (Ricoeur, 1977, p. 836-37).[27] He continues,

> This screening through speech in the analytic situation also functions as a criterion for what will be held to be the object of this science: not instinct as a physiological phenomenon, not even desire as energy, but desire as a meaning capable of being deciphered, translated, and interpreted. Hence the theory necessarily has to account for what we may call the semantic dimension of desire. (Ricoeur, 1977, p. 837)

The second criterion singles out the fact that what is said is said to another person. In Ricoeur's view this is a central feature of analytic technique, and the transference stage is significant within it because of its epistemological implications. Having noted Freud's likening of transference to the creation of a playground, Ricoeur indicates that what is factually significant, psychoanalytically, is that, "*In this 'playground', this 'intermediate region," in effect, we can read the relationship with the other as constituting an erotic demand addressed to another person'* (Ricoeur, 1977, p. 838; Ricoeur's italics). As he then explains, this reveals the constructive aspect of desire, not only is it able to be spoken, but it is addressed to another—to another desire which is capable of rejecting it, i.e., what is being identified here is the inter-subjective dimension of desire—but in particular, desire within the therapeutic situation. This explanation is a striking aspect of Dolto's case studies, since she is often drawn to comment on the significance of the counter-transference, in terms of ultimate success and failure.[28] Ricoeur's third criterion introduces circumstances which are often judged to be central to Freud's project—the conclusion that in the case of neurosis, it is "psychic reality" which is decisive. Ricoeur stresses that it is the analytic situation itself which necessitates the use of this conception as an explanatory term. The criterion is not that it is observable, but that it presents itself as having both coherence and a capacity for resistance comparable to that of material reality, i.e., it constitutes an equivalent to the "objects" of the physical sciences. Ricoeur's concluding comment identifies a trajectory that runs from fantasy to the lost object, the substitute object, and then to the work of mourning, which he considers to be close to the core of psychoanalytic experience within the therapeutic setting:

> Far from restricting itself to vanquishing the fantasy to the benefit of reality, the cure also recovers it as fantasy in order to situate it, without confusing it with what is real, on the level of the imaginary. This kinship between the cure and the work of mourning confirms, if any further confirmation is required, that it is the analytic experience which requires that we add the reference to fantasies to the two preceding criteria. (Ricoeur, 1977, pp. 842–43)

It seems appropriate here to remind the reader of the opening paragraphs of this section. Dolto's faith, if I am correct in the interpretation I give to it, effectively mandates her psychoanalytic practice with children to be one which must always open out to a reality figured by loss—loss of past Selves, loss of Self as a purely familial agency, and ultimately, loss of Self as a member of society without obligation. But this notion of what might be thought tragic for childhood and for the "independent" adult is ultimately twisted by therapy into a source of joy through a gain in the form and depth of social agency. This leads naturally to Ricoeur's fourth criterion, which is that the analytic situation selects from the subject's experience that which is capable of being narrativized; the making of "case histories," as histories, constitute the *primary* texts of psychoanalysis.[29] However, this form of explanation is misleading. Ricoeur makes a crucial point when he indicates that:

> Broadly speaking, we may say that the investigatory procedure tends to give preference to relations of *meaning* between mental productions, while the method of treatment tends to give preference to relations of *force* between systems. (Ricoeur, 1977, p. 846; Ricoeur's italics)

For Dolto, these relations of force are to be understood, I think, within the context of the "pressures" of testimony and faith, although the issue of meaning suggests more a discipline of textual interpretation—a form of hermeneutics. But as Ricoeur stresses, "Freud never doubted that however inaccessible the unconscious might be, it still participates in the same psychic structures as does consciousness" (Ricoeur, 1977, p. 846). This implies that dream formation and symptom formation are both "sayable" and substitutable, and by extension, it suggests connections with daydreams, myths, fables, proverbs, puns, and jokes. But clinical experience also led Freud to develop the terms repression, condensation, displacement, and deformation, i.e., treatment was experienced, above all else, as a struggle against resistances—and this reflexion returns us to a contextualised form of truth. Ricoeur concludes that psychoanalytic theorization is torn between these two poles: between text and translation on one side, and "mechanics" and the interplay of forces on the other. It is clinical practice in general, and the experience of transference in particular, which demands that theory must overcome this antinomy. Ricoeur closes with a return to the nature of psychoanalytic fact:

> . . . if analytic experience is desire coming to discourse, the sort of truth that best answers to it is that of a saying-true rather than a being-true . . . if the analytic situation elicits—principally by means of transference—what is said *to the other,* the truth claims of psychoanalysis can legitimately be placed within the field of intersubjective communication . . . what is psychoanalytically relevant is what a subject makes of his fantasies . . . to explain here is to reorganize facts into a meaningful whole which constitutes a single and continuous history. (Ricoeur, 1977, pp. 858–861; Ricoeur's italics, my ellipses)

My suggestion is, therefore, that Ricoeur not only provides a guide to thinking about the project of psychoanalysis itself, but in so doing implies a particular location for Dolto within it. Her faith is no longer a reason for exclusion. Her interest is to place the child in time of narrative—in the time of its own family, within the child's sense of its own timeliness, and in a unique Self-placing of time within the Symbolic Order as a whole. The therapeutic relation is educative in that what one strives for is the utterance of truth, and this is not, ultimately, just a matter of individual choice but of recognition of the larger frameworks of the symbolic order. This is also much more an entry into a community, however re-constituted through the therapeutic engagement, than it is a narcissistic search for Self; and equally, fantasy in this relationship has work to do, and the erotic message of this "staged event" is closer to that of a "mourning play" than it is to a farce—the child/patient is brought to witness the acting out of a tragedy that, through treatment, can be recognized as an allegory of its own past, i.e., a past that is now valued and "recovered" by a story of its own present. The analyst, meanwhile, is left to reflect upon the doubled meaning for themselves of a play within a play.[30]

DOLTO AND SCHOOLING: *LA MAISON VERTE*

Towards the end of her life, Dolto became associated with the setting up and running of a pre-school site in Paris—a transitional day-care center that would take children accompanied by a principal carer up to the age of three, i.e., before entry into a crèche or nursery school.[31] Started after Dolto had retired, the *Maison Verte* (The Green House) opened its doors on the sixth of January h, 1979 after several years of planning amongst a group of analysts and educationists. It was not really a house, but rather the spacious ground-floor of a flat—complete with green doors and pillars, and furnished with green cushions and curtains. The initial rationale of the center was the prevention of the traumas of separation brought about by the extended social and institutional demands of education. But Dolto also had another preventative intention. In various interviews she stressed her view that too often when children were identified as needing psychoanalytic treatment it was almost too late. And even if the child could be treated successfully, much of the child's psychological "location" within the family was likely to still remain in place—and it was probably this that had created the problem in the first place—perhaps also hindering the identification—if not the admission—of the child's difficulties.[32] She therefore planned for the *Maison Verte* to be a place where such early identification take place, but also where early interventions could be initiated in a normal social setting, i.e., in a non-clinical setting. In terms of actual practice, each child would typically attend once a week, and would always be accompanied with a principal carer who would stay with the child for the whole time. On arriving, the pair was welcomed by three "welcoming" adults, and none of this three would insist upon the recognition of their official affiliation. Only the child's first name was recorded on a board by the door while it was present so as to remove any suggestion of there being any official documentation, or implied dependency on the part of the child. One of the welcoming adults would be a man, and one a psychoanalyst whose role in this, and in any subsequent relationship, was to act, primarily, in a social, rather than professional capacity. However, Dolto also likened their task to anxiety dish-cloths, since much of their work involved "cleaning up" potentially dramatic situations as they occurred. Eventually, at a time initiated by the child or its carer, their task would also be to help elicit painful stories and memories from this dyad without immediately moving into any professional intervention. Often all that the child needed was a context within which certain things could be said to another, could be felt, and could be acted upon.

The *Maison Verte* was, then, never intended as a crèche, a child-minding center, nor even an activity center. Instead, and particularly after her death, the separate and distinct "houses" that were set up in the cities and towns of France and French-speaking Belgium became multi-disciplinary centers where very young children and their carers could informally interact with a variety of professionals, e.g., educationists, social workers, psychoanalysts, etc. Typically, each center had a different professional focus depending on the perceived nature of local needs.[33] However, despite this eventual diversity, certain institutional characteriztics were retained. The guiding principle was then, as it is now, to let the children explore the "house" and its inmates at their own pace. This could be done through play, through verbal and non-verbal exchanges with other children, by playfully distancing from accompanying adults, by interacting with other carers, and also by engaging with the professionals if the desire was there, or if the situation demanded. In this respect, Dolto was clear that there was an essential social function to the *Maison Verte;* this was as a place where the individual child could make a safe and unthreatening initial encounter with the exigencies of social life outside of the family: there were "rules" of conduct that had to be learnt and respected—these having mainly to do with various forms of mutual respect. Equally, the professional focus was not just turned upon the infants, but included pregnant women—married or otherwise, single parents, siblings, aunts, and grandparents, etc.—any of whom might be troubled, unprepared, or simply unaware of the developing needs of the child in their care. And as in so much of Dolto's clinical work, the *Maison Verte* was a place of speech and speaking, but it was also one of careful listening and, particularly, of watching. In other words, the clinically precocious interpretation of symptom presentation was directed towards the child's physical and emotional comportment in so far as this could be spoken of within the child-carer dyadic relationship. Ideally, psychoanalytic, social, and broadly educational concerns would be combined so as to identify a uniquely appropriate nurturing context for the child's secure growth and development.

In terms of its location within the psychoanalytic tradition, then, one might start by characterizing the *Maison Verte* as an informal social site for psychoanalytic intervention. But more precisely, it might be likened to a collective environment—a dynamic social and physical structure—designed to provide successive transitional encounters—a safe preparation for the child to experience the subsequent parting and independence that was inevitably to be its lot. At this point in explanation one might be reminded of Donald Winnicott's explanations of transitional objects, and later accounts of transitional spaces within institutional settings (Winnicott, 1971). However, Dolto's notion of the composition of language results in a rather different emphasis in the description of these transitional spaces. For her, the symbol-generating capacity of every child is seen to rest upon the child's capacity to symbolize an awareness of its own embodiment as half of a composition—the other half being made up of its equivalent attempts to symbolize the world that surrounds it. This "fabric" of daily experience is essentially symbolic, rather than figurative, and the sense of "transition" is therefore shifted towards the progressive recognition of possible subject positions within public discourse, rather than the more individualistic emphasis that Winnicott gives to a child's experience in transition. As must also be clear, what Dolto was advocating for children's experience in the *Maison Verte* was what she also advocated for education in general. The educational task was to assist each child to achieve his or her own form of unique social meaning and social responsiveness; but in fact in most cases she thought educational systems did exactly the reverse. In sum, Dolto considered that her work at the *Maison Verte* was the high-point of her career. From the wider psychoanalytic perspective it can be claimed, I think, that it generated what Freud had lacked: a public demonstration of the cultural need for psychoanalytic understanding to inform cultural life, particularly in relation to early childhood. This was so much the case that Dolto thought other psychoanalysts should pay to work in such a setting.

Her intention, then, was to make the center a place which had language, and the acquisition of language, at its heart, i.e., truthful speaking about ever deeper understandings of the social world. Dolto used her base in the *Maison Verte* to deploy an extended understanding of language as the means to characterize the unconscious, as she explained in her publication of 1984, *L'image inconsciente du corps* [*The Unconscious Image of the Body*]. Through her extensive clinical work with very young children, who were often psychologically disturbed, Dolto came to recognize that the psychodynamic descriptions of the state of infancy available at the time assumed far too great a degree of passivity and under-development. In particular, she concluded that infants often understood far more of their immediate domestic circumstances than was normally allowed, either by professionals or the child's primary carers. However, her conclusions were not directed towards gaining greater recognition for neonate cognitive development—such work was largely American in origin and fitted into a another scientific paradigm. Instead, her growing conviction moved along a path that Jung might have recognized.[34] She came to believe that the infant mind had access to an unconscious history of its place in the family setting where it was soon to be born. This was a history that spanned generations and social structures; it was also more than simply the "space" within adult and sibling inter-generational discourse that it would later attempt to fill in its search for meaning. As a result of this relatively concrete form of access, Dolto argued that even at the fetal stage of development the child-to-be formed a figuration of its own desiring, unconscious being which could gain information about the external domestic environment of symbolic exchange into which it would emerge. In particular, Dolto argued that familial relationships needed to be reproduced in the discourse forms preceding the child's birth, and enveloping it after birth.[35] Stated like this, almost as a form of rehearsal, Dolto's promotion of direct communication to the developing fetus sounds unexceptional, since whatever its effects on the fetus, it would inevitably have the side-effect of making less traumatic to the family as a whole the infant's actual arrival at the time of birth.

Dolto's understanding of the functionality of the unconscious therefore differed from Lacan's. In relation to the life of the child after birth, she was ambivalent about his interpretation of the mirror stage—the state of infant dependency in which its supposedly fragmented understanding of embodiment—fragmented between itself and its mother's partially recognized body—was held by a literal image of self-wholeness. Lacan had argued that by this means the child gained a form of functional integration that, in turn, facilitated the child's own Self-figuring in fantasy, i.e., the child gained a location for agency through an encounter with an "other." Dolto thought that such a visual image, if it played the role that Lacan suggested, would disrupt what for her remained an extended sensory field existing between mother and infant, i.e., bringing about a greater degree of fragmentation than that which Lacan's theory attempted to remove. For Dolto, then, what was significant about the mirror stage was the destruction of the dyadic sensory field that had previously existed between the child and its mother (or principal carer)—a first symbolic castration. The mirror stage broke the mutual regard of mother and child in such a way that although functionally discrete figural components were produced, the intimacy of the previous sensory field was replaced by one in which the child's *embodiment in discourse* came to the fore as a substitute for a now lost sensory immediacy: the child's language was from now on located within its own, discrete, sensory being. According to Dolto, it was the critical loss of this image field which initiated the growth of complexity within the child's unconscious image of its own sensory embodiment, since at the same time that which was sensory had also to be rendered with ever greater precision in discourse: each symbolic castration conferred both growth and loss upon the body it sought to integrate with the world. Dolto's further conviction was that only within such states of integration could the subject maintain an authentic being and remain truly educable and educated. Truthful saying was therefore a constant feature of Dolto's "message"—a duty to speak from the heart, and for the heart, conferring a greater understanding of the heart.[36] It is difficult not to draw a parallel, in ending this chapter, with Rousseau's intentions towards his Émile; but Dolto did not need an entire countryside to bring success to her own enterprise, only a group of friends in a city, and a lifetime of devotion to a single idea.[37]

NOTES

1. This comparison is discussed in Guillerault, 2007. It is hard to over-estimate the importance of Ernest Jones in this history. Apart from being Freud's official biographer, he was particularly instrumental in setting up and managing the institutional structures which sustained the international growth of psychoanalytic study. He co-founded the American Psychoanalytic Association in 1910, and was President of both the British Psychoanalytic Association and the International Psychoanalytic Association during the 1920s and 30s, but with the latter extending through to 1949.

2. There was an official history of psychoanalysis during this period in England, and there is the contemporary one which features the many rebels who, having once worked alongside Freud, often as his most valuable co-workers, then rejected the primacy of his interpretations. In relation to the North American tradition, it is hard to overestimate the influence of Otto Rank, who is today largely credited with providing the foundation for the growth of social and psychotherapeutic counseling; his particular "sin" was to reject the centrality of the Oedipus complex and the sex drive, and for this reason his name was subsequently ignored in official accounts of psychoanalysis. In terms of innovation, and apart from extending Freudian psychoanalytic study into the areas of legend, myth, and art, Rank proposed a pre-Oedipal phase as a significant source of affect and neuroses, and introduced the basic elements of Object Relations theory, leading to an emphasis on the inter-subjective significance of the here-and-now in therapeutic encounters, rather than assuming the analyst's neutrality and a necessary delving into the analyst's childhood.

3. The work of Konrad Lorenz had started before the Second World War, although his publication in popular form in England was delayed, e.g., his *King Solomon's Ring*, of 1949, and Niko Tinbergen's *The Study of Instinct* of 1951. However, before the war there had been an extensive exchange of ideas on the nature of ethology and the role played by instinctive patterns of behavior—subsequently this aspect of their work was important in influencing the development of psychoanalytic theory, as I discuss below.

4. The phenomenon of "cultural studies" itself has been variously commented upon. Fredric Jameson's essay of 1984, "Periodizing the 60s," remains an essential starting point. In Film Studies, an interest in psychoanalysis was long-standing, while in Media Studies the ground was prepared for Lacanian theory through an equivalent interest in anthropology and semiotics—in the 1960s, Roland Barthes's brand of this discipline became particularly dominant, e.g., his *Mythologies* of 1957, but so also did Claude Lévi-Strauss's "structural" anthropology, e.g., his *Tristes Tropiques* of 1955.

5. This was before the contemporary recognition of brain "plasticity" had been added to the case for directly materialistic explanations of brain function.

6. The success of Elizabeth Grosz's prospective and retrospective review of 1990, *Lacan: a feminist introduction*, is typical of both the broad interest by then being generated for his work, and the specific difficulties it posed by retaining an apparently explicit patriarchal reference point for his "Symbolic Order."

7. From hereon, for ease of reading, I use the term "Self" as a variation on "ego," and as the principal substitution used in British Object Relations theorizing; my use of "self" continues its non-specialist meaning.

8. Freud recognized through his early work with Charcot, in Paris, that the ego-concept of the body did not correspond to the "body" of the anatomists or physiologists, but instead to the common understandings of anatomy that existed in everyday conversation.

9. Several theorists have been tempted to combine Marxism with Freudianism, e.g., Wilhelm Reich, Erich Fromm, and Herbert Marcuse (Reich, 1929; Fromm, 1955; Marcuse, 1955).

10. The word "tactical" is used here to emphasize that within Freud's initial characterization of the drives, the overall "strategy" of the human mind existed as a constellation of pre-given dispositions to act in particular ways in relation to specific objects within the environment—mediated by the ego. It is through mediation that the human animal becomes an "I" living within a social environment.

11. This is most effectively presented in Freud's extended essay of 1930, his *Civilization and its Discontents*; but it also returns us to the Ancient Greeks and their notion of *phronesis*.

12. A further level of detail leads onto Freud's assumption that the passage through the Oedipus complex results in a much clearer distinction being created between the ego, the unconscious, and a new entity, the superego—an internalized version of parental and social prohibitions that constrains the ego's operations—Kant's "moral voice within."

13. At this point it is worth noting Winnicott's development of the notion of transitional objects and transitional spaces—aspects of the world that support projection by being deemed to exist in a transitional state between me and not-me, or more properly, between the Self and the not-Self (Winnicott, 1971, 1988).

14. Putting the matter simply, the child has to move from a perceptual state in which the "goodness" and "badness" of things entails separate objects—separate realities—to one in which the unity of things is grasped through their intrinsic ambiguity of meaning—rather like the proverbial curate's egg: good and bad in parts.

15. In particular, he met Wilfred Bion and was stimulated by Bion's account of working with groups (Bion, 1961).

16. This offers a close parallel to Dolto's own interpretation of the influence of instinctive life, but for her this "shaping" process is focused through an unconscious "body-image" as I discuss below.

17. It is worth noting that John Bowlby and his "attachment theory" should be added to this general trend in analytic explanation—perhaps as an antidote. Although originally affiliated with the School, Bowlby's first version of the theory, his *Maternal Care and Mental Health* of 1951, was rejected by most analysts on the grounds that it went too far in emphasizing the empirical aspects of the child's social circumstances. Bowlby's later publication, *Attachment: Attachment and Loss* of 1969, is still widely respected, although the theory itself has been substantially revised.

18. There are interesting parallels to make here between Klein's guiding pre-figurations of reality, relative to each drive, and Dolto's sense of there being a unified body image. Both are subject to modification by reality testing, both are pre-verbal, and both are understood to be the foundation of the child's capacity to eventually conceptualize the world.

19. In one sense, this was no different than most other psychoanalysts. The primary evidence for her interpretations was the language used within a specific inter-subjective formation being generated by the child/patient and therapist while seeking to wrest meaning from the confusions and misleading pronouncements of the surrounding adult world. Because what was to be questioned was language's truthfulness, Dolto—in this respect at least—was closer to both of the other traditions than was Lacan.

20. There have been no recent translations of Dolto's work, and only a few were translated into English some years ago. The following comments are therefore based on my own translation of the original French texts.

21. Dolto, F. (1994) *Tout est langage*. Paris: Gallimard. Gérard Guillerault's careful preface to this text indicates that the original discussion in Grenoble, from which the book is derived, had an extended title which ended with, "The importance of words said to children and said in front of them."

22. The principal texts here are those of 1996 and 2000, *The Gospels and Faith at Risk from Psychoanalysis*. Guy Hall, in a collection of essays brought together by Hall, Hivernal, and Morgan, treats this aspect of Dolto's work very effectively (Hall, G., Hivernal, F., & Morgan, S. eds., 2009).

23. It should be added that Dolto consistently assumes a French cultural context in which the predominant place of the Catholic Church is taken for granted.

24. My use of the term "ego/libido" is to signal my uncertainty about terminology. Dolto clearly intends that the therapist should respect the child's agency of the Self in every encounter.

25. However, it should be recalled that an aspect of Freud's "Copernican revolution" was the assertion that there could be psychic causation, and that this was distinct from physical causation. The split from the I.P.A. had other causes. It was triggered by the re-formulation of the rules governing the induction of new analysts within the French Psychoanalytic Society in 1963—a move aimed primarily at excluding Lacan and anyone tempted to side with him in the ensuing dispute about teaching and therapeutic standards. Dolto herself provides an interesting if depressing account of this split, involving the accusation that she was a member of the Communist Party, passed her weekends with her patients, and had become a Jungian, see Dolto, F. (1989) pp. 138–143. See also the fourth letter in the correspondance between Althusser and Lacan in Corpet, O. & Matheron, E. (1996) pp. 151–158, and also in Roudinesco, (1994) p. 329. Other accounts of this event are more critical of Dolto, and of Lacan.

26. Both men built their initial reputations by reporting on investigations in which they were judge, jury, and also principal witness, i.e., they were their own, and often only, experimental subjects.

27. Note immediately the implication this has for working with very young children. Although like Klein and Anna Freud, Dolto experimented with children's drawings and games, her emphasis on language as the final arbitrator is a striking feature of her case histories with very young children, as much as with older, deeply disturbed ones.

28. From the notion of there being always a potential "community of faith," this might have been anticipated in relation to Dolto's practice, I think. However, the idea that Ricoeur expresses here was already "in the air" as a general focus of French intellectual thought at the time, e.g., Louis Marin's study of utopias as culturally neutral spaces within which the antinomies and contradictions of cultural life might be figured (Marin, 1973), but this, too, is pre-dated by Lévi-Strauss's explanation of Caduveo body painting (Lévi-Strauss, 1955).

29. The reader familiar with more recent trends of psychoanalysis will have been able to associate each of Ricouer's criteria with the emphasis placed within a particular form of practice, e.g., the last matches Donald Spence's interest in narrative truth and historical truth (Spence, 1982).

30. This is not to suggest that Dolto attempted to indoctrinate her child patients; she was always very clear that the child's own capacity for meaning-making was central to the therapeutic enterprise—and the same should be added for the therapist. With regards to the "mourning play," Walter Benjamin identifies Shakespeare's *Hamlet* as the most brilliant example of these, and this was a play which, of course, contained a play within itself—a case of "heal thyself, physician"? (Benjamin, 1998).

31. The first *Maison Verte* was followed by the independent setting up of a number of others with which Dolto had a much more distanced association while she was alive, and many of which have been developed since her death. A very good first-hand account of work alongside Françoise Dolto at one of the centers is provided by Anne-Marie Canu in Hall et al. (2009), pp. 143–162. Binet, previously referenced, also refers to her work in the school at Neuville, which also furthered her educational thinking. This is documented (in French) in D' Ortoli & Amram, 2001, as the review of the later versions of the *Maison Verte* in Neyrand, 1995.

32. In this respect, Dolto's arguments for the earliest possible forms of intervention—before the appearance of recognizable clinical symptoms—parallels some of the early work of R. D. Laing, e.g., (Laing & Esterson, 1964).

33. Apart from each center having no formal organization, Dolto also insisted that there was no such thing as a "Dolto method" which could be duplicated in each of the centers. Each group of co-workers had to define their own pattern of support and intervention, and in particular, their mode of "watchfulness" for the children who attended.

34. Famously, Jung (1959) introduced the concept of there being a "collective unconscious"—one that was not merely supra-individual—a kind of race or "folk" memory—but a means by which access was gained to a dimension beyond conventional understandings of space, time, causation, and identity.

35. An essential aspect of this argument is the recognition that discourse refers to much more than the words that are spoken; it entails the discourse practices of the speakers, their embodiment, and their various forms of agency relative to the discourse in progress.

36. Obviously this is intended metaphorically, but work with my students inclines me to believe that this is a metaphor that will be widely understood, correctly.

37. Rousseau—a self-confessed auto-didact—published his *Social Contract* in the same year as he published *Émile*. Whereas the former argued for a more just and rational organization of civic life, the latter—in its description of the secluded upbringing of a single boy in the country—is probably best understood as an allegory in which the text of *Émile*, as a description of a civilised equivalent to Rousseau's "noble savage," presents an ideal formation intended to inspire and guide more practical, urban forms of education.

REFERENCES

Barthes, R. (2009 [1957]). *Mythologies*. London: Vintage.

Benjamin, W. (1998). *The Origin of German Tragic Drama*. Trans. John Osborne. New York: Verso.

Binet, E. (1999). Françoise Dolto: 1908–1988. In *Prospects: the quarterly review of comparative education.* Paris: UNESCO: International Bureau of Education, vol. XXIX, no. 3, 1999, pp. 445–454.

Bion, W. (2009 [1961]). *Experiences in Groups.* London: Routledge.

Bowlby, J. (1951). *Maternal Care and Mental Health.* London : Jason Aronsen.

Bowlby, J. (1969). *Attachment: Attachment & Loss.* Vol. 1. New York: Basic Books.

Corpet, O. & Matheron, E. eds. (1996). *Writings on Psychoanalysis: Freud and Lacan. Louis Althusser.* New York: Columbia University Press.

Dolto, F. (1984). *L'image inconsciente du corps.* Paris: Éditions de Seuil.

Dolto, F. (1986). *Enfances.* Paris: Éditions de Seuil.

Dolto, F. (1989). *Autoportrait d'une psychanalyste: 1934*–1988. Paris: Éditions de Seuil.

Dolto, F. (1994). *Les chemins de l'éducation.* Paris: Gallimard.

Dolto, F. (1994). *Tout est langage.* Paris: Gallimard.

Dolto, F. (1996). *Les Évangiles et la Foi au risque de la psychoanalyze.* Volume 1. Paris: Gallimard.

Dolto, F. (2000). *Les Évangiles et la Foi au risqué de la psychoanalyze.* Volume 2. Paris : Gallimard.

D'Ortoli, F. & Amram, M. (2001). *La Neuville: l'école avec Françoise Dolto, suivi de Dix ans aprés: roman d'aventures pédagogiques.* Issy-les-Moulineaux: ESF.

Freud, S. (1955 [1922]). Psycho-analysis and the libido theory. *Standard Edition,* 18: 235–259. London: Hogarth Press.

Freud, S. (1989 [1927]). *The Future of an Illusion.* New York: W. W. Norton & Co.

Freud, S. (2004 [1930]). *Civilization and its Discontents.* London: Penguin.

Freud, S. (1955 [1938]) Some elementary lessons in psychoanalysis. *Standard Edition,* 23: 279–285. London: Hogarth Press.

Freud, S. (2003 [1940]). *An Outline of Psychoanalysis.* London: Penguin.

Fromm, E. (1955). *The Sane Society.* New York: Henry Holt & Co.

Grosz, E. (1990). *Jacques Lacan: a feminist introduction.* London: Routledge.

Guillerault, G. (2007). *Dolto/Winnicott: le bébé dans la psychanalyze.* Paris : Gallimard.

Hall, G., Hivernal, F., Morgan, S. (eds.) (2009). *Theory and Practice in Child Psychoanalysis: an introduction to the work of Francoise Dolto.* London: Karnac.

Jameson, F. (1984). Periodizing the 60s. In *Social Text, The 60s without Apology.* Duke University Press, pp. 178–209.

Jung, C. G. (1959). The archetypes and the collective unconscious. *Collected Works,* 9: pt. 1. London: Routledge & Kegan Paul.

Klein, M. (1961). *Narrative of a Child Analysis.* London: Hogarth Press.

Laing, R. D. & Esterson, A. (1964). *Sanity, Madness, and the Family.* London: Penguin.

Lévi-Strauss, C. (2011 [1955]). *Tristes Tropiques.* London: Penguin.

Lorenz, K. (2002 [1949]). *King Solomon's Ring.* London: Routledge.

Marcuse, H. (1987 [1955]). *Eros and Civilization: a philosophical inquiry into Freud.* London : Routledge.

Marin, L. (1973). *Utopiques: Jeux D'Espaces.* Paris: Éditions de Minuet.

Neyrand, G. (1995). Sur les pas de la *Maison Verte.* Paris: Syros.

Phillips, A. (1993). *On Kissing, Tickling and Being Bored: psychoanalytic essays on the unexamined life.* London: Faber & Faber.

Reich, W. (1929). Dialektischer Materialismus und Psychoanalyze in *Unter dem Banner des Marxism,* Berlin/Moscow (untraced pamphlet).

Ricoeur, P. (1977). The Question of Proof in Freud's Psychoanalytic Writings. *Journal of American Psychoanalytic Association.* Vol. 25, 1977, pp. 835–77.

Roudinesco, E. (1994). *Histoire de la psychoanalyze en France.* Paris: Fayard.

Saussure, F. de (2006 [1916]). (eds. Bouquet, S. & Engler, R.). *Writings in General Linguistics.* Oxford: Oxford University Press.

Spence, D. P. (1982). *Narrative and Historical Truth: meaning and interpretation in psychoanalysis.* New York: W. W. Norton & Co.

Tinbergen, N. (1951). *The Study of Instinct.* Oxford: Clarendon Press.

Winnicott, D. W. (1971). *Playing and Reality.* London: Tavistock Publications Ltd.

Winnicott, D. W. (1988). *Human Nature.* London: Free Association Books.

Chapter Five

Ghostly Presences in Children's Lives

Toward a Psychoanalysis of the Social

Michael O'Loughlin

A child walks into my psychotherapy practice. I get to know her over a period of time. We play games together. She may draw pictures. She may speak about the difficulties and pleasures of her life. She may reveal anxieties, worries, or fears. She may give me clues to the difficulties of being in her family by recreating those same difficulties in her relationship with me so that we have an opportunity to resolve them. She is a unique person with a unique sense of self, yet, early on I begin to see that she is also a person who is developing her sense of self through her insertion into a particular constellation of relationships and experiences.

It might make a big difference in what evolves between this girl and me if she is named Tiffany or Jane, Nipa or A'isah, Ngozi or Huei. Each name will come with certain cultural and gendered expectations and will be suggestive of birth into a particular community of cultural meanings. The emotional predispositions this girl brings with her also have the potential to open up a window into the vast range of sociohistorical events that have shaped her preoccupations. Since, as Catherine Mathelin deftly illustrates in *The Broken Piano* (1999), so many children come to therapy because of the anxious internalization of parental desire as their demand (cf. O'Loughlin, 2009), it is to be expected that this child will have formed her emotional dispositions around her parents' anxieties and emotional preoccupations. As Harry Stack Sullivan (1953) once noted, it is as if each child is a pebble shaped by the rushing waters of the brook of parental anxiety which envelops it and actively sculpts its shape.

In speaking of children, therefore, I prefer to use the term *subjectivity* to *self*. "Self" is essentialist in that it implies a fixedness and unity. It is as if there is a core self that has existed since the beginning that is unvarying in its essence and that is over-laid with culture. While children certainly seem to inherit certain temperamental dispositions that can surprise their parents and thwart parental ambitions—and hence suggest perhaps a certain amount of internal agency in even the youngest child—I prefer to think of children as *becoming* rather than *being*. The term *subjectivity* permits a certain fluidity in conceptualizing the formation of our subjective sense of being, and it allows us to imagine subject formation as multiple, constantly in the process of becoming, and socio-historically and ancestrally located. In this chapter I will explore the sociohistorical and ancestral/familial constitutedness of children's coming-to-be, and I will conclude with some implications for our work with children in early childhood educational settings.

PICTURE THIS: A GHOSTLY SIGNIFIER

I spent most of the first two years of my life in a hospital with a life-threatening illness (See O'Loughlin, 2007, for further detail). This was in Ireland in the 1950s. The psychic consequences of this trauma were sufficiently severe that I went into arrested development . . . a sort of suspended animation. I attained most of my developmental milestones well behind schedule, and some things, such as playing ping pong or hitting a golf ball, elude me to this day. I began to read, however, at age four. More than thirty years later I was teaching a university extension course in a rural campus of Bowling Green State University in Ohio. I taught a course on Human Development, and the latter part of the course focused on loss and death. This was especially poignant for me as my best friend, Patrick Buckheister, was dying of leukemia that summer. I spent many evenings at his bedside in Ypsilanti, Michigan, and my struggle with loss was palpable.

At the end of the course one of my students, Bill Baker, came forward and graciously presented me with a gift. Bill was a talented amateur photographer, and he had chosen a picture from his collection and framed it for me. I thanked him and thought no more about it. That winter, as I prepared to move back to New York, I packed the picture without further thought, and it then hung unnoticed in an out-of-the-way spot in my university office for a long time thereafter.

Some years later, while my mother was visiting from Ireland, I began to query her about my hospital experience. In the process of describing my early life she casually mentioned that I got so upset when she and my dad visited me in the hospital that the nurses recommended that whenever possible my parents should stand by the window and peer through the glass so that they could visit with me without upsetting me. Later that week, as I ruminated over this haunting story, I found myself staring dumbfounded at the picture on my office wall. The picture Bill had given me (see figure 5.1) was a photograph of a chalk statuette of a 1940s-style woman peering solemnly and with downcast expression through the grimy window of an antiques store in Northwest Ohio. The longing and loss in the picture spoke immediately to me and evoked powerful feelings of my early separation. This picture is so evocative for me that when I brought it in to share with students in my advanced trauma class this year, many years later, I became quite choked up as I shared this story.

In psychoanalytic parlance, one might say that that picture was a signifier that rendered speakable parts of my presymbolic traumatic memory. Experiences like this offer profound hope for the power of psychoanalysis. Since we are often rendered mute by our own traumatic experiences—or those ghosts of ancestral trauma we unconsciously embody—there is consolation in the fact that healing may be possible through the unconscious transmission of our unspeakable experiences to a receptive Other who can then give them back to us in speakable form. Although I had not discussed my childhood history with my students in Northwest Ohio that summer—and indeed I could not as I had not yet learned the details of my childhood hospitalization—wrestling with teaching about loss and dealing with the impending death of my close friend had surfaced my own deepest losses. Bill had picked this up through his uncanny receptivity to my unconscious. Bill *knew* my ghost and—no doubt unconsciously—he gave the picture to me to assist me in *meeting* my own experience. My childhood loss was of the kind that Christopher Bollas (1987) refers to as *an unthought known*—knowledge that we *know* in some experiential sense but that we do not yet *know that we know*. It was only when I had equipped myself with new knowledge of my childhood hospitalization from my mother and only after I had developed an incipient curiosity about my origins that I was finally able to recognize the signifier embodied in Bill's photograph.

ANOTHER GHOSTLY SIGNIFIER

In recent years I engaged my mother in a series of interviews that helped me formulate my understanding of my origins as I was working on *The Subject of Childhood* (2009). In one of those interviews she casually mentioned that her older brother, Thomas, living in a world of very severe material deprivation in rural Ireland, used to express one ambition as a child: "He said that if he were rich all he'd want is a settle bed full of apples and two pots of jam." Pots of jam (preserves) were extraordinarily significant in the economy of my childhood too. Coming home from his construction job on his bicycle on Fridays—payday—my father always brought an eagerly awaited pot of lemon curd or marmalade. To this day I keep four or five pots of jam in my

Figure 5.1. The Woman Behind the Glass. Michael O'Loughlin received the picture from which this photograph was taken as a gift in 1986 from a photographer who was a student in his class. Published in O'Loughlin 2010.

pantry at all times—often lemon curd or marmalade—and when Margaret, my wife, started noticing my tendency to buy multiple pots of jam at the grocery store I cut down my purchasing and bought additional pots at another time to hide my shame yet ensure that I never ran out! This very morning, as I sat down to write, Margaret, now privy to my inherited jam deprivation said: "I bought you three pots of jam. Different flavors. I hope you like them."

Oh, the memory of jam! Or, more precisely, the wonder of the unconscious reenactment of familial deprivation through embodied memory, in this case through an act as apparently innocuous as buying a jar of preserves!

THE TENSION BETWEEN SUBJECTIFICATION AND SUBJECTION

As Roger Waters suggests in Pink Floyd's (1979) song "Mother," the process of becoming socialized involves the insertion of the infant into a series of parental and societal expectations that are tantamount to bricks in a wall that ultimately imprison the child. Parents grieve when they have an autistic type child who has difficulties entering language and culture because acknowledging a world outside of self—the world of "not-me"—is so essential to the growth into being fully human of which Sullivan and Winnicott speak so eloquently. Entering culture and language, however, is fraught with assimilatory demands. Early childhood teachers and child therapists know the frustration that parents experience when their children refuse to live up to parental expectations. Laurent Danon-Boileau (2001) and Catherine Mathelin (1999) remind us that our responsibility as therapists is to make a space for the child *to be,* in opposition to the demand from parents that the child *be a certain way*. Following Lacan, Mathelin noted that "what the parent is unable to express . . . is expressed through their child" (1999, p. 5). It is possible to take this argument to quite deterministic ends, arguing, as does Karen Coats, that children are "prodigiously porous" (2004, p. 4) or, as Eva Hoffman says, that "we are nothing more—or less—than an encoded memory of our heritage" (2000, p. 50).

I would like to frame the issue more problematically. Following Avery Gordon in *Ghostly Matters,* I would like to pose the problem of the relation between freedom and domination more complexly as a study of the mediating processes "that link an institution and an individual, a social structure and a subject, and history and biography" (1997, p. 19). Binary divisions between inside (e.g., Kleinian phantasy) and outside (e.g., Althusserian interpellation) miss the point. We are both. We are present, past, and future. We are ourselves and we are the Other. Gordon argues for the importance of unearthing the unsettling and difficult knowledges in our pasts:

> If we want to study social life well, and in addition, if we want to contribute in however small a measure, to changing it, we must learn how to identify hauntings and reckon with ghosts, must learn how to make contact with what is without doubt often painful, difficult, and unsettling." (1997, p. 23)

I believe that processes of *subjectification*—coming to be—are enriched, and processes of *subjection* attenuated, when we employ notions from what Derrida (1994) calls *hauntology* to allow children to access deep-seated, unthought, and intergenerationally transmitted forms of embodied knowledges—often traumatic ancestral experiences. Aboriginal and indigenous groups who have long valued spirit knowledge would have little difficulty with this argument (e.g., Allen, 1998; Atkinson, 2002; Battiste, 2000; Deloria, 1988; Fixico, 2003; Graveline, 1998; Hulan & Eigenbrod, 2008; King, 2003; McConaghy, 2000; Smith, 1999). I will develop this idea further below.

INTERPELLATION AND ENTRY INTO LANGUAGE

As students of Lacan and Althusser have noted, becoming a subject is an interpellative process requiring us to encounter and incorporate the Other. Bruce Fink, commenting on Lacan, notes the potentially determinative and alienating nature of this entry into language: "We are all born into a language that is not of our own making. If we are to express ourselves to those around us, we are obliged to learn their language, which we can refer to here as the Other's discourse—and in this process this language shapes us: it shapes our thoughts, demands, and desires. . . . " (1997, p. 86). Begging the question as to whether there is a primordial "I" prior to entry into language, Fink describes a child's entry into language as "choosing one's own disappearance" (1995, p. 51). Fink also speaks of the child being "subjugated by signifiers" and how people's lives are determined by "their 'purloined letters' . . . the snatches of their parents' conversations (that is, of the Other's discourse) often not intended for their ears, that were indelibly etched in their memories and sealed their fates" (1997, pp. 205–06). This notion of alienation is a very tricky concept. One could take it—as Julia Kristeva apparently does in *Strangers to Ourselves*—as romantically suggesting that there is an essential or primordial self which has become alienated through processes of subjection: "A child confides in his analyst that the finest day of his life was that of his birth 'Because on that day it was me and I like being me. I don't like being an other'" (1991, p. 189).

In *The Psychic Life of Power* Judith Butler explores the issue in a more nuanced fashion. She recognizes that "subjection is literally the making of a subject" (1997, p. 85), but then she pokes around to try to articulate where in the acculturation process there might be room for the emergence of agency.

In doing so she draws on Mladen Dolar's critique of interpellation, arguing that there is "a kernel of interiority" (p. 121), a piece of our subjectivity that resists symbolization, resides in the unconscious, and enables us instead of claiming an identity to "*refuse what we are*" (p. 101). Teachers and therapists who work with young children will recognize the powerful interpellative effects of family discursive practices. Children are often very willing participants in ingesting the Otherness of their significant Others. A brief perusal of the cases in Mathelin's book and in the writings of Mannoni (1970, 1999) makes the point. Tension seems to break out most easily in children who resist the Other but who, lacking the means of tapping into an imaginary reservoir, become emotionally constricted, voiceless and, in the most extreme cases, potentially psychotic. I think as a child I saved myself from such a fate by burying myself in books, thereby grabbing a symbolic lifeline.

The Lacanian solution, in therapy is precisely to get at the residue that resists symbolization, as this is the place where the child's desire is likely to be released. Unfortunately, as Vivian Paley (2004a) notes in *A Child's Work: The Importance of Fantasy Play,* the opportunity for children to gain access to this kind of freeing space outside of psychodynamic therapy is diminishing rapidly as early childhood centers eliminate play and fantasy in favor of academic tasks that place adult demands on children and squash their capacity to experience or express desires in that precious "kernel of interiority."

THE PROBLEM OF THE BOURGEOIS SUBJECT

The Lacanian notion that we become subjects through the Other, most particularly through entry into symbols such as language, is useful. So too is the idea that the determinism implicit in the adoption of the Other's language can be countered by tapping into the unsymbolized residue in the unconscious. Nevertheless the theory has limitations. Stuart Hall notes, for example, "how racially neutral, how strikingly *un-raced* Lacan's discourse is, and how rarely this unmarked whiteness of his language has received comment" (1996, p. 27). Couze Venn (2002) argues that notions of Otherness are insufficiently theorized to take account of the asymmetries in relations between whites and blacks as a result of capitalist and colonial relations. The black person's Other and the white person's Other are asymmetrically different. What if, as Frantz Fanon (1967) suggested, the performance of the black person's subjectivity is scripted by the colonizer? Fanon's description of a white Parisian child shrieking in terror as the black Fanon strode down the street reminds us how Fanon's black subjectivity was inscribed on the surface of his skin . . . a process Fanon described as *epidermalization*. Blackness is indeed a fact.

Toni Morrison points out in *Playing in the Dark* how whiteness inherently calls for the existence of a black Other into whom all of the unwanted aspects of the white self can be deposited. The "voluptuous illegality" of blackness "is enforced by the association constantly made between darkness and desire, darkness and irrationality, and darkness and the thrill of evil" (1992, p. 87). The creation of Sambo and the black minstrel movement provided containers into which illicit white desire was projected. As Philip Cushman noted, Sambo "was the antithesis of the American success symbol, the individualist" (1995, p. 51).

What we are talking about then, in the generic subject, is a bourgeois person who, benefiting from power relations, does not need to problematize his or her own origins and being, and who is disciplined through discursive practices to experience *being* as *being a certain way.* The result is that all aspects of the carnivalesque and transgressive are either expelled or else incorporated in disguised ways, for example, through the vicarious enjoyment of sexual licentiousness in minstrel shows. Stallybrass and White sum up the workings of bourgeois normativity this way: "The demonization and the exclusion of the carnival-esque has to be related to the victorious emergence of specifically bourgeois practices and languages which reinflected and reincorporated this material within a negative individualist framework. . . . The language of bourgeois neurosis both disavows and appropriates the domain of calendrical practices" (1993, p. 288).

To take an analogous case, in discussing the meaning of voices that persons designated schizophrenic hear, Lisa Blackman (2001, 2002) argues against the narrowness of narrative theories of subjectivity that focus exclusively on language as the mediator of subjectivity. She argues that subjectivity is embodied (cf. Fanon's epidermalization) and evokes rich images of the potential significance of voices if we only take the trouble to understand them in sociohistorical context: "Voices are not a problem in and of themselves and indeed may have something to say about a person's life, their present and past and even about levels of existence beyond the material world" (2002, p. 137). It is, therefore, crassly simplistic to assume that subjectivity simply requires "entry into language" as discursive practices are embedded in history, culture, and ideology as well as language, and indeed they are inscribed on our very bodies.

Many authors have noted that psychoanalysis and psychology are profoundly Eurocentric and notoriously tone-deaf to issues of culture, class, place, politics, and economic disparity (cf. Derrida, 1998; Morawski, 1997; O'Loughlin, 2002). What is the subjective experience of the black child? . . . of the transgender child? . . . of the immigrant child? . . . of the exiled child? . . . of the creole-speaking child? . . . of the formerly colonized child? . . . of the currently colonized child? . . . of the working-class child? . . . of the disabled/invalid child? . . . of the child deemed psychotic? . . . of a particular child in a particular society? . . . of the child embodying a multiplicity of the foregoing characteristics? Are they all indeed *invalid* because of perceived deviance from a norm? Or can we develop notions of subjectivity that are sufficiently displaced from the bourgeois center to include subaltern and contrarian experiences?

Can we speak of a generic process of subjectification in any kind of positive sense if indeed whiteness is an identity premised on a negative? What if David Roediger is correct that whiteness is "the empty and therefore terrifying attempt to build an identity based on what one isn't and on whom one can hold back"? (Quoted in Ware, 1996, p. 144). What if our entire theory of subjectivity is premised on this negative?

What appears to be needed, therefore, is a much more historically located subject, "a radical historicization of the process of becoming" as Couze Venn (2002, p. 52) puts it. Venn suggests that behind much of the logocentric discussion of subjectivity is a nostalgic longing for the autonomous (i.e., European, capitalist, rational) subject it ostensibly displaced. In what follows I will focus on one particular aspect of this "historicization of the process of becoming," namely a consideration of the contribution of ancestral knowledges and spectral inheritances in the lives of children. And later I will take up the challenge for schooling of creating spaces where diverse identities can be imagined, inscribed, and invented.

A PSYCHOANALYSIS OF THE SOCIAL

Although psychoanalysis is often deservedly criticized for an exclusive focus on intrapsychic processes to the exclusion of social, cultural, and historical contexts, there is a long tradition within clinical psychoanalytic child work of exploration of the sociohistorical origins of psychic pain. This is most evident in the literature on intergenerational trauma, a literature that has emanated from clinical work with children and families, from intensive clinical work with child Holocaust survivors, and from theoretical work on the social origins of psychic suffering. Clinical inquiry in this area dates back to the earliest years of psychoanalysis, represented particularly in the writings of Sándor Ferenczi (1932 ; 1988), a decidedly nonconformist associate of Sigmund Freud.

Here I will explore spectral aspects of experience. I am interested in ghostly traces, spectral remnants, uncanny events, and silences and intrusions that suggest that we need to take seriously aspects of experience beyond the here and now . . . the neat temporal dichotomies of past and present, present and future. What if time is not linear, and experience is neither sequential nor cumulative? What if there are dimensions beyond time? What if Derrida (1994) is correct that a *revenant* is simultaneously a jarring new event and a return/*revenant* of spectral memory? Perhaps because of his intellectual stature, Derrida was able to get away with making an argument that could be considered anathema to the scientific/scientistic traditions of academia, namely that we should carefully explore *hauntology*, as a more comprehensive study of being than mere *ontology*. As Derrida wryly noted about our positivist ways, "As theoreticians or witnesses, spectators, observers, and intellectuals, scholars believe that looking is sufficient. Therefore they are not always in the most competent position to do what is necessary: speak to the specter" (p. 11).

In Derrida's understanding, Lisa Gye notes, past and present are not as easily separable as rational thought would suggest:

> In the figure of the ghost, we see that past and present cannot be neatly separated from one another, as any idea of the present is always constituted through the difference and deferral of the past, as well as anticipations of the future. And so the liminal spirit, or to use Derrida's favored term, revenant, the thing that comes to represent a mobilization of familiar Derridean concepts such as trace, iteration, and the deferral of presence. (Gye, 2010)

From the perspective of subjectivity, Gye says, Derrida's notion captures "the impossibility of conceptually solidifying the past" and the idea of hauntology refers to things *appearing for the first time* that were *already there all the time*. As Toni Morrison noted, "invisible things are not necessarily not there" [quoted in Gordon, 1997, p. 17]. Gordon is passionate in making a claim for respecting and interrogating ghostly knowledges:

> If haunting describes how that which appears to be not there is often a seething presence, acting on and often meddling with taken-for-granted realities, the ghost is just the sign, or the empirical evidence if you like, that tells you a haunting is taking place. The ghost is not just simply a dead or missing person, but a social figure, and investigating it can lead to that dense site where history and subjectivity make social life . . . . The way of the ghost is haunting and haunting is a very particular way of knowing what has happened or is happening. Being haunted draws us affectively, sometimes against our will and always a bit magically, into the structure of feeling a reality we come to experience, not as cold knowledge, but as transformative recognition. (p. 8)

HUNGRY GHOSTS

In the 1840s in Ireland a catastrophic event known as the Great Hunger took place. The failure of the potato crop in three consecutive years, together with ineffective famine relief and the inadequate export of other staple foods by the British colonial authority led to the death of in excess of a million people and the mass migration of three million more. Within fifteen years the population of Ireland was halved under most traumatic circumstances. In a recent paper (O'Loughlin, 2012) I explore the effects of this tragedy on the contemporary Irish psyche. In my paper I offer the following remarkable illustration of the presence of hungry ghosts:

> To take just one illustrative story, consider the case of Irish-American journalist, Carolyn Ramsay. She offers a visceral account of the workings of hungry ghosts in her daily life. Having discussed how her grandmother, a child of Famine survivors, developed an obsession for feeding sandwiches to imaginary people in her old age, Ramsay begins to ruminate on her own "need to feed":
>
> I don't know another working mother who worries about feeding people the way I do. . . . It has taken me years, on the other hand, to focus on just feeding my family—not the whole world. On late nights when I've pounded chicken and chopped vegetables alone in my kitchen while my family sleeps, I've wondered precisely what my problem is. . . . Part of me passes off the feeding urge as a slightly embarrassing compulsion, although its emotional depth and power indicate otherwise. After dropping food at a soup kitchen for the first time a decade ago, I had to steer my car to the side of the street because I was sobbing so hard I couldn't see. There's such unremitting sadness at the root of this drive to feed people that I've come to assume that it links me somehow to the dark events in Ireland in the mid 1800s. I can't know this. No famine stories made their way from my migrating great-grandparents to me, or even to my parents. "The Irish aren't real talkers," my mother once said. When I consider how my grandmother's need to feed imagined ghosts has followed me for thirty years though, it seems likely her famine-surviving parents' attitudes towards food made a deep impression on her. How could they not? (quoted from Ramsay, 1997, in O'Loughlin, 2012, p. 138)

Carolyn Ramsay's story suggests that psychic trauma that has not been absorbed, processed, or resolved in some way lives on in an embodied or disembodied form and travels across generations. Free-floating anxieties of the kind I discuss with respect to my own childhood (e.g., O'Loughlin, 2007; 2012) are an example of disembodied or spectral echoes. Carolyn Ramsay's "need to feed," eating disorders in concentration camp descendants, and anxieties about money and spending among descendants of people raised with severe deprivation can be viewed as examples of embodied spectral presences. I will now explore theoretical explanations of such phenomena.

THEORIES OF PHANTOMIC AND SPECTRAL PRESENCE

What appears to be universal in all theories of phantomic experience is silence, secretiveness, or some form of unspeakability as precipitant for transgenerational effects. In *The Shell and the Kernel* (1994), for example, Nicolas Abraham and Maria Torok speak of people inheriting "the secret psychic substance of their ancestors' lives" (Rand, 1994, p. 167). Nicholas Rand tells us that, in Abraham and Torok's understanding, the voices of previous generations ventriloquate through us in the present, haunting us with the collective memory of our ancestors, Abraham and Torok suggest, consistent with other folkloric traditions, that only "certain categories of the dead return to torment the living: those who were denied the rite of burial or died an unnatural or abnormal death, were criminals or outcasts, or suffered injustice in their lifetime" (Rand, 1994, p. 167). In therapy, therefore, Abraham and Torok argue for "the psychoanalysis *in absentia* of several generations" (Rand, 1994, p. 168). This is not actually a radical practice of psychoanalysis in that Freud himself spoke of the collective archive, and Jung of the collective unconscious, but it is certainly at odds with much of contemporary psychoanalytic practice, probably with the exception of Lacanian approaches, in that the patient is often viewed as disembodied and thought of as an intrapsychic entity or else as a participant in a circumscribed interpersonal dyad. The image of psychoanalysis as arid, omniscient, exclusively intrapsychic, and not very interested in the contexts out of which being arises has contributed considerably to the perception of psychoanalysis as irrelevant to the concerns of educators.

Turning to the origins of phantomic experience, Abraham and Torok suggest that instead of receiving a history or narrative in some area of experience the child instead receives a gap. This gap represents the unspeakable in the parent's experience. We know, as Carolyn Ramsay stated, that "The Irish aren't real talkers." We know too, as Lawrence Langer illustrates in *Holocaust Testimonies* (1991), that for many surviving Jews the shadow of the Holocaust was and is unspeakable. Shosh Shlam's (2001) documentary *Long Journey Into Silence* provides eloquent testimony to the intergenerational consequences of Holocaust silence. I also know that my own mother, responding in anguish to my personal disclosures in *The Subject of Childhood*, asked why I just couldn't forget the past and move on: "What else is there to do?" she queried (O'Loughlin, 2012).

Abraham and Torok argue, to the contrary, that the unthought and unnamed knowledge within us acts as witness to ancestral privation and suffering. If the phantom is not addressed, it provides for endless repetition. Seeking an outlet for the trauma, this phantomic knowledge then attaches itself to some aspect of our living being to gain expression:

> At best, phantom words of this kind can be invested with libido and determine the choice of hobbies, leisure activities, or professional pursuits. One carrier of a phantom became a nature lover on weekends, acting out the fate of his mother's beloved. The loved one had been denounced by the grandmother (an unspeakable and secret fact) and, having been sent to "break rocks" [*caisser les cailloux* = do forced labor—*Trans.*], he later died in the gas chamber. What does our man do on weekends? A lover of geology, he "breaks rocks," catches

> butterflies, and proceeds to kill them in a can of cyanide. (Abraham & Torok, 1994, p. 175)

Apparent oddities such as Carolyn Ramsay's "need to feed," my obsession with accumulating supplies of preserves, one person's predilection for hoarding, another's urge to starve herself, can be viewed quite usefully as signifiers of the presence of active phantoms seeking expression by piggybacking on what can often appear to be benign or eccentric everyday dispositions.

In *The Telescoping of Generations* (2005a) and related writings (1988, 2005b) Haydée Faimberg approaches the same issue a little differently. She revisits Freud's notion of *nachträglichkeit*, popularized in English under the French term *après coup*. This refers to the coming to awareness and hence to significance of something that was experienced or absorbed at an earlier time without its full emotional significance having been registered at that time. Faimberg explains, referencing Winnicott that the psychic crisis the patient fears experiencing is anxiety-provoking because the actual crisis took place in the past but was never registered at that time. Thus, for example, a child could experience or witness a serious catastrophic event and apparently go on being. However, the psychic burden of that experience would foreshadow the child's future, and the weight of foreboding that I might encounter, for example, in an excessively anxious child in my practice, might not come from fear of the future but rather from a fear of a repetition of a frightening unsymbolized past event (cf. Faimberg, 2005a, b). An implication of this work is that, when working with children, we need to be aware that what seems to us history (either events from the current generation or ancestral history) might not be history at all for the child. If the material has not been symbolized and worked through, to use a Freudian term, then it is really not history at all. It is present experience in the child's psyche. I will explore below the implications of this insight for working with young children who have been victims of the kind of collective trauma that has been a notable feature of the lives of indigenous groups in North America and elsewhere in the world.

Faimberg also speaks of a "telescoping of generations" when a person becomes the unconscious recipient of traumatic knowledge from a parent. The identification with this unspoken knowledge telescopes generational time and traps the person in an unconscious identification with the suffering of that parent or even with an earlier ancestor whose trauma the parent had inherited. A clue to this difficulty, Faimberg notes, is that the person's desire becomes organized around the blank space where the trauma or gap is located. Hence the person, locked into an identification with an unmourned loss, has difficulty "going on being," to use a favorite Winnicottian expression.

DWELLING IN THE VICINITY OF THE UNKNOWN

"Where do you live? In the vicinity of the unknown." "What do you do? I try to guess the presence of secrets."

—Pontalis, 2002, translated by and quoted in Garon, 2004, p. 85

Josette Garon, drawing on the writings of Sándor Ferenczi, also addresses the complex psychic problems produced by family secrets. Garon speaks of the "implantation of something alien in the child's psyche" (p. 85), a blank thing that represents the disavowal by parents of some terrible knowledge. As we saw in the Carolyn Ramsay tale, what is key is that the knowledge that is implanted is simultaneously both inaccessible and active. Garon notes that "[t]he alien transplant is never so alien or foreign, and never so active as when it carries *transgenerational traumas*" (p. 88). The disavowal that Garon sees as at the heart of the alien implant takes different forms across generations, shifting from being unspeakable in the first generation, to being unnamable in the second, to being unthinkable in the third. Trauma that cannot be talked about and hence symbolized, inevitably ends in foreclosure, and the trauma manifests in highly disguised signifiers and symptoms. The only solution, Garon concludes, is to "lift the law of silence" (p. 92), and allow the child (or the child within the adult) to come to voice. She poses this problem in a way that resonates for all professionals working with children:

> If every child is confronted with the internal necessity to create their own story, the task is particularly harsh for children who carry alien transplant. They are stuck with family secrets that generate anxiety and the simple fact of thinking about it is forbidden . . . . Regarding the skeletons in the closet, the most that we can do in analysis is access the reality of suffering, anxiety, and constraints thus accessing the subject's truth. What seems most important is to be able to open the closet door, to lift the law of silence, thus freeing the skeletons, to ensure that things are said, named. (pp. 91–92)

THE ARCHEOLOGY OF ANGUISH

In an influential book, *History beyond Trauma,* authors Françoise Davoine and Jean-Max Gaudillière (2004) theorize subjectivity from the case of those who have lost language and contact with the Other through madness. In the language of psychoanalysis, such persons lack a capacity for symbolization at least in the area affected by trauma. Davoine and Gaudillière address this as a destruction of "autobiographic consciousness":

> In that way, most of them give evidence of a strange modification of the arrow of time, whose course sometimes seems to go backward or stand still without past or future. This anomaly could be described as the destruction of "an

> autobiographic consciousness. . . ." But what the destruction actually affects in these patients is the very precarious Other of good faith. Thus, the dimension of a broken, petrified time persists in the catastrophic zones of several generations, which remain present for certain descendants even, as it happens, in the middle of success stories. (2004, p. 78)

What is notable of course, as psychoanalysts understand, is that the very silence of such patients clearly speaks of the trauma, whether that trauma is autobiographical or ancestral in origin. What is needed is an analyst who is capable of recognizing the communication and thereby serving as a new Other for the psychotic person. Lacking an Other with the capability to respond truthfully, the suffering person is destined to experience "an interiority invaded by annihilation, anxiety, and stress" (p. 129). Speaking of psychically injured children, for whom trauma is almost invariably embodied rather than cognitively encoded, Davoine and Gaudillière describe the psychosis in this haunting manner:

> As the child psychiatrist Lionel Bailly puts it, when "children hear the voices of the dead" they are most often the voices of those who died without burial, without a rite. This brief hallucination will cease as soon as it is heard by a therapist in whom the voices of the dead can resonate instead of remaining in a dead letter. If the voice finds no echo, he says, "we have the seed of psychosis." (p.145)

In *The Subject of Childhood* I explored the significance of Davoine and Gaudillière's work for our thinking about children this way:

> Davoine and Gaudillière argue that dehistoricization of experience is particularly traumatic in that it causes people to lose the social link with their pasts and they suggest that we must assist such people in "regaining a foothold in history" (p. 47). Drawing on Wittgenstein, they employ the concept of petrification, arguing that people's bodies can be so numbed by trauma that, as Wittgenstein said, "I turn into stone and my pain goes on" (quoted in Davoine and Gaudillière, p. 49). The authors note that children are particularly susceptible to noticing the blank affect of petrified adults, and are likely to absorb that pain into themselves, "becoming," as they note, "the subject of the other's suffering" (p. 49). This is how trauma is transmitted intergenerationally both within families and in whole communities (cf. Kaplan, 1996). As to the psychosocial effects of such a calamity on people, Davoine and Gaudillière are very clear:
>
> Our patients are perpetuating such a hell, one that continues on in the anesthesia of several generations . . . these descendants may manifest only an omnipresent shame, unalloyed misfortune, a sense of radical injustice, and a global sadness, all these being signs of an imminent catastrophe that they can neither name or dispel. (p. 50)

How might we address traumatic events that cannot be recounted because they were never recorded as past—events that are still "suspended like a present without time"? (p. 52) How does one re-vitalize an individual or community weighed down by events that, on a conscious level, they simply do not know that they know? The psychoanalytic answer is to assist the anguished person or community in turning these *unthought knowns* (Bollas, 1987) of their *foreclosed history* (Davoine and Gaudillière, p. 54) into narrative. This is not an easy task since the disturbing events have never been encoded in narrative memory. Psychoanalysts rely on their own unconscious to serve as a receptor for the patient's anguish, and, through free association the analyst gives voice to the trauma the patient cannot speak and thereby returns it to the patient in speakable form (O'Loughlin, 2009, pp. 152–53).

GHOSTLY ECHOES IN CHILDREN'S LIVES

In a ground-breaking study, "Ghosts in the Nursery," Selma Fraiberg and colleagues (1975) describe how through work with distressed children and their parents they gained insight into the intergenerational trauma that haunts some children. In addition to working therapeutically with children in distress Fraiberg dispatched her therapists to visit parents in their kitchens. From this work Fraiberg was able to discern repetitive patterns in families where the impasses of one generation, not having been resolved, were passed on to the next generation. The ghosts of the past "take up residence and conduct the rehearsal of the family tragedy from a tattered script" (p. 388). The ghosts, therefore, represent a repetition of past unsymbolized trauma, a process that will likely continue uninterrupted unless caregivers or therapists recognize the spectral etiology underlying current difficulties and impasses and generate therapeutic or pedagogical remedies that allow such ghosts to be finally laid to rest.

Very specific insight into the mechanisms underlying such transmission is offered by Louise Kaplan in *No Voice Is Ever Wholly Lost* (1996), her study of the effects of Holocaust trauma on children. Consistent with the theories discussed earlier, Kaplan recognizes silence and secrecy as crucial components in the transmission of spectral trauma. Parents, seeking to protect their children from traumatization, keep the terrible knowledge of their suffering to themselves. The tragedy is that the children, experiencing the absence and emptiness of the parents, absorb the parental terror: "The child of the survivor had been sheltered from the truth. But the child was living the nightmare" (p. 223). Among children of survivors, Kaplan tells us, phobias, self-mutilation, psychosomatic illnesses, dreams and fantasies of bodily mutilation were pervasive, giving clinicians a feeling that, in speaking with children of Holocaust survivors, they were "speaking with the dead": "Our consulting rooms were filled with voices and gestures of the dead. The terrors in our patients' fantasies and dreams were only partially theirs. The children of survivors were living out and dreaming out their parents' nightmares" (p. 222).

The puzzling question, as Kaplan notes, is how a child, in the presence of a parent who either refuses to speak of a trauma or who cannot speak of the trauma because it is has either been dissociated or else received as a blank and unspeakable legacy from ancestors nonetheless comes to embody their suffering. The answer appears to be that the blankness in parental affect elicits a caretaking response from the child. This can be detected, Kaplan notes, in the disproportionate space that the parent occupies in the child's mind. Children who refuse school, for example, often do so because concern for a parent looms so large that the child simply cannot dare to leave her side. The *parentified* child, then, suppresses the possibility of articulating a desire for its own growth and wellbeing in order to attempt to secure the future of the parent.

Such an inversion of the normal symmetry of familial relations is precipitated by an incapacity for dialogue on the parent's part and results in an unhealthy "precocious attunement" (p. 226) on the child's part. Kaplan summarizes the process elegantly: "Because of these abrupt and unexpected derailments in dialogue, the child becomes a witness to what happened to the parent" (p. 227). Kaplan illustrates the terrifyingly ordinary ways in which children may become possessed by such ghosts, and again note here the parallel to Carolyn Ramsay's "need to feed" and even to my obsession with hoarding jars of preserves:

> The survivor parents unconsciously focus on the issues that were and still are crucial to their salvation. Though the mother still cannot remember her starvation, she transmits the emotional experience of starvation through her preoccupation with buying, preparing, serving, and eating food. The father transmits the physical degradations he endured by being preoccupied with cleanliness and the elimination of feces. . . . When a girl is innocently competing with her mother for her father's attentions, the mother may suddenly decide to snip off her daughter's ponytail and send her to school with a crew cut. Of course, when the mother arrived at the camp at the same age the daughter is now, that is what her captors did to her. To survive the psychological trauma of her mother's hostile gesture, the daughter develops an unconscious fantasy that she has been selected by her mother to perform a special mission. She, and she alone, can repair her mother's trauma by sacrificing her own desires and longings. She becomes obese, thus effectively concealing her beauty under layers of fat. Or she starves herself until her body is transformed into the body of a concentration camp prisoner. (pp. 226–27)

Although it may seem impossible to find *trauma trails* (cf. Atkinson, 2002) in children's lives for specific parental trauma, not to mention for trauma that has been passing through families and communities for generations, in looking closely at the everydayness of children's lived lives it is apparent that signifiers for pain, loss, and absence are indeed hidden in plain sight. Psychoanalysts are trained to engage with such spectral presences. It would seem that this is an endeavor which all adults who work with children might find worthwhile.

FROM SYMPTOM TO ORIGIN: PSYCHODYNAMIC APPLICATIONS TO CHILD WORK

What makes psychoanalytic work distinctive is a commitment to the fundamental rule that symptoms are only of interest in relation to what they have to say about origins. In contrast to behaviorist and cognitivist traditions, psychoanalysis explicitly acknowledges the workings of unconscious processes and, in Lacanian terms, recognizes surface characteristics as signifiers pointing to deeper meanings that demand decoding and interpretation. Anxiety, sometimes accompanied by a parentifying urge to take care of parents or siblings or to mediate family conflicts—a role I occupied all too readily in my family of origin—often points to a child's identification with and libidinal investment in parental or ancestral trauma or loss. Acknowledging this possibility suggests that reactive or instrumental approaches to symptoms such as anger, depression, anxiety, enuresis, psychosomatic complaints, phobias, school refusal, obsessive and compulsive behaviors, and so on in children are likely to be futile. A symptom that is driven underground will simply seek another form of expression.

An alternative is to seek to understand the reasons why a particular child is so heavily invested in a particular behavior or disposition. Opportunities are thus created for internal loss to surface and for the child to have an opportunity to work through that loss in ways that may allow the symptom to eventually be relinquished or at least better managed. This calls for the creation of a space where the child is sufficiently free of what Lacan calls *demand* that the child's *desire* has an opportunity to surface. The analyst relies upon an absolute receptivity to the child's being, patience to move at the child's pace, and an awareness that if the analyst's own unconscious is opened up to playfulness and freedom that this will elicit some kind of unconscious response in the child. On the whole, as Laurent Danon-Boileau (2001) notes, the analyst cultivates silence but relies upon resonance from her or his own unconscious to offer moments of playful disruption that enable the child to re-punctuate his or her own narrative as my experience with Alison illustrates.

Alison came to me for therapy at age 11. She came from a home where there was considerable conflict. She did not know how to manage this conflict and she often became either uncontrollably angry or paralyzed with anxiety. She had been referred to therapy when she started having interpersonal difficulties with peers at school. Her progress in therapy was positive, but she continued to experience fluctuating conflict and distress. Then one day she proposed playing Candyland. This game is suitable for very young children, but older children play it surprisingly often in the regressed space of the consulting office. As we began playing I noticed that Alison was cheating quite aggressively. She moved the Ice Princess to the top of the pile so that when the card came up on her turn, she could move to the top of the board where she was assured victory. I made no comment, but, sensing an opportunity to produce change, I secretly moved the discarded Ice Princess back into play so that it came up on my turn, too. "Oh look, I got the Ice Princess, too," I said, sounding surprised. Alison knew that because there was only one Ice Princess, this was impossible. She knew of my trickery. More importantly, she also knew that I had knowledge of her sleight of hand. She flew into a rage. She shredded a dozen playing cards, including the Ice Princess. Then she fled screaming to the waiting room. She climbed onto her mother's lap and stayed there, curled up in a fetal position, sobbing uncontrollably. When Alison returned to therapy the following week she chose not to address the incident, nor did she subsequently speak If it. We continued as before for about another six months. Then one day Alison arrived at my office and offered me something. "I made this for you," she said, proffering me an exquisitely drawn replacement Ice Princess (see figure 5.2).

I thanked Alison, and I marveled at the capacity for repair she had exhibited by creating the new Ice Princess. For a girl who had been raised in a home where conflict was ongoing and repair never possible, she had somehow managed to acquire reparative capacity and to share her new insight with me in such a beautiful way. Her work in therapy was done. She had faced the ghosts of her inherited emotional paralysis and triumphed.

While schools and early childhood centers are different milieu from psychotherapy offices, Vivian Paley's writings (e.g., 2008, 2004a, 2004b, 1992, 1986; Paley & Coles, 1991) serve as beacons to the psychic possibilities when children work in freeing spaces that facilitate emotional expression. Her work and Max Van Manen's (1986) also remind us of the appalling loss to the emotional lives of children when education is structured so that it is exclusively about curriculum imperatives and behavioral expectations—*demand*—with no space allotted for children to write themselves and their histories into schooling. If the "kernel of interiority" remains untouched, if the child is constrained to enact a part from "a tattered script," of what consequence is schooling? In *The Subject of Childhood* I develop this idea further, borrowing Britzman's (2007) notion of the *question child* and arguing for a *liveable pedagogy*, i.e., a pedagogy that speaks to the unconscious in the manner that I suggest here.

Figure 5.2. **The Ice Princess Published in O'Loughlin 2010 with parental permission.**

SPEAKING TO THE GHOST: ADDRESSING THE SOCIOHISTORICAL DIMENSIONS OF SUBJECTIVITY

Locating children in history is, of course, more complex than merely addressing the emotional underpinnings of individual experience. As I illustrated earlier, children are born into sociopolitical and familial systems, and they may be recipients of intergenerationally transmitted individual or communal trauma. There is the issue too that nursery schools, early childhood centers, and indeed all schools are agents of socialization and agents for the communication of dominant culture values. There is inevitable tension between the desire of individual teachers or schools to enable children to construct their own subjectivities and to locate themselves sociohistorically and the acculturative and assimilative imperatives of schooling. This tension is increasing exponentially in Western countries as governments seek to globalize learning objectives, standardize curricula, and reduce all learning to what are deemed to be "evidence-based" units of achievement, often reductionistic test scores.

This tension comes into sharpest relief in the case of education for indigenous peoples for a number of reasons. First, the gap between indigenous epistemologies and westernized narratives of technology, individualization, capitalism, and progress is exceedingly wide. Second, the insult to indigenous people from the kind of collective trauma produced by the Indian conquest in North America, the seizure of indigenous resources and the annihilation of indigenous economies and ways of life worldwide (e.g., see Lear, 2006; O'Loughlin, 2008), and the incalculable damage caused by the residential school movement in Australia, the United States, and Canada have left indigenous children vulnerable on many fronts. Is recovery in such contexts possible?

In *The Subject of Childhood* (see esp. chapter 9) I explore the possibility in terms of two possibilities, evocative pedagogy and regenerative curriculum.

EVOCATIVE PEDAGOGY AND REGENERATIVE CURRICULUM

Evocative pedagogy requires a specific acknowledgment of the collective history of a people, tribe, or community. Teachers who work with such children would benefit from a working knowledge of how collective traumas produced by war, displacements, genocides, annihilation of religious and cultural values, and the systemic erasure of ancestral memory and language can have profound traumatic effects on contemporary members of the community. Teachers and others who work with children could be trained (as Judy Atkinson is doing for Aboriginal child professionals at Gnibi College of Indigenous Australian Peoples—see http://www.scu.edu.au/schools/gnibi/

vv) in local history, culture, music, ancestral spirit knowledge, etc. so that they can create opportunities with community children and elders to evoke the spectral memory of both past injury and ancestral knowledge in the service of allowing children to fully identify with the origins of their own coming-to-be. As I noted:

> However, the epistemological and identificatory possibilities of narrative are enhanced by introducing children to multiple modes of narrating, privileging particularly narrative modes that embody the ancestral lore, rituals, and world-views that particular indigenous children have inherited. Curriculum, in this conceptualization, is an organic process that gets constructed with children and with community stakeholders for the children of that particular community. Teachers might then consider themselves as documentarians of the collective unconscious of the community, documentarians of existing lore, and documentarians of the processes and products involved in constructing new forms of lore with children and community members. The work of Myles Horton and Paulo Freire (Freire, 1969, 1972; Horton & Freire, 1990) and Eliot Wigginton's oral history (e.g., Wigginton, 1972) offer pointers to what might be possible in this area. (2009, p. 162)

If indeed we can acknowledge subjectivity as sociohistorically constituted and spectrally located, then an engaging, revivifying, and ancestrally anchored curriculum process would seem to be indicated if we aspire to re-create social links and give children of a particular community a possibility of moving forward with a sense of history, pride, and belonging. Children who have been rendered *loreless,* to use Judy Atkinson's (2002) term need opportunities to re-inscribe themselves in their history in order to heal soul wounds and fully experience their own subjective possibilities.

If severance of the social link comes from the foreclosure of history, then a major focus of curriculum ought to be on the regeneration of those links by assisting children in experiencing their latent historical subjectivities and in claiming a specific indigenous identity (cf. Lear, 2006). Reanimation of ancestral memories, and reconnection to latent pasts can be facilitated by drama, performance, participation in rituals, viewing of films, reading novels, poetry and myths, and by experiencing and retelling folklore (O'Loughlin, 2009. p. 162).

ACKNOWLEDGMENTS

This chapter was originally published in M. O'Loughlin & R. Johnson (Eds.), *Imagining children otherwise: Theoretical and critical perspectives on childhood subjectivity*. New York: Peter Lang Publishing. It is re-printed by kind permission of Peter Lang Publishing.

REFERENCES

Abraham, N. & Torok, M. (1994). *The shell and the kernel.* [Edited, translated and with an Introduction by N. Rand]. Chicago: University of Chicago Press.

Allen P. G. (1998). *Off the reservation: Reflections on boundary-busting, border crossing, loose canons.* Boston: Beacon Press.

Atkinson, J. (2002). *Trauma trails: Recreating song lines: The transgenerational effects of trauma in Indigenous Australia.* North Melbourne, Australia: Spinifex Press.

Battiste, M. (Ed.). (2000). *Reclaiming indigenous voice and vision.* Vancouver: UBC Press.

Blackman, L. (2001). *Hearing voices: Embodiment and experience.* London: Free Association Press.

Blackman, L. (2002). A psychophysics of the imagination. In V. Walkerdine (Ed.),*Challenging subjects: Critical psychology for a new millennium.* New York: Palgrave.

Bollas, C. (1987). *The shadow of the object: Psychoanalysis of the unthought known.* New York: Columbia University Press.

Britzman, D. (2007). Little Hans, Fritz, and Ludo: On the curious history of gender in the psychoanalytic archive. *Studies in Gender and Sexuality, 7*, 2, 113–140.

Butler, J. (1997). *The psychic life of power: Theories in subjection.* Stanford, CA: Stanford University Press.

Coats, K. (2004). Looking glasses and neverlands: Lacan, desire, and subjectivity in children's literature. Iowa City: University of Iowa Press.

Cushman, P. (1995). *Constructing the self, constructing America: A social history of psychotherapy.* New York: Perseus Publishing.

Danon-Boileau, L. (2001). *The silent child: Bringing language to children who cannot speak.* New York: Oxford University Press.

Davoine, F. & Gaudillière, J. (2004).*History beyond trauma.* New York: Other Press.

Deloria, V. (1988). *Custer died for your sins: An Indian manifesto.* Norman, OK: University of Oklahoma Press.

Derrida, J. (1994). *Specters of Marx: The state of the debt, the work of mourning, and the new international.* New York: Routledge.

Derrida, J. (1998). Geopsychoanalysis: "...and the rest of the world." In C. Lane (Ed.), *The psychoanalysis of race.* New York: Columbia University Press.

Faimberg, H. (2005a). *The telescoping of generations.* London & New York: Routledge.

Faimberg, H. (2005b). Après coup. *International Journal of Psychoanalysis, 86*, 1–6.

Faimberg, H. (1988). The telescoping of generations: Genealogy of certain identifications. *Contemporary Psychoanalysis, 24*, 99–117.

Fanon, F. (1967). *Black skin, white masks.* New York: Grove Press.

Ferenczi, S. (1932). *The clinical diary.* Cambridge, MA: Harvard University Press, 1988.

Fink, B. (1995). *The Lacanian subject.* Princeton: Princeton University Press.

Fink, B. (1997). *A clinical introduction to Lacanian Psychoanalysis.* Cambridge: Harvard University Press.

Fixico, D. L. (2003). *The American Indian mind in a linear world.* New York & London: Routledge.

Fraiberg, S., Adelson, E. & Shapiro, V. (1975). Ghosts in the nursery. *Journal of the American Academy of Child Psychiatry, 14*, 387–421.

Freire, P. (1972). *Pedagogy of the oppressed.* New York: Continuum.

Freire, P. (1969). *Education for critical consciousness.* New York: Continuum.

Garon, J. (2004). Skeletons in the closet. *International Forum of Psychoanalysis, 13*, 84–92.

Gordon, A. (1997). *Ghostly matters: Haunting and the sociological imagination.* Minneapolis: University of Minnesota Press.

Graveline, F. J. (1998). *Circle works: Transforming Eurocentric consciousness.* Halifax, NS: Fernwood Publishing.

Gye, L. (2010). http://halflives.lisagye.net/haunt/hl033.html [Retrieved February 4, 2010]

Hall, S. (1996). The after-life of Frantz Fanon: Why Fanon? Why now? Why *Black skin, white masks?* In A. Read, (Ed.), *The fact of blackness.* Seattle: Bay Press, and London: Institute of Contemporary Arts.

Hoffman, A. (2000). The new nomads.In A. Aciman (Ed.), *Letters of Transit.* New York: New Press.
Horton, M. (1990). *The long haul: An autobiography*. New York: Doubleday.
Horton, M. & Freire, P. (1990). *We make the road by walking: Conversations on education and social change.* Philadelphia: Temple University Press.
Hulan, R. & Eigenbrod, R. (2008). *Aboriginal oral traditions: Theory, practice, ethics*. Halifax, NS: Fernwood Publishing.
Kaplan, L. (1996). *No voice is ever wholly lost: An exploration of the everlasting attachment between parent and child.* New York: Simon & Schuster.
King, T. (2003). *The truth about stories: A Native narrative.* Toronto: House of Anansi Press.
Kristeva, J. (1991). *Strangers to ourselves.* New York: Columbia University Press.
Langer, L. (1991). *Holocaust testimonies: The ruins of memory.* New Haven:Yale University Press.
Lear, J. (2006).*Radical hope: Ethics in the face of cultural devastation.* Cambridge, MA: Harvard University Press.
Mannoni, M. (1970). *The child, his 'illness,' and the others.* London: Karnac.
Mannoni, M. (1999). *Separation and creativity: Refinding the lost language of childhood.* New York: Other Press.
Mathelin, C. (1999). *The broken piano: Lacanian psychotherapy with children.* New York: Other Press.
McConaghy, C. (2000). *Rethinking indigenous education: Culturalism, colonialism and the politics of knowing.* Flaxton, Qld.: Post Pressed.
Morawski, J. (1997). White experimenters, white blood, and other white conditions: Locating the psychologist's race. In M. Fine et al., *Off white: Readings on race, power, and society.* New York: Routledge.
Morrison, T. (1992). *Playing in the dark: Whiteness and the literary imagination.* New York: Vintage.
O'Loughlin, M. (2012). Trauma trails from Ireland's Great Hunger: A psychoanalytic inquiry. In B. Willock, R. Curtis, & L. Bohm, (Eds.). *Loneliness and longings: Psychoanalytic perspectives on a crucial dimension of the human condition. New York: Routledge.*
O'Loughlin, M. (2009). *The subject of childhood.* New York: Peter Lang Publishing.
O'Loughlin, M. (2008). Radical hope or death by a thousand cuts?: The future for Indigenous Australians. *Arena Journal, 29/30*, 175–201.
O'Loughlin, M. (2007). On losses that are not easily mourned. In B. Willock, L. Bohm, & R. Curtis (Eds.). *On deaths and endings: Psychoanalysts' reflections on finality, transformations and new beginnings*. London: Routledge.
O'Loughlin, M. (2002). Is a socially responsible and critical psychology of difference possible? *Race, Gender & Class. 9* (4) 175-202.
Paley, V. (2008). *Wally's stories*. Cambridge, MA: Harvard University Press.
Paley, V. (2004a). *A child's work: The importance of fantasy play.* Chicago: University of Chicago Press.
Paley, V. (2004b). *Bad guys don't have birthdays: Fantasy play at four*. Chicago: University of Chicago Press.
Paley, V. (1992). *You can't say you can't play*. Chicago: University of Chicago Press.
Paley, V. (1986). *Mollie is three: Growing up in school*. Chicago: University of Chicago Press.
Paley, V. & Coles, R. (1991). *The boy who would be a helicopter*. Cambridge, MA: Harvard University Press.
Pontalis, J-B. (2002). En marge des jours (In the margins of the days). Paris: Gallimard.
Ramsay, C. (1997). The need to feed. In T. Hayden, (Ed.). *Irish Hunger: Personal reflections on the legacy of the famine.* Boulder, CO: Roberts Rinehart Publishers.
Rand, N. (1994). Introduction & Editor's notes. In N. Abraham & M. Torok. *The shell and the kernel*. Chicago: University of Chicago Press.
Shlam, S. (2001) *Last journey into silence*. [DVD]. National Center for Jewish Film, Brandeis University.
Smith, L. (1999). *Decolonizing methodologies: Research and indigenous peoples*. London: Zed Books.

Stallybrass, P. & White, A. (1993). Bourgeois hysteria and the carnivalesque. In S. During (Ed.), *The cultural studies reader.* New York: Routledge.
Sullivan, H. S. (1953). *The interpersonal theory of psychiatry.*New York: Norton.
Van Manen, M. (1986). *The tone of teaching.* Portsmouth, NH: Heinemann.
Venn, C. (2002). Refiguring subjectivity after modernity. In V. Walkerdine (Ed.), *Challenging subjects: Critical psychology for a new millennium.* New York: Palgrave.
Ware, V. (1996). Defining forces: 'race,' gender and memories of empire. In I. Chambers & L. Curti, (Eds.), *The post-colonial question.* New York and London: Routledge.
Waters, R. (1970). Mother. In Pink Floyd's *The Wall.* [CD]. Capitol Records.
Wigginton, E. (1972). *The Foxfire book: Hog dressing; Log cabin building; Mountain crafts and foods; Planting by the signs; Snake lore, hunting tales, faith healing; Moonshining; and other affairs of plain living.* New York: Doubleday.

Chapter Six

The Family Unconscious[1]

Karen Lupe Ilinanoa

Some mental health professionals consider Edward Bruce Bynum to be the premier practitioner and researcher to focus on "the family unconscious" in the field of psychology. Bynum—a psychologist, family therapist, and the director of Behavioural Medicine and Biofeedback Clinic at the University of Massachusetts Health Services—is a clinician of many years' standing and a spiritual seeker. Both interests inform his theories on the power of the family unconscious, and the importance of its exploration in the counseling room. As Bynum's works are not widely-known in this country (i.e., Aotearoa/ New Zealand), this essay will explore his and my own understandings on this important topic.

WHAT IS THE FAMILY UNCONSCIOUS?

I first came across Bynum's work when doing research for my chapter in the recently published book *Penina uliuli: Contemporary Challenges in Mental Health for Pacific Peoples* (Culbertson, Agee, & Makasiale, 2007). I found that his ideas on the family unconscious shed light on my experiences of my own family and became a valuable resource in my clinical practice. His theory of the family unconscious was helpful in strengthening my ability to hold my clients, not only as individuals but also as members of a particular family group.

> In a very real sense each family member is deeply interwoven into our intimate psychological functioning. Each is enfolded and reflected in the other. The fragments of past dreamers are the living tissue of our present lives and all are unfolding toward some new extended identity in the future. This system of

> shared meaning, shared feeling and shared emotion is generally termed the family unconscious level of the psyche. (Bynum, 2003, p. 23)

This "common or shared field" is an intimate web connecting our parents and children, spouses and lovers, friends, and the wider community. The family unconscious is a field with energies that transmit images, feelings, and thoughts among family members and beyond. (Readers with a scientific "bent" will find Lynne McTaggart's book, *The Field*, very helpful. This book has been meticulously researched and provides up-to-date findings from quantum, or sub-atomic, physics on the nature of fields, including human transmission of information at the quantum level.)

The family unconscious is not a modern discovery. It is "old knowledge" carried by indigenous cultures for many thousands of years. Bynum makes reference to the Australian Aborigines and the African peoples, and their understandings of the family unconscious.

For the Australian Aborigines, the Dreaming, or dreamtime, is conceived of as the eternally present life-principle that must be personally sustained and reinvigorated by human beings by way of sacred ritual and belief. The purpose of ritual and ceremony itself is to make a place in the waking world where dreamtime is dynamically active in their lives. This includes the dynamically experienced presence of ancestors and other family members. Here, their family unconscious stretches out to enfold not only the living, but also the mythic and powerful deceased. . . .

> In Africa, the importance of dreams—and family dreams in particular—also has a long cultural, clinical, and psychospiritual history. It is a given in many religious societies that family members, both living and deceased, and also the gods themselves, can and do communicate with the dreamer in the dream. (Bynum, 2003, p. 30)

In traditional Samoan culture, the concept of dream-dialogue is called *moe manatunatu*. It is believed that through moe manatunatu, the ancestors and family gods communicate with the dreamer (usually a chief) to give spiritual support for important decision-making processes (Tupua Tamasese Ta'isi Efi, 2006, p. 4).

Bynum emphasizes that we are born into the field of an already existing family unconscious, then through our own unfolding we make subtle changes to the field. After our death, the field continues to exist. Jungian analyst James Hillman (1989) comments on the themes of the continuation of the family and the interconnectedness of family members:

> We are born into a family and, at last, we rejoin its full extension when gathered to the ancestors. Family grave, family altar, family trust, family secrets, and family pride. Our names are family names, our physiognomies

> (physical characteristics) bear family traits and our dreams never let us depart from home—father and mother, brother and sister—from those faces and those rooms. Even alone and only ourselves, we are also part of them, partly them. . . . (p. 196)

The interweaving patterns of intelligence, energy, and motivation within the field of the family unconscious are not only located within the individual; they are also located between individuals and hence are non-local in nature. Within this field, the psyche is understood to be an open system rather than a closed, intrapsychic system, and is constantly interacting with other psyches in the field, mostly below the threshold of waking consciousness. Each family member is reflected and enfolded into the intimate psychological functioning of other family members. The imprints from previous generations are alive and active in the current generation. The field is both vast and intimate. Bynum empahsizes that the field of the family unconscious originates prior to and deeper than the individualized mental-egoic experience. He also raises the very important subject of individuation; the ongoing personal struggles we all face in differentiating ourselves from our families and the collective. From my own understanding, the individuated person is not detached from the group and is able to accommodate dependent/independent needs of self and others from the mature level of interdependence.

Biologist Rupert Shaldrake's ground-breaking work on *morphic fields* and *morphic resonance* in the plant and animal worlds has brought to public awareness the concept of vast fields of stored information potentials that guide the evolution of biological systems. *Morphic resonance* refers to the process of transmission of information from the past across a whole species. This information is carried in a dynamic and evolving morphic field of energy.

Perhaps a real life example will help clarify the concepts of morphic field and resonance. Sheldrake (1995) tells the story of a group of rats in a laboratory at Harvard University. These rats were taught a new trick. Not too long after the first group learned the tricks, researchers in other laboratories located in Scotland and Australia were astonished to discover "their" rats learned the new trick even faster than the first group. Using Sheldrake's theory, we could say that the new information learned by the Harvard rats was transmitted by morphic resonance (like radio signals beaming out into the atmosphere) across the morphic field of the whole species of rats. Hence, by the time the later groups were shown the trick for the first time, they had already received the new information via their morphic field (http://www.sheldrake.org/homepage.html).

From this perspective, the family unconscious also functions as a morphic field for the transmission of information from the past. Sometimes there are moments of instantaneous communication between family members when there is a life-threatening situation. However, the family unconscious is not species-wide across the whole of humanity; this is the *collective* unconscious. The *family* unconscious is specific to family groups, or can sometimes be experienced in groups that function in a family-like manner. Whether our parents, grandparents, and other relatives are alive or deceased, and whether there was a relationship built and experienced or not, we carry their stories, which are imprinted into the woven fabric of our family lineage. Our ancestors are the human ground that we stand upon. Our psychological growth and development has been, and continues to be, unconsciously shaped by our forebears' experiences of love, loss, triumph, and tragedy. Their patterns of relating, not only *how* they thought but *what* they thought, their life experiences, and perhaps more importantly, how they responded to those experiences and much more: we carry these stories from the past, whether or not they form part of our consciousness.

In a recent interview, Chilean film-maker Alejandro Jodorowsky (1999) speaks with deep feeling about his perception of his own family unconscious:

> I realized that we had a family unconscious . . . I am thinking family. My illnesses were created by my family. My behavior, the way I live, my conception of money, my emotional and sexual relationships are all created by my family. Indeed the psychological and genetic field that I come from marks my whole life. . . . If I want to understand myself; I have to understand my family tree, because I am permanently possessed as in voodoo. Even when we cut ties with our family, we carry it. In our unconscious the persons are always alive. The dead live with us. (http://www.jaybabcock.com/jodomean.html)

DISMANTLING OF THE EXTENDED FAMILY SYSTEM

Until very recently in human history, the normal living arrangement was an extended family group. This is still the situation for a large percentage of the world's population. It was in the United States, however, that the associated concepts of suburbia and nuclear family first emerged, and the rest of the Western world then rapidly followed suit. In his book, *The Biology of Transcendence*, Joseph Chilton Pearce (2002) observes:

> In the 1890s roughly 94% of Americans lived on farms where the extended family was the rule because it was economically expedient. One hundred years later, 96% of all Americans live in cities and towns, which is most expedient for corporate, political, or state-religious concerns, but is unviable and disruptive to the nuclear family. . . . Michel Odent points out that the nuclear family by itself is an unnatural and nonviable relationship, but when the nuclear family is at the nucleus of the extended family, and the extended family of society, the systems works beautifully. It you strip away the extended family however, as we have largely done, the nucleus implodes. (p. 253)

The break-down of the extended family system has occurred throughout the West in a relatively short time frame. Previously, individual consciousness emerged from the nest of the family unconscious where it was embedded. The extended family system where three generations lived, loved, and fought together, provided a strong and unified holding matrix for each family member. Jungian analyst Donald Kalsched (1996) clarifies this sense of "holding":

> To have a childhood requires a holding environment in which the child can fall back on caretaking parents. The child does not have to "hold itself together," there is someone else present to do this. D. W. Winnicott has shown that when this "good-enough" facilitating environment is provided, growth of the child's personality can occur. (p. 48)

The obvious disadvantage of living in an extending family system, from a Western perspective, is the lack of freedom from fairly rigid family roles. However, the pressure on parents today in a nuclear family system, without extended family support, is enormous. As well as providing a cushion of practical and emotional support, in Bynum's (1984) view, the extended family also provides a significant benefit to psychological health. A healthy connection to one's family unconscious provides a buffer from the field of the collective unconscious. The invasion of such contents into an individual psyche seriously disturbs psychological functioning, as in a psychotic episode.

> When we lose the intimate connection to the field of energy of the family unconscious and fall prey to the illusion of absolute autonomy or individuality, we run the risk of real illness and a sense of being grounded. Dynamic interconnection and interdependence is vital to our well-being. (Bynum, 1984, p. 22)

HEALTH AND PATHOLOGY

In the family unconscious field, there is a shared body of imagery, affect, ideation, and feeling that influences the functioning of family members. If this shared body has developed in a significantly unbalanced way, a symptomatic disturbance will arise in family members. The symptomatic disturbance, according to Bynum (1994), is really a contraction of life-force around a shared dysfunctional family unconscious image.

> The family's influence on health and illness is immense. Whether it be a physical illness or disease process, an emotional or behavioral problem, or that elusive somatizing or psychosomatic disorder, the reactivity of the family matrix is crucial to its outcome on many levels. (p. 283)

One of my clients exhibited a significant pattern of paranoid ideation running through his family system over several generations. The shared unconscious image that *the world is a very dangerous place,* together with a powerful affective charge, emerged in different family members in a diverse array of symptoms, such as agoraphobia, depression, and the high use of alcohol to manage anxiety. Another example includes the recurrence in an individual of a symptom or event that also occurred in a parent at a similar age. I recall one of my clients who suffered a psychological breakdown at age 38. This turned out to be the same age at which her mother went through a similar experience.

A friend of mine recounted a comparable event in his larger family system. When his father was 5 years old, his grandfather moved the family (including the only child) to a rural farm and "disappeared" into the long hours of agricultural labor. When my friend, the eldest child, was 5 years old, his father got a major job promotion, and began to be gone frequently from the rest of the family. When my friend got divorced, he realized that his eldest child was 5 years old. In the unconscious of that intergenerational system, that age of 5 seems to be a dangerous age for eldest, or only, children.

> Research into the field of family systems and psychosomatic illnesses have uncovered a plethora of conditions spread across several generations of family groups including asthma, diabetes, chronic muscular pain, migraine headaches, gastrointestinal disorders, ulcers, even cancer and leukemia. (Bynum, 1994, p. 284)

In the field of family systems theory this phenomenon is known as the multigenerational transmission of symptomology (Bynum, 2003, p. 285). Alberto Villoldo, a psychologist and medical anthropologist, underwent shamanic initiations with Inca and Amazonian shamans. He writes about the transmission of psychological wounds across the generations:

> We can also suffer from ancestral wounds that have been passed down from one generation to the next—perhaps endured during the Holocaust, the Great Depression, or a revolution. No matter what the cause, we inherit a set of beliefs from our wounded ancestors that we take for our own. Negative attitudes about abundance, scarcity, success, failure, security, sexuality and intimacy can all come from this ancestral wounding. When this kind of generational soul loss is handed down, children are plagued by issues they didn't even experience in their own lifetimes, yet they end up suffering from despair and self-judgement as a result. (Villoldo, 2005, p. 49)

I have found in my counseling work that the notion of ancestral wounds/trauma has given my clients a sense of relief and comfort. It helped them to know that not all their difficulties were personal. For those clients who were mothers with dependent children, it has been moving for them to realize that, through the counseling process, they had the opportunity to transcend the limiting beliefs and behaviors they had inherited, thus releasing their children as well as themselves. Considering the influence of the family unconscious, I have found it invaluable in the counseling process to undertake a genogram with each new client. Genograms are most important tools for uncovering these repetitive, unconscious, intergenerational patterns in families, and many counselor education programs in New Zealand now incorporate routine training in constructing and reading genograms. In the United States, virtually every credentialing organization for mental health professionals requires that case studies for qualification include a genogram of the client under discussion. (For more information on genograms, see McGoldrick, Gerson, & Shellenberger, 1999.)

DREAMS AND PSI EVENTS

Dreams are an important form of communication between members within the family unconscious. When working therapeutically with families, Bynum requests that each family member keep a dream journal to bring to session each week. One of the benefits of this method is that there is plenty of unconscious material to work with. Secondly, as a family dream reflects the unique perspective of the dreamer within the life of the family, each family member has the opportunity to "feel with" the inner experiences of their significant others. In his book, *Families and the Interpretation of Dreams*, Bynum (2003) provides clear guidelines for practitioners working with family dreams with an individual, a couple or family group:

> Bynum emphasizes the normality of "psi events" (such as telepathy and precognition) among family members. He posits that this is simply another way that information is transmitted through the field of the family unconscious. Also significant is Bynum's finding that psi events are most likely to occur where high levels of compassion and altruistic concern for family members prevail in a family group.
>
> There's much evidence to support the argument that the healthier the family is, the more likely they are able to communicate deeply (psi) not only in waking state but also in dream state, including communication about powerful subjects. (Bynum, 2003, pp. 90–91)

I recall working with one of my clients who brought such a dream to session. In the dream she saw her brother's car crash into a tree. She ran to the car and found him slumped over the wheel, unconscious and seriously injured. She knew he would die. In session, my client reported that in the dream she had felt dead inside. We looked at her dream from a symbolic perspective: what was the dream pointing to about her own psycho-dynamics? We also explored the historical and current relationship between her and her brother and the family patterns of dealing with powerful emotion. After the session, I was puzzled by the dream. It was powerful and gripping, and yet I felt somehow that we'd missed the essence of the dream.

Roughly four weeks later my client rang up, deeply shaken, to tell me that she couldn't come to session that day as she was on her way to hospital. Her brother (who was in his mid twenties) was in intensive care due to multiple injuries he'd suffered in a car accident. Sadly, he died several days later. My client told me afterwards that the dream had helped her to cope with the tragedy of his death; it had prepared her for the shock of his sudden demise and she was able to support other family members who didn't fare as well as she did. World-renowned physicist Stephen Hawking (2002) came to the conclusion, from his research on the nature of the space-time continuum, that the near future sends ripples (waves) into the present. Seen from this perspective, we could say that the waves from the near future about the fatal accident were transmitted through the field of their family unconscious (client and her brother) and the information then communicated to my client in her dream. As Bynum (1984) says, "The dream is more primary process mode and closer to the heart-beat of the family" (p. 34).

Perhaps unwisely, I started writing this article two days before my late mother's birthday. As counselors, we are aware that anniversaries can activate the memories and emotional field connected to a significant other. Not surprisingly, I found it hard to focus on writing when feelings of loss and sadness continually rose up. However, instead of these feelings gradually dissipating, I felt increasingly raw inside and heavy in my body to the point of physical lethargy. With this listlessness, I also began to experience vague fears about the future which hadn't been there before. During this time my computer crashed so I couldn't write anyway. I decided simply to be with this experience. I had no idea where this raw heaviness and lethargy was coming from. It felt qualitatively different from the grief associated with my mother's death. After several days in this emotional/somatic fog, I had a dream which helped me to understand what was going on.

> *The dream begins on a large sports field in the middle of the night. I'm walking across the field and find my male cousin sitting alone on the ground (In the dream he's about 4 years old, however his actual age is mid forties). He is confused and distressed. When I kneel down besides him I know that he's infected with intestinal parasites. I carry him back to his family home where his mother and sisters are waiting.*

To give a context to the dream, my cousin's mother is the sister of my mother. His mother and my mother happen to share the same birthday. My cousin's family had lost their father suddenly the previous year, so at the time of this recent birthday my aunt experienced the double loss of her sister and husband. As explained by Bynum, the psyche relaxes and opens during sleep. At this time, communication occurs when psyches within the field of the family unconscious "touch" one another. A clue that some form of communication has taken place is either through a dream or strong felt-sense of the other person upon waking. I understood from my dream that, at a deep level, my psyche had touched my cousin's psyche. This occurred, I believe, due to the shared themes of the death of a parent and the shared birthdays of our mothers, which were often celebrated together with both families. My psychic field was very likely resonating at a similar enough frequency to my cousin's psyche to allow morphic resonance to occur. In the field of our shared family unconscious, I became "infected" with the grief of my cousin's family.

The motif of intestinal parasites is an interesting one. In the body, they cause problems at the level of base chakra, which focuses on life/death events, the drive for survival, and kinship themes of the family group (for Bynum's model of the chakras as a developmental schema for the family group, see 1984, pp. 100–113). The death of a parent sends powerful waves through the family unconscious. Death and birth are archetypal events that register strongly across this matrix. The death of a parent, even in adult-age children, stirs up very early survival fears that are held in the body. The eggs and larvae of the most common types of intestinal parasites reside in the soil and are usually spread by children. In my dream I walk across a field and find my young cousin who is infected. The field/soil in my dream is a metaphor for the field of the family unconscious and the parasites from that field are those deep survival fears that "eat away on the inside," taking energy from the body-mind system. I had this dream just when the "infection" had run its course. This experience confirmed to me how deeply we are affected by family members and that this influence is beyond the usual constraints of time and space. Of course the reverse is true: that I am also affecting others within the field of my family unconscious. (My own understanding of working with dreams has developed from having undertaken several years of Jungian dream-work as well as participating in numerous courses on dream logic and symbolism, myths and fairytales).

During a counseling session, one of my Pasifika clients reported that she could see (in an inward sense) a large group of her ancestors in the room. I couldn't see them, although I felt an energy shift in the room when they appeared. They stood in a half circle around her, which my client experienced as comforting. I welcomed her ancestors into the room, where they remained standing quietly in the same place. My client described in detail the clothing worn by each ancestor. Many of the outfits puzzled her as she'd never seen these styles before. The same group of ancestors, in the same clothing, appeared in sessions on many later occasions. Mostly they remained silent, but sometimes she asked them for advice on current matters.

One of the ancestors appeared to be the spokesperson for the group and readily responded to her concerns. It then struck me that perhaps my client would benefit by doing a family tree. She liked the idea and set to work straight away. She found it a meaningful process and especially exciting when she recognized one of the ancestors from a very old book she found in the library. It turned out that some of her ancestors' clothes were worn by members of the royal family. Their story was long and complex, filled with betrayal and heart-break.

Undertaking the construction of the family tree gave her a new sense of dignity and belonging. Her identity as a Pasifka woman living in New Zealand's multicultural society was strengthened. The earlier despair from feeling overwhelmed by the impact of colonization was lessened. Her deepest fear was that the cultural treasures from the past were rapidly disappearing. In one very emotional session she sobbed, "It's all gone!" We wept together. The undertaking of her family tree gave her another perspective, in which "it" (the cultural treasures) hadn't gone at all. She needed only to turn around and look for them. At the time I was a new counselor and did not know about Bynum's works on the family unconscious. However, many years later, I now understand that our cultural treasures are accessible through the family unconscious—that each one of us carries cultural and other knowledge reaching back many generations. Such experiences serve as a reminder that there is so much we don't know. There are times in the counseling relationship when it can seem that we are called to witness a great Mystery.

THE OEDIPUS MYTH AND THE FAMILY CURSE

Due to the writings of Freud, most of us are familiar with the concept of the oedipal triangle: a young boy's unconscious desire to kill his father and marry his mother. However, there are other ways of interpreting the classical Greek myth, in addition to the Freudian interpretation, which focus on the intrapsychic perspective.

We carry the mystery of our history that reaches back, beyond our current lives, directly to the family lineage. As well as our genetic blueprint, we inherit deeply entrenched emotional and cognitive styles, and natural talents such as in the field of poetry and mathematics. On the shadow side of the family legacy, there are those dark secrets (skeletons in the closet) and a whole raft of pathologies (using this word its original meaning, "sufferings of the soul") that no family unconscious is completely free of. Perhaps one of the most disturbing patterns in a family unconscious is what is known as the family curse. Both the Oedipus and Elektra myths share the same mythic theme of the family curse. I have decided to focus on the Oedipus myth, as it is more well-known, to explore the family curse and its relevance to the family unconscious.

> *King Laius (father of Oedipus) is head of the House of Thebes. He offends both Apollo and Artemis, who are the divine protectors of children, by raping a youth who is the son of his friend. The Oracle informs King Laius of the divine deities whom he has offended. He is told that he will meet his death at the hands of his own son. At this point it is possible for Laius to stop the curse by admitting his crime and humbly making an offering to the god and goddess to expatiate his wrong-doing. Out of arrogance he refuses to accept the sentence. He secretly tries to avoid punishment by curtailing sexual relations with his wife, Queen Jocasta, without explaining the reason. She feels hurt and rejected, and manages to seduce Laius when he's drunk. She becomes pregnant and eventually gives birth to a baby boy. Laius again tries to cheat the oracle by leaving the new-born baby on a hillside to die. He nails the baby's feet with a stake into the ground. The wrath of Apollo and Artemis is compounded by this cruel act, and now the entire city of Thebes is cursed by the presence of a giant Sphinx. The abandoned boy is rescued by a kind shepherd, who gives him the name Oedipus, meaning "swollen foot." He grows up believing that his parents are the King and Queen of Corinth. As a young man Oedipus also consults the Oracle and is told that he will one day kill his father and marry his mother. Oedipus, like his father, tries to cheat the Oracle. He flees Corinth and runs straight into his destiny. He meets his birth father on the road. The unknown older man has blocked his way and speaks to him in an abusive way. In a fit of rage, Oedipus kills Laius. He then confronts the Sphinx and through this heroic act frees the city of Thebes. Thus he wins the kingship and, unknowingly, the hand of his mother, the Queen. When Oedipus discovers the truth, he is so horrified that he blinds himself and eventually dies an outcast. His mother commits suicide. However the curse continues on through his children and is not spent until every last member of the House of Thebes is dead.*

The myth of Oedipus, in all its shocking brutality, provides an excellent example of a disturbed family unconscious. The story can be read on the symbolic and literal levels. On the symbolic level, the abuse of one's God-given gifts and talents (the creative inner children) out of greed, arrogance, or ruthless ambition is essentially self-destructive. Such an attitude, compounded by wrong-action, flows through the family unconscious to future generations. The flow-on effect to descendents may cause major disruptions to their unfolding individuation process by the contraction of life-force into symptomology (as discussed earlier) or by diverting life-force through unconsciously "acting out" the family myth. On the literal level, we are aware, as counselors, that cruelty towards children in the form of physical and/or sexual abuse has serious consequences for several generations. Although the myth contains a severe warning, it also hints that by taking a different approach from that of Laius and Oedipus, a better outcome is possible.

By being willing to struggle honestly and humbly when confronting the reality of one's family myth or curse, in all its ugliness, it is possible to make choices that are life-enhancing. These life-enhancing choices then flow back into the family unconscious and have a positive effect on other family members, including descendents. This is relevant to our work as counselors, as there are many clients who come from family systems that have been unhealthy over many generations, and whose family members appear to be "cursed" in one way or another. Exploration of the mythic themes of a client's family patterns—the deeper stories that are enacted and often disguised by personal experience—can facilitate the healing process within the counseling relationship. Rather than deny our family roots, it is vital that we counselors and clients understand, live with, and address them as creatively as possible.

CONCLUSION

Within the scope of this article, it has only been possible to touch lightly upon the concept of the family unconscious, it's "field" nature, and the diverse associated activities within the personal sphere. For further reading, Bynum's books that provided the backbone for this discussion are listed in the bibliography. Bynum's website, the Obelisk Foundation (http://www.obelisk-foundation.com/), also provides information on the family unconscious, as well as his ongoing research project on family dreams.

The final words rightly belong to Bynum (1984): "In its healthy form the family unconscious is the taproot of compassion" (p. 196).

ACKNOWLEDGMENTS

This chapter was originally published in *New Zealand Journal of Counselling*, Vol. 28, No. 1, June 2008. It is reprinted by kind permission of the co-editors of *New Zealand Journal of Counselling*.

NOTE

1. Readers please note: the form of this paper more closely resembles the style of a Samoan tale called a su'ifeifiloi, than it does an academic paper. A su'ifeifiloi has a central theme which is expressed as a medley of ideas that, initially, appear to be disconnected. It is through the telling of the story that the ideas become woven together in a meaningful way.

REFERENCES

Bynum, E. B. (1994). *The roots of transcendence: Transcending psychoneurotic disturbances.* New York: Cosimo Books.

Bynum, E. B. (2003). *Families and the interpretation of dreams: Awakening the intimate web.* New York: Paraview.
Bynum, E. B. (1984). *The family unconscious: An invisible bond.* Wheaton: The Theosophical Publishing House.
Culbertson, P. L., Agee, M. N., & Makasiale, C. O. (2007). *Penina uliuli: Contemporary challenges in mental health for Pacific peoples.* Honolulu: University of Hawai'i Press.
Hawking, S. W., Thorne, K. S., Novokov, I., Ferris, T., & Lightman R. (2002). *The future of spacetime.* New York: W. W. Norton.
Hillman, J. (1989) *A blue fire: Selected writings.* New York: Harper Collins.
Jodorowsky, A. (1999, December). Your brain is a crazy guy. *Mean Magazine, 6.* Retrieved on February 14, 2008 from http://www.jaybabcock.com/jodomean.html.
Kalsched, D. (1996). *The inner world of trauma: Archetypal defences of the personal spirit.* London: Routledge.
McGoldrick, M., Gerson, R., & Shellenberger, S. (1999). *Genograms: Assessment and intervention* (2nd ed.). New York: W. W. Norton.
McTaggart, L. (2002). *The field: The quest for the secret force of the universe.* New York: HarperCollins.
Pearce, J. C. (2002). *The biology of transcendence: A blueprint of the human spirit.* Rochester: Park Street Press.
Sheldrake, R. (1995). *A new science of life.* South Parish, ME: Park Street Press.
Sheldrake, R. (2008). *Research on morphic fields, morphic resonance and unexplained phenomena (1974-present).* Retrieved on February 20, 2008 from http://www.sheldrake.org/Research/morphic/.
Tamasese Efi, Tui Atua Tupua. (2006, June 28). *Navigating our future together.* Keynote address at the Emerging Pacific Leaders Dialogue Conference, Brisbane, Australia. Retrieved March 30, 2008, from http://www.cscaustralia.com/epld/doco/Tui%20Atua%20Tupua%20Tamasese%20Taisi%20Efi%20%20-%20Presentation.pdf.
Villoldo, A. (2005). *Mending the past and healing the future with soul retrieval.* New York: Hay House.

Chapter Seven

Working at the Interface of Education and Trauma in an Indigenous Preschool

The Importance of "Deep Soul Listening"[1]

Norma Tracey

The preschool as a therapeutic Community—a psychic space to heal early childhood trauma.

When Father Ted Kennedy defied his Bishop and stood in the streets of Redfern, publicly proclaiming, "I will not sleep in a warm safe bed while my black brother sleeps on the cold street!" he represented the awakening conscience of a nation. As a result, every night, up to a hundred homeless Aboriginal people drawn to Sydney by the lure of the city after the Missions were disbanded in the 1960s, slept on the presbytery floor, ate in the church and viewed the church as their own. They were married there and buried there with no concern for creed or background. That warmth of community abounded alongside their massive problems of dislocation. Ted Kennedy's vision of community became the vision for how we at Gunawirra[2] would extend care to over thirty preschools for Aboriginal children throughout country New South Wales (NSW).

BACKGROUND

In 1940, the New South Wales Aborigines Protection Board was given powers to remove Aboriginal children without a court hearing. This heralded one of the darkest chapters of Australian History—the forced removal of Aboriginal children from their families. Children as young as babies were stolen from their families to be placed in girls and boys homes, foster families, or missions. At the age of 18 they were "released" into white society, often scarred for life by their experiences. Between 1995 and 1996 the Australian Government conducted a National Inquiry into the Separation of Aboriginal and Torres Strait Islander Children from Their Families to examine the effects of separation, to identify what should be done in response, to find justification for any compensation, and to look at the laws of that time affecting child separation. The findings were published in 1997 as the *Bringing Them Home Report.* Today these Aboriginal people are collectively known as the "Stolen Generations" because several generations were affected.

Many Aboriginal people are still searching for their fathers, mothers, and siblings. "Four generations of my family went without parental love, without mother or father. I myself found it very hard to show any love to my children because I wasn't given that, so was my mother and grandmother" (Carol, personal story in the *Bringing Them Home Report 1997*).

The report showed that 10 to 33 percent of Aboriginal children were removed from their families between 1910 and 1970 and often suffered physical and sexual abuse. All were traumatized by the forced separation from family and community. The Government had failed in its duty of care. In 2010 the Australian Labour Government issued a formal national apology to the Aboriginal people of Australia.

A HISTORY OF MASSIVE DEPRIVATION AND SUFFERING

Indigenous people are the most disadvantaged group within Australia across the full spectrum of socio-economic indicators. —NIELNS, 2001

I write here not only of traumatized children, but traumatized mothers and fathers, traumatized teachers and sometimes a transgenerationally traumatized community where past and present experiences have created the suffering.

Family and sexual violence continues to devastate Indigenous families and communities at a much higher rate than the broader community. Indigenous people are eleven times more likely than non-Indigenous people to be hospitalized with assault-related injuries and are five to ten times more likely to die as a result of assault-related incidents (Bryant, 2009). The presence of family violence is a strong predictor of child abuse. The causes of domestic and sexual violence are well known to all of us: financial problems and poverty, unemployment, physical illness, lack of education, racism-induced stress, single-parent families, parenting at an early age, substance and drug abuse (e.g., alcohol, glue sniffing), poor or inadequate housing, social isolation, loss of identity and self esteem, abusive styles of conflict resolution, sexual jealousy, oppression, which turns them into oppressors, imbalance and inequity within male and female roles, lack of respect within families, marginalization and dispossession, poor physical and mental health, loss of land and traditional culture, breakdown of community kinship systems and Aboriginal law, childhood experience of violence and abuse, pornography, geographic location with poor access to services.

A PATH TO HEALING: PROFESSIONAL EXPERIENCE JOINS WITH CULTURAL WAYS

I was challenged to use my forty-six years of working with infants, young children and mothers to seek a method of healing from within a culture steeped in ancient art, ritual, and myth; programs that would give our Aboriginal children a better start in living experience and in learning.

My professional colleagues at Gunawirra and I felt supported by the knowledge that the responsiveness of the psyche at this tender age allows growth, which may never again be available in their lifetime.

Using a Therapeutic Community as a Means of Healing the Distress—the Birth of Gunawirra

In 2008, Aboriginal representatives and elders from around New South Wales and Sydney, as well as twenty-six professionals from psychiatry, psychology, social work and psychoanalytic therapy, and concerned Directors of country preschools, gathered at the Grail Centre in North Sydney. The group wanted to design programs that would work in predominantly Aboriginal outback preschools. Gunawirra was born.

With a vision of informed practice born out of psychoanalysis, we attempted to make sense of our role. If the problem lay in the community in the religious zeal of the colonisers in converting the Aboriginal people, then the healing should take place in the community.

What Better Place than in the Community Classroom?

Our thoughts were to empower the child who is struggling against an internalized lack of value and worth, a sense of being unacceptable and inferior. Dislocation of the people from their own spiritual and cultural center through a forced Credo that at best makes no sense to them and at worst is destructive of their own spirituality, creates a powerful unconscious disturbance and is the cause of deep intra-psychic suffering.

What we try to create in our work in over twenty-five preschools around the country is the restoration of pride in culture and a sense of valued ancestry. The problem is of a people who are now either by force, or desire, impregnated physically, emotionally, socially, and spiritually by a race that has subjugated them, a race they hate, fear, and also paradoxically regard as superior and to be emulated. It is a race whose blood now flows in their veins, since very few are pure Aboriginal.

Our first effort was to hold in our own minds a sacred and safe place, mirrored in the preschool. This space would be free from hostility and intrusions; a space where dreaming could occur; a space to develop and use imagination and play. In such a space we have the potential to create the meaning of our world from out of our own thinking. We imagine ourselves, our world into being. Aboriginal people have been doing this for centuries. In the Dreamtime were the creation stories.

> In the Dreamtime where the creation of the world is continually being sung into existence, the unknown invisible seed (Gunewari), Gunawirra engenders the energy of new life. (Atkinson, 2002).

> The people of this land, within the boundaries of their own countries, were intimately familiar with each rock and cave, watercourse and waterhole, mountain peak and headland, all humanized in the process of dreaming. (Berndt and Berndt 1988, cited in Atkinson, 2002, p. 136).

> Here the bandicoot man went and fought with the native cat man to make this valley: there the kangaroo man scrambled over the range to form this saddle. Here the pigeon women menstruated to form this large deposit of red ochre: there the caterpillar men and women marched through the range to form this gap (Flood, 2006)

A RECREATING OF OUR WORLD FROM OUR IMAGINING

We have two ancient gifts from the Aboriginal people: "the Dreaming" and "Dadirri" embody ancient Aboriginal concepts of space. These were the underpinnings for all our thinking on healing.

The Dreaming

The Dreaming imbues the world around us with meaning. This meaning is born out of our internal imagining; it becomes a wisdom transposed through generations by Aboriginal elders in oral and cave art form. An ancient spirituality, it gives historic continuity to the inner self, giving links to ancestors and elders in the past and in the present living community. It creates a link from the internal world to the external world, giving relationship a meaning, between nature, environment, and the inner person. It gives value to selfhood, community, and culture. The rules or laws that bind these meanings become sacred, the symbols born of them are precious because they create a boundary in which to contain and hold that meaning. *It is the dislocation from their spirituality and culture that we see as the basis of all disasters for Aboriginal people. We workers in preschools direct all our energies to restoration of spiritual values of their own culture and a seeking of reconciliation with the "white man's" culture.*

We dream! Our dreams are all-important. Without our dreams by day and by night we would have no meaning in our lives. One of the most amazing capacities human beings have is the ability to project emotional meaning into people and objects in their external world. Love, hate, all interactions and all symbols are born out of this psychic capacity. We create the meaning of our world from our own psyche. From this, the dream can have a space in which to be dreamt. Here is Barry's story. I have his permission to tell it here.

> I have never shared this with a white man, but because you are my special friend I want to share this with you, Norma, a secret no one else knows outside of black fellas. This is our story.
> In the beginning all the black fellas were the one tribe, one family; and they all lived in the middle of the desert and they all spread out like this. [Barry drew a picture of spokes radiating from the circle centre.] And then the white fellas killed them off here and here and here. [He showed places where indeed massacres had occurred] But what no one knows, and I am sharing with you—see all these lines [pointing to the lines radiating from the centre], they only killed the people; they couldn't kill the song lines, they are the dreaming and the secret is, the dreaming is all still there. You white fellas are stupid. You can't kill dreaming; dreaming lives after everyone is dead! That is our secret. (Barry Smith, Manager at Aboriginal Children's Services in private conversation 2008)

The Dreaming and the Pre-creative Space in Different Traditions

Before the Dreaming is a pre-creative space, a particular psychic space, a primordial abyss. It is the nothingness, a nowhere space known in most religions as the primary abyss, "and the earth was without form, and void" (Genesis 1:2, The Bible). This space was before all creative experiencing, before all ambivalence; in Tao "before is and is not" (Mitchell, 1988, p. 21); in Hebrew "tehom" abyss or "bottomless sea." Rose Ungunmer, an Australian Aboriginal elder writes, "It is the place before we were born, before we were in our mother's womb. So we let God touch this deep pain place and begin to heal us in this space. . . . It is the space in which the potential to dream may occur. It is the space where 'we sing our self into creation'" (Farrelly, 2003).

The Other Dark Abyss

There is another psychic space—the dark abyss resulting from unresolved trauma. It has no growth, no movement. In it, death becomes more active than life, annihilates life. At the center is terror—the autistic-like space—the nothing space where nothing grows. This is Frances Tustin's autism (Tustin, 1995). Tustin was one of the first analysts to become aware of the loss of meaning for the person who is autistic.

Aboriginal people understand this dead "no-faith" space. In the Kimberly Region of Western Australia, paintings by the Wandjina tribe, are retouched. "I don't know all what happened to you, but all your spirit has gone out of you. No men or women watch over you, for the people who belong to this place—my aunties, sisters, fathers and grannies—they are all dead now. Only I, who belong to another place, came to visit you, but you are lonely for all those people who died and your spirit has gone away now. Because you are looking all dull—you are not looking bright. . . . Don't get wild! Don't send rain! My eye it has life, and your eye has life too, because I make it new" (Isaacs, 2006, p. 71).

In trauma non-existence enters the psyche, "thingifying" and robbing the "other" of personhood. This "thingifying" makes sense of the senseless and inhumane treatment one human, or even one race metes out to another. I propose that this trauma of dislocation kills meaning, nullifies the internal illusion; destroys the capacity to sublimate into art and story; destroys the psychic binding that symbol formation gives. It denudes the experience of a living self; the person experiences themselves as a no person, an autistic defense protects against an overwhelming internal chaos; but then it concretizes. Sometimes it does not hold and the chaos breaks loose. Dreaming is lost; it is replaced by a living nightmare. We think here of a dead mother, and therefore a dead foetal self. The sacred is taken from everyone and everything. Non-existence enters the psyche, robbing self and "other" of personhood. How to build bridges across the dead black hole in the center of trauma; how to restore a sense of personhood became our challenge.

Ghia

> Preschool teacher has warned me that Ghia seems distressed. I sit a little distant holding a comfortable observing stance. He draws a picture and then covers it with red scribble which gets stronger and stronger. "What is that?" I ask. "That is blood because you are all killed and killed." He waves his hand around the room at all the teachers. "Why?" "You won't sleep with my dad and be his girl friend so I can come and sleep with you in the night and get cuddles when I am scared." The teacher comes over and tells me he told her the same story that morning. The father is a miner and the mother left when he was two and ran away with another man to an unknown town. She bends down to him and says, "What if I give you some hugs now Ghia and then when you are afraid in the night you can remember them and remember I will have some more ready for you in the morning." Ghia broke into tears. My thoughts were they were tears of relief that he could be a frightened little boy if someone cared, not a murderous monster.

In this very simple story are many theoretical constructs. One concerns me particularly. It asks what occurs when the autistic defense "*breaks down.*" For Ghia this powerful "close down" defense did not work in the night. Could the chaos, the murderous rage depicted in his painting, become enacted when he is in adolescence or later as an adult? The thought I had is that such unresolved intense emotions might result in serious addiction, to quell the nightmare of mad instincts, or worse may lead to instinctual acting of domestic violence, rape, murder, suicide, far too common among Aboriginal teenagers and adults with no place to work through their pain.

Trauma "*break out*" is different and one sees it in Ghia's story and in his teacher's response. She acknowledges and validates his pain of aloneness. She hears his suffering and in so doing allows a presence in his mind to ease that suffering. She creates a transitional bridging of the space between; she gives him the possibility of holding memory and desire. There is faith and hope in fulfilment at a later time.

It reminds us of the black hole in the center of trauma, "The heartbreak at the center of existence means there lives not one single man who is not to some extent in despair, in whose inmost parts there does not dwell a disquietude, a perturbation, a discord, and anxious dread of an unknown something" (Kierkegaard, Lowrie, & Payne, 1941, p. 155). Tustin (1995) wrote further," The nameless dread of not existing, of extension of the spirit, fits with the theory of normal primary autism. How does this universal experience of sickness and death, of primal depression regain meaning out of meaningless?"

For some the autistic defense holds and it becomes a dead center; for some the "autistic close down" does not work and the pain is experienced but with no repair—it just continues without abatement to a degree that creates a sense of death being better than life. Aboriginal people have a suicide rate five times higher than their white counterparts. So could we imagine a future for Ghia without his preschool as a space to express anger, hurt, fear and where actual help in the form of "desired cuddles" come to protect him from his own inner dark center, laid bare by his mother's absence?

Disturbing cases from our preschools show that trauma does kill meaning and nullifies illusion and symbol formation. Trauma turns dreams into nightmares; trauma concretizes the dream; trauma kills the capacity to dream. So the state of non-existence comes about.

Dadirri

Dadirri is the ancient name given to restoration in dealing with trauma. It is a ritualized form of "deep listening," not an ordinary witnessing, but an empathic psychic action. A version of this is known to the modern world as psychotherapy. Like Dadirri, psychoanalytic therapy used even in these simplest of situations creates through the therapeutic encounter, a relationship that allows the suffering in the suffering to be experienced and shared by another hearing it. In Dadirri the elders gather around the traumatized troubled one and listen for hours in deep silence while the traumatized person talks and talks. It is called "deep soul listening."

> Dadirri is about tapping into the dead springs within us. We have a strong sense of community. All persons matter. All of us belong.
> In the Dadirri circle, the person in pain or trouble speaks out of his pain and trouble. We sit in a circle around the person. We hear it in the depth of our inner spring. We do not talk, we own the story, we own his pain, the owning makes us all one with him, it heals. This is Dadirri. (Tribal elder)

Dadirri transposes to the living situation the skills of the therapy room.

Transgenerational Trauma and Loss

> The willful denigration and destruction of Aboriginal ceremonial responsibilities and processes by the colonizers has therefore had profound transgenerational effects on the people of this land. Aboriginal people have been prevented from engaging in ceremonial processes for healing from the trauma. The distressed feelings that accompany loss, death and devastation remain as destructive forces within the land and the people. (Atkinson, 2002, p. 35)

The issue of how much is their trauma and how much is the trauma of their family is relevant. In *History Beyond Trauma (2004)*, Davoine and Gaudillière say that the experiences that families cannot know, process or integrate, are implicitly passed on to the next generation. They then become one's own trauma and one is part of it. But it is often not their story but the story of their race, told by the only means they know how: to relive it, to enact it, and to seek for it to be witnessed and validated.

In trauma, one faces terror of one's own death. One feels betrayed by those one loves: one's parents, who fail to protect the child from the real. Consequently, the field of the experience fragments with no guarantee of trust, leaving uncertainty to pervade one's life space. This telling of the story and the witnessing of it is at the root of Dadirri as it undoes the uncanny burden of one being alone with the burden. Trauma speaks to trauma.

Alana

> A young Aboriginal couple sit with me in my clinic room. Their three year old, Alana, plays happily on the floor with a teddy. She has a shawl she wraps teddy in, putting him to sleep and tending most caringly for him. She seems oblivious to the doors that have opened to pain in both her parents, I think. She is in a bubble, safe from it, but then I think she *is* the sleeping teddy protected

from the pain. A palpable blackness fills the room. I cannot avoid it. I am in it. I feel and see and smell it. I wish I was anywhere but in that space.

Her mother Chrissie looks at me and cries, "When I have to beg for a hug from Tom, I feel degraded. I feel like a piece of sh . . . , like I am a nothing and no one, and still he can't see or hear me." She sobs. "All my life I have felt like a piece of useless sh . . . , and he just makes sure that I keep feeling that way. He reminds me every day I am worthless, a no one."

Pain meets pain. But the silence is deadly and I am sure he is not speaking because he has no words. It is a relief when after five minutes he finds some: "So do you think I was born with a silver spoon in my mouth or somethin'? There weren't no father around, just my mother. I had to take care of myself, there wasn't anyone else. I work for you like a bloody dog but it is never enough, never good enough. Sometimes I get home and you are on the computer and I feel I just wanna break that bloody computer to pieces. There is bloody dog shit everywhere, no room for me, your bloody dogs are more important than I am. On the $4000 lounge there is dog shit, can't get to the toilet to do a piss without walking in dog shit! I feel like kicking the buggers out. No room for me—the dogs have all the room!!" (This is true the two poodle dogs are totally un-toilet trained.)

He is the dog shit. The beautiful preschool Aboriginal child plays on the floor, awakens teddy, plays with him a little then wraps Teddy up and puts him to bed again, talking gently and comfortingly to him.

I feel their anger and hurt, rage and blackness palpably as they leave me. How much pain can any human being suffer? They look accusingly at me for exposing and witnessing their suffering, but they are grateful someone has heard it. Did it free the little girl to have me carry it for them?

One could sense the psychic wound in both Alana's parents. It was enormous! Was it the loss of country, the trauma of war, or the loss of a loved one or a parent. An excess of psychic pain floods the psychic sense in the room. Projective identification fails; the psychic pain became unbearable and I wanted to be anywhere but there. It took me days to process what was going on and it looked so harmless. In that simple event there was no mourning, only unthinkable fear. One senses a non living space where knowing would be if it could be known, where thought would be if it could be thought. This space has an autistic deadening quality. Its cause is demonstrably similar to that described by Tustin (1981, 1988) in autistic children. To treat trauma as in the case of Alana's parents, the dosage and the timing is all too important. The pain of opening those doors in small doses, the initial primitive anger, like yelps of animal pain at hurt inflicted initially, but then a process of acceptance of suffering, acceptance of the hurt as I witness and validate, is powerful medicine indeed.

THE UNPROTECTED CHILD—ANGELS AND BAD GHOSTS IN THE PRESCHOOL

Why are children in orphanages or in institutions more open to abuse than in other childhood places? It is my belief that when there are no internal protective parents, the message given out is "This is an unprotected child," available to be used for one's selfish needs.

The absence of a parent creates the presence of an abuser. When psychoanalysis began, Freud thought that our instincts were the psychic center from which our personality developed. Klein shone the torch on internal objects and saw the psychic center as the internal battle acted out between good and bad spirits whom we internalized. The good internalized objects protected us from the bad objects. More recently Bion (1977) in his writings gave us a new basis: someone, a self within us, not known to us, called "the ineffable unknown," thought our thoughts, and did our dreaming. Without a thinker, thoughts become perverted, destructive, and undeveloped. This is the paradigm of the unprotected child. Is this what is happening in this people who kill their own thoughts, their own value, their own life meaning?

Dadirri's Opposite

Go down to the local park on a Saturday night and you will find a dozen Aboriginals sitting in a circle. This is not the traditional sacred Dadirri circle where all pain is shared and held and transformed by the care of the others. Not this circle! They drink until Sunday night or until the cops come—whichever is first. Some do drugs as well. Pain is not suffered. Pain is numbed—too many have suffered too much already. That is what happens when people lose that which is meaningful and sacred to them. Vena is one such person in the group. She has a son, Jeremiah.

Jeremiah

> Vena's grandmother bought her to us for help. Her grandmother however is a drug addict and an alcoholic herself. Vena saw her father stab her mother to death and lost speech until adulthood. Vena's son, Jeremiah, is at one of our Preschool centers.He is labeled autistic and possibly retarded. We work with Vena in psychoanalytic therapy and she is encouraged to come into the center. She sees the therapist as "my new lifeline" (her umbilical cord to a live mother?) She lets go of her alcoholic grandmother more and more, and gets a job for three days a week and spends the other two days in our center with Jeremiah. Jeremiah is no longer considered in the "autistic spectrum"; he blossoms now that she is giving him a womb place in her mind. You can't stop him talking, and he smiles and he plays: a transformation from dead mother, dead womb to live mother, live womb! Dead child, now live child!

Dead center: The psychoanalyst Andre Green holds that the "dead mother" of infancy, resulting from neglect and absence, remains as a blank or dead space in our psyche, a space where love and desire once held life and potential (Green, 1986). Central to trauma is a deadened and deadening internal mother. I see this over and over again in our young Aboriginal mothers. The internalized good mother's containing womb is shattered. The internal holding psychic womb becomes a sterile womb that deadens all emotion. That which holds the unknown and unknowable "core self" part of us is violated and ruptured in a horrifying way—the foetal self is aborted. The central core becomes a "non-person." There is no creative space. The inner world becomes a dark, frightening abyss instead of a safe and protective place. Life is rooted in abject fear and terror, freezing all emotion and joy in living. Sometimes bits of emotional breakthroughs present in the form of flashbacks or dark daydreaming or in nightmares. This is passed on to the next generation, with terrible consequences. It is passed on because the mother, not having her core self, cannot hold the child in a way that sustains the child's core self (LaMothe, 2006, p. 450). In therapy a long slow process sometimes of repair, sometimes for the first time, brings the curative aspects of the "caring" nurturing other. Its transformational qualities allow a positive introjection to hold one, to allow sublimation, to allow a sense of value and protection. It is a long slow and sometimes never achievable process.

Working Together

While the teacher creates the ongoing experience for the child in the preschool, often trauma requires a special worker: a therapist who is able to work one-on-one with the child. But Gunawirra also seeks methods for teachers and especially for parents to utilize when faced with trauma in the child." MarteMeo," a strength-based positive reinforcement therapy, assists with finding the strengths in the child in the here and now relationship with the teacher and in the child's relationship with the parent. Teacher, therapist and most of all parent, all work together. The therapist may use art therapy as a medium in which she allows the child's emotional life to be expressed through art in a one-on-one or very small group situation. This is not about positive reinforcement but rather allows the darkest fears and emotions to find expression. This is the interface of education and trauma. Access to the parents is hard for the teacher and this is where the worker becomes also relevant. This working together is at the core of all successful work. All bring their strengths to bear for the benefit of the child. Here is an example:

Serena: Big Troubles at Home

Will, the father, sleeps on the back veranda on a couch. He and his wife Serena are in therapy. His wife asks, "So why doesn't he take the space in my bed?" Will looked like he had got an electric shock; such a thought as taking or asserting his place was unknown to him. It is the father that teaches the son to demand, to assert, to have rights, to deserve respect. Will didn't have his father there when he was a child to teach him this. He taught him that the only way you can be yourself was to free yourself from the woman, by leaving and never returning, which he did when Will was three years old.

Will calls me, although it is his partner I see. He is going to leave if she does not treat him better. Three weekends later Will walks out, telling me on the phone that she had robbed him of his adolescence and friends and life and her jealous possessiveness was choking the life from him. Serena thinks he left in spite of every effort she made to be good, including coming to see me. For her, in the end everything, everyone dies. You are left in the end.

Serena is a total mess, hyperventilating, having massive anxiety attacks, crying that all her life she had never been loved. Our concern is the three and a half year old in our preschool.

The little child lay on the floor screaming, "I want my daddy! I want my daddy!" for hours on end. She had not eaten for two days. Her mother is now past the screaming and yelling and excited stage, she is in silent mourning. "In my head I am hanging with a strap around my neck. There is no other way out . . . the image haunts me day and night. I cannot cry anymore! I am all washed out. I know now I'm a nothing!"

Will says, "I feel free like I am out of jail when I leave you. Nothing I ever do is good enough. Stuff everywhere, no room, no space. She won't give him his things. She cannot bear the intolerable pain of losing him. He gets the police in. They stand protective witness as she is humiliated, destroyed and powerless again. Little girl lies on the floor. She cries and cries. She screams and screams . . . powerless also. In the end they have to physically restrain her. Her 10 year old brother says, as rage and hurt vie for supremacy in his young frame. "He doesn't want us!" His 10 year old mind is enraged.

Every evening is the same. "I want my daddy! I want my daddy! Don't let the crocodile eat me."

Sometimes he would come home and sit and comfort her. He would wait until she slept and then leave.

They come for a session. The little girl cannot, does not eat. She looks numb and is no more the happy free child I observed before. It's like all joy has left her. The mother is screaming, rude words all over the neighbourhood from my clinic room. Then I see she actually has no words underneath. It is a loud nothingness. She has no power. I show her this. She sees her own impotence. It shocks her. I show her how everything she says to her partner is threats and ultimatums which just drive him away. She cannot ask for him. She cannot let him know her need of him. She is crying for him and yet doing the very things that disempowered and drove him away. She leaves that session thinking. Within a week he is back home and much more involved in the relationship than before.

I was left with a whole lot of questions. Can we only murder if we have already murdered ourselves? What part of us closes down so that we have no idea of the impact of our actions on the other? He damages the people he loves unknowingly and yet in some part of him, he knows, someone in there knows. I am sure he comes home to save that child, the child in his partner also. Some never come home. How do we murder without knowing we are murdering? How can anyone forgive ignorance of this profound nature? My mind moves to the stolen generation. How did those people take the children from their parents, with the mother screaming, the child screaming, every bond of attachment ripped apart in the anguish and trauma and not know what they did? Why did Will leave? Was it because that part of him was already dead? His father had left, never to return, when Will was the age his daughter was now. Has that got something to do with it? Did he need her to know his pain or him to know his pain through her?

Nathaniel

> One of our preschoolers was badly burnt. He said he had taken the lid off the petrol from a machine near where his father was lighting a barbecue (barbecues are a common form of outdoor eating all over Australia). He was so badly burnt that any movement was pure agony. In the Burns Ward, contractions could set in without movement, but he was terrified of movement. Two physiotherapists thought up the idea of creating a hammock with a soft cotton-wool-like center. Each held one end and very gently, almost imperceptibly at first, rocked him a little more each day until he could discover again pleasure in movement.

This is what our teachers do with traumatized children: gently bring them towards the joy of a liberated space where it is safe to have fun, to experiment, to learn again.

As we began to think and to ask, "How do we as therapists work with pain, our pain, the pain of others?" we realize that sharing the pain with them is not enough. Recovering means suffering the suffering in the suffering. This means not a flood of characters on to the stage, but a careful monitoring of how much the audience, the ego can tolerate what is happening and process it. The timing and dosage, the knowing of it by another as empathic witness, neutralizes the pain. It is what a mother does for her infant in reverie. The central psychosis of terror of annihilation is dispelled by psychic holding. The mother does that; the healing circle does that; the good enough therapist does that.

Like Dadirri, psychoanalytic therapy creates through the therapeutic encounter, a relationship that allows the suffering in the suffering to be experienced, liberating the capacity to dream, to live, to give a renewed womb, a new foetus evolved from the therapeutic couple. This is Tustin's movement out of the autistic state.

Creating a space in which to experience through play and imagination in the preschool.

> The humanization of schooling through increasing the social competence and sensitivity of teachers and other child professionals as frontline workers with children can greatly enhance the psychic well-being of children and serve as a critical adjunct to more formal mental health services. The same, of course, could be said for increasing opportunities for parents to understand how to respond sensitively to their children's psychic distress. (O'Loughlin, in press).

How does the Child Care Centre, long day stay preschool help and support the traumatized child, parent, community, staff to survive and to cope with this enormous task?

Valuing the center and its capacity to give to the traumatized child became something more and more important to us; valuing the workers was at the basis of this. What we have tried to create is a space in which to work with free play, stories, song and dance, art, growing things and crafting things—*recreates the dreaming space*. The presence of the teachers, visits by our professional worker, visits and mentoring by phone, create a presence of space and allows our preschool children to create the world as they want to, instead of through harsh imposition from without by trauma. In the preschool center is the concept of the sacred site— a sacred, safe, secure space where trauma heals. The order in that space gives holding, the preschool teacher's reliability gives security, their handling of stimulus that is appropriate in timing and dose and so allows the possibility of life and creativity in what I call the pre-creative space.

Sam

> The Director of one center told of Sam, a boy of three, who had not been going well, was acting out, was destructive towards the other children's play and sometimes violent with them but had responded well to play therapy for many weeks. That morning however, Sam's mother, Melina told Sam's teacher that she had had an abortion. She talked freely about it in Sam's presence, saying, "I'm 40 years of age, you'd think I would have learnt how to look after myself by now, imagine getting pregnant and having to have an abortion."
>
> The staff would have liked to believe that Sam didn't understand, although he was standing with his mother the whole time. When Sam's chosen worker arrived at the discussion group to present her session with him she had no idea that Sam's mother had had an abortion, and was amazed by the revelation made after she presented her session with Sam. She reported:

> When I approached Sam he saw that I had his play box and knew this was his special time. He came straight to me and decided that what he wanted to play with this morning were the little plastic bears. There are about 30 small baby and bigger adult bears, all the same shape and colour. He took two bears, telling me, "This is a mummy bear and a baby bear," and he put them in a box which was open on the side. He got a hard covered book to use as a blocking wall on the box. I asked, "What are you doing?" He said, "I'm making the mummy and baby bear safe from all the bad bears outside." He got all the rest of the bears out of the container and he put them outside the box and he said, "See, they want to attack the mummy and the baby bear." Then with violently aggressive stamping he tried to crush the other bears. He told me, "These are very naughty bears they want to attack and kill the mummy's baby and the mummy too. I have to stop them."

The group was stunned, thinking it extraordinary that Sam should be so conscious of the protection of the mother and baby, at a time when the mother had aborted a baby. Did he fear to be aborted? We asked each other. How aware was this three and a half year old?

Later in the week, I observed the children queued up taking turns jumping from a springboard to a box, with the space between the board and the box widening each turn. All the other children could cope and enjoy it, but Sam could not. He was obviously terrified he would fall in the space between. We suggested that I put the box as close to the board as he felt comfortable to jump. That was right alongside the board, with no gap between. In the play was revealed an extremely frightened little boy: Death was too close and one could fall into the abyss the space between too easily.

The psychological self develops through perception of oneself in another person's mind as thinking and feeling. Teachers who cannot reflect with understanding on the children's inner experiences and respond accordingly, deprive their children of a core psychological structure which they need to build a viable self.

Being alone in the presence of another is central to Winnicott's thinking (1976, p. 29). That presence is needed but it must be unobtrusive so that the preschool child can have a space for self exploration which lies at the root of solitary play. In attachment theory, the balance between exploration and contact maintenance is the paradigm. This is the relevance of the therapist: being there but leaving room for self exploration, a space in which to think. The worker provides such a space.

Jeremiah

> The teacher sits on the floor, legs spread slightly, as Jeremiah, who has a slight intellectual disability, puts large wooden pieces together on the floor with her careful non-intrusive help. She asks what it is he is making. "It is my boat," he says with a degree of pride. "Oh I will get on the boat," says Nathan, and

> jumps on the blocks. Jeremiah angrily pushes Nathan over. "He got on my boat!" he cries. The teacher goes to both children and holds them both. "Jeremiah, remember the rule, we never push—we share! You have such a nice boat, Nathan wanted to share it with you. Why don't the three of us sing a song about sharing and then maybe you can both get on the boat." As they clap and hold hands and sing some of the others wander over and join in the song. Jeremiah is gifted with music and singing. They sing a song about a crocodile, who we all know is not good at sharing. The teacher tells me, "Because Jeremiah is a really big boy, I have to teach him how to control and use his strength for good things or he may end up not accepted at any school or by any kids! He has no awareness of how to use his strength, but he is much improved and we try to give him one-on-one time each day. We are going to keep him here another year so that he will be more ready for school in an intellectual and social sense.

These are the "building blocks" of emotional learning that help so much to develop maturity.

Caring for the Carers

The most important people in the Aboriginal nation are the carers, the healers giving emotional empowerment to the children, and hence the future.

We were always surprised by the amount of trauma the Aboriginal workers themselves had gone through as children. One director told us she decided not to have children so that they would not suffer as she did. But, she devoted her life to the pre-school center. So who takes care of the carers while the carers take care of the children? How do we work when our work touches the core of our own traumas?

For the staff, trauma workshops, debriefing, drama enactments, and supportive supervision must be integral parts of our centers. The staff need to take care of themselves to avoid burnout. A supportive family life helps, space to play themselves helps, not overworking helps. Being with young children in this sensitive state of development and trauma demands a listening and supporting and encouraging that is incredibly exhausting. Carers need debriefing and support. They need someone to talk to. They need supportive workshops. They need a sympathetic Board. They need to not be used and abused. They need a good wage. They need acknowledgement of the good work they do.

Staff need their fellow workers to hear and respect what each other has suffered. The traumatized child touches a depth of emotion in carers that exposes their own trauma. Providing debriefing for the staff in a child care center is the role of the Director. This begs the question: whose role is it to support the Director?

With Aboriginal Directors, we have a paradox here. They tell us, "We are the best people to know and look after our 'own,' we are the ones that know of our background of our losses. This makes us invaluable in helping our own children. They are our own and we are community. But what if we are suffering ourselves? What if our own pain is opened by their pain, what if our space is so cluttered with domestic violence and hurt that we do not have the mind-space ourselves? What if all our own dreams have turned to nightmares? How do we help our children to dare to dream? This is why we professionals must learn to trust each other, must learn to develop groups and boundaries where we can share and neutralize our pain, our trauma. All too often, the dominance of the white fella has taught us a culture of power and we think we are above the parents or the children."

What makes any center work is the commitment of staff and their support of each other. In our research, mothers liked it "that most of the staff are Indigenous and they like seeing the same known faces when they come in." They like you to use their name to greet them, they like to see you enjoying their children and involved in their children. The culture of domination and power must die as the powerless experience more power.

Training professional staff means supporting and hearing about their work with the children, hearing their traumas, and allowing expression of them so they no longer suffer the sense of shame that trauma brings.

CONCLUSION

Imagine if you will, a center in a small isolated town where the summers are scorching hot with parched land, sometimes no rain for a few years, and then the land changes to flood and all is devastation. The town is under water. This is a harsh country. Distance is the worst tyrant of all; more than an hour or two by plane, then by car for two or three hours.

For us as professionals entering the preschool classroom, no amount of care, regardless of our professionalism and sensitivity, seems able to alter the years of distrust earned by white man's intrusion and subjugation. The divide remains. Prejudices are even worse in the country areas. White and black ignore each other in the streets. Asked what was the singular most relevant gain of a three day camp run by Gunawirra professionals and preschool teachers for mothers and their preschool children, all made similar comments, "We talk in the street when we see each other now. We stop and have a chat and laugh about things that happened at the camp." And another one from the teachers, "That mother used to stand outside the gate and push her child in. She comes in after school now, makes a cup of tea and talks about her problems. We share our day with her too." A moment when Aboriginal and non-Aboriginal could come together. Traveling together is still a long way away.

Gunawirra embeds in and springs from the community: it has joined with Directors in thirty country pre-schools to grow gardens with bush tucker (i.e., naturally-growing bush food that Aboriginal people have survived on) and vegetables side by side. We have created a mentoring program where a professional speaks with an outback director on a weekly or fortnightly basis to give her a space to share problems, to debrief and simply to not feel alone and isolated.

Most exciting has been the Activities Website, *Tracking the Milky Way*.[3] This website, created by ten outback preschool centers, offers ideas and educational videos to assist teachers in remote preschool centers with new approaches for "healing" the children in an enjoyable way. Our Gunawirra puppets model culturally sensitive play activities that are educative and follow our basic tenet of working at the interface of trauma and education. Equally important, the website provides the feeling of being part of a community of preschool teachers instead of being isolated, as is so often the case.

It may not seem much when Gunawirra sponsors a child who would otherwise never go to preschool, or pay and help with breakfast and packed lunch for twenty to thirty children for a year. Many of our preschool children come to school without breakfast and sometimes with no dinner the night before. We thought it a wonderful breakthrough when mothers with the preschool teacher's support would do the shopping and buy fresh healthy food and prepare breakfasts that were nourishing.

Gunawirra's intense Art program is another way of providing psychotherapy as a treatment of trauma. The Strong Man project, in which Gunawirra pays for the employment of a male Aboriginal sports teacher to create a physical education program and provide a strong male role model for the Aboriginal boys, has been a success—not only do the boys admire and look up to him, but the little girls also have a male model to look up to and adore.

Many of Gunawirra's efforts are small, funding is very low, government support is locked in a system where the help can only be given by throwing money at the problem, unaware of what the children need emotionally to allow learning to succeed. Somehow politics comes to the forefront and the need to appear to be following a prescription, despite the fact that it does not work, is alarming.

Sometimes we have no idea where we were going. A quilting group in a small town preschool about five hours from Sydney became a group where every single woman shared stories of childhood sexual abuse and present domestic violence. Five of the six women in the group had experienced rape. We knew we had to create a new physical and psychic space for these women and their infants and children and their partners, if they were still with them. The focus in group and individual therapy was around a space to heal, a space to be held, a space to be heard and a space to give care to each other. Dadirri was alive and well.

The space where a dead autistic defense was at work became a space where the families could imagine, creating in their mind a world of future imagining. In one preschool a mother was crying and the other mothers came to comfort her. Empowered by her friends in the group, a woman talked with her husband about how his violence made her feel. Once he knew a whole group of his own people, a group of women, were watching him, the transformations that resulted were amazing. We held in our mind the concept of sacred site, a safe, secure space where healing could take place and a new growing begin. The group and the psychotherapy gave holding and our reliability gave security.

It will take generations, but for every moment of connection there is a future where it is remembered and sought out again. With healing, dreams can be dreamed and emotions that were too painful can be held and suffered. So much energy for so few and with such little hope of "success." But we knew that anything one does in this work is measurable in minute moments of personal empathy, in moments of psychic pain shared between two people and in the witnessing presence that allows pain to be suffered. It may take generations, yet in any moment of healing between two people, moments of transgenerational trauma are healed, the dream is allowed to be dreamt, hope has the potential to come into being, and the preschool child has the potential to live a meaningful life.

NOTE

1. I wish to acknowledge the workers of Gunawirraand—the director and staff of the preschools with whom I have been privileged to work.
2. Gunawirra is an organization made up of Aboriginal and non-Aboriginal professionals formed to work with young Aboriginal families with a focus on children from pregnancy—5 years of age. www.gunawirra.org.au. In order to protect the confidentiality of the children and parents discussed in this chapter all names and identifying information have been altered.
3. http://trackingthemilkyway.com/about-us/about-gunawirra/.

REFERENCES

Atkinson, J. (2002). *Trauma trails, recreating song lines: the transgenerational effects of trauma in Indigenous Australia*. North Melbourne: Spinifex Press.

Bion, W. R. (1977). *Seven servants: Four works*. Northvale, N. J.: Jason Aronson.

Bryant, C. (2009). *Identifying the risks for Indigenous violent victimisation.* In I. J. Clearinghouse (Ed.): Department of Justice and Attorney General (NSW).

Farrelly, E. (2003). *Dadirri: The Spring Within: The Spiritual Art of the Aboriginal People from Australia's Daly River Region*. Darwin: Terry Knight & Associates.

Flood, J. (2006). *The original Australians: story of the Aboriginal people*. Sydney: Allen & Unwin.

Davoine, F. & Gaudillière, J.-M. (2004). *History beyond trauma: Whereof one cannot speak, thereof one cannot stay silent*. New York: Other Press.

Green, A. (1986). *On private madness* (Vol. 117). London: Hogarth Press.

Isaacs, J. (2006). *Australian Dreaming: 40,000 Years of Aboriginal History*. Sydney: New Holland.

Kierkegaard, S., Lowrie, W., & Payne, R. (1941). *Fear and trembling: a dialectical lyric*: Princeton, N. J.: Princeton University Press.

LaMothe, R. (2006). Constructing Infants: Anthropological Realities And Analytic Horizons. *The Psychoanalytic Review, 93, 3*, 437–462.

Mitchell, S. (1988). *Tao Te Ching*: New York: HarperCollins.

NIELNS. (2001). *Working together for indigenous youth. A national framework*. Canberra: Commonwealth of Australia.

O'Loughlin, M. (In press). Countering the rush to medication: Psychodynamic, intergenerational, and cultural considerations in understanding children's distress.In U.S. Nayar (Ed.). *International Handbook on Mental Health of Children and Adolescents: Culture, Policy & Practices*. Delhi, India: Sage.

Tustin, F. (1981). *Autistic states in children*. London: Routledge & Kegan Paul.

Tustin, F. (1988). Psychotherapy with Children who cannot Play. *The International Review of Psycho-analysis, 15, 1*, 93–106.

Tustin, F. (1995). *Autism and childhood psychosis*. London: Hogarth Press.

Winnicott, D. W. (1976). The Capacity to be Alone. In *The Maturational Process and the Facilitating Environment*. London: Hogarth Press.

Chapter Eight

Self-Containment versus Fragmentation

Helping Parents Understand Their Child's Language of Play

Donna Wolf-Palacio

For many years, there has been an evolution of clinical theories about the treatment of children and families who have experienced trauma or developmental delays. The role of the therapist in the treatment has also gone through many variations. From Freud's treatment of Little Hans, where Freud (S. Freud, 1909) designated the child's father as the "therapist" who did the therapeutic interventions, through Winnicott's analytical approach to working with children through their play (e.g., Winnicott, 1971), through Anna Freud's use of play and analysis of child defense (A. Freud, 1966), through expanded theories of systems and family therapy. In the systems approaches, as put forth by Minuchin in the early 1970s, (Minuchin, 1974), the focus shifted to the therapist's role while the child's role shifted to that of the *identified patient*, meaning the child was playing a role in the family like everyone else, and the therapist was treating not the child but the whole family system.

Child development and family systems development continue to be somewhat of a moving target from a psychobiological point of view, but there is also the culture and environment to consider in making an assessment for purposes of designing and implementing an effective treatment strategy. For example, several years ago, there was a traumatic event in one of the neighborhoods we serve, and the therapists at our community mental health center were collected into an "intervention team" to help the children and families deal with the trauma. The population of the neighborhood was primarily blue collar, and the treatment team had been trained clinically in a more expressive dynamic therapeutic model. Several models of therapy were discussed among our team: (1) encouraging the parents to openly show their feelings about the trauma to their children, including crying if appropriate; (2) having an art therapist work, but only with the children, to help them express their feelings through art; and (3) to have the parents participate in expression through art together with their children.

The young team returned to our agency very confused and upset. When they told the parents it was okay to cry in front of their children, these particular parents became enraged and lambasted the therapists for not understanding that crying in front of their children was not socially acceptable in their community and represented a sign of weakness. As it turned out, expressing feelings in artwork with an art therapist (that is primarily nonverbally and at some psychological distance) worked best for this community. Likewise, in working with families from cultures different than the cultural backgrounds of team members, I have learned that the therapist can be most effective when he or she is a kind of "culture broker," interpreting between parent and child and between the family and the larger environment.

Thus, there is a wide range of roles a therapist can assume when dealing with children and families. On one end of the spectrum the therapist is actually in the role of a parent (such as in residential settings), giving the child what has been called a "corrective emotional experience" (Alexander & French, 1946) to make up for the perceived lack of good enough parenting in the home. This type of therapy is often supplemented by behavioral interventions. On the other end of the spectrum, the therapist is joined to but maintains a "metaposition" within the family, treating the system rather than the child, who has come to be known as the identified patient or symptom bearer for the family's difficulty. In the middle is the individual therapist, who may, in the case of the younger child use the child's communication through play, art, and talk to help the child express what is perceived to be difficult to express in a family context, and who also works with parents to help them to understand the child's communication and how to address their child to the best of their ability according to the child's own developmental level and needs.

One day, several years ago, when I was supervising, from behind a one-way mirror, an intern in individual play therapy with a young child, one of our respected family therapists joined me in the observation room to watch the process. After observing for a while he remarked, "I will never understand the point of seeing a child alone." For him, family context was all. And in many ways, I agreed with him.

Practicing these various modalities over the years, I have learned that the parents' level of ego function, their developmental and trauma history, and their attachment to the child all contribute to the therapist's assessment of what kind of therapy or intervention will be most effective in removing developmental obstacles and allowing the child and family to continue growing in a healthy direction—or at least move toward a direction that is less unhealthy. In some cases I have found that working with a parent alone and a child alone reveals more quickly and clearly where the developmental gaps between parent and child overlap. In other cases, seeing the dynamic between parent and child gives a more dramatic and workable assessment.

In this chapter, I will give two examples of approaches to dealing with a parent-child dyad in crisis. The differences in approach are determined by the availability of the parent or parent-figure to take in the child's communication. Both examples include work with the child, but one is a more "individual" model, and the other uses a more "family-based" approach.

What the two examples share is a view of the therapist's role. Whether working individually or conjointly with parent and child, the therapist maintains the role of "system regulator." In this role, all the developmental levels of the participants are balanced in the mind of the therapist so decisions can be made that reveal and modify areas of dysregulation that impede the child's and the family's growth

As a psychotherapist at a community mental health center in Philadelphia, I often see variations on how both adults and children cope with ongoing and past trauma. In play therapy, children bring evidence of their reaction to trauma into the play-space through their drawings and their play. These messages are close enough in time to the actual trauma as to still cause pain and fear, so they unfold slowly and cryptically.

What is especially delicate is the tie between the message of the play and the environment of the child. These messages can give us a blueprint of the crisis, and illustrate the disruptions and frustration of the child. However, some families lack the ability to receive these messages. These caretakers are too anxious to see how their own behavior interacts with that of the child. In other families, the caretaker is able to manage his or her own anxiety sufficiently to be open to and use the messages of the play, particularly with the help of the interpretations of the psychotherapist.

I present two cases, both of which are examples of a psychotherapist trying to help a parent understand the play of the child to facilitate the child's getting their emotional needs met. In the first case, Rashid,[1] the mother has more difficulty using the therapist this way. In the second, the mother was better able to absorb the therapist's feedback and use it to help her child. In the first case, the therapist has to take a more active role in assisting the child to use his resources to reconnect with himself and move on. In the second case, the mother is able to do more of this work, with some prompting from the therapist.

CASE #1: RASHID AND THE RESISTANT MOTHER

In some cases, even with more traumatized families, we are fortunate enough to see a child who has the inner resources to enable his ruthless drive for growth to insist on surfacing. Just such a child is a boy I will call Rashid.

When I first saw him in therapy accompanied by his great-aunt, Rashid was a four year old with big brown eyes and a shy smile. His great-aunt had taken guardianship when his mother had lost her home and was unable to care for him. Under the great-aunt's care Rashid did very well. However, as the years progressed, mother wanted him to come back with her, causing tension with the great-aunt and stress for Rashid. During the custody conflict, which went on for several years, Rashid's great-aunt, a woman in her forties, brought him for therapy. In those sessions Rashid would make drawings, and it soon became apparent that he had a gift for conveying in those drawings his inner life, his feelings and conflicts, his suppressed rage and the defenses he used to protect himself. He would draw himself in various poses of openness or guardedness, sometimes in the image of a dog, who might be sad, or angry, or scared. While he lived with his great-aunt, with whom he felt secure and stable, the drawings reflected feelings about his visits with his mother and his attempt to withstand the stress of his loyalty conflict in relation to his caretakers.

The drawings allowed us to talk about Rashid's fears and confusion. It was significant that his great-aunt was able to respond to these feelings in a way that made him feel safe. She would acknowledge the feeling he was expressing and tell him it was okay to feel that way. Sometimes she would put her arm around him, or even cry with him when he was sad. The drawings had become a language that could guard Rashid's internal sense of integration by allowing his feelings to emerge and permit others to offer comfort and validation. However, there came a time when Rashid's mother went back to court and was granted physical custody and shared legal custody with her aunt. Part of the court's ruling was that Rashid would continue in therapy with me. His mother tried to bring him in to see me, but the visits were irregular. Once Rashid was living with his mother his drawings became highly charged and full of anxiety. They often portrayed a very concrete system of defense, such as rigid body armor, exaggerated muscles, sunglasses and hats on the figures.

Rashid's messages were communicated clearly, but his mother needed more help accepting and responding to them than his aunt had. His frustration grew. His drawings began to reflect a frantic search for defenses against his growing anxiety, including some manic rigidity and dark depressive configurations. I could not help but wonder, what was the use of this wonderful gift if it could not affect any change in his situation? And I wondered if it was cruel to continue to get to the nature of things through these evocative pictures, only to have Rashid move more and more towards despair and rage at having so little control?

One could say the drawings were themselves a compromise, a coping mechanism, even a symptom—in other words, a way of discharging his affects so that he would not "blow up." But in fact, when the stress became too intense, he did blow up. He physically enacted his anger at an impossible situation by punching a wall and falling down the stairs without remembering how this had happened. In this crisis he was brought to see me. His drawings that day were jagged and shaky; there was a feeling of disintegration and fragmentation that I had never seen in his artwork before. He seemed, in fact, from his affect and the way he drew, to be either dissociating or on the verge of doing so.

So here he was, bringing up from inside himself a message of great distress, and it was increasingly clear that his mother, although present in the room, could not, because of her own anxiety, respond to this message in a way that would bring him relief. There was in that moment a hopelessness and frustration that was palpable.

In an attempt to keep him grounded, I pulled out the file of Rashid's pictures and began reconstructing, with Rashid, the events and feelings that were reflected in them. I did this chronologically, retelling his story through the progression of the drawings. As we went over this past "history," he became noticeably more himself, more relaxed, and more in contact with his body. He then drew an integrated coherent picture of himself and his situation, as if he were reminded by his past work of what his ego was capable of doing.

After this session, he did not dissociate again or punch any walls. He had shown himself that he could survive not just by compromising and repressing, but also by being able to move back and forth in two worlds. He could draw on various internal personae (the characters in his drawings) that allowed him the integrity of his feelings and sense of self.

In reviewing Rashid's progress, one could say that punching that wall and drawing pictures of his inner states both were affirmations of the body and its ability to express feelings that were intolerable. One might even say that the body took back its right to have a say in how it was treated, even if it didn't have the power to change it. In this session, Rashid seemed to tremble on the brink of fragmentation and then was able to regroup. As the session ended, he appeared to have found an adaptation that would allow him to withstand the stress of trauma without risking the disintegration of his sense of himself, in spite of the unavailability of his mother.

CASE #2: CHARLES AND THE AVAILABLE MOTHER

At the time of our work, Charles was a three-and-a-half year old boy who lived with his mother, maternal grandmother, maternal grandfather, and thirteen-year-old aunt. He was brought by mother and grandmother because he had become symptomatic after he started supervised visitations with his father. His mother had gone to court to try to get full custody, and father was then ordered to have two hour supervised visitation at family court every other Sunday.

Charles'ss father had many mental health and substance abuse problems. His mother had felt trapped in the relationship with Charles'ss father and she was afraid of him because of threats and obsessive harassment, coupled with threats of suicide if she would leave him. With the support of her mother, she was finally able to separate herself from Charles's father. She was in therapy and working her way through college with the help of her parents. Charles was very attached to his mother and grandmother, but his attachment to his mother was more ambivalent. With his mother he would be clingy, then pull her hair or call her names. This may be in part because he had seen his father be emotionally and verbally abusive to his mother. For a while after the separation, father left the state, and during that time Charles was less anxious and symptomatic, though he still could be very negative and oppositional with mother. Once his father returned and was given supervised visitation every two weeks, Charles's anxiety increased.

After the first visit with his father, Charles began to regress. He became angry and more aggressive with his mother, and he developed other regressive symptoms such as bedwetting and fear of going down the stairs by himself. He is a very bright little boy who was able to verbalize his dislike of the visits and his anxiety about having to see his father. Though his father failed to show up at subsequent visits, Charles'ss mother was still obligated to bring Charles to the family courthouse at the designated time, and Charles's anxiety and anger continued.

The situation caused such great distress and guilt for his mother that it was difficult at times for her to help Charles manage his anxiety. In a number of parent-child sessions, Charles would play out with me and his mother his anger and frustration at having to go to the visits, experience intense anticipatory anxiety, and then, when father didn't show, be left with a great feeling of stress and lack of control. He also was reacting to how the mandatory visits stressed and upset his mother. In one of these sessions, Charles decided he wanted to draw an "angry robot." Since this was hard, I drew it for him, and he turned the paper over and traced it, placing very angry features in the robot's face. At this point, his mother could not absorb and acknowledge the anger in the drawing. She put it aside and asked him to draw something else. Charles became enraged, and started throwing figures and toys around the room and at her, something she had described but that had never happened in our sessions.

In this situation, as the therapist, I held several technical choices. I could help his mother work on containing the acting out with rules and boundaries in order to bring the child back to feeling his feelings. This can be effective with a child who has totally lost control and needs outside help to regain focus. Another technique is to make verbal meaning of the acting out to bring it back into the interactive arena between mother and child. Charles's mother is very bright and sensitive but in that moment her anxiety blocked her from connecting the throwing of figures with her response to the drawing.

While Charles was throwing the toys I decided to speak to the mother about the connection between the acting out and his need for a response to his anger. I asked her to take out the drawing of the "angry robot" and bring it to him while talking about how it might have something to do with the visitations with his father and his grave disappointment and frustration at having no control over them. When she did this, he immediately calmed down and was eager to talk about the drawing and how he felt about the visitations. In this case, in contrast to the previous case presented, we see the positive effect of a mother who is willing to read the signals of her child not as simply defiance, but as a communication with which she can help him to verbalize and thereby express his inner conflicts.

However, in cases like these where the mother's anxiety is high, it does help to have a "meaning broker" such as a therapist to facilitate communication between parent and child. The grandmother did have some skill in this also, but she had more difficulty because of Charles's mother's experience of perceiving her own mother's feedback as critical and undermining of her authority. This was something we were able work on in other sessions, to allow mother and grandmother to work more as a team using self-observation of the ways they might trigger defenses in each other.

The use of interpretation of the metacommunication (one might almost see it as subtext) of a child's acting out to a more attuned self-observant caregiver is effective and long-lasting. But when the ego of the parent is temporarily compromised due to anxiety, it is important that feedback be given in the context of a trusting therapeutic alliance. This is best developed over time in supportive therapy with the parent, although it can be achieved in a shorter time if the transference to the therapist is highly idealized.

It is interesting to note, in terms of developmental evolution, that the mother's resistance to understanding due to her own overwhelming anxiety and guilt, in spite of her best intentions, does not seem to be an adaptive functional mechanism for either mother or child. It does not even serve the function of reducing the mother's anxiety through the mechanism of avoidance, since this child does not accept the avoidance without making sure his mother suffers more. What this resistance may do, however, is allow the mother to convert her own anxiety to anger which could end up being displaced onto her child in response to his aggression. It is possible to view mother's anger as more mobilizing and tolerable for her, thus allowing her to switch from a passive to an active stance. Thus the symptom of the child may be said to have a function, which in most cases is to change the attempted solution of the problem of anxiety (avoidance) to one that is closer to the target of the cause of the anxiety in the first place. Parents who do not tolerate their child's anger and then focus on the child's reactive regression to their response of avoidance, risk getting increasingly embedded in power struggles that are a distraction from the underlying developmental disruptions and frustrations.

THEORETICAL AND CLINICAL CONSIDERATIONS IN WORKING WITH CHILDREN AND MOTHERS

Differentiating between a child's acting out as pure limit-testing, appropriate to the age, or as a communication that cannot be verbalized, is a skill that can be developed with some coaching for parents who are amenable to feedback in this area. As grown-ups, we may take for granted the ability to present ourselves adaptively to the various people and situations we encounter. This may even be seen as a sort of "healthy splitting," which comes increasingly under our control as we mature. For children this is not such an easy task. Conscious splitting-off of affects for the sake of survival has its price, but children do not always have an alternative. It is very much in the repertoire of the "healthy" adult to protect bodily and psychological integrity through this adaptation. For this reason, children are dependent on adult caretakers to help with their "demons," their traumas and fears. Children may split off their affect in play or drawing, but, like firemen going into a fire, they cannot help having feelings about the trauma and stressors. In general, insecure parents find their children's negative emotions difficult to handle. They often respond negatively with aggression or by turning away. They have trouble separating themselves from the child's fear or anger and cannot "metabolize it" with their own processes in order to give feedback that could help the child master his or her fears.

In his article, "The Psychoanalytic Theory of Play," Robert Walder (1933) explores the function of play in relation to the playing child and the caregiving adult. He notes that "Play, as a fundamental and purposeful phenomenon, is encountered only in children, that is, during a period of growth, in which the traumata of life touch the ascending limb of the vitality curve" (Walder, p. 220). Walder implies the function of mastery in his exploration of the uses of play, but when trauma is involved, interpretation of the play by an accepting adult is important to the integration and abreaction of the traumatized feelings. His question is an interesting one: Why would a child play out a painful scene (such as going to the dentist) if play followed the "pleasure principle" as fantasizing and wish-fulfillment dreams do? His answer is that "this merging of reality and fantasy . . . makes possible the abreaction of an experience in play" (Walder, p. 221). It is the adult whom Walder feels is in "the position to help the child obtain this kind of abreaction." In a phrase that seems to predict Winnicott's thinking in *Playing and Reality* (1971), Walder says "the antithesis of play is reality, not seriousness." (Walder, 1933, p. 223).

Attachment issues play a major role in the interface between the parent's and child's ability to cope with disruptions and trauma. If a parent has only marginally worked through his or her own attachment issues from childhood, the parent might have a "blind spot" with respect the child's attachment needs and difficulties. Thus, an area of anxiety for the child that overlaps with an area of unresolved issues for a parent may lessen the parent's availability. In child developmental theory, when we talk about attachment, we are talking about affect. And when we speak of affect in children, this generally translates into action. We can observe the ways a child expresses and communicates feelings and what actions the child takes when prompted by feelings. We can also observe when feelings shut the child down or cause him or her to withdraw to avoid interaction.

I am suggesting that we apply these criteria to parents also in terms of where they fall on the spectrum of healthy/resolved attachment and unresolved/disrupted attachment. The focus would then be on the interface between the influence these affects have on the child and how they affect the parent's actions and reactions. In other words, does a child's anger or anxiety cause the parent to withdraw or shut down because it touches an unfinished corner of the parent's affect regulation system?

If one imagines a graph in which the child's affect and the parent's level of affect regulation interact, one observe the parent's way of responding as inevitable, even predetermined. This is a way in which the defenses described by Sigmund and Anna Freud are useful to compare in parents and children. For instance, the child's affect of panic and defense of disengagement may set off in the parent a kind of paralysis. A wall goes up to guard the parent from being flooded with affect that cannot be modulated.

One way of thinking about this is an emergency situation on an airplane. The usual directions are that if a parent is sitting next to a child and the oxygen masks drop down, the parent is to put a mask on himself or herself before putting a mask on the child. This is a logical rule for preservation but may go against the protective instinct of the parent. Putting the mask on the parent is a form of "system regulation." It implies that the parent who loses control in the face of the child's being in danger is of no use to the child.

The role of the therapist in the misattuned parent-child dyad is to become a stable attachment object for parent and child to help regulate the system. With the help of the therapist's stance, the parent does not have to rely so heavily on defenses and can modulate his/her anxiety enough to cope effectively. The therapist can also help the parent when he/she is in a calmer state to explore the meaning of the child's distress. This can lead to more creative and flexible problem-solving responses. A parent's ability to respond effectively to a child's affect in or out of play is a building block not only for the relationship but also for the child's ability to enhance his/her expansive view of the world and the child's place in it.

ACKNOWLEDGMENT

Portions of this chapter were previously published in *Voices: The Art and Science of Psychotherapy*, *46*, No. 2, in an article "Self-Containment Versus Fragmentation: Coping with Crisis Through the Language of Drawing." I am grateful to the editors for permission to revise and reprint it.

NOTE

1. All names and identifying information have been changed to protect the identities of participants.

REFERENCES

Alexander, F. & French, T. M. (1946). *Psychoanalytic Therapy: Principles and Application.* New York: Ronald Press.
Freud, A. (1966). *The Ego and the Mechanisms of Defense.* Vol. 2 of *The Writings of Anna Freud.* Rev. ed. New York: International Universities Press.
Freud, A. (1965). *Normality and Pathology in Childhood: Assessments of Development.* Vol. 6 of *The Writings of Anna Freud.* New York: International Universities Press.
Freud, S. (1909). Analysis of a Phoia of a Five-Year Old Boy. In *Standard Edition of the Works of Sigmund Freud,* 10: 5–149.
Minuchin, S. (1974). *Families and Family Therapy.* Canbridge, MA: Harvard University Press.
Walder, Robert. (1933). The Psychoanalytic Theory of Play, *Psychoanalytic Quarterly, 2,* 208–224.
Winnicott, D.W. (1971). *Playing and Reality.* New York: Basic Books.

Chapter Nine

The Hidden Allies

Parents as Collaborators

Carola Chase

With all the tools often available to teachers—extensive training, supervision, resource rooms, updated technology—there remain problems in the classroom that can feel endless and unresolvable. This chapter will demonstrate how a deeper understanding of the children who present these difficulties can be a teacher's greatest asset. Further, it will provide evidence that the establishment of strong alliances with parents assists in this effort. Finally, because working with parents is not invariably smooth and productive, the chapter will briefly address strategies for dealing with more difficult interactions with parents.

STANDARD APPROACHES TO CLASSROOM DIFFICULTIES

Any reluctance on the part of teachers to delve into a more in-depth perspective on the children in their classrooms would be understandable, given their days motivating, managing, and, naturally, teaching. Most teachers are dealing with not only the stress of the school day, but also pressure from administration to comply with regulations, adhere to school policy, and to bring in strong results on standardized tests. To achieve these goals, teachers ideally need a cohesive, well-functioning group in an environment conducive to learning, and with highly motivated, cooperative students. Introducing psychodynamics into this complicated and demanding picture is not necessarily part of the teacher's arsenal or training, and requires additional time and energy, factors which are generally in short supply for teachers.

At the same time, the effect of a difficult child, or a problematic situation in the classroom, can be profound, upsetting the balance of the classroom, exhausting the teacher, and delaying or derailing the learning process. Teachers feel frustrated and helpless to both affect a change in the face of these difficulties, and to maintain order in the room. The need to focus on the child who is presenting a challenge takes valuable time from other children who also need a teacher's attention. Perhaps a different perspective on these problems, and the children themselves, via work with parents, could provide useful answers and also relieve a teacher of the arduous task of solving them alone. Watson states that, "Meeting and talking with our students' parents or caregivers early and throughout the year will help us understand our students' lives outside of school and the kind of relationship each child has with the most important adults in his or her life." (p. 43)

Traditional approaches to dealing with classroom problems, such as sending children out of the room, giving them extra work, or restricting activities, are often ineffective for many children. As Kohn points out (1996, p. xiii), "Some of these programs are remarkably autocratic, urging teachers to lay down the law with children and coerce them into compliance." He further addresses the dilemma of using either punishments or rewards which "can be quite effective indeed—but only to get one thing: temporary compliance." (p. 25) So while these tactics work in many instances, "through manipulation" (Kohn, p. 36) there are also children for whom they will fail. Worse, in some cases it may backfire, increasing a child's shame and lowering his/her self-esteem. The end result is a child who, feeling threatened, escalates the battle with the teacher, ultimately resulting in not fewer, but more, problems.

Behavioral approaches utilizing rewards and punishments may be effective with children who respond to these incentives or disincentives, work harder to earn some privileges, and avoid doing anything that is likely to result in negative consequences. While one can sympathize with the use of these remedies, in that they often lead to greater compliance, they also focus exclusively on behavior, success, and performance, bypassing underlying problems which, unheeded, tend to mount. O'Loughlin (2009, p. 75) speaks of the problem with focusing primarily on performance and learning in schools. He states, "Imagine for a moment that instead of thinking in terms of normalization, individual achievement, and totalizing forms of pedagogy that seek to shape all children inexorably in predetermined ways, we entertain a notion of child growth that acknowledges that children grow up in contexts" (2009, p. 14).

Desperate, teachers may turn to parents, not with requests for assistance and mutual problem solving, but with complaints and exasperation. Here, not only does the teacher and possibly the school appear impotent to deal with the problem at hand, but this approach instantly puts parents at a disadvantage, leaving them to feel simultaneously powerless and responsible for a "bad" child. Calls to parents are used punitively, with children threatened with these contacts and parents predictably defensive and angry. They blame the teacher and/or the school for not handling the problem adequately, leading teachers to believe that these parents not only have no answers to the problems, but are also unaware of the actual, ongoing pressures in the classroom. Here, what could be an opportunity for collaboration instead leads to a less cooperative dialogue, a misalliance.

THE INNER LIFE OF THE CHILD

Children are different from adults and generally do not yet have the capacity to understand, let alone to explain or even show, what they feel like inside. It can be difficult, and painful, to think of children as having complicated emotional lives. "Could it be that in ascribing 'cuteness' and 'innocence' to children we are trying to ward off the possibility that little people can experience anger, rage, desire, loss, worry, terror and so on?" (O'Loughlin, 2009, p. 28). So although teachers see these children five days a week, and already have a basic understanding of their personalities, their habits, and their idiosyncrasies, it is still advantageous to obtain additional information from the parents who can provide many of the missing links. Much of what goes on with children is still masked in their behavior. While children want to learn, succeed, make friends, and discover new interests, they are still in the process of developing and growing, with ego development continuing throughout childhood and into adolescence and early adulthood. Along with this development comes a gradual increase in regulation of impulses, capacity for warm, sustained relationships with others, and relinquishment of primitive thought processes, such as magical or omnipotent thinking.

In healthy situations, children continue to gain mastery of their environments, allowing for occasional regressions. But because children's lives are never smooth or free of conflict and stresses, both the normal ups and downs in a child's life as well as more serious impediments to growth—such as problematic home environments, illness, and trauma—need to be considered when evaluating interferences with development or behavior.

Even under the best of circumstances, children are still lacking tools for managing not just everyday tasks, but also intense feelings. Children who are struggling with familial conflicts, for example, may be unaware of, or unable to articulate, these concerns, either due to immaturity, confusion, or anxiety. They therefore communicate what is occurring through behavior, often indirectly, and frequently in direct opposition to their own needs and wishes. For example, a child in emotional pain, which he or she does not understand, may become aggressive, displaying evidence of distress with no indication of its source.

It is therefore incumbent upon the adults in a child's life, ideally working together, to look beyond what is readily apparent (this behavior) to see what the child cannot, and to then begin to fill in the missing pieces and help the child feel understood. This in turn assists the student to work through problems in ways that allow ongoing learning and development.

Externally, children may be witness to situations, behaviors, and conversations which may confuse and/or distress them. These may include parental fighting, financial stressors in the home, or anxieties related to family illness. Children often misunderstand and misinterpret the events and activities around them so that parents arguing, for example, may be instantly viewed as a sign of divorce. Concerns over money may be heard as financial ruin to a child. How do children simultaneously negotiate their place at home and in school, while attempting to comprehend the world and their place in it when faced with such worries? Given the difficulties that many children have to contend with, one might wonder how they can accomplish very much at all.

Three smart, verbal children of a family[1] —Harry, Eva, and Jon, ages 8, 10, and 12—who had recently moved from another state, began at their new school. The teachers of these three children noticed significant differences in their coping skills and adjustments to their new school. Whereas Jon presented his teachers with an almost disdainful façade and a reluctance to seek help or acknowledge problems with any academic material, Eva was almost the opposite. She worked hard, made friends readily, and went overboard in trying to please her teacher. Harry, in contrast to both siblings, argued constantly with his teacher and questioned everything she said in class.

As Jon was the most challenging, it was *his* teacher who arranged a meeting with the mother. Although his mother was not surprised, she was also troubled by Jon's behavior, as she'd seen the same *I-don't-need-anyone* attitude at home. Furthermore, she spoke of her other children with similar concern, detailing the factors that helped explain what the teachers were seeing in school.

Two years prior to coming to this school, the children's father had died suddenly, when the children were 6, 8, and 10 years old. Due to financial constraints, the family moved shortly thereafter, to live with relatives of the mother's. There, conflicts arose which made this arrangement untenable. The mother moved twice more with her children before settling in this new town, which the mother found comfortable and welcoming. Already she had a few friends and was in a support group for single parents. The children, however, were adjusting to the traumas and upheavals of their lives with more difficulty. Jon, as the oldest, had always been loath to turn to others (even his mother) with problems, thereby avoiding any appearance of reliance on others and protecting himself with a tough veneer. Eva, compliant and easy, had found that the best way to feel safe was by causing no problems and being vigilant about the welfare of her family. Finally, Harry, who openly longed for his father, had developed a unique, generally ineffective, way of engaging adults, particularly men, by verbally challenging and attacking them.

With the mother's permission, Jon's teacher spoke with the teachers of Eva and Harry, explaining what she'd learned. This teacher also worked with Jon throughout the year to establish a greater level of trust, for example arranging special teacher-student meetings to discuss progress, during which she provided support and encouragement. Eva's teacher, now recognizing the unhealthy aspects of Eva's exemplary behavior, subtly pushed Eva toward more independence at school with classmates and less reliance on the teachers' approval. In Harry's case, his testing behavior was accepted without the teacher becoming riled or threatened. Ironically, this resulted in Harry's increased capacity to engage with the teacher in more productive ways.

As with these three children, worries about external events often contribute to children's stress. Yet it is usually what happens within a child, i.e., the *interpretation* of these events and the child's perceived role in them that can result in interferences with a capacity to manage impulses. Jon, for example, felt mostly anger about his father's death, with no awareness of his own suffering. Eva believed she alone could hold the family together, with an intense, exaggerated sense of responsibility. And Harry, who felt both hurt by and furious with his father's "abandonment" of him, struggled with his own ambivalence. These feelings can be especially frightening to young children who still believe in magical thinking and who are sometimes convinced that angry thoughts in themselves cause real harm.

Arthur, age 11, was a fifth grader who, while not the easiest of children in the classroom under normal circumstances, was beginning to show marked deterioration in his behavior. He was becoming more confrontational and argumentative with his teacher, and he was escalating his usual clowning with peers, inciting them to engage in disruptive classroom antics. Interestingly, Arthur's teacher, a man in his early twenties, was not initially put off by Arthur's provocations and was impressed by his creativity, particularly in writing. The teacher therefore did nothing to curb the behavior or bring it to anyone's attention, enjoying Arthur's liveliness and failing to recognize the fact that Arthur was, unconsciously, trying to communicate something through his behavior.

Eventually however, the teacher did become frustrated with the behavior, which had continued unabated, and arranged to speak with Arthur's mother. In their meeting, she revealed that she and Arthur's father had recently separated and that the father was now living in another state and was only minimally involved in Arthur's life. She explained that Arthur was sad and confused about his father's limited interest in maintaining contact with him.

After this meeting, and with a better understanding of Arthur's distress (which, it later turned out, included anger, self doubts, guilt about his own anger, and fear of losing his father forever) the teacher was able to rethink his strategy with Arthur. Having allowed, even encouraged, Arthur's difficult behavior, viewing it as creative and typically preadolescent, the teacher decided that what Arthur needed was more, not less, guidance and structure, with clearer boundaries. Subsequent to the meeting with the mother, the teacher was able, with considerable sensitivity, to set reasonable limits in class, resulting in a major turn around in Arthur's behavior, noticed by other teachers in the school as well.

UNDERSTANDING THE MEANING OF BEHAVIORS IN THE CLASSROOM

What could explain the difficulty in deciphering the behavior of a child in the classroom? Clearly children are often unaware of the underlying sources of their behavior. They do not always examine the meanings of their disruptiveness, clowning, teasing, aggressiveness, or withdrawal. Even if they had the capacity for such introspection and understanding of their own behavior it is unlikely that they would be able to articulate this to others.

In an effort to protect themselves from dangerous, forbidden wishes and thoughts, children, like adults, use defenses to keep these thoughts and wishes within the realm of the unconscious with some alteration, or denial, of reality. And while these defenses are often to some degree successful in protecting children from painful or unacceptable thoughts, children are unaware of both the process and the resulting behavior.

One example is that of a child who, experiencing feelings of jealousy and/or hatred towards a younger sibling, becomes suddenly and excessively solicitous with the sibling. Here, a behavior that appears to be showing one thing, love and concern, may represent the exact opposite. The apparent altruism masks unacceptable feelings of anger and hostility.

A more primitive method of self-protection is denial, normal in childhood, in which uncomfortable thoughts and realities are eradicated from consciousness. Children may, for example, develop fantasies that they possess superpowers, temporarily eliminating feelings of vulnerability.

Another common defense used in childhood is identification with the aggressor. Here the child, in an effort to reduce anxiety, takes on the attributes and behavior of the aggressor—perhaps an angry and/or punitive parent—and lashes out at a younger sibling. As a result, the child no longer feels like the victim of the aggression, but the perpetrator.

A less adaptive defense is a reversal of the aggressive impulse or hostile thought, so that the intended focus of the anger, say a parent whom the child also loves, is protected from the child's anger. Cathy, for example, whose mother is at times verbally abusive—repeatedly pointing out and exaggerating Cathy's flaws—responds by turning her anger with her mother toward herself. To save the mother from her rage, Cathy heaps abuse onto herself instead. Here the child becomes the object of her own anger and aggression, with the criticisms and rage meant for another, in this case the parent, leveled at herself.

Because these self-protective devices are not always apparent, problems with which a child is struggling may be manifested in confusing, at times paradoxical ways, generally signaling that the child's feelings and thoughts have not been warded off successfully. The disruptive child in school who behaves in provocative, incendiary, or aggressive ways suggests some inner turmoil, indicating anything from an effort to mask feelings of insecurity to fears about learning or a need for attention. Angry outbursts and wild or uncooperative behavior can signal sadness or depression just as withdrawal, clinginess, and excessive compliance can hide enormous rage.

Timothy, age 11 was just such a child. He battled constantly with his teacher, arguing with him about every point, provoking him with sarcastic, scornful remarks when called on in class, and regularly failing to finish work. Exasperated, the teacher called the parents to discuss Timothy's difficult behavior, explaining that it had begun to infect other children in the class. The parents were not surprised, as these problems had been raised in other classes. But the teacher witnessed a father who, while devoted and loving, spoke in a punitive, almost militaristic way about his handling of his children's chores and homework assignments. Timothy's mother in fact corroborated the teacher's impressions by gently and supportively challenging some of her husband's thinking about child rearing, suggesting other strategies.

Timothy's experience of feeling bullied at home had manifested itself in Timothy's taking on the aggressive role with the teacher (an example of identification with the aggressor). Yet this meeting with the parents also highlighted some of Timothy's interests, of which the teacher had not been aware. The teacher subsequently used this information, gearing occasional assignments to these interests, which were shared by other children in the class. Additionally, he praised Timothy's highly unconventional and imaginative writing and requested that Timothy, when finished with his own work, help other children who had problems with math (a subject in which Timothy was quite strong). The father benefited from this meeting also. Seeing Timothy become a far more engaged, enthusiastic, and cooperative student, the father was able to let up to some degree on his firm control at home.

Another example of a difficult child in a classroom was Daniel, age 10, who expressed his anger and aggression in his drawings of battle scenes. These illustrations were largely of bombs exploding, and wounded soldiers screaming for help, their bodies dismembered and spouting blood. When he was not drawing, which he did at every opportunity, he *talked* about guns, explosives, and mayhem, raising concern in the teacher as Daniel at times engaged other children in his fantasies, escalating the level of chaos in the room. Here too, talking with the parents revealed something the teacher had not known, namely that Daniel's older sister suffered from epilepsy. Daniel often witnessed her seizures, trips to the emergency room, and the accompanying parental anxiety. While at times angry with his sister for the frequent disruptions at home, Daniel was also confused, sad, and fearful of developing epilepsy himself. All of these feelings were reflected in his drawings and his preoccupation with violence and destruction.

After meeting with the parents, the teacher was able to see the behavior more in the context of events at home. With the assistance of the parents, who had been unaware of Daniel's obsessive drawing in school due to their understandable preoccupation with their daughter, the teacher helped Daniel refocus his drawing, praising his enthusiasm but also allowing him to begin to talk about his sister. Genuine concern and caring crept into Daniel's comments about her and his drawings gradually evolved into a serious interest in art, eventually helping him to contain and manage some of his anger and fear.

Sometimes persistent problems with learning are in fact unrelated to any actual learning disability. Lauren, an intelligent, sensitive six-and-a-half year old girl, could not seem to pay attention at all in class. She looked out the window during assignments, or stared blankly ahead when her teacher was giving lessons on basic arithmetic and reading skills to the class. When questioned about what she'd learned, Lauren showed a pervasive lack of retention for any of the material. This was in contrast to the sense the teacher had of a thoughtful and bright child. After conferring with the parents and with the school psychologist, who also met with Lauren to rule out any learning disability, the teacher and parents, learned that an older male cousin of Lauren's had molested her during a summer vacation shortly before the start of the school year. Fearful and full of shame and guilt about what had occurred, and with no capacity to understand, let alone articulate it, Lauren had been distracted and in a state of panic, unable to focus or learn anything. Learning had become linked for her to "seeing" what had happened to her over the summer, resulting in an inhibition concerning any new learning. She could not take in any additional information while still coping with the trauma of the previous summer.

Children with actual learning disabilities may also present with behavior problems not specifically connected with the disability. Melissa, diagnosed at age nine with dyslexia and dysgraphia, received extra help from a learning specialist, which resulted in progress in both reading and writing. Nevertheless, Melissa was sullen in class. She cried readily and complained of stomachaches so often that she became a regular visitor to the school nurse, who, knowing that there was nothing medically wrong, usually let Melissa rest for a few minutes before having her return to the classroom. This behavior made no sense to the teacher, who had been impressed with Melissa's academic improvements. Talking with the parents, the teacher learned that at home Melissa complained bitterly about not being smart enough. The other children did not need outside tutoring, she told her parents, and everyone else finished reading or writing assignments quickly and easily. She said, "I don't want to go to school. I'm stupid!" While her parents had never even inadvertently communicated disappointment about Melissa's disabilities, she nonetheless felt bad about herself. The teacher explained that she had seen other children with learning difficulties who suffered from problems with self-esteem, even though she hadn't been aware of such a problem with Melissa until this meeting.

The teacher subsequently spoke privately with Melissa about her difficulties, not only explaining that they had nothing to do with how intelligent she truly was, but also showing Melissa areas in which she clearly excelled. In addition, the teacher directed Melissa to a website that listed famous people with learning difficulties, which allowed Melissa to talk more openly about her own, even showing the website to her friends.

Another problem with which teachers are often presented is the area of social problems, where children appear withdrawn, preoccupied, needy, or victimized. While an aggressive child requires more active interventions at school, a child who withdraws emotionally or a child who is excessively compliant should also raise alarms as their symptoms, too, may signal problems with self-esteem. The scapegoated or overly dependent child may drain a teacher's energy and attention as much as an aggressive child, and should prompt a teacher to speak with the child's parents.

Emma was a nine year old girl who told her parents that she hated school. She complained of various ailments, ranging from stomach distress, allergies, and aches and pains, all so that she might be allowed to stay home. In school Emma was shy, quiet, and cooperative, never failing to do instantly whatever the teacher requested. However she was also socially withdrawn. When her parents finally approached the teacher, explaining that Emma had always loved school but was now dreading each school day, the teacher was astonished, even given Emma's withdrawn behavior. He was even more surprised to learn that Emma believed the teacher, who had also taught Emma's older brother, disliked her. Emma's parents, quite perceptive about their daughter, believed that Emma compared herself, usually negatively, to her high achieving, assertive, and outgoing brother. This unfavorable opinion of herself, formed partly in response to her parents' idealization of the older brother, of which they were not initially aware, was projected onto the teacher, who therefore must similarly dislike her. This is another example of turning aggression (anger towards her brother, with whom she felt she could not compete, and with her parents for appearing to favor him) against herself.

Armed with this information, the teacher praised Emma more openly in class, urged her to talk more, and gave her extra jobs to do. Emma responded so enthusiastically to these encouragements that when the teacher broke the class into groups for a final history project, he made Emma the leader of her group. She took on the role eagerly and soon gained the respect of the other children in her group. Here again, collaboration with the child's parents helped clarify ways in which the child's inner experience was interfering with her academic and social skills. Further, it suggested strategies for assisting Emma in overcoming these difficulties.

TEACHERS AND PARENTS AS COLLABORATORS

What aspects of these collaborative efforts lead to success and what factors hinder the process? To begin to answer these questions, it is helpful to look at the main players in these dramas, the parents and teachers, along with their capacities to empathize with and understand the child.

Children are not miniature grownups, able to recognize their own feelings, be aware of ways in which emotions affect them, and adapt accordingly. While adults can learn to contain and manage their feelings to the extent that they do not impinge on work or relationships, children—when worried, angry, sad, or agitated—are often unable, even if attuned to these feelings, to express them. Their emotions at times feel confusing, unwanted, and frightening, but this does not protect the child from having these feelings. Emotions continue to affect behavior, mood, interpersonal relationships, and self-esteem. It is therefore the job of the adults in a child's life to help sort out and translate these perplexing parts of a child's inner world.

How can one accomplish this so that children can gain tools to cope with feelings and attain greater control over when and how they are expressed? Children who misdirect, avoid, or express feelings in ways that interfere with classroom functioning (whether with disruptive behavior, refusal to do work, or conflicts with peers) pose particular challenges. With parents as collaborators and a clearer psychological understanding of a child, a teacher can curtail the struggle to contain or control a difficult behavior in the classroom, and begin to find solutions that address underlying pressures.

Parents also, when provided with information about a child's behavior in school can recognize and explain features of the child's personality that help teachers work more effectively. Although there are parents who may be unwilling to acknowledge concerns about a child, many will respond proactively when made aware of issues their child struggles with in school.

While there are children who exhibit difficult or oppositional behaviors at home while remaining cooperative and motivated in school, there are other children whose behavior at home is exemplary, setting off no alarms to parents. These children are the ones who bring to school problems and worries they experience but that they are unable to express at home. In these cases parents may in fact be unaware of what occurs in school until alerted to problems by a teacher or other school staff. Here a teacher can initiate the process of exploring a difficulty and the parents can provide help in finding a wider range of options when the usual approaches are proving ineffectual.

Although it is not the premise of this chapter that teachers should spend inordinate amounts of time attempting to decode a child's emotional life, there are benefits to a greater understanding of these factors. Teachers are drawn to the field not only because of their investment in academic learning, but also because of their enthusiasm about and interest in children themselves, what motivates them, what causes them stress, what upsets or excites them, what is most conducive to the development of new academic and social skills. Therefore a basic understanding of children—their personalities, home life, fears, and idiosyncrasies—gleaned from communication with parents, can provide a broader and more effective framework for thinking about those who present difficulties.

Not surprisingly, many parents have goals for their children that are strikingly similar to those of most teachers. With an investment in a child's success, both academic and social, parents experience children as extensions of themselves, reflecting parental skills, intelligence, and commitment as well as limitations, emotional problems, and failures. If used tactfully, a teacher's comments about a child can be powerful and productive. For parents, who look to the teacher for reassurance that a child is hard-working, likeable, and motivated, the teacher's praise or concern carries considerable weight. As the one person who sees the child all day, the teacher can attempt to either form a strong alliance with parents, or sidestep this possible connection. Avoidance of this option, however tempting it may be due to classroom responsibilities (particularly with complicated or difficult parents themselves), risks missing a potentially strong resource.

As much as teachers find parent-teacher meetings stressful, many parents similarly dread them, fearing criticism of themselves, particularly with a child about whom parents have heard repeated complaints. In these situations, parents may arrive at a conference already defensive and angry, feeling they too will be criticized. However, when included in the process of pinpointing the source of the problem for the child, parents have the potential to be valuable, or perhaps invaluable, consultants about their child. Furthermore, teachers and other school staff who tap into the parents' vast knowledge of a child, learn clues about how best to manage a child's difficulties in the classroom. By making this connection with parents, teachers find that parents become strong champions of the teacher's own classroom goals. Such parents are often likely to reinforce, at home, many of the solutions arrived at in these meetings with teachers.

Samantha T, at age 7, was a creative child who loved school and particularly enjoyed art projects. She became uncharacteristically provocative with other children in her second grade class, teasing and distracting them during work periods and causing minor conflicts on the playground. Additionally, Samantha began refusing to do work in the classroom—including artwork—and avoiding assignments in a number of ingenious but ultimately frustrating ways that tried the teacher's patience. Here the teacher, who had Samantha's older sister in class a few years earlier, relied on her excellent working relationship with Samantha's mother. This mother had always respected the teacher's observations and responded quickly whenever a problem needed to be addressed.

The mother stated that she was not completely surprised by either the telephone call from the teacher or Samantha's behavior in school, as she'd been acting up at home as well. Initially baffled as to possible causes of such a change, Mrs. T mentioned casually that her husband was in Japan on an unusually lengthy business trip that had already been extended twice. Samantha, who had voiced some anger and disappointment when Mr. T left, and then again at the first extension of the trip, had stopped complaining, which is why Mrs. T had not considered this as a reason for the change in Samantha's behavior. Together, the teacher and Mrs. T were able to recognize that Samantha was reacting to her father's absence, which the occasional phone calls did nothing to alleviate.

As a result of this conversation, the teacher was able to verbalize for Samantha, in school, how hard it must be to have her father away. She suggested that Samantha write letters to her father and send him some of her drawings, a suggestion Samantha eagerly accepted, renewing her former interest in art (which continued until long after the father had returned home). The mother also benefited from this meeting with the teacher, making sure, for example, to talk more openly with Samantha about the father's trip. She also encouraged Samantha to speak regularly with her father, and she even added a video chat component to their communications with him. Samantha's anger and provocations quickly subsided, allowing her to return to her former functioning.

However overwhelmed and distressed a parent is at home with an uncooperative, trying, or oppositional child, that parent has had to find techniques for dealing with these problems. It is true that over time a teacher will figure out what approaches work best with individual children in order for them to function well in the classroom. The teacher will learn, for example, that transitions are particularly difficult for Sally who does better when reminded ahead of time about a change in activity, while Joey must be very tactfully approached about his teasing behavior as any public reprimand sets off an escalation of distress. Yet, despite a teacher's capacity to learn about the children in a given class, coordinating efforts with parents can help to speed the process.

Even the most skilled, experienced, and caring teacher cannot have the window into the inner life of the child that parents have. New information that a parent shares about a child enables a teacher to be even more empathic with a child and to help broaden the child's repertoire for managing his or her stress in school. Teachers therefore have the potential to encourage and support new, more effective coping techniques. This not only provides relief to a child who is suffering, but gives the child tools that can be utilized for many years to come.

An example of this lasting effect from an important teacher is Cecilia, a ninty-two year old woman who sought psychotherapy for help with depression and reported a childhood in which she felt constantly criticized at home by her family, ostracized and scapegoated by peers, and often immobilized at school, unable to complete work. She thought she was unlikable, and withdrew from people to avoid feeling even worse. Although she eventually overcame many of her early struggles by making a number of friends, having a successful career, and upon retirement joining an amateur theater group, some parts of Cecilia's early suffering never entirely vanished.

In exploring this woman's painful early history as well as her successes, her therapist wondered about positive experiences that helped her develop some degree of self-esteem. At first insisting that no one in her childhood had provided any support or encouragement, she suddenly stopped, saying, "Wait. Mrs. Moore, my second grade teacher." She then explained that as a child she had been given to frequent bouts of crying, often further annoying and alienating both children and teachers. Mrs. Moore had been different, however, especially after speaking with Cecilia's parents and learning about some of her problems at home. Mrs. Moore came out of that meeting with more compassion for Cecilia. Seeing the child with her head on the desk, crying and miserable, Mrs. Moore had come over to her, patted her gently on the back and reassured her, telling her how smart and capable she was. Mrs. Moore was able to respond empathically to Cecilia's fears and sensitivities by encouraging this child who had experienced minimal support in her life. The impact of this one teacher, who helped Cecilia emerge from her shell in second grade, had a profound and lasting effect. Eighty-five years later, the memory of Mrs. Moore still made Cecilia smile, reminding her that this one caring teacher had been a beacon of hope. She'd begun to think that the world *might* offer some kindness and support and that she might discover strengths in herself she had never known.

HOW TO TALK WITH PARENTS ABOUT A CHILD'S DIFFICULTIES

Reaching out to parents about a child's problems, or raising such concerns in the context of a parent-teacher conference, can be challenging. Even "constructive criticism" is not usually taken as such. Hearing anything negative or critical about their child can cause parents to become defensive and angry. So how does one address such problems in ways that also encourage cooperation and interest from the parents?

The most important aspect of these conversations with parents is, obviously, tact. There are painful realities about a child that a teacher needs to communicate; realities that can make the parent feel that he or she is being criticized. Thus, even the phrasing of the concern can make a significant difference as to how it will be perceived and what effect it will have. This is not to suggest that teachers need to walk on eggshells with parents, but rather to emphasize that a teacher's perceptions of a child have a powerful impact on parents. Ideally, a teacher will present as well rounded a sense of the child as possible, not limit their discussion with parents to a problem area.

Establishing a working relationship with parents early in the year can go a long way toward forming a strong alliance, with or without any specific concerns. This can be done by maintaining regular contact through notes sent home about a child's progress, brief interactions at drop-off or pick-up, emails, and phone calls. A parent-teacher relationship that is cordial and collaborative allows for casual observations and questions. Further, it gives the teacher an ongoing window into a child's home life, and it gives the parent a better picture of a child's life at school. A teacher who has set the groundwork for communication with parents will have an easier time working with them if and when a problem does arise.

Eliciting information about children as a matter of course, even without any specific troubling issues in school provides teachers with a better sense of a child's life and personality. Information from parents about vacations, weekends, illnesses, births of siblings, etc. convey a great deal. Briefly following up with parents when a child mentions something exciting, disturbing, frightening, or perplexing in school demonstrates an interest in the child's life and further encourages collaboration. A teacher might say to a parent, "You know, Ginny mentioned that her grandmother is very sick, but couldn't really explain. I was wondering about what's happening. Is she very close with her grandmother?" That parent is instantly drawn in and can quickly clarify Ginny's relationship with her grandmother and the nature of the illness. The parent might explain the child's misunderstanding and anxiety about the grandmother's relatively minor medical procedure; or, should the grandmother be more seriously ill, that the child has become completely preoccupied with the grandmother's impending death, and the subject of mortality in general. These simple exchanges assist the teacher who sees a child who is sad, withdrawn, or having trouble focusing, in better understanding these moods.

How does a teacher broach the subject of a child's difficulty with parents? Certainly not in the way three-year-old Patty's teachers spoke with her parents about her first school experience by immediately telling them that their child was difficult and uncooperative. Although in her case the parents were able to rise above the hurt and anger this engendered and they ultimately offered their own suggestions for ameliorating the situation, such comments would alienate many parents. A teacher's praise of a child at the onset of a meeting or conversation sets a different tone, one that allows and encourages a parent to take in painful information and to ally with the teacher in confronting the difficulty. Starting with some positive attribute of the child communicates that the teacher has some warmth toward that child, enabling the parent to hear problems that need to be addressed.

What about the child who is so difficult or unpleasant that a teacher finds him or her hard to like? Even with this child, a teacher needs to think about positive traits and remember that the child, no matter how difficult, is also struggling. Perhaps the boy who is disruptive and oppositional can also be funny. Perhaps he is generous and helpful at times to another child, or is athletic, or knows a lot about science. Anything can be brought up to demonstrate to the parent that one sees something worthwhile in this child. One should approach the problem with compassion and empathy, commenting that the child seems upset and unhappy, rather than focusing exclusively on the negative behavior. Then the teacher can inquire about what the parents think might be happening. In this way a teacher encourages a deeper understanding of the issues and expresses an interest and concern for the whole child. Essentially, whatever strategy works for forming an alliance with parents benefits both the child and the teacher.

PROBLEMATIC COLLABORATIONS

This chapter has not focused on the truly difficult, uncooperative parent with whom it may be virtually impossible to establish a working relationship. Such a parent may withhold important family history or information that is crucial to an understanding of the child's functioning and state of mind. An equally problematic parent is one who rejects any suggestions, flatly denies any problems, or refuses suggestions outright. Even in the case of a clear learning disability when a teacher recommends testing, parents may adamantly reject this idea unless mandated by the school.

When Jack's teacher noticed the nine year old's lack of focus in class, his tendency to sit passively while the other children completed their assignments, and his apparent unwillingness or inability to do any work in the classroom, she initially assumed Jack was having a difficult adjustment to the new school year. She had seen many children who needed time to acclimate and was not alarmed. As a perceptive, sympathetic, and experienced teacher, she felt certain that she could find a creative way of helping Jack.

By October, when the situation with Jack had not abated despite all her efforts, the teacher became concerned and called the parents, whom she had met once or twice. The parents responded defensively, despite the teacher's tact and sensitivity, insisting that Jack had no difficulty at all doing work at home. They concluded that as a quiet, reserved child, Jack must just be distracted by the commotion in the classroom and suggested that he be permitted to do all of his work at home. This they felt would allow him to work in a calmer environment. The teacher, after initial explanations to the parents about the disadvantages of such an approach for Jack's learning process, reluctantly agreed to try this on a temporary trial basis. She found, however, that Jack would return to school with all of his assignments done perfectly with no errors, erasures, etc.—this was clearly not the work of a nine year old. While the teacher met regularly with Jack's parents throughout the year in an attempt to help Jack, she found them uncooperative and defensive. Jack's work continued to suffer along with his social adjustment. Here the parents were inflexible, refusing to acknowledge and deal openly with their child's problems in school, thwarting the teacher's best efforts.

Rather than continuing to attempt some communication, there may be little one can do in these instances. However, before reaching such a conclusion one might try speaking with the child him or herself to try to understand what is getting in the way, such as a conflict with another child or difficulty organizing work assignments. The teacher may also be able to find a solution to a difficulty in school with the child as an ally. Encouraging the child to meet with a school psychologist is another viable option. Additionally, the school administration can often offer support or encourage parents to become more engaged. Finally, it is important to keep in mind the impact of an obstructive and uncooperative parent on the life of the child. While a teacher may find assistance from other staff, and try various techniques for dealing with such a parent, it is the child who suffers most in this situation. The child has few resources to rally the support and engagement necessary from such a parent.

CONCLUSION

While looking more deeply at a child's inner life is time consuming for the teacher, the results, in addition to being profoundly fascinating and rewarding, can also make a significant impact on a child's life.

Angeline, age 11, had been diagnosed with Asperger's syndrome. Although smart and verbal, she consistently saw herself as having no positive traits or strengths, and she verbalized these self-perceptions to others. Given Angeline's musical talents and her intelligence, the teacher was struck by her negative feelings about herself. Meeting with Angeline's parents, the teacher quickly saw that despite genuine support and love for Angeline, they were prone to speaking glowingly of Angeline's more successful, athletic, and beautiful younger sister, even in the midst of a conversation about Angeline. They seemed completely unaware of what this might be communicating. The teacher, by pointing out Angeline's skills and particularly highlighting her rather extraordinary musical abilities, was able to help the parents deal with their own narcissistic wound in having a child with a disability.

In this small class, the teacher worked to actively rebuild Angeline's confidence by reiterating her talents until Angeline herself could see them. The parents in turn began to praise her sister less often, releasing Angeline from the constant need to excel in order to make up for her disability. Ultimately, the teacher was able to turn the relationship with the parents into a collaborative one. While Angeline had not been a difficult child (by disturbing the class or interfering with the teacher's work), she had been suffering needlessly with low self-esteem. The teacher's capacity to look at this child in terms of both academic and emotional functioning ultimately made a significant difference in Angeline's school year. The teacher was able to talk sensitively with the parents toward a better understanding of Angeline's internal state, enabling them in turn to help alter Angeline's perception of herself. This resulted in a vast improvement in the school year for Angeline and hopefully helped her think differently about herself for years to come.

While this chapter has stressed the collaborative role a teacher can have with parents, there are obviously other sources of support for the teacher coping with classroom difficulties. Speaking with other teachers, either in a supervisory or a less formal forum, can be invaluable. Other teachers are usually able to understand classroom pressures and offer sympathy and strategies for dealing with them. School support staff such as guidance counselors and administrators can also offer backup with problematic situations. Finally, for many children with difficulties, psychotherapy may be able to help them cope more effectively with emotional and/or learning difficulties. Therapists are generally open to collaboration as well, eager and willing to talk with a child's teacher (with parental consent of course). This alliance with yet another person in the child's life often provides fresh insights about a child.

Often though an alliance with parents is sufficient not only in providing the extra support that a teacher needs, but also in supplying information that allows the teacher to affect a powerful and lasting, often life-long impact on the children in his or her classroom. How many people are fortunate enough to be able to make such a profound difference in a child's life ?

FOR THOSE INTERESTED IN FURTHER READING

Although this chapter reflects my own thinking and experience in working with children and parents over the years, many of the early pioneers in psychoanalytic thinking continue to inform my understanding of child development. I am indebted, for example, to Anna Freud for her groundbreaking work on ego development, defenses, and clinical applications of psychoanalytic concepts in working with children. In "The Relationship Between Psychoanalysis and Education" (1930) she elucidates some of the ways psychoanalysts and educators can work effectively together to help children who are in difficulty. Also in *Normality and Pathology in Childhood: Assessments of Development* (1965), she explains and describes the various defense mechanisms available to a child and how such defenses might manifest themselves in the child's behavior. Ms. Freud invariably provides sharp, clinically astute examples, whether she is talking about studies from the Hampstead Clinic, or the impact of early relationships on a child's emotional growth. *War and Children* (1943), written in collaboration with Dorothy Burlingham provides fascinating case examples from the groups of children they observed in their nursery in wartime England.

Both Margaret Mahler and Renee Spitz strongly influenced my thinking about the earliest life experiences, including the areas of separation anxiety, early attachment theory, and primitive depressive states in infants. In his studies of hospitalized infants, reported in *The First Year of Life* (1965), Spitz recognized the profound emotional effect of maternal deprivation on a baby's development. Mahler, co-author of the *The Psychological Birth of the Human Infant* (Mahler, Pine, and Bergman, 1975) was one of the first psychoanalysts to clearly delineate and describe the stages of early separation in the infant and toddler.

While Selma Fraiberg is particularly known for *The Magic Years* (1959), a book accessible to any lay person interested in children, her writings in the journal *The Psychoanalytic Study of the Child* are also compelling reading. For example, in "Clinical Notes on the nature of Transference" (1951) she presents the case of a 7 year old in treatment, offering unusual glimpses into the treatment and the thought processes of the psychoanalyst. Berta Bornstein, a prolific writer and also a frequent contributor to *The Psychoanalytic Study of the Child*, provides some of the most fascinating, poignant, and beautifully written clinical contributions to the literature, particularly in her famous case of Frankie (Bornstein, 1950). Though there are many other psychoanalytic scholars who have strongly influenced my understanding of children, I will end by citing D.W. Winnicott (e.g., *Playing and Reality*, 1971), who is certainly one of the most unique and innovative thinkers about early mother-child bonding, play, and fantasy, and creative ways of working with children in treatment.

NOTE

1. In order to protect the confidentiality of the children and parents discussed in this chapter all names and identifying information have been altered.

REFERENCES

Bornstein, B. (1950). The analysis of a phobic child. Some problems of theory and technique in child analysis. *The Psychoanalytic Study of the Child, 3/4,* 181–226.

Fraiberg, S. H. (1951). Clinical notes on the nature of transference in child analysis. *The Psychoanalytic Study of the Child, 6,* 286–306.

Fraiberg, S. H. (1959). *The magic years*. New York: Charles Scribner's Sons

Freud A. & Burlingham, D. T. (1943) *War and children. New York: Medical Warbooks.*

Freud, A. (1930). The relationship between psychoanalysis and education. In *The writings of Anna Freud*, (*Volume I*, Part II, Lecture 4), 121–133.

Freud, A. (1965) *Normality and pathology in childhood: Assessments of development.The writings of Anna Freud, 6.*

Kohn.A. (1996). *Beyond discipline: From compliance to community:* Alexandria, Virginia: Association for Supervision and Curriculum Development.

Mahler, M. S., Pine, F., & Bergman, A. (1975). *The psychological birth of the human infant.* New York: Basic Books, Inc.

O'Loughlin, M. (2009). *The subject of childhood.* New York: Peter Lang Publishing, Inc.

Spitz, R. A. (1965). *The first year of life.* New York: International Universities Press, Inc.

Watson, M. In Collaboration with Ecken, L. (2003). *Learning to trust: Transforming difficult elementary classrooms through developmental discipline.* San Francisco: John Wiley & Sons.

Winnicott, D.W. (1971). *Playing and reality.* New York: Tavistock Pulications Ltd.

Chapter Ten

Even When Things Go Well They Are Difficult

A Psychoanalytic Approach to the Relationship between School and Family

Ana Archangelo and
Fabio Camargo Bandeira Villela

The "subject of learning"—the "cognizant student," who is the focus of the school's attention, is, first and foremost, a child, a young person, a "being of flesh and blood," as Borgogno (2007) puts it, although his/her parents and teachers are also involved. The encounters and mismatching experienced in the relation between family and school involve multiple determinants and many vertices of understanding. When viewed in the light of psychoanalytic theory, the relationship between family and school gains some perspectives in which the "beings of flesh and blood" are present, with their minds and bodies, their sufferings, often lived out in secret. They are still present even when concealed behind terms like "institution," "school," "cognizant subject," or "family."

The relationship between school and family is complex, for although these institutions may have similar missions, they approach them in different ways. In addition, fantasies and anxieties crucial to the success or failure of the bond of trust, and mutual recognition vital to the proper conduct of educational work, permeate the imaginary constructions, one over the other.

This is a relationship marked by intense subjective processes, often unconscious and of a persecutory nature. In day-to-day life, school and family not only show their "ways of being" and internal contradictions, but also make demands of one another that are congruent with their fantasies. When things go well, the normal strains can lead to trust, or at least be mitigated by acceptance of differences and by actions that make clear their specificity, so that any eventual dispute or jealousy of one institution relative to the other can be handled.

When things go badly, it is common for one institution to want to set out "modes of being" for the other, and large scale projective processes become part of everyday life, for example, through mechanisms of projective identification in order to control, destroy, or exacerbate the differences.

An investigation of the relationships established between school and family-based defense mechanisms and unconscious control is a field as broad as it is interesting. In certain cases, it may be possible to refer to problems resulting from isolated aspects of the interaction between school and parents. Even when serious, these problems tend to be episodic, and therefore generally transient. In other cases, it may refer to relatively persistent trends resulting from marked psychological characteristics, whether of the school or the family. In these situations, relations become repetitive in character, as opposed to the episodic nature of the cases mentioned above. Even when taking different forms, they show what, in this article, will be called "features," a "manner of being" with consistent traits that tend to establish the "rules of the game" of relations, setting the basis on which others may take part. In one respect, these "features" can be found at both extremes. It would be possible to address this issue in terms of "features of the school," "family features," or both, creating a huge number of research opportunities that fall outside the limits and objectives of this discussion. This chapter has as its objective the investigation of the second type of situation, thus referring to typical and recurrent situations brought by families into the relationship with the school. This brings up some relatively common but important situations with reference to certain emotional dispositions present in some families, which tend to impact on the school and its staff. We have therefore addressed some hypothetical situations with reference to the family in its relationship with the school. Since these typical situations do not refer to any specific case, the discussion presented is based on reflection, empathy, and, in particular, clinical experience transposed to the school. These situations are presented through scenarios or pictures that we offer as objects of analysis.

We also seek to investigate the effect of certain family expectations concerning the school and the effect of marked psychological characteristics in the family, when in the school. We are aware, however, that different schools respond differently to the specific demands and requirements of particular families. In addition, we are sure that such reactions are sometimes likely to aggravate the difficulties and impede the relationship, which should always be aimed at establishing and deepening the child's welfare.

However, so as not to lose focus on the family, we will discuss the supposed effects of certain scenarios as pertaining to a relatively calm school, well set up for its task of teaching and well disposed to interact with the student and the family. In other words, the reflection proposed here presupposes, on the one hand, a school that acts as one would expect a psychoanalyst or a "good enough mother" (Winnicott, 1999) to act, that is, a school in which fantasies, defense mechanisms, and attack do not start in the first place. On the other hand, it is presupposed that the institution has the psychological resources to manage and overcome conflicts. However, just like an analyst or a mother (or any caregiver), the school is not assumed here to be immune to problems, be they caused directly by its own fantasies or triggered by countertransferential[1] reactions intensified to the point of hindering a relationship based on mutual recognition.

In this chapter, therefore, we deal with the reaction of the school to some of these scenarios. We wish to describe some of the psychological dynamics usually found in the family in its relationship with the school, and to elucidate some of the supposed effects of such dynamics on the school itself. We also seek to point out some appropriate technical or clinical management for the proposed scenarios. In so doing, a second meaning is given to the metaphor of the school seen as a psychoanalyst or a "good enough mother."

THE CHILD IN THE SCHOOL

To parents, a child is not just another human being, but, in a sense, an extension of their own selves, a catalyst for the experiences which they had as a child or as a student. The unfulfilled promises of our childhood are strongly re-awakened to give life to the dreams we have about the future of our children ("he will have everything I didn't have," "he will not have to go through what I went through"). Through the future that the child has, it seems possible to reshape his or her own life story to the extent that we define what we offer and with what we expect of the child. This is the unconscious fantasy that regulates parenthood, for good or ill. This desire, which we communicate through our care and affection, is one of the most powerful mechanisms in the development of the child. Through this, the child can hold on to people and objects and explore them, becomes capable of moving towards others and, therefore, of constituting as a person. On the other hand, it is this desire that shapes the conditions imposed on the child, including parental fantasies about the child and the path s/he ought to follow. By the time we are born, our parents have already imagined not only the color of our eyes, but our profession, our loves, our adventures, our capabilities, and our limitations. To a great extent, parents will relate to their child from this imaginary script.

Going to school, therefore, is a fundamental experience of separation for the child; his psyche is challenged by "being in the world" on his own, without the mental and emotional support offered by the psyche of the mother or father (or other caregiver). Additionally, his psyche finds other desires and fantasies circulating, and he experiences occupying a place in the web of relationships among these psyches. But most of all, the child's start at school is an important experience for the parents, who have to adapt to a well-established organization no matter whether it matches their fantasies or not.

Sooner or later, these parents need to understand that their son or daughter cannot have their care at all times, forever, in part because of the immediate demands the world of work imposes on the parents and in part because parents realize that the needs of their children will be better served at another institution.

Hence, a first step towards a relationship between school and family is taken when the parents realize that the task of educating their child is not totally within their capacity and must be shared with another institution. The way this understanding is arrived at and takes shape within the family will certainly denote the real contact between these institutions and will define the kind of approach the family adopts. There are many starting points, and it is important to bear in mind that the many considerations that go into to defining the "right time" for the child to go to school are rational constructions beneath which powerful unconscious forces are at play. To anticipate or postpone the moment of beginning, to explain the child's crying or lack of crying, or the mother's insistence on waiting at the school when, after the first few days of classes, the professionals are encouraging parents to leave the environment, are just a few examples. So, standard remarks such as "I need to leave my child at school because I have to work," or "I have to take my child to school because it's time," or "my child won't stay without me," or even "it's not worth leaving school for so short a time if I have to come back soon to fetch my child," contain many dynamics that need to be heard differently by the school. Many objective elements of life concerning what we want rationally and consciously for our children's futures as well as unconscious aspects stemming from our own childhood experiences and the place our children occupy in the web of our lives are synthesized in these common everyday expressions.

The image the family has of the school is also infused with desires and fears in advance of the child's physical presence in the school. It is clear, however, that this image tends to be rebuilt following the child's entry into school and in the course of participating in educational activities. Consequently, concrete experiences and the data of reality result in impacting on family fantasies concerning the school and in compounding with these fantasies to create new impressions about the care the school devotes to their child.

But it is always necessary to highlight certain points that the school must not forget if it is aiming to build a relationship with the family for the benefit of the student/child. First, the task of educating is grounded in the fantasies and fears already mentioned. Second, these impressions, these fantasies, and these fears, produce different requests and demands that the family brings to the school. In the end, the way the school listens to such requests and demands cannot be just administrative or prescriptive. It is not enough to listen to parental requests and to merely try to decide what can or cannot be done, or worse, whether this is the school's job or the responsibility of the parents.

First Feature: *"Excessive Presence"*

Although nowadays the school's biggest complaint about the family is the absence of parents in the school, we propose to start with the feature of excessive presence. The excessive presence is not surprising in schools for very young children, given the fact that the parents are supposed to be more insecure regarding the right time to send their child to school, to leave him or her there, and regarding the effects of that initiative. However, this excessive presence is often a warning sign when persistent in older children's parents. Generally, this "excess" takes the form of visits or frequent phone calls, questions, requests for guidance, and, in many cases, information about how to proceed "correctly" in relation to the child in different situations. Such families, however, fall into two types: (1) families who appear to want to conform to the structure and culture of the school and (2) families who, subtly but repeatedly, try to make the school conform to the ways of the family. At first, it is common for the school not to bother about this, especially when the parents are of the first type.

In both cases, parents are helpful and attentive to any call the school gives. They tend to accept and accommodate all the institution's characteristics, often uncritically, seeking to avoid any tension. The second type of parents, although they are also kind to the school, little by little build a relationship that leads the school to do whatever is asked by the parents. And it seems the only sensible option. In both cases, there is an initial sympathy. These are parents who adhere to the institutional project, respect what the professionals say, and therefore tend to mobilize important narcissistic elements in teachers and administrators. It is therefore common for the school to perceive these parents initially as a model to which all others should aspire. Where the complementary nature of this tendency of parents and the narcissism of members of the school is kept up, the school will face its first serious problem, namely that of reacting unconsciously, in countertransference, according to their overwhelming omnipotent fantasies, their desire to know everything, instead of in terms of establishing a healthy relationship with parents. The relationship in which one institution apparently "completes" the other is marked by fantasies of omnipotence and of fusion in which "I'm really the greatest" and "all parents who are not completely aligned with me are wrong." There is the risk of the school becoming excessively indulgent and permissive with these parents who adhere to these fantasies, while being extremely intolerant and severe with the others. As we shall see, the intolerance and severity directed to other parents in this case can be a reaction to finding "I'm really the greatest" is no more than a fantasy. They are also a reaction to these same "over-present" parents but displaced and projected onto the "other parents."

The first situation is a fairly familiar scenario, which points out the difficulty we have in accepting our incompleteness and our limitations, and, furthermore, our difficulty in accepting those who challenge us about them. The second situation occurs because, in general, the initial seduction contains a nameless, but nonetheless present, malaise: the professionals agree to satisfy the expectations of parents, even though doing so goes against some of their own convictions. The school personnel consequently feel subjugated to parental demands and gradually they come to feel annihilated within the relationship.

If the school does not recognize these processes, it will continue to divide the parents into "good" and "bad." The parents who apparently complete the school are seen as "good," but in order to keep this image they are supposed to keep the school image of perfection, ignoring some of its features, that is, ignoring parts of the real and existing institution. Any complaint or demand may collapse this idealized relationship.

That is why the "honeymoon" between the "good parents" and the school may come to an early end as parents tend, little by little, to harass or irritate teachers, coordinators, and directors. The trouble comes primarily with parents of the second kind. They will seek out the professional at any time and any place, initially just hinting at their recommendations on how to deal with their child but progressively wanting to define what the school should or should not do, giving precise instructions on how their child should be treated, cared for, and handled. This input by the parents has been present since the beginning, but it is often fragmented, making it impossible to detect. After a time, however, the personnel begin to aggressively respond to the unconscious perception relating to this input and to the risk of being annihilated by the parental demands.

Concerning the "good" parents of the first type, harassment and irritation will also be noted after a time. And the reason is much the same: it concerns the situation in which the presence of the one inevitably undermines the position of the other. However, in this instance, the parents put the professionals in a position of subjugating and not of being subjugated. In a way, we can say that the school is put in a situation of "aggressor" as if trying to undermine the parents. Although our putative ideal school has done nothing specific for this blemish to appear in the relationship, it easily occupies this place by responding with irritation to this scenario of submission. We can say, in psychoanalytic terms, that projective identification processes are in operation on the part of the parents towards the school and its staff. This concept was originally enunciated by Klein (1946) as something inherent in a mother-baby relationship. It would be noted when the baby deposits his or her anxieties and fears related to survival into the mother, making her feel what the baby feels. This concept was deepened and expanded in particular by Bion (2000b), who puts it in the terms used here. We are speaking of the mechanism through which the subject forces his or her own anxieties, fears, feelings, parts of the self *into* the other's psyche, in order to make this other react in accordance with these feelings. In this sense, it is, notwithstanding, a violent and unconscious mechanism of control. Unconsciously, the "psyche of the school" tends to react violently and with annoyance to this, thereby fulfilling a script as the aggressor that invalidates parents who seek at all times to follow the recommendations of the school. The "excessive presence" of both types of parents may suggest that anxieties and fantasies concerning separation are very powerful, especially when it comes to letting the child go to school.

According to Bick (1964, 1968), "being in pieces" is our earliest experience and we have a basic need for integration, which can only be achieved through physical contact with the caregiver, as well as through care and affection. This contact is responsible for a gradual sense of integration and the progressive ability to hold on to our scattered parts. It is this sense of integration that allows, little by little, and simultaneously, a sense of "I" to be formed and the care and affection offered by someone else (the caregiver) to be introjected.

Through this process, the subject gains important aspects of personality. One is the capacity to see self both as unified with and as distinct from others and, at the same time, to see others as units distinct from himself. Another is the ability to recognize dependence on the caregiver and a gradual move toward independence, in that the child develops internally those same attributes that were initially offered by the parent. By successfully mastering these periods of development the subject will be able to "be with the other" or even to "separate from the other," without there being any threat to psychic integrity.

For Bick, only when the boundary is achieved, is the early ego supposed to develop its capacity to introject. In Bick's words:

> This internal function of containing the parts of the self is dependent initially on the introjection of an external object experienced as capable of fulfilling this function. . . . Until the containing functions have been introjected, the concept of space within the self cannot arise. Introjection, i.e., construction of an object in an internal space, is therefore impaired.
>
> . . . Disturbance in the primal skin function can lead to a development of a "second skin" formation through which dependence on the object is replaced

> by a pseudo-independence, by the inappropriate use of certain mental functions. (Bick. 1968, p. 484)

Hence, the first object relation is a passive experience and is the one that will bring the sense of integration from outside. Although the infant is incapable of striving for this experience, she or he will benefit as it is a means for development of the ego (Briggs, 2002).

The problem is that things do not always run smoothly. Failures in reception of this sense of unintegration could lead, according to the author, to the development of pseudo-independent personalities. They seek, in mimicry and imitation of the surface qualities of the other, a replacement for what Bion (2004) called the ability to "learn from experience." Bick (1968) gave the name "adhesive personality" to the psychological result of this process. Making use of Bick's work, we can draw a parallel between the attempt to achieve total identity between the care offered to children at home and at school and the strategies of imitation mentioned by Bick.

As mentioned, this is quite a common feature, particularly in schools for young children, and is even expected with first-time parents. But what to say and what to do when this relationship with the school continues into the later stages of student life? How do we understand and manage the irritation, which, in psychoanalytical terms, we can call countertransference, caused by the difficulties of parents who cannot easily separate from their children?

It is clearly necessary to take account of the discontinuity between the separate ambiences of home and school. If parents make an effort to annihilate this discontinuity in fantasy, so that the separation between the "I" (parents) and "other" (school) does not exist, the school has to build space for the discontinuity to be demarcated. However, it must be borne in mind that such demarcation should not be done on impulse because of the greater or lesser degree of irritation caused to the institution. It is important that the school be able to anticipate the dynamics that mobilize their impulsive reactions and to think of responses and actions to communicate that the institution recognizes the existence and dependence of the other, and, above all, listens to and welcomes their existence "as it is." At the same time, it is necessary to make clear that listening, acceptance, and recognition are actions that come from an institution with resources and tools distinct from those of the family. This difference is manifest not only on the level of the specific task itself within the institution, but also on a psychic level, since the student does not represent for teachers the same thing that the child represents for parents.

Confronted with parents who "just say yes" to the school, or parents who expect the school will "just say yes" to them, the school must deliberately be a "dissenting voice" that offers the chance for diverse thinking to be considered and which encourages parents to try something different. It is the school that has the responsibility for expanding the "mental space" in which new thoughts can be accepted by parents. With "submissive parents" who wait to hear from the school "what is the right thing to do," the school might, for example, use an approach in which the concept "what you, the parent, would do" can be communicated. It is not productive for the family or the student if the school either responds promptly about what to do, or flatly refuses to offer a structured response. On the other hand, for parents who, either clandestinely or openly, seek the school's submission, their attempts to make this happen have to find room for reverberation and problematization. In general, if the school merely opposes or refuses a suggestion from the parents, it is taken by them as confrontational and not as the normal school search for pedagogical coherence. Consequently, it is necessary for openings to be created in which "thinking it over" is possible, particularly when this reflection can be supported from experiences the child is having in school, which can bring new elements into consideration.

This should take the form of a contrast, not a confrontation. The contrast between "selves" is a measure of difference. Handled properly by the school, this also presents the possibility of introjection of qualities of the "other," thereby preventing intrusion by the experience of that "other." Recognizing that the school does not depend on the submission of the "other," neither become hostile in the face of disagreement, parents can try out new, more autonomous approaches in relation to broader school issues, and, in all probability, in relation to their own child. The school must gamble on this as it also means gambling on the possibility that the child will gradually find greater mental space from the parents' minds to accommodate the differences that she or he will show in relation to them. When the school does not recognize this scenario, there is a huge risk of reactively becoming intrusive. To put it another way, if it is necessary for someone to die for another to live, I will destroy in order not to be destroyed.

Second Feature: The Permanent Complaint

Some families are characterized by a permanent complaint in relation to school. Evidently, leaving aside the possibility of an appropriate complaint concerning negligence, indisposition, or even constant hostility from the school towards some student or groups of students, there are families in which one or more members always have something with which to charge the institution. These complaints are explained either as relating to certain teachers or as accusations against the school. To these parents, there is always something lacking, some error to be made good, although this attitude bears no direct relationship to how well or poorly the child is doing in school. It seems these parents have doubts as to the reliability of the school, regardless of whether this or that is done, and this can be seen, in terms more appropriate to psychoanalysis, as doubts about how "loving" those in authority are. Unlike the parents of the second type, discussed above, in which the attitude seems often to be inclusive and seeking harmony, here there is no attempt to adjust to the school's methods and actions. They complain about the school and object to its policies and practices.

But thinking of the scenario of a welcoming, favorable institution, these parents tend to trigger precisely what they want to avoid: alienation, indifference, at times even hostility. It is difficult for the school to remain consistently calm in the face of such complaints. In such cases, the question "what is missing?" might help.

It is common for all humans to dwell on the fantasy of not having been loved enough. How many of us remember episodes from childhood when, having been told off by a parent, we came to the conclusion that we were not loved and were not wanted in the family? On becoming parents or caregivers, this fantasy often returns in the form of anxiety about our ability to love our children. When this happens, it is to be expected that the "unloving" or "unreliable" parts of the parents, whether or not this is fantasy, will be projected onto the institution. This turns the question about what is lacking into the following equation: "Love is lacking" and "it is the 'other' who does not love." But this is not all. Although such projective processes[2] are in operation, the original fantasy about not being loved is still alive. And in relation to it, the question: "what is missing?" remains, with another equation: "Love is lacking"; but the "love that is lacking is what I did not have, that maybe I have not given to my child, and that my child might get at school."

That is, on the one hand, projective processes impose on the school the "lack of love" that comprises the parents' fantasies regarding themselves. On the other hand, on the part of the parents there are processes of identification concerning the child "not sufficiently loved by the family," which tend to provoke envy of "the love the child receives from the school." In this case, it is impossible to treat the parents' complaints regarding the school in strict terms, because the "lack of love" on the part of the institution towards the parents stems from the fact that the school is not aimed at meeting the needs of the parents as much as it is at meeting those of the students.

These mechanisms may appear more or less frequently in a family. They also appear in different degrees: complaints may be more or less mild and subtle, or more or less overt and even violent. In the latter case the complaint may be associated not only with jealousy concerning what the parents feel about what the child receives at school, but also with the persecutory fantasies about the risk of losing their child to the "loving" institution.

Severe and traumatic experiences lived through by loving and caring parents can trigger and augment these fantasies. Among parents who survived experiences of neglect and actual abandonment, for example, in situations of social exclusion or humiliation, this reaction can be quite common.

The concept of trauma is traditionally dear to psychoanalysis and can have many meanings. For this discussion, a useful interpretation conceives of trauma not only as an excessively intense experience of great impact but also as the reproduction of times that gave rise to great anxiety. Trauma is not only the presence of an aggressive external agent that imposes a deep rupture on the psychic stability of the subject, or puts into conflict their natural tendencies of self-preservation and aggression (wanting to make peace with the aggressor, as if responsibility for the attack lay with the victim *versus* wanting to kill or annihilate the aggressor). The absence of structuring elements of the personality or something that is missing also becomes traumatic: the lack of care, an absent mother, an absent father, lack of a good breast, in terms used by Klein (1975). In this model, what is real is the non-object, because the non-existence takes the place of reality. It is important to note that in this case, it is possible to imagine that the absence of something good might be more harmful than the presence of something bad, which we can come into contact with and rebel against. The psyche can react to this, but not to what was not given.

Ferenczi (1955) and Borgogno (2004) add to trauma a dimension of omission of support for the developing mind. Here, the traumatic event is the absence of some other significant and important person effectively capable of legitimizing the perception the subject has of the aggression suffered. Once more, it is evidenced as development within absence. This absence becomes present, either in the void left by others who should be the container to such an unbearable and not processable burden, or in the violence that the lack of recognition of pain represents. It is at some level what social exclusion and social humiliation are about.

The individual who is born into socially excluding processes is denied any effective recourse in the process of psychic development and growth. That individual is forced to occupy a place that does not exist for the other. In not existing, no links are triggered and, consequently, experiences of *social reverie* (Archangelo 2010) are practically absent. From this non-place, there seems to be no choice for the subject but to withdraw or to act out violently as "if to be recognized as a legitimate contained." In doing either one or the other, one ends up entangled in both neglect and intrusion, from which shame and humiliation arise.

The concept of *social reverie* is born from Bion's concept of reverie (2000a), which deals with the mother's ability to support and give meaning to the anxieties and fears the infant finds intolerable and meaningless. It is an ideological choice—as Borgogno (2004) points out—concerning the importance of the environment to psychic birth and development. However, differently from Borgogno's idea, social reverie refers to an environment that is broader than the family. It regards the social group to which the one belongs and within which he/she has to find several opportunities to "be with" (as

Bick, 1968, says), to have meaningful relationships and symbolically "inhabit the other's mind." This means that the one—be it child or adult—has to testify to somebody being fulfilled by his/her presence and being positively challenged by his/her autonomous existence. That is to say, this testimony would be an enriching and structuring experience of existence.

We all know that familial suffering is not only for those who are poor or socially excluded. However, among the latter, the lack of social opportunities may prevent them from having good enough experiences in contexts outside the family.

A "good enough" social environment opens up several possible relationships. These relationships are not supposed to be a fortuitous combination of circumstances, but a result of public policies aimed at reaching different needs that come from different social groups. From this perspective, professionals in charge of health or other facilities are not there "by chance": there is a purpose, there are attempts to know and to understand what each group or person needs and how to offer what is best for them. The "other" is a person who intentionally makes use of his/her mind to grasp what is going on and what one's needs are. These are not necessarily clearly given at first: if a patient goes to a doctor, for example, she or he may complain about a pain, but there have to be different levels of communication for the doctor to make a diagnosis. The doctor does not have to be perfect or to know what is going on. It is the shared search that is meaningful as the doctor shares his or her mental capacities with the person "in need" with the aim of finding what is important for both. Different "others" offer different possibilities for getting to know different mental capacities, different mistakes, different levels of comprehension and emotional contact. The recognition involved in this process is what makes the experience of becoming part of the human group possible.

Social exclusion prevents the person from having meaningful people to relate to. There are people around, but they are not concerned with the "being of flesh and blood" before them. It is as if they were there by chance, with no interest at all. Keeping with the example given above, in social exclusion contexts, the doctor prescribes a pill and sends the person back home, no matter how much pain the person is in and what this pain means—physically and emotionally. The doctor's main purpose is to get rid of the patient. When there is social inclusion, health care, leisure, security system, schools, and other educational institutions are all aimed at offering real and meaningful relationships. It can be said that the discontinuity between one's needs and the social services apparatus is only to the same and inevitable level that is present in all relationships, but without jeopardizing the match between them.

The effects of what is described above on parents who have suffered the violence of absence and lack of support are many. It is not surprising that they hope this help will come from the nearest institution. Similarly, it is not unusual that they envy the attention given to the child. However, even while envying, it is possible that, in an ambivalent way, they also fear that, in its place, there is the constant risk of something traumatic and catastrophic to come, such as they have experienced in the past.

Arising from these different developments are several approaches from parents who constantly complain to the school. They may demand that something be offered to them or their children. At the same time, and paradoxically, they may unconsciously lay claim to what they perceive the school is offering to the child. In such cases, what is offered to the child is often perceived as indifference to them, the parents. They also constantly complain about the school because they fear that nothing will come about, like the absence already experienced. Or, again, they may complain out of fear that what is offered is something bad, like their accumulated traumatic experiences, that is, something malevolent.

The school's approach towards these parents requires, first, that it seeks to identify where, when, and how it responds evasively and/or with hostility to the confrontational attitudes of parents toward the school's initiatives. Although it may seem justifiable to the eyes of the injured professionals who "do everything for the student" and "only get complaints in return," the school's indifference and hostility repeat the parents' experiences of absence and of the presence of an aggressor exacerbating the difficulties of the parents in approaching the school. Another point with which the school should concern itself in the case of these parents is to be constant and consistent, so that the fragile bond already contaminated with distrust is not allowed to be further diminished and may actually be improved. Small and unimportant changes or discontinuities, such as postponing a meeting or leaving a parent waiting on the telephone can greatly upset these parents and can therefore be disastrous for their relationship with the school. If the school complains about the parents as a payback for their complaints, it has to be prepared for a devastating effect on the relation between school and the parents. As Borgogno (2011) commented with regard to his patients, a subject in a helpless situation speedily comes to identify with the parties most harmful of the personality of the others, even though they are, relatively speaking, far less active than the constructive parties, and far less intense and extensive.

Hence, the school must be able to fulfill what we have called *social reverie*. As a social facility, the school must represent a positive presence of "the social" and identify and welcome small, imperceptible, suspicions, and any ambivalent signs of respect and recognition these parents give. As well as this, it is necessary to "dream" some of the needs of these parents and to anticipate and legitimize them to provide an experience in which the parents meet, on the part of the institution, "a containing mind" for the fears that make their anxiety intolerable.

Third Feature: Parents Identified with the Aggressor

Yet more complex is the situation in which the victims of lack of support identify with the aggressor. If we bear in mind that most of the time the violence preceding the lack of support comes from an emotionally significant "other," we must consider how painful it would be for the victim to hate or reject the aggressor. One of the psychological outcomes of this dilemma is "identification with the aggressor"—a concept first developed by Ferenczi (1955) and further explored by Anna Freud (1993) and by contemporary psychoanalysts, such as Borgogno (2001). Through it, the dilemma between loving and hating the aggressor is resolved by the suppression, on the conscious level, of the aggression suffered and by the victims assuming the place of the aggressor.

In cases where neglected and traumatized parents identify with the aggressor and turn themselves into negligent, traumatizing parents, deeper difficulties are added to the ones described above, likely creating difficulties with the students themselves. The children, once neglected and deprived of loving primary care, tend to perform at the school in a more agitated way or show the delinquency characteristics typically associated with deprivation, as described by Winnicott (1990). This student profile, in its turn, causes the school to turn more quickly to strict disciplinary measures at the expense of proper educational procedures. In these cases, the school is, at best, very ambivalent about the student: while it still wants to help, there is already a sense of resentment towards the child and, often, a considerable amount of hostility has been noted, not only with regard to the parents, as discussed earlier, but also towards the child/student. At this point, it is common for fantasies about the parents not having sufficient love for the child to come into play again. The parents feel a lot of guilt, conscious and unconscious. It is as if the parents intuitively understand that the disciplinary measures were also doomed to failure as the problems would not be the school's fault but a result of their mistakes. Often, before eventual failure, the parents start fighting with the school, making demands and even threatening the institution. They react unconsciously to the possibility of being trapped by the school, or other organs triggered by the institution, concerning what is happening with the child. If this tension between school and parents is not well handled, it can eventually lead, on the part of the school, to very vindictive measures towards the child within the school, as well as external measures, without, in fact, having exhausted the possibilities of intervention aimed at both the child and parents.

In fact, when confronting the school, these parents tell us of two processes that are at work. The first is the fantasy that any and all contact with the school regarding these parents will be about what they "did not or could not do." In other words, these parents no longer expect the institution to offer them a friendly (or loving) approach, as, perhaps, they have not expected this of any other person or institution. The second process involves the fantasies concerning how "spoiled" and "damaged" their child is, and how vulnerable the parents feel when faced with possible allegations about something bad they have done to their child. In all of the situations described here, the challenge for the school is to slowly reverse the constant expectation of disaster. For this reason, it must put up with many ups and downs and many attacks it may regard as unfair.

If the school is not thoroughly prepared, it will tend to retaliate against the parents with an aggressive approach to the student, who is the weakest available link. The school runs the serious risk of reacting contratransferentially, either through neglect and absence, or by way of revenge. In either of these situations, the school will cause these parents to relive their traumatic catastrophe, often resulting in a final breakdown of relations with these parents, but, above all, with the children.

However, when the handling of the situation does not seem catastrophic (in other words, does not repeat the neglect, aggression, or absence), the setbacks should not be seen as going back to square one but as part of a slow building of links. In this process, trust in the love of another is established on unstable basis and is constantly checked, and re-evaluation takes place at every new modest step. At the setback, there are certainly psychic forces which recall the persecutory anxieties that amplify the mutual distrust. That is why the school is apt to be discouraged and question whether the effort is worthwhile. But such anxieties are not without a balance: there are also forces that believe it is possible to forge a new relationship with the school and its professionals. When well received, these parents will take a step back in time and space as required to take stock of the welcoming presence as compared to the aggression and violence characteristic of earlier traumatic experiences.

If the school can achieve good contact with parents in situations that are neither stressed nor fraught with a sense of urgency, it can also provide a model of relationships for the parents, which will enable them to enjoy good, relatively stable relational experiences. This not only improves future communication and contact but also, in particular, acts as a "second education" for those parents who had difficulties in their emotional development and bear elements of the suffering of the children in need they once were. The school may see this as a step too far: not only to care for the emotional problems of the students but also of their parents. However, in many cases just a little judicious care that does not involve any serious tension or drastic measures in relation to the child or his behavior is enough. A noticeable change can be seen in the parents' relationship with the school, and, perhaps with their own child, when freer and more relaxed listening to the parents or real pedagogical and instructive conversations take place. Although this is not the only answer and conflict management will continue to be required in the school day-to-day, the child and everyone involved with him or her will often benefit from this broader approach to education. In some cases, as mentioned above, a special understanding of conflict and emotional aspects at play allows a reasonable anticipation of the likely effects of certain interactive measures, expanding the possibilities not only in relation to the parents but also to the child's education.

FINAL CONSIDERATIONS

School is an institution which, from its beginnings, evokes profound contradictions - admiration and revolt, love and hate. Admiration for the things it may offer. Revolt for the things it cannot offer, either because of its specific nature or because of the intrinsic impossibility of adapting to the fantasies of each of its members and clients. Both in admiration and revolt, rapport between family and school depends on overcoming the gaps between the expectations created, consciously and unconsciously, on both sides, and the data that reality requires.

One of the aspects of creating distance from the family in relation to school is the deprivation of a sense of belonging. This deprivation can impede processes of identification through which relations between people and between people and institutions are made possible. Any relationship has as its starting point the capacity of at least one of the parties, to recognize part of himself in the other, or vice versa.

This is equally true when we are talking about school-family relationships; the latter needs to be recognized in some manner by the institution. Given the difficulty caused by the deprivation of a sense of belonging, identification tends to give rise to estrangement. Although children and young people attend school, in many cases, they and their families can feel like aliens there.

The relationship between school and parents, therefore, needs to consider how the school operates, always with a view to reducing any tensions present. Three maxims should be kept in our hearts and minds when thinking about the relationship between school and parents and/or about the actions of the school jointly with or for the family:

1. The significance of the school for parents goes beyond the limits of its functions and purposes as explicitly outlined, and is accompanied by representations and conscious and unconscious fantasies through which the family relates to the school.

2. Whatever this meaning is, it comes loaded with positive and/or negative emotions, which can derive from admiration, but also from envy and anger.
3. The relationship between school and family begins under the sign of estrangement, but this can be overcome if the school is aware of this element and is prepared to deal with it. The school's disposition will certainly influence the concrete forms of life for the school as an institution and for the individuals within it.

NOTES

1. Countertransference refers to a set of unconscious reactions of the analyst towards the patient, particularly towards the patient's transference. According to Hinshelwood (1991, p. 255), "Countertransference underwent a remarkable metamorphosis. Heimann, in the 1950s, emphasized the human side of the patient/analyst transaction, pointing out that '. . . comparing the feelings roused in himself with the content of the patient's associations and the qualities of his mood and behavior, the analyst has the means for checking whether he has understood or failed to understand his patient.'" (Heimann, 1960)

2. In a broad sense, projection is the process through which the subject gets rid of some of his or her own emotions—usually the unwelcome ones—by depositing them onto another and perceiving them as the other's state. This operation is mostly unconscious and tends to temporarily alleviate the subject's anxiety.

REFERENCES

Archangelo, A. (2010). Social exclusion, difficulties with learning and symbol formation: A Bionian approach. *Psychoanalysis, Culture and Society, 15*, 315–327.

Bick, E. (1964). Notes on infant observation in psycho-analytic training. *International Journal of Psycho-Analysis, 45*, 558–566.

Bick, E. (1968). The experience of the skin in early object relations. *International Journal of Psycho-Analysis, 49*, 484–486.

Bion, W. R. (2000a). Attacks on linking [1959]. In: E. B. Spillius, *Melanie Klein Today: developments in theory and practice. Volume I: Mainly practice.* (1st ed., Vol. 1, pp. 87–101). London: Routledge.

Bion, W. R. (2000b). A theory of thinking [1962]. In: E. B. Spillius, *Melanie Klein Today: developments in theory and practice.Volume I: Mainly practice.* (1st ed., Vol. 1, pp. 178-186). London: Routledge.

Bion, W. R. (2004). *Learning from experience*. USA: Jason Aronson.

Borgogno, F. (2001). La "lunga onda" della catastrofe e le "condizioni" del cambiamento psichico nel pensiero clinico de S. Ferenczi. In: F. Borgogno, & C. Bonomi, *La catastrofe e i suoi simboli* (1a ed., pp. 171–186). Torino, Italia: UTET.

Borgogno, F. (2004). "Spoilt children." L'intrusione e l'estrazione parentale come fatores di distruttività. In: F. Borgogno, *Psicoanalisi come percorso* (2a ed., pp. 90–115). Torino, Italia: Bollati Boringhieri.

Borgogno, F. (2007). *The Vancouver interview: frammenti di vita e opere d'una vocazione psicoanalitica* (1a ed., Vol. 1). Roma, Italia: Borla.

Borgogno, F. (2011). Diventare una persona: l'importanza della risposta affettiva dell'analista a una paziente schizoide e ai suoi sogni. In: F. Borgogno, *La signorina che faceva Hara Kiri e altri saggi* (1a ed., pp. 21–45). Torino, Italia: Bollati Boringhieri.

Briggs, A. (2002). *Surviving space: papers on infant observation.* London, UK: Karnac.

Ferenczi, S. (1955). Some thoughts on trauma [1934]. In: S. Ferenczi, & M. Balint (Ed.), *Final contributions to the problems and methods of psychoanalysis.* New York: Basic Books.
Freud, A. (1993). *The ego and the mechanisms of defence [1936].* London: Karnac.
Heimann, P. (1960). Counter-transference. *Br. J. Med. Psychol., 33,* 9–15.
Hinshelwood, R. D. (1991). *A dictionary of kleinian thought* (2a ed.). London, UK: Aronson.
Klein, M. (1946). Notes on some schizoid mechanisms. In: M. Klein, *The writings of Melanie Klein* (Vol. 3, pp. 1–24). London: Hogarth.
Klein, M. (1975). *Envy and gratitude and other works* (Vol. 3). New York, USA: Free Press.
Winnicott, D. W. (1990). *Deprivations and delinquency.* (C. Winnicott, R. Shepherd, & M. Davis, Eds.) London, UK: Routledge.
Winnicott, D. W. (1999). *Playing and reality* (7a ed.). London, UK: Routledge.

Chapter Eleven

Integrative Role of Psychodynamic Principles in an Interdisciplinary Elementary School

Leon Hoffman, Carrie Catapano, and Katy Meyer

West End Day School provides an unusual elementary school environment in that the collaboration among the staff, parents, and children provides an exceptional experience for the children who attend. The basic mission of the school was developed in 1917 when the program was the "Godmothers' League," a non-sectarian day and night shelter. It was a place to support children and their families in the Upper West Side of New York City. As foster homes became more widespread, the need for nursery programs declined.

In 1956, a day treatment center and school (Children's Day Treatment Center) for emotionally disturbed young children was founded as a joint project between the Godmother's League and Mount Sinai Hospital (LaVietes, et al., 1960). In the center, psychiatric treatment of the children and their parents were combined with a therapeutic school program. The original program attempted to serve both what were described as autistic children as well as other children with less severe emotional disorders.

Over time, the program evolved from a psychiatrically-focused center to a therapeutic educational program for bright students with good potential who were not being well served in a traditional school setting. There was a need for a school that was therapeutic but could academically support students who are uneven learners. In 1984, West End Day School was developed. West End Day School was created to teach these uneven learners how to develop their own strengths, overcome obstacles at their own pace, understand their learning style, pay attention to what others are asking them, and form positive relationships.

A psychodynamic developmental approach unifies the diagnostic and therapeutic work with the children and their families. The diagnostic approach which was developed is in-depth and multimodal in which a variety of functions are considered and evaluated in order to develop a comprehensive plan to work with the parents and children. Several facets are stressed.

Most importantly, this approach recognizes the importance of understanding how parents feel when they bring their child to a psychiatrist, psychologist, social worker, psychoanalyst, or any other person who is going to help parents understand the nature of their children's problems. Mental health professionals have to be fully aware that parents may be frightened, anxious, puzzled; they may not even know what questions to ask, especially if they are worried or if it is their first contact with a professional. As way to deal with their difficult, at times turbulent, emotions, parents use a variety of defensive responses, some adaptive and socially appropriate and some maladaptive and difficult to work with.

In order to engage parents as partners in the therapeutic work with their children, we try to ascertain their ideas about their children's symptoms: the major areas in their children's lives that are worrisome to them, the impact of their children's symptoms on their families, and how family interactions affect the children.

We also try to understand how the parents view their children's perceptions of the problems. In this way, parents begin to understand how children communicate—that most children do not always express their problems directly because unlike adults, most children don't complain directly. In young children the nature of their games and play activities can provide clues as to what is on their mind; for example, a young child may play out a scene of family discord. Some children who are very anxious and/or worried will complain about the worries or describe difficult sleep patterns. Children who are depressed may very well say that they feel very sad. Children who express their problems through activity and oppositional behavior will usually not subjectively feel as if they have problems.

Since social development is such an important part of childhood, it is crucial to understand how children interact with people around them: with their parents, siblings, relatives, other children, other significant adults; as well as, how others interact with them. In other words, a central part of our work entails trying to understand how the children's social development has proceeded in order to develop a plan to improve their socialization capacities.

Finally, the children's skills are evaluated: sensory, motor, and cognitive development. This evaluation includes understanding the nature of the child's responses to sensory stimuli (appropriate, under-reactive, over-reactive); fine motor and gross motor development; language development (receptive, expressive, and processing abilities); memory; fund of knowledge;

ability to understand social situations; and academic achievement. Has the child's development proceeded smoothly or unevenly?

In addition to understanding the nature of the child's skill level, we try to understand the child's social and emotional development in order to arrive at both a descriptive (DSM) and dynamic diagnosis. In broad terms we ask the following questions:

a. Does the problem concern mainly the *child's feelings* (is it mainly depression or anxiety)?
b. Is the problem related mainly to the child's sensory, motor, and/or cognitive (including language) *development* with emotional reactions secondary to those problems?
c. Is the problem mainly what's called an "externalizing" kind of problem? In other words, does the child express his problems primarily through *action* rather than through expressing subjective distressful feelings, particularly with words? We are always aware that there is a psychological meaning behind a child's behavior.
d. Is there a problem with the child's ability to differentiate his or her *fantasy life* from the rest of his experience?
e. Does the child experience a *conflict* within him or herself or does he or she only feel a conflict with other people?
f. What is the nature of the child's *defenses?* To what extent are they adaptive and to what extent, maladaptive?
g. Is there a *mixture* that is hard to tease apart?
h. How do the child's problems *impact* on and interact with the family's feelings and functions?
i. Are cognitive and learning problems secondary to *emotional* issues?

In sum, we understand that there are always interactions between executive functions, such as attention, planning, organizations, and delay of gratification with emotional states.

It is crucial to remember that a diagnostic assessment is always a "work in progress." As treatment evolves, one always needs to be sensitive and allow for modifications and changes in direction.

THE VOICE OF A FIRST-GRADER

Here is a real first-grader during his first year at West End Day—in his words:

> I didn't have any problems until kindergarten. But when I first started kindergarten, my teachers didn't understand me at all. There was no teaching for me there. I just could not learn because I felt worried, I ran around a lot, and

> moved all the time. The teachers were very strict. Most of the time I would get time-outs and I sat in the hallway. I was sent home often. That was my old school. They didn't give me any chances like I now have at West End Day School.
>
> How did I get to West End Day School? I have no idea. My mom found it. I'm just so happy she did. Here, everybody is really nice including the custodians. At my old school, not so much. I was a bit scared when I first came here last year. But once I met some of the grown-ups, I became more relaxed. I met Ms. D, and she told me that she would be my special grown-up who could help me deal with my feelings. Ms. D can really handle feelings. I'm still trying to get to know her pretty well. Last year, I was still adjusting to West End Day School. I still felt upset and angry about what I had to go through at my previous school. I realize now that I wasn't ready to be a student, I still wanted to play.
>
> Here at West End Day, I can take breaks when I need them. Mostly what helped is that I feel comfortable. Now I do most of my work and even have special jobs to do. It's so much easier to learn when I don't have to think about my worries all of the time.

Why is there such a contrast between this child's old school and West End Day?

- We listened to this student in order to try to understand why he was nervous and worried.
- We recognized that his behavior problems were a result of his worries and anxieties.
- We understood that the child needed to play, which eased him into to being a better group learner.
- We talked about his feelings about his previous school (they did not go away easily).
- We emphasized the importance of making choices for himself. With this child, taking planned breaks was a decision we came to together.
- We provided an outlet where this student could express himself, offered planned breaks, and provided a comfortable and safe learning environment—all of which led to successful learning.

A crucial aspect of the approach at West Day School involves the idea that trying to understand the meaning of a child's actions is crucial for the promotion of the child's ability to develop autonomous functioning. Fonagy and Target (1998) suggest that the development of a mentalizing capacity (finding meaning in one's own and others' psychic experiences) "underlies affect regulation, impulse control, self-monitoring, and the experience of self-agency" (p. 92).

THE SETTING

Many of us who work with children with school difficulties are convinced that because such difficulties are broad based and complex a unitary approach is not as effective as a multidisciplinary approach. West End Day School[1] is an elementary school for children with emotional problems in New York City which utilizes such a multi-disciplinary approach. The school provides an academic elementary school program for up to fifty intelligent children who have learning and social issues. In our small school, students are prepared for entry into mainstream schools whenever possible.

The school stresses that to be able to feel successful is essential to a child's healthy development. We know that children with learning and social issues are often denied the very elemental feeling of success that accomplishment brings. The West End Day School is a small nurturing school. Here children can gain success in achieving the vital academic and social foundations on which their future depends.

We address a variety of needs during the important elementary school years:

- To learn
- Develop friendships
- Explore inner talents
- Grow into a confident, productive member of the community.

EVALUATION PROCESS

The Evaluation Process at West End Day School is a multi-step process which involves many of the staff members over a period of time and is ongoing throughout the children's stay. As described on our web page (http://www.westenddayschool.org/admissions.html), the admission process introduces the parents to our collaborative approach where we see them as partners in trying to help their child. On our web page, we address parents as follows:

1. Our admissions process is a time when we get to learn more about each other and make sure the fit is a good one. So if you feel your 5-11 year old child is cognitively capable, has the capacity to take advantage of an academic program, but needs therapeutic interventions to address vulnerabilities that cannot be accommodated in the mainstream, then let's get to know each other. We accept admissions and enrollment on a rolling basis.

2. Call our Admissions Department to review a snapshot view of your child. This just means that you'll tell us a bit more about your child and his or her specific needs. If it seems like a good match for both of us, then we'll move on to:
3. Visit us for a Mini Open House session where you can walk our halls and get a feel for West End Day School. Does West End Day seem like a beneficial program for your child? Could you see your child here? Yes? Then it's on to the next step.
4. Pick up our application packet and return it with the required material as soon as soon as you can.
5. Now, let's talk about how we should proceed together. What's next? Should your child come for a play-date with our Speech-Language Pathologist? Should your child visit a classroom? What would work best for your child?

Once parents feel comfortable, they complete an admission packet which includes "AN OVERVIEW OF YOUR FAMILY AND YOUR CHILD FROM BIRTH TO THE PRESENT" (http://www.westenddayschool.org/pdfs/WEDS_Admissions_Packet.pdf). The Admissions Director meets with the parents along with other staff, including the Social Worker who will be working with the family, the Speech and Language Pathologist, Teacher, and other relevant staff members. A bond is established with the parents and significant historical data is reviewed, including past school experiences and prior psychological and psychiatric treatment.

Once parents feel comfortable to proceed with the admission process, the child visits the school and participates in class activities for one or more days. As part of this orientation process, the child is discussed at a clinical meeting.

THE CLINICAL MEETING WITH THE PSYCHIATRIST/ PSYCHOANALYST

The participation of a psychoanalyst as part of the team allows for an infusion of a psychoanalytic perspective in the evaluation, educational, and treatment components of the program. Psychoanalytic principles include: that a child's behavior, activity, or misbehavior has meaning; that each child's personality is uniquely developed within a particular family unit; and that the child's modes of adaptation/mal-adaptation are a result of ongoing lifelong processes (interactions among inborn constitutional factors, familial relationships, and individual intrapsychic meanings which the child imbues to reality events).

A psychoanalytic perspective begins with how one approaches both parents and children. Milton Horowitz (in Richards, 1997) describes the "psychoanalytic atmosphere" (page 1242). With such an approach, one conveys a tone of respect and acceptance where one allows both parents and children to communicate their story in their own way and at their own pace. Children, of course, may communicate through play and activities. After the parent and child finish telling you their story, one may ask questions to fill in the story and see if you can make connections.

Of course, one has to evaluate the mental status of the child, including how the child appears, what is his/her affect state, how logical is his/her thinking—is s/he talkative/quiet? What is the level of activity? What is the level of intelligence? How does he/she relate? If there are questions about psychosis, does he/she have hallucinations/delusions? Is there any suicidal thoughts/action? How is his/her orientation? What are some of the major themes in his/her thoughts?

The key factor in a psychodynamic approach is the *integration* of the psychodynamic principles (what forces in the patient's life—external as well as internal contributing to the situation), behavioral principles, e.g., reinforcements of maladaptive behaviors, cognitive/developmental limitations and strengths, and/or potential obvious biological factors. One needs to address the impact of the child's problems on the parents (and vice versa) and one has to clarify the phenomenology of the disorder and have a dynamic understanding of the child's internal experience. In our school setting, we try to ascertain how to work with the child and with the parents, whether to utilize psychodynamic principles, and/or behavioral principles, and/or cognitive and other techniques, and/or psychopharmacologic intervention.

Leon Hoffman has been involved in the school since November 1993, as the Chief Psychiatrist. His position as co-Director of The Pacella Parent Child Center at The New York Psychoanalytic Society and Institute has allowed for a deepening collaboration between the school, the Center, and the Institute. During this time working collaboratively with the Director of the school and the Director of Admissions, as well as with the other staff, we have developed a working alliance which has allowed the fostering of an atmosphere where the values inherent in psychoanalytic principles have prospered.

A key unifying activity has been an exciting weekly collaborative clinical meeting, conducted by the psychiatrist/psychoanalyst. The meeting at West End Day is a rewarding clinical and educational exercise for all of the staff, which allows for more effective treatment and educational planning for the child. At this time a child is discussed in order to formulate a diagnostic and treatment plan. The child is interviewed with the clinical staff present, including the child's teacher. All new children are interviewed and children are interviewed for periodic updates. This interview format is modeled after "ward rounds" on an inpatient unit (Hoffman, 1982). The aim of these interviews is to learn something about the child which can then be integrated by the staff in the everyday work with the child and family.

In addition to formulating a DSM diagnosis (including the level of the child's Global Assessment of Functioning), one of the goals of the interview with the child is to try to understand, and very judiciously explore, the child's current mental state, including the nature of the defenses the child utilizes to try to protect him or herself against a conscious awareness of the emotional pain that the child seems to be experiencing. By identifying how the child is hiding the emotional pain from him or herself (consciously or unconsciously keeping bad feelings out of awareness, avoiding direct verbalization, or disavowing the painful feeling states), the child's social worker and other staff can discuss ways to address the defenses.

Understanding how the child is protecting him or herself from painful feelings can help all of the staff in their work with the child, particularly helping the child feel understood by the staff. In this meeting, of course, the child's defensive maneuvers cannot be explored. However, thinking about the child's protective devices against painful emotions and communicating our understanding of this will help the child feel less threatened by painful feeling states with an ultimate goal of allowing the child to share the feelings with the social worker and other staff in a more direct way. With greater mastery of feelings and diminishment of maladaptive defenses the child feels less overwhelmed (Hoffman, 2007). With greater mastery, the child is able to improve his socialization with staff and peers as well as attend to his or her academic program:

- It is imperative to stress that these meetings are collaborative meetings. During our discussions, there is input from all who participate (agreements and disagreements about the child's phenomenology, cognitive and other functions, and inferred psychodynamics and family dynamics).
- We outline the nature of the child's productions during the interview, what the phenomenology may indicate, the nature of further evaluations that are needed, and the possible day-to-day interventions that would be helpful.
- In this way a psychoanalytically-oriented interview is modeled for the staff, particularly the utility of sensitive interview techniques (such as, following the child's lead during the interview and methods to reasonably infer the personal meaning of the child's play/fantasy or verbal descriptions of everyday events).
- We demonstrate how to promote a connection and rapport with the child and this allows the child to communicate with us about the issues important in his or her life, including the experience of changing schools and meeting new people.

- The result of the conference discussion is a comprehensive understanding of the child (strengths as well as areas that are problematic) and an attempt to develop an integrated approach to the child.

In addition to the school personnel who attend the meeting (including social work, speech and language, and OT), a Child and Adolescent Psychiatry Fellow from Mount Sinai Medical Center attend the meeting. The New York Psychoanalytic Institute has a formal affiliation with the Mount Sinai Medical Center's Department of Psychiatry. The participation of all of these professionals allows us to implement the most appropriate intervention:

- Emotional support (in the class, by the social worker, by an outside therapists or analysts)
- Cognitive support and enrichment (in the class and outside the class)
- Psychopharmacological intervention (continuation of psychiatric treatment or referral)
- Developing the best transition plan at the end of the stay at the school.

The recent collaboration among Mount Sinai (a return to the collaboration from the past) and The Pacella Parent Child Center New York Psychoanalytic Society and Institute has led to the development of a psychoanalytically informed school consultation module (Compare Kris, 1978). In addition to the work with the staff the psychiatrist/psychoanalyst (as well as guest psychoanalysts) has conducted evening parent workshops. Many topics have been covered, such as: "My baby's growing up and I'm having a hard time with him/her," "How to help my fearful child," "When does loving become disabling: Where's the limit?" "Is play therapy more than play?" "Executive Function and Emotions: A Complex Relationship," and "An Introduction for Parents to an Evaluation of their Children." At each of these discussions a one-page hand-out is used as a starting point for the discussion, driven by the ideas, issues, and feelings that are brought up by the parents.

Most importantly, throughout their stay at the school the children are evaluated in an in-depth manner. The general approach to the children involves gaining an understanding of the child's place and relationship with his or her family, the nature of the child's symptoms, the nature of the child's emotional state, cognitive and other capacities, and social relationships. A psychodynamic picture is formulated (that is, what are the inner struggles with which the child is coping?).

Throughout the child's stay, among the various specific functions which we assess and address are[2]

- Capacities for Regulation, Attention, and Learning (constitutional and maturational contributions), including auditory processing and language,

visual-spatial processing, motor planning and sequencing, sensory modulation, and related capacities for executive functioning, memory (implicit, explicit, semantic, episodic, working), attention, overall intelligence, and processing emotional and social cues.
- Capacity for Relationships (Including Depth, Range, and Consistency)
- Quality of Internal Experience (Level of Confidence and Self-Regard)
- Emotional Experience, Expression, and Communication
- Defensive Patterns and Capacities
- Capacity to Form Internal Representations
- Capacity for Differentiation and Integration
- Self-Observing Capacity (Psychological-Mindedness)
- Capacity for Internal Standards and Ideals: Sense of Morality

THERAPEUTIC EDUCATION: INTEGRATION OF COUNSELING, TEACHING, REMEDIATION

A unique aspect of our school program is the on-site collaboration among social workers who provide counseling (individually outside the classroom, individually within the classroom, and/or in groups), teachers who provide in-class instruction, speech and language pathologists, who provide evaluation, consultation with the staff, and remediation, and a variety of other specialists (computer science, art, music, physical education, and occupational therapy). A question often asked is how does a counseling program help improve a child's learning?

A counseling program enables all of the staff to be aware that we *must* pay attention to the meaning of children's actions, which may be blocking their learning. When children feel understood, they settle down and can move on with their work. Acknowledging that the child has bad feelings validates the child's inner experience and thus eliminates one motivation for maladaptive actions. Since each child has his or her very own grown-up friend (clinical social worker) to help resolve bad feelings and work out problems, the child knows there is someone who can address emotional turmoil when it occurs.

The social workers can help address children's feelings by reflecting them back to the child helping him or her feel understood. This feeling of being listened to leads to an openness in which children can talk about problems. The fact that each child has a grown-up friend that talks about problems outside of the classroom is incorporated into school culture so children enjoy their special time and don't have to worry about feeling stigmatized. Children are taught to understand themselves. Once they have insight and reach an understanding that feels acceptable to them, they can make more effective choices about their activities. At the same time we listen to parents and help parents listen to their children so school and home can work together.

An important part of the program can be conceptualized as "strength-based" whereby we identify children's strengths, stress the strengths to the children and their parents, and explore their inner talents and reinforce them. Children are encouraged to incorporate strengths into their learning style; talents are shown off in school activities such as chess tournaments, art shows, chorus, school plays, and enrichment activities such as track and field. Parents partner with the school to talk and reinforce strengths and talents at school and home. Overall, the program promoted the children's resiliency.

STRUCTURE: PROMOTING RESILIENCE

It is crucial to underscore that all children, but especially children with emotional and cognitive challenges, adapt more effectively when they participate in a structured environment. Needless to say, without structure, a child has difficulty learning.

A clear classroom structure provides a sense of safety for the children so they can develop emotionally, socially, and cognitively. Some of the principles which inform the interactions among the teachers and the children include:

- Helping children function within a group, establishing reciprocity (e.g., giving and taking, turn taking)
- Setting limits while offering explanations for the limits provided. While at the same time helping the child reviewing his/her own role.
- Reducing the child's anxiety into smaller manageable entities which the child can master
- Facilitating the child's thinking process by reducing anxiety and making links between different aspects of thought processes
- Expanding the child's thinking process by stressing cause and effect, particularly within relationships
- Helping children transition and improve ability to regulate
- Helping the children to develop the capacity to delay gratification

CLASSROOM MILIEU AND THE ROLE OF THE SPECIAL EDUCATION TEACHER

The West End Day School provides a dynamic academic curriculum covering Kindergarten through grade six. Classes are academically and socially grouped, rather than by strict grade. Children are placed in the group that will work best for them. Class-size is usually ten students with a head teacher and assistant teacher. The classroom curriculum is developed by the classroom teacher and the Education Head with the special needs of individual students in mind. Having flexibility in the way the students are taught is a key component in the program as the school works with students of varying learning abilities. All students are placed in small reading, writing, and math groups (made up of anywhere between two to five students) based on their ability level as well as their learning style. The students are assessed at the beginning of each school year to determine their group. However, the groups are fluid and are subject to change based on the student's needs. Each group is taught using the method that works best for their learning profile. For example, students that need a phonics based approach in reading and are struggling to decode are taught strictly using a specific Orton-Gillingham based program. On the other hand, students that are fluent readers where reading is a strength for them, are taught using a guided reading program that is more appropriate for their ability level. Having this type of flexibility in the program allows each student to feel more comfortable and less anxious about learning, especially in an area that may be more difficult for them.

Overall, the school uses a multi-sensory approach to teaching where the content is taught using both a visual and hands-on approach so that we are able to reach all types of learners. For the students who have language difficulties we make sure that all of the language in the classroom is broken down for them, aiding in comprehension. For the youngest learners, the curriculum emphasizes the importance of being part of a group learner and the how-tos of building positive relationships. For example, they are taught how to share supplies, how do use the adults in the room for help and what to do during a learning time. Students are asked to stop, think, and listen to each other. As the students get older, we are teaching them how to be more independent in their learning, including teaching study skills and organizational techniques as well as what types of learners they are and how to advocate for themselves in other settings.

Another key component of our curriculum and classroom environment is the structure that is embedded within the program. The schedule is looked at throughout the day and any changes in the schedule are talked about with plenty of time for the students to adjust to the change. Also, each classroom has a motivational plan as part of a class-wide management system with the overall class theme of being a group learner at its core. All of the students have a visual reminder of how they are doing behaviorally and are working on earning something that is meaningful to them, such as lunch with a friend or a homework pass.

The combination of having a small class size, a flexible curriculum, and a structured classroom routine help the students feel comfortable in learning in the group atmosphere and eases the anxiety of academic areas that may be difficult for them.

We cannot stress enough the important role the special education teacher provides by promoting the socio-emotional development of the children. Many of the techniques that teachers use to promote academic and social functioning are in essence modifications of "ego supportive" techniques which have been utilized in psychoanalytically oriented milieus, dating back to ground breaking work of Fritz Redl. In Redl's framework for working with children (Redl and Wineman, 1951, 1952; Redl, 1959), he stresses the importance of the distribution of roles for the staff members working with the children and the need for clear distinctions for the students. At West End Day, it is very clear and obvious to the students who helps them with their "feelings problems" and who their teacher is. They understand who to go to and clear boundaries are made between the two. Another component of this framework is having enough clinical resiliency to vary between flexibility and structure. This is a factor that is discussed frequently at West End Day School. Finding the balance between structure and flexibility is a key element with both teachers and social workers that helps the students feel more comfortable in their learning environment. The structure helps them feel in control while the flexibility allows them to know that they have choices. From Redl's perspective we provide a great deal of "ego support."

The children who attend our school are children who have not been able to navigate the ambiguities of mainstream schools, despite having high intelligence. For a variety of reasons (conflictual, cognitive, developmental, or emotional interference) they lack internal controls (ego controls) for which they require simplifications of their routine and predictability from their teachers and other staff members. Rosenblitt (1996) discusses some of these ideas in detail, particularly the overstimulated states children exhibit when they have difficulties with their affect regulation and attentional difficulties. By creating a structure and a predictable schedule, students feel calmer and understand expectations better. We found that even in the smallest academic group that providing the same basic routine for the lessons presented helps ease students' anxiety about what is expected of them and they don't feel the need to worry about their performance as they always know what would come next. Even when there is a small change in the schedule or something unexpected occurs in a lesson, the students are prepared ahead of time by explaining what the change is and what it will look like. We make sure that our overall program is very similar to what one would find in a mainstream school so the students get the same experiences (science fairs, musical performances, school plays), but the way it is approached is different. We give the students plenty of time to prepare and we celebrate their strengths. If there is a student who has a fear of getting on stage then their contribution to the performance is to work as an art director with our art specialist or as a stage hand behind the scenes. Any type of nervousness or anxiety about an upcoming event is talked about in their social skills groups or individually with a counselor.

In addition to the academic curriculum there is an after-school program, which is customized according to each child's strengths. In sum, the teachers and staff provide a great deal of ego supportive measures which allow the children to:

- Internalize controls
- Internalize a greater sense of accomplishment

Many parents often say that for the first time their children are happy to go to school in contrast to previous schools where they may have been shunned, treated like scapegoats, or repetitively criticized for their difficulties.

It is important to stress, that many of the "ego-supportive" techniques utilized by all of the staff are similar to techniques utilized in a variety of contemporary therapies with children and young adolescents. See Fonagy and Target (1996) and Hoffman (2007).

A clear classroom structure provides a sense of safety for the children so they can develop emotionally, socially, and cognitively. Some of the principles which inform the interactions among the teachers and the children include:

- Setting limits, offering explanations for the limits provided, as well as including the child in reviewing his/her own "choice" whether accepting or rejecting the limit
- Helping children function within a group
- Verbalization of the children's internal states and differentiation of children's emotions
- The teacher attempts to break down the child's unmanageable emotions such as anxiety into smaller manageable entities which the child can master
- The teacher facilitates the child's thinking process by reducing anxiety and making links between different aspects of thought processes
- The teacher facilitates the child's thinking process by stressing cause and effect, particularly within relationships
- Helping children separate internal from external, real from unreal, fantasy from reality
- Establishing reciprocity (e.g., giving and taking, turn taking)
- Helping the children to develop the capacity to delay gratification

In short:

- The faculty and staff focus on helping students learn to interact with peers and adults
- Social skill development emphasizes attitudes towards classmates, the child's effect on the class and being a productive member of the school community
- Our aim is not only the development of an academically competent child but also a socially successful child.

An important part of all of the classrooms includes the utilization of behavioral rewards for appropriate activity. Receiving or not receiving the reward is spelled out from the beginning of the child's participation in the class, so that endless non-productive interpersonal arguments are avoided, especially by oppositional children. Redl (1949) wrote about the value of such "depersonalized controls" where rules can be accepted without loss of face.

Needless to say, teachers are provided with a great deal of emotional support and continuing education in order to brainstorm how to handle problematic situations. Teachers have regular discussions with the social workers about particular issues with specific children and families, support from adminstrators, and have a variety of staff conferences, including the clinical meetings with psychiatrist/psychoanalyst (see Cappella, et al., 2012).

SOCIAL WORK INVOLVEMENT

A key factor which promotes the clinical approach in the school is the presence of an active staff of social workers and social work students. A social worker is assigned to each child and family, the nature of the involvement varying with the needs of the child and emotional availability of the family. The social worker maintains an ongoing collaborative relationship with the child's teachers in order to insure that the development of the child's academic curriculum is informed by the child's emotional and social needs.

Some children are seen individually by the social worker, others are seen in dyadic, triadic, or other group setting, some children are seen in the classroom, particularly during stressful periods. Some parents come weekly or biweekly, whereas others do not meet with the social worker on a regular basis. Some parents meet with one or two of the social workers in early morning small group sessions. Although we encourage regular attendance by the parents and consistently attempt to address resistances to attendance, we do not make attendance at regular parental meetings an absolute condition for the child's continuation at the school.

Social workers have the challenging task of working with parents and/or other important family members who have a variety of responses to their children's difficulties. Working with those parents who utilize significant denial mechanisms may be very difficult. They may attribute the child's problems to a variety of external factors such as the "class is not right or the teacher is too strict" or they may even say that the observations in the school are incorrect. Tactful approaches by the social workers are required to aid these parents because their narcissistic wounds from having a child with problems are too much for them to consciously acknowledge the problems.

Some parents' defensiveness manifests itself in comments such as "he seems so happy at home, he plays well with his best friend, she is good with us." They may express puzzlement and have a hard time understanding what the social worker is trying to explain to them. Other parents may have excessive self-blaming behavior and castigate themselves, "What did we do wrong? Is it because of our divorce? Is it because of my illness? Is it because I went back to work? Is it because I travel too much?"

Others blame the child: "Why can't he listen? Why does she bully the other girls?" Some blame their own or their partner's genes: "There is mental illness in my (his/her) family." Some may blame the birth process. In other words there are innumerable ways in which parents deal with their fright and their anxiety. A major goal of the social worker's task is to try to develop an alliance with the family and eventually gently address some of these difficult defenses.

Since a sizable percentage of the children have "outside" therapists, analysts, psychiatrists, or other professional supports, the social worker is a key player, coordinating the work within the school milieu with the "outside" therapeutic interventions.

SPEECH AND LANGUAGE THERAPIST, PSYCHOEDUCATION EVALUATIONS, OCCUPATIONAL THERAPY

As can be seen from the evaluative process described above, a very important member of the therapeutic team is the speech and language therapist. Many of the children, particularly the younger children, have a variety of linguistic and speech difficulties. Very often in our team meetings we have valuable clinical and educational discussions in which we try to differentiate emotional components from cognitive components with regard to a child's expressive or receptive language difficulties. Does a child have difficulties with his/her thinking process or is it a language problem? Is a child's difficulty learning a result of emotional interference or a result of cognitive problems? Does a child have both language as well as social deficits? More formal psychoeducational evaluations, language evaluations, or occupational therapy evaluations and interventions are conducted.

SUMMARY

As can be seen from the above, the school provides a unique atmosphere whereby:

1. The child and family are the focus of and partners with the staff in the evaluation and treatment
2. A broad interdisciplinary approach to such evaluation and treatment includes a range of professions: psychiatry, psychology, social work, special education, speech and language therapy, occupational therapy, and psychoanalysis.
3. While each profession in our program has its own area of expertise, the school uses psychoanalytic theory as an integrating umbrella. Thus, individual approaches become blended into a broader overall understanding. The whole, therefore, becomes greater than its parts.

The key factor in our psychodynamic approach is the *integration* of the psychodynamic principles (what forces in the patient's life—external as well as internal contributing to the situation), behavioral principles, e.g., reinforcements of maladaptive behaviors, cognitive/developmental limitations and strengths, and/or potential obvious biological factors. We address the impact of the child's problems on the parents (and vice versa) and we clarify the phenomenology of the disorder while incorporating a dynamic understanding of the child's internal experience in our overall treatment plan.

In our school setting, we try to ascertain how to work with the child and with the parents, whether to utilize psychodynamic principles, and/or behavioral principles, and/or cognitive and other techniques, and/or psychopharmacologic intervention. We always try to address the impact of the child's problems on the parents (and vice versa).

NOTES

1. Some of the description of the program are adapted from http://westenddayschool.org/.
2. The functions are explicated in the Psychodynamic Diagnostic Manual (PDM), Greenspan, S., Chair. Leon Hoffman served on the Task Force on Childhood Mental Health Disorders (PDM Task Force, 2006).

REFERENCES

Cappella, E., Hamre, B. K., Kim, H. Y., Henry, D. B., Frazier, S. L., Atkins, M. S., & Schoenwald, S. K. (2012, March 19). Teacher Consultation and Coaching Within Mental Health Practice: Classroom and Child Effects in Urban Elementary Schools. *Journal of Consulting and Clinical Psychology*. Advance online publication. doi: 10.1037/a0027725

Fonagy, P. and Target, M. (1996). Predictors Of Outcome In Child Psychoanalysis: A Retrospective Study Of 763 Cases At The Anna Freud Centre. *Journal of the American Psychoanalytic Association, 44*, 27–77.
Fonagy, P. and Target, M. (1998). Mentalization and the Changing Aims of Child Psychoanalysis. *Psychoanalytic Dialogues, 8*, 87–114.
Hoffman, L. (1982). *Evaluation and Care Of Severely Disturbed Children and Their Families.* New York: Spectrum Publications.
Hoffman, L. (2007) Do Children Get Better When We Interpret Their Defenses Against Painful Feelings? *Psychoanalytic Study of the Child 62*, 291–313.
Kris, K. (1978) The School Consultant as an Object for Externalization. *Psychoanalytic Study of the Child, 33*, 641–651.
Lavietes, R. L., Hulse, W. C., & Blau, A. (1960). A psychiatric day treatment center and school for young children and their parents. *American Journal of Orthopsychiatry, 30*, 468–482. PDM Task Force. (2006). *Psychodynamic Diagnostic Manual.* Silver Spring, MD: Alliance of Psychoanalytic Organizations.
Redl, F. (1949). New Ways of Ego Support in Residential Treatment of Disturbed Children. *Bulletin of the Menninger Clinic, 13*, 60–66.
Redl, F. (1059). Strategy and Techniques of Life-Space Interview *Amer. J. Orthopsychiat. 29*, 1–18.
Redl, F. & Wineman, D. (1951). *Children Who Hate: The Disorganization and Breakdown of Behavior Controls.* New York: Free Press.
Redl, F. & Wineman, D. (1952). *Controls from Within: Techniques for the Treatment of the Aggressive Child.* New York: Free Press.
Richards, A. K. (1997). The Relevance Of Frequency Of Sessions To The Creation Of An Analytic Experience. *Journal of the American Psychoanalytic Association, 45*, 1241–1251.
Rosenblitt, D. L. (1996). States of Overstimulation in Early Childhood. *Psychoanalytic Study of the Child, 51*, 542–561.

Chapter Twelve

Reviving Schools as "Great Good Places"

Robbie Lloyd

When I came to review the first draft of this chapter, I realized there were three main "aunties and uncles" (my borrowed indigenous term for esteemed elders) whose voices kept echoing through the story you are about to read—and they all came from books published in 1964. What a year! The same year that the Righteous Brothers had their all time No. 1 hit, "You've Lost That Lovin' Feelin'" (Spector, Mann, Weil, 1964), which went on to become the U.S.'s most played song on radio and television throughout the twentieth century (Broadcast Music Inc. statistic 1999, Wikipedia). It could have been an epitaph for what school education has achieved during the last three centuries (nineteenth, twentieth and twenty-first).

In that period schools have swung from chalk-encrusted Victorian era discipline factories, through seventies child-centerd free-schooling environments, to contemporary electronic whiteboarded, dog-eat-dog meritocratic, web-published competition-tabled, measurement-obsessed sausage machines of "knowledge." Pink Floyd's meat grinder scene in their number one 1979 hit rock opera*The Wall* (Ezrin, Gilmour, Guthrie, Waters, 1979), captured this pattern perfectly, and it has continued to echo what generations before and since have struggled against, and usually ended up complying with.

This pattern has created a repeated cycle of impression management (Goffman, 1959)—from the nineteenth century student's fear-driven pretense in front of the teacher, through the twenty-first century's school principal's desperate impression management PR (public relations) exercises in the free market of schooling, to current students having to relearn how to impression manage their way through the latest web of measured expectations that adults have produced. It's all pretty hard work! And draining on the emotions.

But maybe there were positive lessons in some of the old patterns prevailing behind the scenes in earlier days. Schools were also informal playgrounds for risk-taking youth development, where bypassing the rules allowed friendship and camaraderie to prevail. While stand-over bullying might have been occurring alongside exploratory kisses behind the toilets, it was less internally colonizing than today's sexting and Facebooked world. And just as adults still revel in their favorite "third places" (i.e., not home and not work)—the club, the pub, coffee shop or general hang out zone—some students enjoyed the schoolyard as "a great good place" in which to gather with friends and chew the fat. I argue that we need to revive that third place, or "great good place" (Oldenberg, 1999) aspect of schooling, to nurture the social and emotional well-being (SEWB) of children (and adults) in these environments, said to be dedicated to developing the whole person. As our first 1964 aunty, one of America's greatest philosophers (as well as being a poet and potter of renown), M. C. Richards, put it in her classic book *Centering: In Pottery, Poetry, and the Person*:

> It is a function of love to provide a continuous environment in which life is permitted to unfold in its entirety. It informs a moment with the sense of eternity that courses through it: seeing in the child their summer and autumn come; in the adult, their spring and winter; in the dying day, its full blaze and dawn. It is this Now which holds in layers of transparency the past and future, and we see ourselves suspended in emptiness, an emptiness which exists in order for fullness to be present. (Richards, 1989/1964, p. 143)

That presence in the Now is what great good places offer. It fits the quantum physics understanding that we are all "in the field," "in the flow" of what Nobel Laureate Henri Bergson called "duration" back in 1908 (Bergson, 1988/1908). Modern day advocates of improving life balance and self-awareness, such as Eckhart Tolle, argue for the same emphasis—bringing us into the Now (Tolle 2005, 2001). And so do good schools—places where children and adults feel that spaces for learning are always being opened up, so everyone can grow with the pleasure of new knowing together, "right now." But sadly, that is not what is being nurtured in too many schools around the world. They have been overtaken by concerns about "achieving outcomes" and, "producing products" which are measured in mountains of tests and skyscrapers of data collection—all projected towards an anxiety-creating future.

This chapter aims to reflect on an approach to whole-school-culture building, which is based on nurturing well-being as the foundation for good learning and growth, among everyone involved. And it is based on a meditation about great good places, because they express something of the vibrant, life-giving, loving energy of acceptance and nurture that we all need, to be able to grow into our full selves.

HOW IT CAN BE?

One of my favorite reflections on what would be called today "value-adding education" comes from our second uncle, author of the 1964 book*In The Early World*, New Zealander Elwyn Richardson (Richardson, 1964). It tells the story of Richardson's twelve years teaching at the one-teacher Oruaiti School, on the northernmost tip of New Zealand's north island in the 50s and 60s, where he originally ventured because he had a private passion to study the molluscs living along that coastline. It is a wonder-filled, uplifting celebration of what can happen when imagination, exploration and natural democratic respect among children and adults is allowed to dominate the learning environment.

The foreword to his book was written by English-born and New Zealand-raised innovative New York Principal John Melser, who pioneered open classrooms, mixed grades, whole-language instruction, and arts-based learning, at Public School 3 on Hudson St in Greenwich Village in the 1970s. He said of Richardson and Oruaiti:

> Oruaiti functioned as a community of artists and scientists who turned a frank and searching gaze on all that came within their ambit. Curiosity and emotional force led them to explore together the natural world and the world of their feelings. They learned to esteem each other's explorations, discoveries, and records with tact and with discriminating enthusiasm, so that a fine collective strength was developed, a strength depending on each child making an individual search and bringing to the group what only *s/he* could give (this author's emphasis). (Richardson, 1964, p.v)

Elwyn Richardson took risks with how young people can be. He allowed them to follow their own path of exploration to a large extent. And by so doing he created a congruent world for them to grow up into. He gave them freedom to be themselves, rather than stressing about "the curriculum, the timetable, the school's behaviour management regime, and the test results." It must have been fun—perish the thought in the 1950s and 60s! But we have lost much of that fun in our classrooms and school grounds today, despite all the technological tools in the world, and advanced standards of teacher education, and more engaged parents in their children's learning . . . what's happened?

JUST CHILLIN'

Working in Australia's remote Northern Territory (NT) communities over the past few years, I have been privileged to engage with indigenous people, culture and spirit that survive despite decades of colonial invasion, stolen generations interference, and contemporary "results-driven," "outcomes oriented" government interventions. Some children may be at school each day, but plenty of others are "down the river" swimming, hunting, chasing each other and exploring the natural world. There are paradoxes in this scenario. Because home lives may be traumatized, violent and suffering abuse of young and old alike. Community morale may be despirited due to waves of whitefella [1] interference, local faction-fighting, lack of ability to escape "humbug" (others demanding "you give if you have") and payback wars. Unemployment is rife, gambling occupies large amounts of each day, grog and gunja (marihuana) each night, and many children wander the streets late after dark. Yet there is passionate connection to country, family, and culture.

Aboriginal people represent strong examples of how mainstream western education needs to provide whole-person, individual-respect-based approaches, rather than demanding compliance with didactic subject instruction and testing-dominated daily routines. There is a natural curiosity in indigenous consciousness, and there are ways of being together than can engage deeply, once respect for feelings and spirit of place have been established.

This is what exists in those adult environments we call "great good places." Those "third places" which are not home or work, but communal gathering spaces where people feel at home being themselves, letting their guard down. Sadly that's not the case in many western and eastern school environments today, where fear and compliance have arisen again, as if we were back in the Victorian era.

John Melser saw Elwyn Richardson achieving something much more effective at Oruaiti:

> In much discussion of teaching there is an assumption that a radical difference of kind exists between work which is variously called "creative," "imaginative," or "expressive"—work which is about children's feelings and sensations—and, on the other hand, work which is distinguished as "factual" and which concerns the "real" or "outside" world. Attitudes that follow from this assumption induce children to write "creatively" by injecting an artificial heightening of tone or spurious fancy into an otherwise straightforward account, and force them into a clipped, inelegantly dull jargon whenever presenting a report. It seems evident from the work at Oruaiti that the distinction has little relevance to the work of children. (Richardson, 1964 pp. v–vi)

My argument is that adults like the relaxed environment of their favorite third place, precisely because that is where they rediscover the part of themselves that can be spontaneous, cheeky, even rude (in a spirit of fun) with their peers. But when it comes to today's schools, the structural forces of performance, monitoring and measurement right across society have created high stress environments for both adults and children. This has led to a loss of trust, that children can benefit from being allowed social and emotional space, and freedom to explore different ways of being, relating, and expressing themselves. Such growth nurtures the sort of social and emotional well-being and development that enhances learning much more than earning good test scores, or brownie points for being compliant in class and thereby easy for teachers in terms of "behavior management." Yet compliance is exactly what an industrial model school demands, in order to efficiently achieve its ultimate purpose, good test results and scores on the comparative, competitive league tables of schools.

It reminds me of a popular saying among some work colleagues in the 1990s, when anyone got overwrought and stressed out—"you need to take a chill pill baby!" So it should be for many contemporary learning environments and those in charge of them.

THE WORRYING TREND

Sadly, many schools I have witnessed are falling under the weight of big-brother government and nervous parental expectations that they compete on the league table, rather than being primarily concerned about the social and emotional well-being of children first, so they can learn effectively as a natural outcome of feeling good about themselves. This tight emphasis on "producing results" creates stress on principals and teachers to comply with the system's requirements first, and worry about children's well-being second. And it can also result in schools becoming not unlike the hollow "non-places" of supermodernity—such as airport departure lounges, supermarkets and freeways. Dominated by mechanistic "professional standards," "duties of care," and "due processes," many learning environments have become stress zones of curriculum-churning, timetable-checking, compliance-demanding routines.

In the semiotics of modernism's history, anthropologist Marc Augérgues that the progression from modernism to post-modernism to supermodernity reflected an increasing abstraction of places and spaces where humans can end up (Augé, 1995).

Three "excessive" trends moved our society towards a distorted experience of identity and reciprocal relations, which previously made up "normal life," according to Augé. People now experience an overabundance of events, spatial overabundance, and excessive individualization of references (Augé, 1995, pp. 18–21, 34, 39). All this leaves us detached from a sense of belonging anywhere.

Augérgues that airport lounges, supermarkets, and freeways are the ultimate examples of this effect of supermodernity. He says that "culture as text" is about "localized society" where people can relate to the scale of events, numbers of people, and activities (Augé, 1995, 49–52). What he calls "anthropological space" is one where the "concrete and symbolic construction of space" can serve the needs of people. Such a perspective contrasts with what has been happening to schools, where professionalized regimes of teaching and learning can end up treating students and staff alike as process workers in a massive machine churning out "educational products."

Assessment regimes, registration, and accreditation of education all emphasize this rigid corralling of learners and teachers, within a system designed for maximum adherence to preset "standards." And "leadership" roles in education have become clones of business management principles and practices, rather than the main role models for caring and wise counsel.

It is this same reductionist, outcomes-focused, measured-and-tested-results approach that designs and manages spaces around a dominant paradigm of "the professional," that now works across all human services, in health, welfare, justice, aged and child care, and schooling.

I argue that it doesn't have to be that way. By "valuing the picture rather than the picture frame" (Herzfeld, 2001, p. 291) we can move away from arid abstraction and measurement of students' learning, to create vital, freed-up social spaces for mutually supported exploration and development—as Elwyn Richardson did at Oruaiti, and as many people still do today in schools across the world, where they choose to resist becoming compliant clones of mechanized, monocultured education production.

WHAT DOES IT TAKE?

Australia has been lucky to have had nearly twenty years of bipartisan reform in its approach to mental health. This has led to educational engagement with a social and emotional learning curriculum (SELC), and the general understanding that social and emotional well-being (SEWB) needs to underpin good schooling. The Australian Curriculum, now a national framework (http://www.australiancurriculum.edu.au; http://www.acara.edu.au/default.asp), includes social and emotional competence (language that sadly still reflects an industrial training era emphasis on "competencies") as one of its core foundations. And there are nationally supported programs to help schools build whole-school cultures of well-being—such as Kidsmatter, Mindmatters and Staffmatters, and Dare To Lead (for indigenous-related communities).[2] I have been working to incorporate versions of these elements in some Northern Territory schools, in a three-pronged approach. First, that every school establishes a weekly Wellbeing Team, involving school leadership, counseling, special education, and so on, in monitoring and supportive intervention for students, families, and staff needing support (see figure 12.1). In remote locations this also involves the local health clinic, cultural leaders, police, and any other significant agencies wanting to support community well-being on a regular, totally confidential basis (with parents' pre-agreement signed each year, for their children to receive such support, which can include people visiting the home to offer support when needed).

Second, added to the whole-school Wellbeing Team, the social and emotional learning curriculum (SELC) highlights the sorts of feelings, values, and behaviors which are encompassed in the national mental health scheme, agreed among local staff and parents, and also translated into local language, concepts, and metaphors that link with local culture. This set of mantras is then used as a reinforcing common language across the school community, to nurture well-being in the way people be with each other (see figure 12.2).

And lastly, The Gathering Place (see figure 12.3) is a regular ritual ceremony, where students, staff, parents, and community come together to share rhythmical occasions of celebrating belonging and identity. This is especially crucial for those who may have been vulnerable or not fitting into the mainstream flow of classroom relations. Which is what I have come to call "having a scratchy life"—i.e., when things for any person (student, teacher, parent) are rubbing up against "normal" expectations of how to behave in groups, usually due to serious exhaustion, trauma at home, or in the overall family and community environment: i.e., things that require compassion and empathy, rather than judgement about someone "being badly behaved," or "not cutting it."

WBT Rationale includes:

- ❑ Any matter coming to this group WILL BE ACTED ON
- ❑ No blaming or shaming anyone, always positive support, and Restorative Justice practices
- ❑ Strengths-based approach to solving problems, with involvement of student, family, teacher & community
- ❑ Whole-school philosophy & practice, involving everyone in supporting those in need – One In: All In.

WBT Structure includes:

- ❑ Wellbeing Officer (keeps weekly chart for monitoring & intervention ; data filed after each meeting to record trends & track effectiveness of outcomes);
- ❑ Principal and Deputies/Assistant Principals;
- ❑ Special Education Coordinator & School Counsellor;
- ❑ Classroom Teachers (with relievers filling in) needing to discuss student issues &/or their own personal concerns;
- ❑ Regular visitors (eg. Clinic; Police &/or other Justice Agencies; Elders; Cultural Centre rep's – generally any Community stakeholders supporting families & community)

WBT Decisions may include:

- ❑ Refer student to School Counsellor or Student Services;
- ❑ Set up Behaviour Support program for student &/or Teacher – designed to decrease stress in class, and bring Self-Management into action by student;
- ❑ Teacher may need a Buddy/Peer Support intervention, or Mental Health Day, or Prof. Dev. to address gaps in classroom practice.

Figure 12.1. The Wellbeing Team Structure and Function. Created by Robbie Lloyd.

THE FIVE SOCIAL & EMOTIONAL LEARNING COMPETENCIES (making up the SEL Curriculum SELC):

•**SELF AWARENESS:** Being aware of our own feelings is what we try to teach children, but do adults remember? Identify & Recognise your emotions.

•**SELF-MANAGEMENT:** Knowing when we are upset, and taking action to be responsible for our feelings, are skills some adults were never taught, and so we too need to learn them. Regulate emotions to handle stress & control impulses.

•**SOCIAL AWARENESS:** Being able to take the perspective of others, and to empathise with their different experiences, are skills that adults need to master. Accept others' differences without having to reject or marginalise them.

•**RELATIONSHIP SKILLS:** If we feel OK about ourselves, we should be able to relate to others without fear, discomfort, or petty resentments. If not, we need to get help to rebalance ourselves. The onus is on us, to create **Respectful Relationships**.

•**RESPONSIBLE DECISION-MAKING:** We need to be able to weigh up our own and others' emotional state, and find ways to relate that are fair and considerate, or else get help to do so. Self reflection is what adults should be able to do, and young people can learn through programs like **Response Ability Pathways** and the **Circle of Courage**.

Figure 12.2. The Five Social & Emotional Learning Competencies (making up the SEL Curriculum SELC). Created by Robbie Lloyd.

By creating special moments and spaces where these individuals can come back into the circle, and receive a witnessing and testimony of their contributions in a setting of communal acknowledgement, schools are doing a full job of "growing up everyone" about "how life goes round, round, round."

The overall whole-school-culture-building effect of such strategies aims to reclaim the social poetics of schools as great good places (Herzfeld, 2001: the concept of social poetics is dealt with more fully below). The diagrams accompanying this text illustrate the linked elements of care, designed to create a foundation and scaffold that will support children and adults in school communities. They all depend on people being prepared to be vulnerable around each other, not trying to "fake it til you make it," but being open an honest when things are going pear shaped.

Elwyn Richardson's gift was to create an environment of social and emotional well-being without even trying. He allowed children to explore and imagine. He opened up the space for mutual caring to arise spontaneously. He created a great good place for learning without trying:

> A matter-of-fact acceptance of a total event in which feelings are involved with all the other facts of the situation permits a growth in awareness, and a search for exactness which the usual view prevents or hinders. These children turned the same dispassionate and unselfconscious regard on to their own

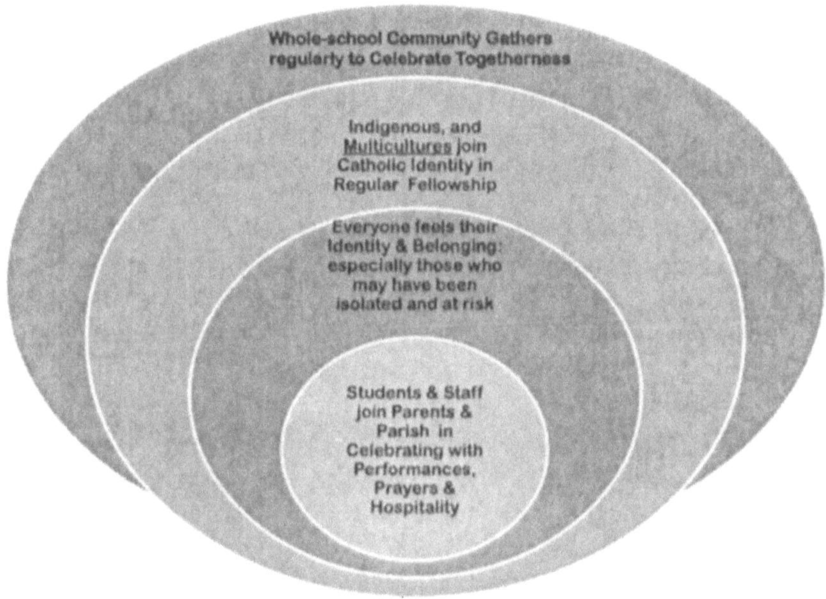

Figure 12.3. The Gathering Place—where regular rituals celebrate community, culture, and communion. Created by Robbie Lloyd.

> feelings as on to other events, and pursued with the same relentless demand for exactitude a fact of natural science or a fact of human response. It is this that made possible the beauty of the poetry, the excellence of the graphic and ceramic work, and the careful scientific observation. (Richardson, 1964, p. vi)

I argue that schools can be rescued from becoming equivalent to places like airport departure lounges, supermarkets, and freeways, in their depersonalized anonymity (Augé, 1995), by educators and parents reclaiming their ownership of the core human value of investing in people first—i.e., the children and the adults in this environment to be allowed to take a chill pill, and not let fear (of test results, places at university, inspectors' assessments, comparisons on "the league table of schools") dominate how schools can run as communities. Richardson saw the vital need for maintaining congruence of our full humanity in this experience:

> Because the children were not required to make a divorce between the parts of their experience, a divorce hostile to their intuitive grasp of situations, they could bend to their work with an enthusiasm and a degree of concentration which ordinary schooling never touches. And always the school functioned as a community, a community of artist-scientists . . . the school functioned as a community not in spite of but because of the individualism of its members—

> each person counted and was expected to make his/her own contribution to its life (this author's emphasis). (Richardson, 1964, p. vi)

And so it is in our favorite pub, diner, coffee shop, or hang-out place. We don't need to prove anything, we can just chew the fat, shoot the breeze, and be ourselves. But in young people's lives, it is increasingly about what they're consuming while being monitored, and then regurgitating under examination and measurement, that is determining their futures. Schools are more like mini boot camps for capitalist consumers, where selfhood is judged by evidence of consumption, rather than by potentially uncomfortable to watch, listen to, or see, self-actualized expressions.

CAN ADULTS DO IT TOO?

In my other community mental health work, I have modeled with young adults living with psychiatric disability and/or intellectual disability (mainly Down Syndrome), a similar community of learners approach as Elwyn Richardson's (Lloyd, 2005, 2009, 2010). Using the cheeky expression "a bunch of fruits" (in the tradition of Queer Theory [Jagose, 1996], deliberately turning upside down the pejorative slang term "fruitloops," often used to refer disparagingly to people living with psychiatric or intellectual disability), I have argued for using voluntary social poetics (Herzfeld 2001) as a refreshing, uplifting way to respirit the spaces known as rehabs or disability support services. Here social poetics means allowing natural cheeky expressions, uninhibited mirroring and feedback of feelings and thoughts in one-on-one and small group interactions. It's about taking risks with how to be together, and how far to tease someone or pull their leg, and so on, because of an underpinning trust in the basic unconditional regard shared between those present.

By creating an open, urban tribe (Watters, 2004) of about sixty people who spent three years together, meeting regularly sharing stories and feelings (2004–2006), we created a new energy of welcome and celebration together, wherever we gathered. And in the Northern Territory (NT) from 2007–2010 I facilitated similar gatherings of people of difference (whether living with mental illness, or combining experiences of multicultural refugees and asylum seekers, who have been through multiple traumas).

The original project was called "Going Walkabout Together Through The Suburbs," after my earlier master's research and book *Going Walkabout Through The Suburbs* (Lloyd 2003/2005), which projected trialing this style of community-based, self-help, peer support. It was built on voluntary participation of multicultural young people (18–35 yrs) living with mental illness and/or intellectual disability, and volunteer buddies and elder mentors ("aunties and uncles" in the indigenous sense).

We used personal narrative sharing, in a witnessing and testimony cycle, developing an exchange I called "working the business of life" (Lloyd, 2005)—whereby people of mixed life experience and consciousness gave each other input and feedback in small group settings, about how life was unfolding for each person—in our self-help peer support group. That experience echoed the story in Ray Oldenburg's 1989 classic book on informal public places, *The Great Good Place* (Oldenburg, 1999/89), which celebrates places where people "hang out." He describes the demise of informal public gathering places, or "third places" in western suburbanized communities. But the decline of such gathering places isn't only a concern for sociologists and demographers. I argue that those interested in nurturing healing, learning, and development in education, health, and community cultural development places need to reassess the sorts of spaces they have created. If these have become places where people have been commodified into "patients, clients or consumers," passively and almost anonymously consuming an objectifying clinical culture created by the psy-ed (psychology and education combined, especially when both are about measuring people's behavior, more than caring for or about them) or clinical/medical model, then we are all in trouble.

Marc Augé's "introduction to an anthropology of supermodernity," (Augé, 1995) unpacks the phenomenon of "anthropological place." This is the "concrete and symbolic construction of space . . . which serves as a reference for all those it assigns to a position . . . (and) is a principle of meaning for the people who live in it." (Augé, 1995, pp. 51–52). Such a perspective is enlightening when one considers the impact of types of place on how well people heal and/or develop in health and rehabilitation spaces. The argument of this chapter is that currently such places and spaces are emptied of the essential elements of hospitality that create a sense of belonging and identity, and nurture the social relations that are a vital part of a healthy human condition. These are the core elements of third places, or informal public gathering places.

My PhD tribe generated "a principle of meaning" and a spirit of mutuality that fostered relaxed identity-reinforcement, a sense of belonging, and spontaneous engagement in fun and celebration on a regular basis. Along with moments of deep shared grief and pain, which became more bearable for being shared with a group of unconditionally supportive peers and elders. In schools, it is possible to allow children to experience the ups and downs of community life, while also providing a pastoral care and well-being support foundation that will allow them to receive support when it may be needed, rather than be ignored if they're not "keeping up with productivity targets." See figure 12.4 for one possible process to realize this support.

INVESTING IN THE SOCIAL POETICS OF SPACE

Linguist Roman Jakobson's Six Functions of Significance included the "poetic" as a "capacity to convey meaning by creatively playing with a recognizable form (Herzfeld, 2001, p. 280)." "Social poetics" are taken here as those relational interactions between people that combine expressive, emotive, and informative exchanges—i.e., "playing with it." Elwyn Richardson's students were involved in this everyday they went to school.

But social poetics can equally include the transition processes inherent in people's lived experience. This was what our PhD tribe explored together, which we then celebrated through shared expression of what had happened to us. And similarly, refugees and asylum seekers share extreme experiences requiring deep emotive exchanges to work through the trauma to healing.

The argument here is that this process is not essentially about retrospective understanding in our thinking, as reflected in the professionalized typology of symptoms and diagnoses, as much as it is involved in the moment by moment transition of our being, as Bergson argued (Bergson 1908/1988). This also fits with R.W. Emerson's work on the processes or events that make up human being.

> Emerson's "abandonment to the nature of things" serves less to indicate the possibility of arriving at an essential nature or core of being, than to figure

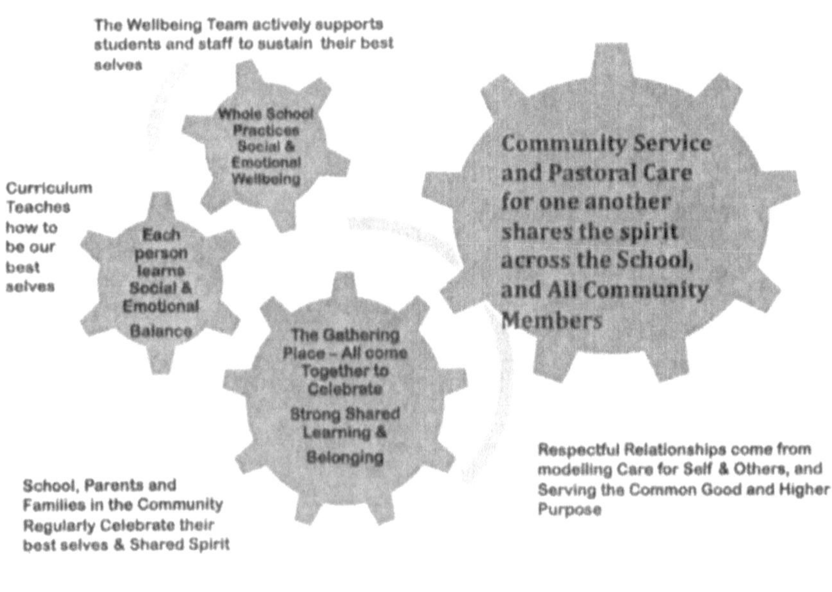

Figure 12.4. Pastoral Care and Wellbeing—Whole Community Cycles. Created by Robbie Lloyd.

> abandonment and transition as the nature of things. Transition and abandonment figure a power that at once supports and shatters the self . . . (they) mark the limit of the self's agency and self-control. (Levin, 1999, p. 3)

Participants in the PhD tribe, or community of belonging, that I helped to facilitate came to know one another and share their being with each other, in an environment of exploration and abandonment to it more than thinking. That is, they shared feelings and experiences, which then generated an energy field that had its own fit and flow, and form. This then influenced the ongoing nature of each person's Structure of Feelings and Experience (Lloyd, 2005), according my direct observations. This was as far removed from the medical, what I dub "the psy-ed model" as we could manage. Everyone participated equally in exploring the mystery and wonder of our individual and shared feelings and experiences. The experience of refugees and asylum seekers has an equivalent potency in the poetic exchange of beingness in moments of transition. In contrast, "psy-ed," to me, means those expert-dominated interchanges between "client and professional," where the client is a passive recipient of the expert-on-high view of how these people are or are not performing, well or badly, in their maneuverings around in the world.

> Everything teaches transition, transference, metamorphosis: therein is human power, in transference, not in creation; and therein is human destiny, not in longevity but in removal. We dive and reappear in new places.(Emerson in "Journals and Miscellaneous Notebooks of R.W. Emerson"). . . . The originality of Emerson's poet and scholar is a function of their transference of prior energies. Transition thus locates human power in a fated destiny of perpetual removal. (Levin, 1999, p. 3)

This perspective came close to my PhD tribe's process. They each went through an experience that involved, firstly, their intention to join in, then their motivation to fully engage, and their openness to go on experiencing. But it was in the actual dynamic of that encounter that "the magic" occurred (as many named it and commented on it throughout their journey together). The tribe generated an energy field of exchange of being, which was seen and felt to be efficacious in itself, as it caught and renewed the vital energy within each of the participants (consumers, carers, volunteer buddies, and professional mentor "aunties and uncles"), as I observed and recorded over seven years (Lloyd, 2004–10).

> Transition should . . . bring the familiar into contact with the unknown, a process that extends knowledge further into the mysterious margin of things even as it defamiliarizes the very categories through which that movement is conducted. By maximising the available "transitional surface," the great artist incessantly familiarises the strange and, at the same time, estranges the familiar. (Levin, 1999, p. 3)

This totally echoes Richardson's students' experience: "In this account we can trace step by step the children's increasing awareness of the world around them and their increasing desire to express its subtleties adequately and vividly, going hand in hand with the glad recognition of high achievement in the expression of others" (Richardson, 1964, p. vii).

The eventual result of my set of observations with the PhD tribe was The All Fruits Theory (Lloyd, 2009; in press; and *The All Fruits Theory*, new book appearing 2012 through Undergrowth Inc. Darwin), akin to Queer Theory (Jagose, 1996), arguing for mixing up people of diverse consciousness in communities of belonging, as they can assist each other's healing, growth, and development through the very transitional diversity of their mixed consciousnesses. By generating the sort of social poetics of transition that occur spontaneously in great good places, like Oruaiti in NZ, and my tribes in Sydney and NT, education, health, and community rehabilitation environments may be able to revitalize their roles through nurturing such diversity.

Wherever collectivities of people gather for the sake of seeking learning, healing, or developing community and culture, their main experience should be one that nurtures goodwill, fun, mutual concern for one another, and a shared sense of belonging and identity. Such was the outcome of the three year journey of the PhD tribe, and continues to be my experience in continuing to create zones of mutual support in different settings across the NT—most especially in whole-school cultures of well-being.

CREATING THE GATHERING PLACE

By creating a rhythmical, symbolic, interactive, cyclical pattern of gatherings, where shared personal stories created a narrative context of witnessing and testimony, my PhD tribe illustrated a different way of creating shared spaces for healing and new learning (Lloyd, 2009). This diverse group of souls was able to generate a vital healing energy field, full of spontaneity and "permission-giving" to be one's natural self. This is the essence of the Oruaiti learning environment, and of Ray Oldenburg's "great good place," where we can most easily be ourselves among others. Each participant in the PhD had their own identity and sense of purpose, role in the group, and reason for coming—i.e., they belonged there.

Marc Augén the other hand says that the "non-places" created by supermodernity actually attract a number of people, who go there deliberately seeking and appreciating the very anonymity that spooks many of us. "What is significant in the experience of non-place is its power of attraction, inversely proportional to territorial attraction, to the gravitational pull of place and tradition." (Augé, 1995, p. 118)

That may be true for adults who feel totally comfortable within themselves, and who have the security of home and family settings to return to. They may appreciate the de-personalized escape of the airport lounge, to get away from the hurly-burly for a while. But those who live in traumatized communities very often may not have such comfortable and secure settings, or senses of self, and have often been institutionally re-traumatized along the way.

Ray Oldenburg says that the attributes of third, or great good places are simple to identify: "Third places exist on neutral ground and serve to level their guests to a condition of social equality" (Oldenburg, 1999, p. 42). So far that is no different from airport lounges or supermarkets, except:

> Within these places, conversation is the primary activity and the major vehicle for the display and appreciation of human personality and individuality. Third places are taken for granted and most have a low profile . . . the character of a third place is determined most of all by its regular clientele and is marked by a playful mood, which contrasts with people's more serious involvement in other spheres. (Oldenburg, 1999, p. 42)

Many people use the anonymous airport lounge to escape into some "me time," where being identity-less is a welcome relief. But participants in my PhD tribe, and in community rehabilitation groups I have facilitated in the NT, have reported feeling that way in the very places they were supposed to be "recovering"—i.e., mental hospital wards, rehabilitation and disability support centers (Lloyd, 2007, 2009). Hence they and their carers showed great appreciation of the opportunity to "just hang out" in our tribe, and to share their Structure of Feelings and Experience (Lloyd, 2005) in a narrative sharing process that generated a rhythm of witnessing and testimony.

Marc Augé says that, "the community of human destinies is experienced in the anonymity of non-place, and solitude" (Augé, 1995, p. 120). This is an understandable reaction to the overwhelming individuated consumer-on-the-prairie experience of the shopping mall, our ant-like presence on the freeway, and the *Mulholland Drive* movie's (Lynch, 2001) trance-inducing effect of the ticky-tacky sameness of our suburban wastelands.

But for places claiming to offer learning, healing, or recovery for vulnerable people, such specters are downright scary. We need something injected into this non-place, this Twilight Zone, to nurture our universal humanity with some hope and purpose. Such as comes from having an identity, a role in the group, and sense of belonging—all elements of the "great good place." That's where The Gathering place in schools in NT aims to generate welcome, hospitality, and unconditional love as a communal setting for strong being and learning. But it takes work to bring this about—the work of effective social and emotional well-being coordinators among school leaders and staffs.

SOCIAL POETICS AND GROWTH

I argue that applying the social poetics of transition to more schools, and community-based rehabilitation and disability support environments, would create hope, remotivation, and purpose for many students, teachers, administrative staff, and families in schools. As well as among mental health "consumers, carers and concerned professionals." When people can share stories together, create dreams together, and experience the social poetics that come from spontaneous exchange of natural being, they find a new form of welcome and nurture—recipients and care providers alike.

This old fashioned "hospitality" is simply the exchange of the structure of feelings and experiences (Lloyd, 2005), in unconditionally "safe" environments, that constitute the same elements as great good places.

Just as great good places have people who rib one another, "take the mickey," and give immediate feedback that won't allow bad moods or long-held resentments to dominate the shared space, so too did my PhD tribe's exercise "working the business of life" (Lloyd, 2005). This sort of mirroring and feedback helps students, staff, leaders, and community participants to know they belong and are wanted, but that they can't get away with messy behavior in this place or this company. This is the same effect that U.S. journalist Ethan Watters identified in his classic book, *Urban Tribes: Are Friends the New Family?* (Watters, 2004), where he found correspondents from around the world who told him that, "my tribe helps me be the best me I can be."

"We need to pay some attention to the changes affecting the major categories people use when they think about their identity and their reciprocal relations" (Augé, 1995, p. 40). This is the core problem in current increasingly objectified settings for education, mental health and disability rehabilitation. Even if people are treated "nicely," and have lots of activities and outings, my argument is that they are basically being told in the subtext of every interaction, "you are less than, and we are here to help you receive a service you need, because we are experts who know best."

There is no reciprocity, no exchange as equals (which Elwyn Richardson created so seamlessly), and which great good places ensure. Currently it's become all one way traffic in these settings for learning, health, and community service.

This contrasts with what Andrew Mawson found were the most important elements in the Bromley-by-Bow community resurgence in London:

> I realized just how deeply we all depend for our sanity on relationships with other people. They give us our sense of reality and equilibrium. Without them we all stumble . . . a community within which (we) could have a role and be valued. (Mawson, 2008, p. 21)

Our tribe created that same relationship base, and it all came from voluntary participation and resourcing. The importance of voluntary social poetics in generating community learning and healing is a much-neglected one. And it is one of the main reasons we need to challenge the system's obsession with experts, measurement, and assessment of professional practice, along with that of mechanistic, rule-bound "duties of care," which allow for no risks to be taken, of entering into moments of deep human exchange. Professional responsibility has been taken to such an extreme that ordinary human exchange and feedback has been denied a role in the lives of "the vulnerable" (i.e., children, and people living with mental illness and/or intellectual disability).

The tribe showed that participants got into what they called a "magical" rhythm of sharing and caring whenever they came together. All this came about through voluntary, informal reciprocal exchange. I summed up its elements as: interactive, intentional and intuitive, rhythmical, reciprocal, relational ritual cycles, of companionship, contemplation, communion and celebration" (Lloyd, 2010).

Such symbolic interaction occurs everyday in great good places, but it is not officially studied or recorded as an efficacious part of society's makeup (except in extraordinary cases such as Ray Oldenburg's book). The elements operating in such places can easily be transferred to schools, and community health settings, if one barrier is removed. The expert-dominated, over-regulated, risk-averse, over-measured fields of education, health and rehabilitation need to "chill out," and allow more active exchange of our natural human attributes of relationality. Then, the social poetics of transition would contribute untold benefits to overall learning, community health, along with job satisfaction among teachers, and health and human service workers.

MAKING IT REAL IN PRACTICE

In several schools where I have worked as the pastoral care and well-being coordinator or adviser, clear evidence has arisen of the benefits from adopting this sort of foundation of social and emotional support. Weekly Wellbeing Teams led to principals showing more care and concern for teachers and administrative staff whom they had previously let "slip through the cracks." This was often due to awkward personality politics between them, or just bad chemistry, both of which needed emotional homework and assertiveness to be worked through to get a genuine communication and relationship affirming result. The adults are most often the problem, because none of us got any help in learning how to express our feelings in a balanced way, without being hurt or taking offence when someone gives us honest feedback about one of our failings. So my job was often to teach adults how to behave, so they could relate to children more respectfully. And when they got into the groove with this, the results were amazing—reduced teacher absences; improved staff room harmony and positive "buzz"; more volunteering to collaborate and help each other during stressful periods; and generally happier classrooms, assemblies, and meetings when parents came into school.

The Gathering Place idea reinforces how much we all respond to rhythmical rituals. When people can rely on there being a flowing set of gatherings with warm feelings and shared opportunities for different ones to lead events, everyone gets a deep lift in spirits. Whether weekly assemblies with little performance items, or short "prayers for the people" followed by news of community events, or visits by community elders to share some old story or a new development in the community—all these elements built what the market-oriented social scientists might call "social capital," but what I prefer to see as our community spirit.

Great good places share that "vibe," that sense of relaxed honoring of each other and "our place." With humour and "getting alongside each other" (i.e., rather than confronting each other head-on) we can be companions on the journey through life. Children want that informal, relaxed way of being around their close family and friends, but also those adults they see everyday, their teachers and general school staff. By creating that sense of being a great good place, school can be become a refreshing place of renewing energy and uplifting spirit, rather than a burdensome factory, expecting measured results and creating stressful lives (with the natural flow-on expectation that, "something bad is going to happen if those results don't come in on time, on budget, and up to the mark!").

CONCLUSION

At the same time as Elwyn Richardson published his poignant book in New York, another uncle and educator of great note was sharing his experiences in a similar vein. David Holbrook published *The Secret Places* (Holbrook, 1964) in the same year, and described therein "the cultural environment of the child," and how to nurture creative expression by getting "in touch with the secret places of the soul" (Holbrook, 1964, p. xiv). I do not believe it is too much to claim this is what we achieve when The Gathering Place works holistically alongside The Wellbeing Team, and a well-woven social and emotional learning curriculum in schools. The aim is to build strong senses of self that can withstand life's knocks by knowing deep down that one is loved and belongs in this world, with the support of all around us. That takes much more than test results, fancy curricula, flash timetabling, and good assessment results of students and teachers:

> The themes of the present book are the cultural environment of the child, and the positive, creative work one may do in school to aid the imagination to develop, as a means of self-realization and literacy. The latter work needs to be in touch with the secret places of the soul; it is here that order may be found, and by what flourishes there potentialities may be released. . . . We need far more teaching-as-art. I argue that, because such work can only be done in sincerity and awe, the teacher will inevitably find *s/he* is working against the environment of commercial culture . . . the mass culture of our mass-production urban society is, it seems, doomed to be trivial . . . (whereas) by their imaginative culture they (students) may grow to become good lovers, good parents, good workers, and creative people in the community, able to let their sympathy flow, to become sustained by self-respect, and possessed of a sense of purpose. (Holbrook 1964, p. xiv) (*current author's emphasis*)

It takes work to achieve this sort of climate of being and social poetics. Work that many adults haven't bothered with, as they didn't receive an education that fostered such perspectives, either at home or at school. Yet that is what we need to undertake—challenging the mechanistic, linear hierarchical thinking that has once again risen to dominate education, health and community services sectors.

Those lessons were reinforced by M.C. Richard's messages in *Centering* (Richards, 1964/1989). Her inspiration to several generations of America's educators, artists, and followers of evolving human consciousness rather than stuck dogmas, continues today. In 1989, Matthew Fox introduced the twenty-fifth anniversary edition of M.C's classic title by reminding us that:

> Because M.C. is so committed to cosmology, she offers morality without moralizing. Morality for her is to "commit ourselves to participation" (Richards, 1964, p. 92), and from this participation derives the development of moral imagination. Another way of naming this capacity for moral participation is compassion "the ability to picture the sufferings of others, to identify. In one's citizenship, or the art of politics, it is part of one's skill to imagine other ways of living than one's own" (Richards 1964, p. 115). Compassion is itself an alternative "mode of perception." It is the ultimate act of centering, of bringing together the known energies of the universe.

This perspective brings together the same awareness Henri Bergson explored and expressed in his notion of "duration" (Bergson, 1908/1988). He saw perception as always inclining us to the future, while our moments of reflection when in the space between perception and action allow us to fill our consciousness with memory images. So we get the best of both worlds by combining action and reflection. M. C. Richards taught what Matthew Fox called "the one way of perception. . . .

> Awakening our perceptions; cleansing our perceptions; celebrating our perceptions; reverencing our perceptions. The artists in us must lead the way into this

> spiritual voyaging—for the artist in us perceives. "We want our minds to be clear—not so we can think clearly, but so we can be open in our perception." (Fox, quoted in Richards, 1989/1964, p. xi)

This is what Elwyn Richardson and David Holbrook were also teaching in 1964. Nearly fifty years later we are struggling to remember the priceless value in those ways of being together in learning and healing environments. Great good places were named by Henry James, whose thought improved by M. C. Richards, as Matthew Fox noted:

> M. C. cites Henry James who said that a writer is a person upon whom nothing is lost—but she improves on James when she adds, "Well, anyone should be: a person upon whom nothing is lost!" (Richards, 1964, p. 106) (Fox in Richards, 1989/1964, p. xi).

Our job, as effective educators, health service providers, parents, and citizens, is to try to rejuvenate that spirit of great good places in schools and healing places, and the open perception of life that flourishes in their convivial, inspiring company for our souls as well as our minds.

NOTES

1. "Whitefella" is the term used by Australia's indigenous peoples to describe the non-indigenous (male and female); it is matched in colloquial conversation by the reciprocal term "blackfella."
2. See websites: www.kidsmatter.edu.au; http://www.mindmatters.edu.au/default.asp; www.mindmatters.edu.au/resources_and_downloads/staff_matters/staff_matters_landing.html; www.daretolead.edu.au/.

REFERENCES

Augé, M. (trans. John Howe). (1995). *Non-places: Introduction to an anthropology of supermodernity* London: Verso.

Bergson, H. (1908/1988) *Matter and Memory*. New York: Zone Books.

Ezrin, Gilmour, Guthrie, Waters. (1979). *The Wall*. Harvest/EMI Records, UK.

Goffman, E. (1959). *The Presentation of Self in Everyday Life*. NY: Doubleday.

Hansen, J. (2005). 'The Devaluation of Inner Subjective Experiences by the Counselling Profession: A Plea to Reclaim the Essence of the Profession'. In the *Journal of Counseling & Development, 83*, accessed 14/05/2010.

Herzfeld, M. (2001). *Anthropology: Theoretical Practice in Culture and Society*, UNESCO. Malden, MA: Blackwell.

Holbrook, D. (1964). *The Secret Places: Essays on Imaginative Work in English Teaching and on the Culture of the Child*. London: Methuen, University Paperbacks.

Jagose, A. (1996). *Queer Theory*. Carlton South: Melbourne University Press.

Lloyd, R. (2004–2010). Personal Journal kept while undertakingPhD field work and continuing community health projects.

Lloyd, R. (2005a). 'Indigenous-style "working the business of life" as tools for active growth and healing reflexivity.' In G. Whiteford, (Ed.), *Voice, Identity and Reflexivity: Proceedings of the Second RIPPLE Qualitative Research as Interpretive Practice Conference*, CSU, Albury, NSW 22–23 Sept. 2005, CSU, Bathurst.

Lloyd, R. (2005b). *Going Walkabout Throughthe Suburbs: Valuing the lessons from alternative consciousness*. Melbourne: Sid Harta Publishers.

Lloyd, R. (2009). '*How the All Fruits Salad creates sweeter futures in rural and remote mental health*'. Paper presented at 'Creating Futures: Research, Practice & Policy' Conference of RANZCP, Cairns, 22–25 Sept. 2008.

Lloyd, R. (2010). Journal kept while working in community and education settings in Darwin and 'the Top End' of Northern Territory, Australia.

Mawson, A. (2008). *The Social Entrepreneur: Making Communities Work*. London: Atlantic Books.

Levin, J. (1999). *The Poetics of Transition: Emerson, Pragmatism, & American Literary Modernism*, Durham, NC: Duke University Press.

Lynch, D. (2001). Writer/Director, *Mulholland Drive*, Universal Pictures, USA.

Oldenburg, R. (1989/99). *The Great Good Place: Cafes, Coffee Shops, Bookstores, Bars, Hair Salons and other Hangouts at the Heart of a Community*. New York: Marlowe & Co.

Richards, M.C. (1989/1964). *Centering: On Pottery, Poetry, and the Present*. Middletown, Connecticut: Wesleyan University Press.

Richardson, E. (1964). *In the Early World*. New York: Pantheon/Random House.

Tolle, E. (2001). *The Power of Now: A Guide to Spiritual Enlightenment*. Mumbai, India: Yogi Impressions.

Tolle, E. (2005). *A New Earth: Awakening to Your Life's Purpose*. Camberwell, Victoria: Michael Joseph/Penguin,.

Watters, E. (2004). *Urban Tribes: Are Friends the New Family?* London: Bloomsbury.

Chapter Thirteen

Not Confronting the Resistances in a Psychoanalytically Guided School

Howard Covitz

Playing in the last quarter of life is replete with mysteries, all their own. Even fully mature people, nevermind grandchildren, betimes imagine the older person as some kind of fixed point, carrying neither past nor future within them. Older psychoanalysts are, by no means, an exception. Patients see the older analyst as he or she is for them . . . in the moment, and in the moment of their need. Supervisees view them, at times, as possessors of oracular vision and, at other times, as relics of previous civilizations. What to say? I object! I object to being seen as an object with a fixed trajectory, someone who landed before recorded time just where I am, today. Reflecting to himself as he grew older, the once poet laureate of the United States, Stanley Kunitz, recommended (*The Layers*, 1995) that we choose to live in life's layers, rather than in its litter, as he protested against those who imagine that he might be done with his life's changes.

I have a complicated past—I have gone through lots of "changes"; we all have. I have lived, I like to think, many lives since as a young man I married Marsha—that was 1965, though I shall be thinking, in these reflections, of a period of glee and sadness and great activity from 1976 to 1978. By that time, I had already studied Theology and Biblical Studies, had run a catechism school, had taught university Mathematics, and had left Mathematics to work with disturbed adolescents—first inpatient and then in a day school for emotionally disturbed inner city children. I had earlier tired of the monastic withdrawal necessary for working in Theoretical Mathematics and decided to seek training in working with people. "What a novel idea," I thought.

The year before that first year in question, I enrolled in a psychoanalytic program. It was an old fashioned program that believed its students should be thoroughly versed in the psychoanalytic literature 1896–1975. To do this reading, I began taking public transportation so as to allow time for reading some 400 pages each week and to make ends meet. As *pater familias*, I taught Calculus part-time in city prisons, in addition to my high school teaching. Oh, yes! And Marsha and I had a dog named Kazimierza,[1] as well as three children: a newborn daughter and 9 and 10 year old sons, the three of whom would eventually combine to make us grandparents, six times over.

A call came in one day from the Director of the four-school special education matrix in which I taught. We were not friends, the Director and I, and indeed there had been considerable friction between us related to my expressed urgings at faculty meetings to racially integrate the school at which I taught. My counterpart in one of the other schools in our little special education chain of schools was the Reverend Paul Washington who had marched with "Brother Martin," making it particularly unseemly to my way of thinking that my school was comprised of poor Whites . . . while Paul Washington enrolled only poor Blacks. In any case, I wasn't popular with our Director.

It was all the more surprising when the call came in: "Would you like to be Principal?" Oh, my gosh! Principal? The school was a mess. Daily attendance was hovering at 50 percent and the probability of hostilities was far greater than that figure on any given day. The Principal who preceded me had lasted for a year and was, as they say, burnt out. The Principal before him had lasted longer. The four schools had been under the gentle guidance of a psychodynamically informed fellow who had initially hired me. He had given up his position to a young EdD who bandied about terms such as: Diagnostic Prescriptive Model[2]; Non-teaching Assistants; and Service Delivery Systems. I was biased by my early psychoanalytic studies to think differently. Learning wasn't the result of discrete simple lessons accumulating one at a time: "Johnny will add 3 digit numbers with 85% accuracy" did not even begin to move me. As an ex-Seminarian, NTA's,[3] non-teaching assistants, that is, could not be distinguished from bar room bouncers and I could not utter the words "service delivery system"[4] without cringing. "Principal?" I queried. "But will I have an open hand, will I be able to integrate the school, and can I abbreviate *Service Delivery System* as SDS?" The Director was about as amused by my little witticism as J. Edgar Hoover might have been, but since the school was such a mess, I surmise, he thought: "What do I got to lose?" And, thus, the die was cast.

That is the short story of how an ex-Seminarian, ex-Mathematician, and psychoanalytic candidate found himself running a previously behaviorally oriented, unracially-integrated school in a run-down part of *White Town, USA*[5] (cf., Binzen, 1971).

IMAGINING CHANGE IN SOME CHILDREN IN FISHTOWN, PHILADELPHIA

Fenichel (1941), one of the third generation analysts, opined that in psychoanalytic treatment we could do most anything as long as we knew why we had chosen to do so. Still and all, some things work and some don't. Thinking back, I claim no advantage other than "the chutzpah" of youth and a few ideas borrowed from psychoanalysis.

After beginning at the end and recounting the situation that motivated me to leave both the school and special education, I shall briefly outline the program that my staff and I put in place during my days as a secondary school principal with inner city emotionally disturbed and delinquent children, and the results of that effort.[6] As someone who spent many years afterwards teaching in a University Department of Statistics, I don't need to remind myself of the difference between anecdotal and controlled-experimental evidence. Neither, however, do I feel obligated to depreciate the anecdotal; all research begins with a hunch that precipitates from such material or, else, accidentally available *ex post facto* from others' experiments.

I might still be running a day school for inner city children if not for L. It was the April of my second year. I had already received multiple pointed inquiries from the Department of Special Education filtered through my Director. A decision was apparently made to dispatch one of the Department's research henchmen, Dr. T He dutifully scheduled a day to come and *discuss* my school's programs. The appointed morning was spent discussing these programs and results from standardized tests. I suspected that he believed that the results may have been fudged (I'll discuss results, later), but, having the training he had, he was not going to show his cards.

Instead, Dr. T took aim specifically at the Math Program. Maxine the Math Teacher had been requested by me to discontinue the teaching of the Algebra sequence until students begged to be taught the conventional components of this ancient discipline. Instead—as this was but several years after the controversial Fisher-Spassky 1972 World Chess Championship in Reykjavik, Iceland—I recommended a move-by-move replaying of the games. Dr. T, having spent part of the morning going through students' files, had wondered out loud if these students were—based on their recorded IQs—bright enough to learn the rules of the game and the moves of the pieces, never mind to benefit from such an experience. I explained to him that I thought they, indeed, were and that I had decided on each component of our school's program based on a now fifty year old maxim in certain treatment circles: *never fight the resistance—you'll lose* (this model was implicit in the early works of August Aichorn with his *Wayward Youth* [1935] and in Freud's introduction to that work). These students were more adept at resisting the learning process, I argued, than teachers were in teaching, pushing my staff and me to choose subject areas to teach in which resistances had not yet developed; he was not convinced.

Dr. T chose L whose recorded IQ was in the Borderline area (as I recall . . . 75 on the WISC). L was a bleach-blonde Ziggy Stardust/David Bowie imitator who, by the very length of his police record, was not a talented thief. He was to become a pipe-fitter, as an adult, earning a solid middle class living but he was a reasonably gifted player of the Game of Kings as a youngster. In any case, if the Department of Special Education wasn't titillated by our programs, Dr. T was obviously excited to demonstrate how a doctoral level educator might summarily do away with such a limited 16 year old youngster over a checkered board. L was asked and agreed; *puer et senex* sat down to play at lunchtime with an audience of L's peers and some staff. A dozen or so moves into the game, L was up a *small piece* . . . a Knight or a Bishop. L noted Dr. T's weak defensive position ("Da way y'playsy'Pawns is important, too") and recommended that he resign. Dr. T refused; I remember his words nearly forty years later: "we'll play it out just to see what happens."

It was Sandor Feldman (1965), the transplanted Hungarian psychoanalytic student of the great innovator Ferenczi, who used to say that whenever the speaker uses the word "just," one could be certain that something much more is in play. L mercilessly trounced Dr. T, who immediately demanded a rematch. The same openings were used, yielding the same initial result and another offer to set the chess pieces up, anew. Again, the good Dr. T refused. This time, however, after it was certain to L that his opponent's skills—combined with careful play and a little *zug-zwang*—would contribute to ending this game, as well, in a rout, paused and stood up from the table. He noted with both poise and clarity and in his adopted Cockney twang: "Dr. T, if you're too fuck'n stupid to resign a losing game, then I resign." L left the building, as the saying goes, and so did Dr. T. I received a friendly call from Carmen the District Supervisor of Special Education the next day hinting that, unless I left the school, additional referrals to the school were unlikely. I submitted my resignation effective the last day of school.

THE PROGRAM: CIRCUMNAVIGATING THE SWEAT-HOG RESISTANCES

It was precisely during those years that a popular TV series was aired in the USA: Welcome Back, Kotter (1975–1979). It highlighted a special education teacher who had a mottled career as a student, himself, and was—when he returned to his alma mater as a teacher—punished by his principal by having to teach the class of "sweat hogs," who Mr. Woodman, the Principal described in his frequent retort: "Kotter, these children couldn't pass a blood test without cheating." Kotter didn't think of them in this way and, as might be expected from an up-beat sitcom, he had great success in teaching them in an atmosphere of mutual—if betimes broken—respect. I think it fair to say that I, too, had a less than typical career. During the last years of high school, I attended on Tuesdays and Thursdays, those days I was responsible for teaching the Calculus class. On Mondays, Wednesdays, and Fridays, I hung out at the Boston Metropolitan Museum of Fine Art and MIT. After proudly not receiving a High School degree, though having a very good relationship with my teachers, I went on to not finish baccalaureate studies, beginning doctoral work in Mathematics after my Freshman undergraduate year. Thus, between a birth certificate from the City of New York and my first graduate degree there was a delay in my collection of conventional credentials. All this is to say that I was well-prepared, just like Gabe Kotter, to embrace students who lived within boundaries that related to respect but who might deviate in the manner in which they expressed their respect for others as subjects in their own right. As an aside, I should add that, just as Gabe Kotter had a beautiful wife to go home to each day for support, I had Marsha, two latency-aged boys and our daughter, whom my staff called The Perfect One, to support my adventures in education.

In any case, now in charge of an inner city school, I had the responsibility for designing a program that met the worldly and educational needs of my own unwashed crew of adolescents and a group of teachers inured to the trainings they gleaned in graduate schools of education. I had no such advantaged education but was sufficiently daring and ignorant of conventional methodologies to freshly consider the problems that arose in our little high school. I will not attempt to describe how exciting a time and task this was.

The singular paradigm that I suggested to my staff, to repeat, was never to resist the resistances. Freud had introduced the notion of "resistances to treatment" very early on, in his 1890s joint treatise on hysteria published with his mentor Breuer (Breuer and Freud, 1895). If complexes were repressed, there was both a theoretical and a practical need to recognize that some force must be keeping disabilities in place. By the time of his *Interpretation of Dreams* (1899–1900, p. 8), Freud had proffered a definition: "Whatever interrupts the progress of analytic work is a resistance." By 1926 in his *Inhibitions, Symptoms and Anxiety,* Freud had postulated the existence of at least five types of resistance. Examination of the Ego (*das Ich*) offered three types: (i) Repression or the removal of conscious access to painful material; (ii) Resistances which he called *transference* related to the wish not to disturb psychical relationship with the analyst borrowed from historical relationships with parents and others[7]; and (iii) Resistances that relate to so-called *secondary gains of illness*, those benefits that accrue to the sufferer due to his or her suffering. There were two additional resistances that were subtypes of the first, namely: (a) Resistances of the Id (*Widerstandfumdas*

Es) that coaxed the psyche into repeating unconsciously mediated scenarios (Freud called them *vorstellungen*, visual scenarios . . . today, we might call them schemata (Slap, 1991), object relations (British Middle School), or RIGS (Stern, 1985 on Representations of Internalized Generalizations); and (b) Resistances of the Conscience (*Widerstandfumdas Uber Ich*) that protect the personality from unmanageable and potentially overwhelming guilt.

As a School Principal, it *was not* within my power or purview to carry on analyses and, indeed, even our consulting psychiatrist[8] was satisfied to limit his interactions to evaluation and consultation with faculty. It *was* my task specifically to take a group of inner-city and disturbed high school students from their then-present skill level (with the bulk of the student body functioning on a primer to third grade level) and help them to attain a functional level of education that would permit them to more fully appreciate daily living and to enter technical training programs, Community Colleges, and higher education, whenever possible.

I did find a first resistance, one about which my beginning psychoanalytic training offered no hint and about which I could do nothing. On my first day, I told faculty that I would show up quite early each day to make coffee and think about the children (aka . . . Service Delivery Recipients). They were welcome to come and think with me and equally welcome not to do so. The next several years found this offer pitted against the local teachers union's sense that I was coercing teachers into working beyond their contract.[9] Some resistances are never resolved; this is such an example. Most of the teachers did, indeed, come to drink coffee and join in a form of mutual supervision related to our work.

It should be noted that the five Ego resistances (listed above) were each identifiable in our students. Our students, especially those who walked blind to the written signs that serve as guideposts in this world—on stores and on roads—had deep pain associated with their effective blindness and any changes to that threatened a *looking inside* at their own deficiencies (see i, above). Similarly, their relationships to significant others in their lives were predicated on older relationships that were of some importance to them (see ii, above, on transference). G never read until he confronted his violent and alcoholic father and explained that he would not ever again stand idly by as their father assaulted G's one-year-older sister. And with these transferences in mind, their limitations had many advantages—the so-called *secondary gains of illness*—not the least of which was extracting themselves from dangerous and violent city schools. The two specific resistances from the Id (the repetition compulsion) and from the Superego (the fear of toxic guilt overwhelming them) played roles, as well.

As to my staff? They identified a number of areas in which *resistances to learning* were in play and standing in the way of educative processes. The ones we spoke of early on in our work, together, were *inter alia* the following:

- a history of failing to learn how to read,[10] in spite of programs staffed by reading experts;
- a related fear of reading out loud, made evident by a refusal to do so;
- a history of failing to learn how to do elementary Mathematics;
- a refusal to cooperate in school processes;
- a tendency to use the long striated musculature of the arms and legs for solving problems between themselves and other students and staff; and
- a refusal to come to school.

Thus, my staff and I began to fascinate about manners in which we might engage our wards without activating these resistances, and without engaging them in either forced restraint (non-Teaching Assistants with weight and muscle on their side, sitting on them in halls) or negative reinforcement schedules.

Reading

As noted above, the inability to read in a sixteen year old or his or her ability to read only on a primer level, is front-loaded with a variety of feelings related to failure and disability. Our students had mostly gone through reading *programs* that had failed to add much at all to their reading facility. How could we, we opined, teach these youngsters to read in their English class without confronting head-on their resistances to learning how to read. Walter the History teacher was also an ex-Seminarian and, as such, suggested that we give up on the process of teaching them how to read English and focus, instead, on teaching them to read Latin.

"Don't bother to confront their resistance to learning how to read English. Don't even, initially, teach them English. Teach them, instead, something which they have never tried and never failed to learn that encapsulates the self-same skill-set that one wishes them to learn. Reading Latin and reading English are indistinguishable skills. The latter they have learned not to do; the former they are resistant to doing."

Ah, Walter! What the Vatican lost, Fishtown gained.

I'll come back to cite the improvements that followed upon this program.

Before I go on, however, I should like to suggest that there is some difficulty in the use of the notion of *a program*, at all. I have been involved in observing people in their educative work, many who were patients of mine. Frequently, when they have introduced successful *programs* or *techniques*, they have been pushed by their Principals and Superintendents to *spread the word*. As if: "if it works for you, think of how many more people can be helped by teaching this program to others." If there is little else that has been learned in the Century of psychoanalysis, it is that *A treating/educating B* is a specifically human and a specific-to-the-practitioner process.[11] Walter was excited about this program and undoubtedly his excitement was contagious. Another Master Teacher would have to find their own catalysts of excitement.

Fear of Reading Out Loud

Being able to present one's Truths by speaking them may well be somewhere near the core of *the Good Life*. As someone who stuttered from age three to the middle of my training analysis, I remain keenly aware of the resistance to reading out loud. I recall with no delight, how my second grade teacher, Miss B, decided that she might break right through my resistance to fluidly read by forcing me to do so. I do not question her good intentions and cannot know whether she lengthened or shortened the duration of my disability, but I do have my suspicions. My high school Math teacher, Mrs B, got (me) further by enlisting me to teach the Calculus class. In any case, Psychoanalysis has its silent patients, as well as its silent analysts.[12] When we worked inpatient with very bright and very disturbed adolescents, my wife taught me the importance of reading to students . . . of being active, oneself. Most of the children who would visit her and the head librarian, Edith, had not been read to in childhood. These librarians read to them. I borrowed this from them.

Several days each week—and likely inconsistent with union policies— a staff member at Columbia School Kensington, Sherri the English Teacher/ Vice Principal or I would read a short story at lunchtime in our library. Resistance was clear and it took weeks before a group of students could be found lying on the floor of the library. I vividly recall one day, however. The reader had chosen Lawrence's (1926) pathos-filled short story—"The Rocking Horse Winner." At the poignant close of the story, R, who had a long history of collecting protection money from weaker students, was on the floor with the others; he was in tears. His right arm was partly covering his red eyes.

It would be several months before R asked if he could become a lunchtime reader from time to time. Others followed.

Fear of Elementary Mathematics

A colleague and friend asked me to meet with his daughter who was being held back in a swank private school due to her failure to pass Trigonometry. She was a poetic young woman who now, decades later, is married and functioning as a City Planner. I knew that as a non-Math-phobe who enjoys building geodesic domes, I have rarely had the occasion to use Trigonometry. Why should her school or I expect other from this young woman? My own children were exposed to most curious requirements and exercises in Math classes. One—years prior to his becoming a successful academic—was failed for not keeping "adequate" notes on his teacher's lectures in Geometry. Fortunate that my son was raised in the suburbs! His father, a guttersnipe from the streets of Brooklyn, might have enlisted the assistance of the notebook *qua* weapon to instill in this teacher a more sanguine notion of good pedagogical technique. Another child was in the generation of "the mad minute," a classroom exercise where students are graded by calculating the percentage of correct answers not based on the complete test but based rather on the number of correct answers prior to their first error. (That was a hard sentence to write; it's a tough concept to comprehend.) An example might clarify. If there were one hundred questions and only the fourth was incorrect, the child's grade was 3 out of 100, i.e., 3 percent.

All this is to say that there is reason to fear learning elementary Mathematics. Coupled with this is a nasty artifact of the passage of time. When the present system of teaching Mathematics was designed, puberty was in the fifteen to sixteen year old range. Today, and in 1976, it was twelve to thirteen years old. And while pre-pubescent children—looked upon developmentally—are fascinated by solving puzzles (Algebra can be thought of as a guided method for solving obfuscating puzzles), pubescent children are not. As one inpatient of mine averred: when I hit puberty, puberty hit back. No attention has been paid to the high school freshman's hierarchy of interests. Who among us cannot recall—upon our entry to puberty—our sudden new focus on the loving potentials and sexual accoutrements of our fellow classmates and the diminution of the previous center of our interests in playing games or solving puzzles? Still, no attention has been paid to this in reformulating the high school Mathematics curriculum and students are being asked to do things, which are not within their abilities to focus upon.

I should add that the anxieties that precipitate from sexual interest and the existential fear of not finding "someone to love" (Queen, 1976), in and of themselves, make many students *neurologically* incapable of doing this work. In our lengthy evolution, the prefrontal cortical areas have learned to partially if temporarily shut down in the presence of anxiety. It is not, need I add, adaptive to be able to think about the Quadratic Formula or to see up-close when the tiger's toothy mouth is poised to eat you. And our neurological apparati are not capable during the teen years (and not much-so, afterwards) of separating out one anxiety from another.

It was with this in mind that I suggested to Maxine[13] that the Game of Chess was far more suitable as a method for increasing analytic acuity than the solution of quadratic equations. The outcome, winning or losing, was more in tune with notions of success in relationship than answering a question such as the following:

> If Hortense has 3 times as many dimes in her pocket as quarters,
> half as many nickels as quarters and twice as many pennies as dimes,
> and if she knows—through some unspecified process of divination—
> that the 62 coins in her pocket add up to $6.24, how many of each coin does she have?

"You've gotta be kidding. And if it turns out there's no solution, what a fool you are for trying."

I say (said): Let them play Chess! And the skill set, as with reading English or else reading Latin, is, just perhaps, the same.

A Resistance to Cooperating in School Processes

The U.S. involvement in Vietnam was just over in the 1970s, but still, most of our students were in the sixteen to nineteen year old range, either near or at enlistment age. They were, that is, deemed mature enough and sufficiently replaceable to follow their First Lieutenant over some foreign hill in the next war. Indeed, they were largely from the socio-economic class that provides the human fodder for our war efforts. An old story! When the tribes arrived in the Land of Canaan and needed to choose a soldier to drive out its previous inhabitants and their idolatrous habits, where did they look but to Jepthah, the muscled son of a poor prostitute (Judges 12–13).

Our students were little different. Working class children, some of whose parents were to be found when I'd make house calls lying on the couch with a bottle of rye or "trucking on a joint." Others held working class or paraprofessional jobs but couldn't leave the neighborhood that they knew as home. The neighborhood was dirty, chocked full of litter. The local tavern was required to serve minorities but after so doing would smash their glass against a brick wall.

A school might design a Civics program or talk loftily about the students' needs to become active members in polities of mutual concern and interest. Their community was a wreck. The drug of choice was tuluol in that neighborhood—a working class drug in a working class neighborhood. I was well familiar with it. When my father and I would need to clean out a gunked carburetor, we'd toss it into a 55-gallon drum of a solvent, sometimes tuluol. My father always warned me not to breathe in the fumes. Some of these children did. They would carry a rag impregnated with what they pronounced "ty-wall." The drug *spaced* them out and calcified massive amounts of brain cells. It was a great carburetor cleaner and a powerful destroyer of brain cells for those who indulged.

Indeed, I recall one of our faculty leaning into a classroom where a "huffer" (someone who frequently breathed in these fumes) was sexually soothing himself. Attempting to lessen the tension in himself and in the lad and in order not to disrupt Sherri the English Teacher, the faculty member quipped: "J, get a hold of yourself." Alas, the humor went right over J's radar.

Back to the program. I could talk to them all day about how Washington and Jefferson and Hamilton struggled over how to apportion members to the House of Representatives and worried, just as some of us do today, about gerrymandering; there was, however, no salient reason for them to be interested. The outside world was frightening to them. The schools they were expelled from in order to have the honor of entering ours were, as I've already noted, violent and threatening, and dirty, too. Out of what I can only presume was fear, when we took them to museums in the outside world, they would typically *act out* and we'd be *thrown out*. The look on a museum guard's face remains with me, thirty five years later. Apparently, one of our Sweat Hogs put a lit cigarette in the mouth of a millennia old Shang Dynasty porcelain guard dog. The guard was far less than amused, even if the guard dog was undamaged. Understandable.

The students, additionally, tended to have what the psychoanalytic anthropologist, Paul Parin (see Parin et al., 1971), identified as a tribal conscience (superego) that he had witnessed in his work with some of the tribes of Africa with which he worked. Conscience existed most obviously in the presence of authority and dissolved in the authority figure's absence. How does one create an external authority that circumvents the resistance to authority while encouraging the behaviors associated with obeisance? When I called a first community meeting, G refused to attend: "I follow all the rules, why should I attend?" The students were not ready to form their own government; history had demonstrated the brevity of their reflex-arc of response as individuals and as a group. On top of this, there was a multiplicity of tensions. The State Board of Special Education was at odds with a psychodynamic perspective, as if it were so much hocus-pocus. The Teachers' Union was interested in discreetly maintaining the contract, even if faculty were open to informal and voluntary modifications that promoted the likelihood for success among the staff. And the central and largest of the matrix of the four special education schools was hostile towards the growing body of evidence that suggested that whatever it was that we were doing . . . was working. Attendance was month-to-month increasing—by the end of my first year as principal moving from under 50 percent to nearly 95 percent. Fighting had all but stopped within the first quarter, though staff numbers had been cut. Let me briefly explain.

On the first day of my second year as principal, the day prior to the arrival of our students, books had not been delivered, as promised. The three teachers, Maxine, Walter, and Sherri—those that I've already mentioned (above)—agreed to go pick them up at the Main School. If one were to believe the reports that came from the administration in my cursorily arranged meeting the following day to which I was summoned, the threesome—a retired and widowed grandmotherly meteorologist, an ex-Seminarian, and a Chaucer-buff who was growing near five feet in stature—had metamorphosed into The Three Bold Marauders. The Director explained, additionally, that since we were obviously over-staffed as demonstrated by my ability to send three teachers out to pick up texts and by our near-95 percent attendance rate the previous year, we could relinquish 10 percent of our staff to the Main School.

THOUGHTS ON HOW TO BUILD AN ALLIANCE

In psychoanalysis—as it was beginning to be practiced in the mid-1970s—there were but two major rules. The participants to the psychoanalytic contract did not make love and did not make war. To paraphrase what Fenichel (1941) had said thirty-five years before: "the rest of the rules we make up along the way."

The agreement with my teaching staff was multi-layered and based in my sense that they had been chosen due to their being consummate professionals, experts in their own fields, and without undue fear of their students:

1. I would exchange places with them whenever they were experiencing battlefield fatigue.
2. They, in turn, would do their best to announce sick-days well in advance, preferably during the first week of school, with my hope being that they would recover in beautiful places.
3. I asked them to enter their classes each day—as Bion (1967) might have it: "without memory or desire" or in this pedagogical setting—without lesson plans.[14]
4. If students became hostile with each other, I asked the teachers to put their hands in their pockets and walk in between the angry students.

The agreement with the students was different.

1. Students agreed to attend community meeting of the complete school and to encourage their fellow students to do the same.
2. These meetings would be announced whenever, as Principal, I felt it necessary to make a unilateral decision or when there had been a major breach in school *etiquette*. Occasions for such meetings were infrequent . . . perhaps, monthly. On two occasions, for instance, I felt it necessary to furlough teachers. One male teacher, in response to a male student's callous description of his female teacher's sexual organs, pushed the very powerful student culminating in the student stumbling down part of a flight of stairs. Another teacher had given a

student a "nickel bag of pot" ($5 worth of marijuana) for his 18th birthday. At these meetings, my decisions might be affirmed or contravened by the community as a whole. No serious decision, curiously, was ever overturned, including decisions to give students mental health days (time off from school when their behavior intruded on the polity's mental health.)

3. I, in turn, promised not to intrude on classrooms uninvited or to throw my weight around, or to pull rank.
4. I promised, as well, to be frank and honest with them, to allow (others and) myself to indulge humorous but non-mean-spirited play and to avoid the usual niceties of disingenuous obsequities. I was quite direct with them, for instance, that I was annoyed by their cursing. It had, for me, a harsh ring. I expressed my wish that they learn to replace their cursing with the curse words of the Arundu tribe. The psychoanalytic world had just begun to consider a place for sharing countertransferences with patients during ongoing analyses, something frowned-upon during and after the days of Sandor Ferenczi's experiments. Ferenczi had famously said (1949):

> Parents and adults, in the same way as we analysts, ought to learn to be constantly aware that behind the submissiveness or even the adoration, just as behind the transference love of our children, patients and pupils, there lies hidden an ardent desire to get rid of this oppressive love. If we can help the child, the patient or pupil to give up the reaction of identification, and to ward off the over-burdening (idealized) transference, then we may be said to have reached the goal of raising the personality to a higher level. (p. 229)

It was fascinating to observe the changes in students as they moved from, for instance, the English "mother-fucker" to the translated Arundu "you were there when you were conceived."

5. I promised, as well, to follow the rules and teachers were expected to do so, as well. When I called one morning to indicate that the tail-pipe on my car had dropped off and I would be late, the entire school congregated outside in the snow in order to celebrate my singular lateness. Their seeing my breaking the agreement for prompt attendance on this one occasion served to highlight my adherence to the same rule, especially on typical days when they knew that I arrived by public transportation.

I did run the community meetings which betimes compared well with the quality, volume, and tone of dialogue in the well of the House of Commons.

A lengthy aside is in order on distinguishing Behavioral Therapies from Psychoanalytic Therapies. Loosely, Cognitive Behavioral Therapy envisions the thought as father to the deed, just as the Nazarene is supposed to have claimed (Matthew 6) that "whosoever commits adultery in his heart has committed adultery." Psychoanalysis, on the other hand, envisions the non-thought as parent to the deed. In my work with patients over these years since the mid-1970s, I have noticed that there are parents who fantasize about abusing their children and there are parents who abuse their children. These two groups have little overlap between them.

Freud's (1915) model for the psyche was quite elegant, though due to mistranslation by Strachey, poorly understood (cf, Covitz, 1998, Ch 4). The Unconscious part of the mind (Syst. Ucs., in Freud's abbreviation) is comprised of visual scenarios or what her he called *vorstellungen*. Each *vorstellung* is comprised of images of subjects acting on objects.When these images move towards consciousness, they precipitate affect. Kernberg, (1976) some sixty years later, would add that these images or endopsychic object relations cohere based on their connection to similar affects.

These internal mages run the gamut from loving to violent and from autistic to socially connected. When stimulated, they rise towards consciousness and appear as feeling. Who among us has not risen from our beds with an inexplicable affect residual from, most likely, a forgotten dream? Thus, we have no surprise that Fairy Tales are chocked full of violence and love and sex and we should not be shocked by the presence of all such thoughts in our students and patients. Freud, in his sociological papers, repeatedly cites the futility of extinguishing these thoughts, though he shows no interest in supporting antisocial behaviors.

Indeed, in his metapsychological papers, Freud describes psychosis as an inability to distinguish *das wortrepraesentanz*, the word, from *das ding repraesentanz*, the thing in itself and whatever action it represents. The mentioned teacher, the one who was revolted by the student's comment about his teacher's genitalia, failed to distinguish between feeling/word and deed and, indeed, was suffering from clear signs of illness for many months, thereafter.

This aside was in response to the reader's imagined query: What's the point of encouraging students to curse in Arundu? Or to curse at all? Were we not encouraging a permissive environment? Shouldn't the *Book of Proverbs* have something to say about caning foul-mouthed children? And shouldn't the staff of a school work against such speech?

Our answer was a qualified *no*. It was not our role to suppress the internal images but, rather, to alter the dominance of the affect that followed their elevation to consciousness and to make that affect recognizable and fungible. Our goal was to circumvent the need to defend against the recognition of this affect by means that were not in support of the working alliance at school, e.g., aggressive acts. I recall a student with a lengthy history of violence in schools and a mouth to serve as adequate counterpoise to the foulest shouting *truck-drivers*. I encouraged him "to try on for size" (an expression I used with some frequency) telling me to "jolly-well indulge in solo sexual horizontal aerobics" rather than exhorting me *to go fuck myself.* What he reportedly noticed was that his anger at me seemed more available to him and, at the same time, "kind of silly." In contemporary psychoanalytic circles, we call this process mentalization and its centrality in change processes has recently been emphasized by Fonagy, Target, and others, though its place in psychoanalysis has been long established (cf, Feldman, 1974).

THE PROGRAM IN BRIEF AND OUTCOME MEASURES

Columbia School Kensington Branch had been run as a conventionally conceptualized behaviorally oriented school for more than a decade before this experiment in giving its directorship over to a then young psychoanalytic candidate. Until the move towards paying attention to avoiding confronting the students' resistances enacted by this new principal:

- attendance hovered just below 50 percent;
- lateness was the rule;
- mean improvements on standardized tests was measured in fractions of a year in and around .25-.30. It would be difficult to put precise values on such a mean as attrition and absenteeism were both quite high; and
- acted-out aggressive behaviors were typical with fights, chairs being thrown inside the building and out windows onto the playground.

The changes enacted during my tenure of several years were limited. The main changes were:

a. Most important to my way of thinking was a tentative recognition by the complete staff that resistance to learning was, akin to other resistances, an expression of the healthy part of the Ego attempting to maintain its integrity rather to risk the unknown consequences of change. Respecting this, the major programs, those in Mathematical and Language Arts skills, were modified to circumvent those areas in which these high school aged students had already failed. And so, we replaced Algebra with Chess and reading English and studying Literature with reading Latin and being read to in English.
b. The content of behavior was not confronted in the manner in which it had previously been approached. Instead, emphasis was placed on the therapeutic alliance. Every attempt was made to bring the individual student and the polity that we collectively comprised into an active cooperative alliance in which we were all—students, teachers, staff, and principal—working together to bring about changes in our com-

munity. Among these changes that we hoped to enact, assuredly, were improvements in educational skills, but these were not the only changes to which we aspired. Behavior was evaluated in terms of its influence on the alliance and not in terms of a one-person evaluative psycho-pedagogy.

c. Major decisions were now the prerogative and the responsibility of the polity as a whole, acting whenever possible, as a unit. Roles were not interchangeable, but the Latin Teacher might run the office while the Principal taught Latin, a student might, as noted above, take on an active role as reader rather than listener, and everyone might be heard at Community Meeting. The Principal's role, additionally, was to set a model for protecting the alliance from intrusions from both inside and outside, above and below.

APOLOGIA AND RESULTS

It is important to repeat that such field work, as outlined in the above description of modifications to programming in an inner-city school for emotionally disturbed adolescents, carries a different weight than empirical experimental research. Indeed, the above is closer to a therapeutic case-study in which the operant conditions that brought about change are never known. On many occasions, patients and analysands have told me that previous practitioners seemed obviously prideful of the changes that their therapeutic work had brought about in their treatments. Some appeared disappointed that I did not appear to take that credit. Truth be told, in even controlled experimentation, we are most often in the position of evaluating modification of certain presumed indicators of the hypothesis we wish to test. Rarely—and then most often in the most uninteresting of studies—are we able, for instance, to test whether a depressed person's life is improved by the introduction of something as measurable as a chemical that alters this or that neurotransmitter. Is our nomenclature even well-defined? Can we agree on what is and what isn't depression? Not yet. In addition, so many of our published experimental studies present verified hypotheses that are, in their verification, statistically significant, even though many of the results demonstrate trivial and, therefore, insignificant treatment effects?

Our work thirty-five years ago with our little group of Sweat Hogs was followed by the following numerical measures that may or may not have been the product of our efforts.

As I've noted, I left Columbia School in summer 1978, as did the new Director; he indeed left during the months before I did. However, while we may have disagreed, we had managed to integrate a school and to avoid the threats from anonymous members of the neighborhood against my family

Table 13.1.

Years	**Prior to 1976**	**1976-1977**	**1977-1978**
Attendance	< 50%—est.	94%	93%
Lateness	20%—est.	~20%	18%
Math—CAT	~ .25	1.4	2.1
Verbal—CAT	~ .30	1.7	2.5
Violence	3-4 x week	1 incident	3 incidents

and myself. He had given me a rather wide berth for experimentation and, indeed, apologized for the "hard time" he gave me, as he was leaving. And he kept the school alive, no small feat in those difficult years.

As to the above-listed data. I've previously explained my view that anecdotal data—however numerical it may look—ought not be conflated with similar-looking data from controlled experimental studies, nor should it be discounted. Such results may suggest hypotheses-worth-testing (if I may string together a German-looking word) about whether a broadly interpreted psychoanalytically informed educational model may have something to contribute to the conversation about education, in general, and education of disadvantaged and/or disturbed inner-city children, in particular.

I do not wish to be in the position of Lewis Carroll's gardener—in the Gardener's Song *Sylvie and Bruno,* (Carroll, 1889)—about whom the refraining choristers mouthed:

> He thought he saw an Argument
> That proved he was the Pope;
> He looked again, and found it was
> A Bar of Mottled Soap.
> "A fact so dread," he faintly said,
> "Extinguishes all hope."

No. Unlike the gardener, I am satisfied to present these thoughts as the reflections of a psychoanalyst and Pyrrhonian skeptic who thirty-five years ago—in years when he still might be described as a *fallen mathematician* . . . fallen into *psychoanalytic candidacy*, that is—stumbled upon an opportunity to learn from a group of inner-city children and his colleagues.

I don't have follow-up, except on a few dozen or so students. So, let me close by sharing from what I know, beginning with some of our failures.

Of the students—now in their 50s—who have contacted me or that I have heard about from other students, I am aware of one suicide (some thirty-three years ago), expectedly discouraging results in the lives of the tuluol huffers, and one young lady who endured her season in hell before turning to a life in healthcare. During my tenure at the school, the student who suicided was encouraged by his teachers and by myself to "find his own way." This was for him a knife that cut two ways. He became increasingly conflicted about losing his culture, on the one hand, and being, perhaps, rejected by a new culture, on the other. S turned to opiates and died from an overdose of heroin. It was Fenichel (1941), whom I've cited before, who reminded us that if you want to do surgery, you cannot be afraid of blood or of cutting. S was a wonderful young man and I would hope that future generations of educators find a manner wherein the therapy is less often lethal. Still, I carry his picture in my mind always.

Of the successes, I have already mentioned L, the Chess playing ringer to whom I owe my career move into psychoanalytic private practice, the youngster who became a pipe fitter. A number of the young women and one of our few gay students became hair-dressers. Many went to community college, at least two became small business owners and I've already noted a lady who became a caretaker. None that I know became renowned doctors or won prizes. Our goal was to prepare a group of failing children for the rigors of life in the real world. Perhaps, it is sufficient to note, in closing, that a number of the faculty and I feel that we accomplished much of that goal.

NOTES

1. Named after my mentor, the retired head of the Polish Academy of Sciences, at his request.

2. DPM or Diagnostic Prescriptive Model was, in many ways, similar to components of the contemporary medical model. It sought to identify discrete disabilities and then to prescribe actions to remedy these. It is such a model which has our patients arriving with a cocktail of drugs. The patient has anxiety? Give them an anti-anxielitic. The patient is sad? An antidepressant. Their moods are labile? A mood stabilizer. And their thoughts are odd, too? Add an atypical anti-psychotic medication. This, need I add, ran counter to my sense that my students, then, and my patients, now, are more complex than the sum of their symptoms.

3. Abbreviations seemed to be in vogue. NTA's or non-teaching assistants were BBF (Big Beefy Folk) who were made available in schools to "Civilization to its Discontents" with other means beyond their intellectual gravitas.

4. Service Delivery System, indeed! The professionalization of teaching was arriving in the 1970s with the professionalization of therapy. Our *patients* (from the Latin for sufferers) became *clients*. Advocates of the word *client* claimed that it took the patient out of a subordinate role. Little attention was paid to the dehumanization inherent to moving these relationships closer to the cash nexus, nor was there interest in the origin of the word *client*. In ancient Rome, a citizen with less power, a *cliens*, would promise his vote to his *patron* in exchange for the protections afforded by his relationship to this person of means.

5. Peter Binzen, at that time a Philadelphia journalist, had written about pockets of unracially integrated poor White working class neighborhoods in major American cities, including Philadelphia's riverside Fishtown where my school was situated and from which it drew most of its students.

6. The word *results* is used casually. No controlled experiments were planned and the report contained in this chapter is heuristic and anecdotal, in nature.

7. It is oftentime difficult to distinguish transference from the real relationship that develops between people who work and fight together in the trenches. Not so many years ago, Marsha and I were invited to the wedding of one of our inpatient students from the early 1970s.

He was now a fifty-something PhD in Mathematics and a bank executive and was marrying a beautiful young woman. A group of our other students were *lying in wait* for us to arrive. They had built a yurt, reminiscent of the geodesics we had built, together, nearly a lifetime ago. When it became time for us to change into our wedding clothes at this *wedding in the woods*, these middle-aged men acted as an honor guard, protecting our privacy (Marsha says it was *her* privacy) as we changed in their yurt. Is it the transference that never dies as the obiter dicta from Florida case law suggests? Or is it the real relationship? I don't know.

8. Dr. S was a training analyst in the local medical society and I was a candidate in the local Lay Psychoanalytic institute that I would later direct for many years.

9. I think of myself as a staunch supporter of labor unions and the rights of workers. My boundaries, however, tend to be porous. I think, for instance, of the complexity of the ending of fifty minute sessions. Assuming that no one else is waiting, I feel it my right, in conjunction with analysands, to extend that time. My teachers were interested—outside of the parameters set out in their contract—in our work, together and, as a group, tended not to see their relationship to the school as adversarial. That said: the Union was doing its job.

10. Need I say that such reading disabilities had consequences in their studies of History, Science, and all other Secondary Studies.

11. Until Glover's seminal paper on "Inexact Interpretations" in 1931, it was more or less unthinkable to suggest that different analysts might produce different results with the same patient. The view that psychoanalysts have of psychoanalysis, too, has evolved from a well-defined technique to a human art-form. I am not hiding my belief that education, too, is a human art-form.

12. Another one of Ferenczi's students, Edmund Bergler, used to say something like: "These silent analysts? Chances are they don't have much to say."

13. Marsha and I had lunch with Maxine just as I was writing this and three months after her nintieth birthday. Her memory and mine differ and hers may well be correct. She recalls having no facility with Chess, herself, and recalls that I led these sessions. This chapter is, alas, based on memory which we know to be, as we age, like wicker in a Spring storm: while it may get wet, it holds little water.

14. As I'm confident that the statute of limitations has long-expired for the betimes cavalier style of this author and his staff and for crimes committed between 1976 and 1978, this author can shamelessly admit that the school secretary was enlisted in writing lesson plans for the State to read. Had I had the time, I would have written them in Aramaic; I suppose Linear B would have been preferable but Seminary offered no preparation in that language. My staff was welcome to think about an opening question for the students and then to proceed to interact with the students based on the *unfoldings* that precipitated from that initial question.

REFERENCES

Aichorn, A. (1935). *Wayward Youth*. London: Penguin.

Binzen, P. (1970). *Whitetown, USA*. New York: Vintage.

Bion, W. (1967). *Second Thoughts*. New York: Jason Aronson.

Carroll, L. (1889). *Sylvie and Bruno* in Lewis Caroll (1982), *The Complete Fully Illustrated Works*, London: Gramercy Books.

Covitz, H. (1998). OEdipal Paradigms in Collision: a centennial emendation of a piece of Freudian canon (1897–1997). New York: Peter Lang.

Feldman, H. (1974). "A psychoanalytic addition to human nature." New York: *Psychoanalytic Review*, *61*, 133–139.

Feldman, S. (1965). *Mannerisms and Gestures of Speech*. New York: International Universities Press.

Fenichel, Otto (1941). *Problems of Psychoanalytic Technique*. New York: The Psychoanalytic Quarterly Press.

Ferenczi, S. (1949). Confusion of the Tongues between the Adults and the Child (the language of tenderness and of passion). *International Journal of Psychoanalysis*, *30*, 225–230.

Freud, S. and Breuer (1895). *Studies on Hysteria. From The Standard Edition of the Complete Psychological Works of Sigmund Freud*, Vols. II (J. Strachey, Ed.). London: Hogarth, London.

Freud, S. (1900). *Interpretation of Dreams. From The Standard Edition of the Complete Psychological Works of Sigmund Freud*, Vols IV-V (J. Strachey, Ed.). London: Hogarth,

Freud, S. (1926). "Symptoms, inhibitions, and anxiety." *From The Standard Edition of the Complete Psychological Works of Sigmund Freud*, Vol. XX (J. Strachey, Ed.). London: Hogarth.

Glover, E. (1931). "The Therapeutic Effect of Inexact Interpretation: A Contribution to the Theory of Suggestion." *International Journal of Psychoanalysis, 12,* 397-411.

Kunitz, S. (1995). *The Collected Poems.* New York: W. W. Norton.

Kernberg, O. (1976). *Object Relations Theory and Clinical Psychoanalysis.* New York: Jason Aronson.

Lawrence, DH (1926). "The rocking horse winner." *Harpers Magazine*, July.

Parin, P. et al (1971) *Fürchte Deinen Nächsten Wie DichSelbest: Psychoanalyse Und Gesellschaft Am Modell Der Agni in Westafrika* [fear Your Neighbor as Yourself: Psychoanalysis and Society as Exemplified by the Agni in West Africa]. Frankfurt am Main: Suhrkamp, 1971, 582 pp. DM20.

Chapter Fourteen

Psychoanalytic Understandings of Classroom Life and Learning

Devin Thornburg

Over the years, I have been involved as a teacher educator and psychologist in school reform work, particularly in schools where there have been alarming decreases in students' academic achievement, increases in student suspensions, absenteeism or dropping out, or all of these trends. While there have been reforms in those schools at the levels of both policy and program, it has been the realm of practice of teaching that has been the most challenging for the schools and for me.

The individual work of educators with students and their families, and with each other, are the areas in greatest need of attention as change at this level is the most complex. Curriculum and instruction can improve rather readily in comparison to the ways in which teachers understand their students' learning needs and their interactions with them. This is the level of change that must be examined and understood for other reforms to be effective. In the narrative that follows, I look to psychoanalytic understandings of teaching and learning as a valuable paradigm for facilitating change that has been relatively ignored by those in school reform work, let alone those who teach and lead in schools.

I am not making a case here for teachers to become therapists or psychoanalysts. There is—and there always has been—a debate over whether it is necessary to make any connection between psychoanalysis and education (e.g., Cifali Bega, 2007). My view is that teachers would benefit greatly from bringing a psychoanalytic perspective to their work as teachers and their students' learning.

No small part of this examination should be the process of looking at my own motives in this project. While I have studied and read psychoanalytic theory over the years, I was an even more enthusiastic student of critical and post-structural theories that emerged, in part, from psychoanalytic writings. And while I underwent psychoanalysis as well as having worked for several years as a therapist of children and adults supervised by those who were, themselves, psychoanalytically-trained, I see myself primarily as an educator who respects the work of clinicians but who no longer does clinical work. There is, therefore, a theme of ambivalence running throughout my personal and professional life about a psychoanalytic understanding of the world. However, as I have gotten older, I have begun to appreciate more the power of Freud's work and hope to illuminate that power for myself and for the reader.

A BRIEF HISTORY

The place to begin an inquiry, it seems to me, is with a historical overview of the relationship between psychoanalysis and learning. This is, of course, my interpretation through my own biased perspective (cf., Cifali Bega, 2007). During the past century there has been a considerable amount of ambivalence towards psychoanalytic theory as it pertains to education. For the most part, the insights gained from other human service professions about the psychodynamics of helping relationships have not been embraced in education. It is even less considered in the current era of economic crises with intensified demands for school and teacher accountability. As Taubman (2007) has pointed out, it would seem "anachronistic" to talk of psychoanalysis in an era ". . . shaped largely by cognitive science and behaviorism, and reflective of the larger globalization of capitalism . . ." (p. 5). In the current era, the focus on learning is narrowed to academic achievement as an outcome ("test scores") rather than remaining open to a wider lens where learning is seen as a dynamic between teachers and students that is part of ongoing emotional as well as intellectual experience. Psychoanalytic perspectives imply that the dynamic of the student-teacher relationship is integral to the learning experience rather than apart from and secondary to it.

My intention is not primarily to provide a detailed overview of this history here but to provide some context for speculating as to why, until rather recently, there has been little in-depth (re)consideration of the potential contribution of psychoanalytic understandings of teaching and learning (e.g., Cohler, 2006; Taubman, 2007). There are some notable exceptions, to this, such as the use of psychoanalytic frameworks for conceptualizing early childhood education, both philosophically and pedagogically (Tobin, 2001). The approach to early childhood learning developed at Bank Street College in New York, where psychoanalytic theory has been one of the contributions to their developmental rationale, is one such example (Dean, 2008).

In many respects, the developmental approach was adopted in the earlier part of the twentieth century by psychoanalytic writers who sought to bring this perspective to the creation of schools. Freud (1905) called this "the princely education along psychoanalytic lines" (quoted in Finkelstein, 1979, p. 185). While Freud had little to do with the direct application of psychoanalysis to education, he argued that its insights about children should attract educators. Freud was unclear about whether he advocated for a harsh or lenient education but he encouraged an approach that was based on an understanding of development and an avoidance of neuroses (Dean, 2008).

Several years later Freud wrote that, "Whatever we can expect in the way of prophylaxis against neurosis in the individual lies in the hands of a psychoanalytically enlightened education" (1913, p. 189). In that same writing, Freud wrote that, "only someone who can feel his way into the minds of children can be capable of educating them; and we grown-up people cannot understand children because we no longer understand our own childhood" (1913, p. 189). This quote is an important element in the overall position I am taking in this work: that teachers should understand their own childhoods to be successful as teachers and that psychoanalysis can provide a way towards that understanding (cf., Britzman, 1998; Taubman, 2007).

The child analysis movement that emerged in the 1920s and 1930s in Europe helped to support a fusion of psychoanalysis and education (Dean, 2008). Psychoanalytic educational programs began in the 1920s, described by some as "progressive education," and were addressed by Freud in *The Question of Lay Analysis* (1928) in terms of the application of psychoanalysis to the education of young children. Many saw Anna Freud's work on psychology and education as emancipatory and aligned with child-centered approaches (Britzman, 1998). She sought to combine psychoanalysis and education into what she termed, "a science for upbringing and education" (A. Freud, 1927, p. 65).

Suggesting that teachers should focus on channeling instinctive impulses into materials and play that would result in both pleasure and problem-solving, Anna Freud argued that later developmental difficulties would be avoided. Melanie Klein sought to lessen the punitive aspects of the superego and related anxiety through education, strengthen the ego for future healthy adjustment. For both, psychoanalytic theory was to be transformed into methods and strategies for achieving educational goals and practices (Dean, 2008). Erik Erikson and his wife, Joan, were teachers in Anna Freud's school (Coles, 1970), a place in which children planned the day's activities and the subject matter ranged from science, to history, geography, English, poetry, and the arts. No grades were given in the school with Erikson emphasizing individual uniquenesses—particularly unconscious motivations.

Similar schools were attempted in other parts of Europe. Teachers would interpret the unconscious and helped to separate the unconscious attributes from conscious manifestations. They would attempt to create a relationship founded on affection and trust rather than on authority (Angelini, 2008). Many of those involved with psychoanalysis and education saw themselves as part of a larger social project building a democratic socialism (Ascher, 2005). An example of such a venture was a co-educational school for Jewish refugee children in Vienna that sought to maximize their psychological development and used a permissive milieu (Rolnick, 2012).

However, some of these schools were closed down by authorities with the rationale given as being too sexually permissive (e.g., Vera Schmidt, 1924). By the late 1930s, many in the psychoanalytic community, themselves, were disillusioned with the psychoanalytically informed schools and there were several reports of children from these schools developing personality problems. At the "Four Countries Conference" in 1937, Anna Freud, herself, declared that the years of intensive work and trial error had failed to achieve the goals of psychoanalytic pedagogy (Dean, 2008). The struggle to specify immediate and ultimate purposes of early childhood education from psychoanalytic pedagogy largely ended in Europe and the movement overall was halted in Europe by the advent of World War II when many Jewish activists in the movement had to flee Nazism (Ascher, 2005).

In the United States, "permissive" schools drew from psychoanalytic theory to establish goals for "mental health" or "mental hygiene." American educators were as drawn to the goal of preventing neurosis in children as their European counterparts (Cohen, 1979). Through the early 1940s the argument was that teachers who had the capacity to protect a child from neurosis were teachers who were not neurotic, themselves (e.g., Tiegs and Katz, 1941). This was taken to mean that teachers should be hired who were found to be healthy. It was not an argument for any form of psychotherapeutic treatment to help current teachers to become less neurotic and more attuned to children.

After World War II, the criticisms of a psychoanalytic pedagogy increased in the United States. Its focus on the emotional rather than the academic life of the child was regarded as ideologically liberal and therefore out of step with the Cold War era (Milton et al., 2004). Psychoanalytic theory has been seen at various times as authoritarian, conformist, and radical by its detractors, depending on the version of psychoanalysis and the ideological viewpoint of the critic (Weiner, 2006). It was certainly overtaken—as was progressive education, in general—by the behavioral views of learning that emphasized objectives that were to be supported by curriculum, lesson planning, instruction and finally, assessments determining whether objectives were met. While by no means wrong-minded as a method of structuring classroom curriculum, behavioral approaches explicitly denied the emotional lives of children, objectifying them, and making the teacher a behavioral engineer whose role was to impart knowledge.

After a brief return to both humanistic and progressive educational philosophies in the 1960s and 1970s, the cognitive-behavioral view of learning arose, coinciding with the educational "crisis" in the early 1980s that noted the United States' poor showing globally in levels of student achievement (Sizer, 1983). It was assumed that approaches to learning based on a cognitive, empirically-based view of children's minds, drawn from a "Human Information Processing" paradigm, would lead to a more efficient and effective approaches to student learning. Again, children's emotional lives became a shadow to their objectification and teachers were engineers—this time with the help of technology—whose goal was to understand the mind.

During the late 1980s, there was renewed interest in psychoanalytic understanding of the educational process, shifting from the earlier views of a psychoanalytic pedagogy that would enhance the reality principle over the pleasure principle as part of mental development (e.g., A. Freud, 1930) to psychoanalysis as a way for understanding the classroom milieu and the teacher's personality, identity, motivations, and lived experience (Boldt and Salvio, 2006; Cohler and Galatzer-Levy, 2006). This shift was supported by larger social changes during the past several decades, including the feminist movement (Weiner, 2006), leading to an emphasis on "relationships and interdependence in social life and personal well-being rather than the autonomy earlier presumed as the foundation of mental health" (Weiner, 2006, p. 1).

TRANSFERENCE AND LEARNING

The importance of the learning relationship has become a rationale for research in the psychoanalytic literature and for my own reflections as a teacher and professional working with teachers. Perhaps there is no more important element of psychoanalytic theory for understanding teacher motivations and the relationship with students than transference. While there are other structures that have been cited as important in the learning process—including defense mechanisms, such as repression and projection, and the various drives and psychic agencies (Taubman, 2007)—the unconscious reproduction of previous emotional patterns onto a current teacher-student relationship is viewed as both pervasive and contributing to the intensity that is part of the power of teaching (Britzman and Pitt, 1996; Daloz, 1986; Robertson, 1999). Cohler and Galatzer-Levy (2006) have described transference as "often at the heart of the student's desire to engage and learn" (p. 342).

In 1895, Freud wrote about transference as the "false connection" between the physician and figures in the patient's past (Freud, 1955, p. 302). Within a decade, he had elaborated the concept and termed transference an "inevitable necessity" in psychoanalysis (Freud, 1953, p. 116). Viewing transference as a common, everyday phenomenon, he wrote, "Transference arises spontaneously in all human relationships . . . and the less its presence is suspected, the more powerfully it operates" (1957a, p. 51). Following Freud, Jung (1966) viewed transference as a very frequent natural occurrence. "Indeed, in any human relationship that is at all intimate, certain transference phenomena will almost always operate as helpful or disturbing factors" (p. 171). In 1915, Freud wrote about students loving or hating or experiencing emotional ambivalence towards their teachers because of earlier relationships, suggesting that "educational spaces are quite . . . explosive" (Freud as quoted by Stebbins, 2010, p. 3).

Post-structuralist and psychoanalyst Jacques Lacan, (Lacan, 1977a; 1988a, p. 271), emphasized knowledge and authority in describing transference such as the notion of ignorance "as a passion" (p. 271), a resistance to learning that teachers often face. Lacan (1977b) elaborated this view in terms of the "subject who is supposed to know," proposing that "whenever this function may be, for the subject . . . the transference . . . is established" (1988a, pp. 232–233). Felman (1987) concluded that the application of Lacanian understanding of this to teaching means that the teacher, like the therapist, should make herself "a student of the patient's knowledge" (p. 83) and that the teacher is taught by the student's own process. So, in this sense, the teacher *and* the student are both "subjects who are supposed to know." This approach appeals to those who are constructivists, as well as those embracing a feminist or post-structural pedagogy, allowing for a desconstruction of an authoritarian view of teaching (Robertson, 1999).

The paradox is that without transference—or this "subject supposed to know"—teaching cannot occur. So the participants must both construct and deconstruct the "supposed to know" of transference (Moi, 1992). There have been some fruitful discussions about the dynamics of transference in teacher-student relationships extending Lacan's work in this regard, such as the idea that teachers see deficiencies in their students in order to fulfill their own rescue fantasies, seeking, for example an unconscious need for love and gratification (O'Loughlin, 2011; Pianta, 1999).

In 1910, Freud described "countertransference" as a way to refer to a physician's unconscious response to the patient but not further than one's "own complexes and internal resistances permit" (p. 145). Freud (1915) addressed patient's affections for the physician and noted that a second type of countertransference might occur—failing to recognize the patient's transference—and taking such affection as without historical meaning. As Robertson (1999) noted, Freud did not acknowledge that physicians could generate transference on their own without it being "a result of the patient's influence." Kernberg (1965) proposed dividing countertransference into two categories: (1) the classical approach that involves the unconscious response to the patient's transference and (2) the totalistic approach, representing the total emotional reaction of the physician to the patient within psychoanalytic treatment. Following the arguments I make here, the second category of countertransference will be used and, in fact, that there is no meaningful distinction made between transference and countertransference as concepts in the teacher-student relationship (McLaughlin, 1981; Robertson, 1999).

Psychoanalytic thought supports educators in the examination of their unconscious and how it affects their interaction with their students, the curriculum, and the meanings they they give their experience (Taubman, 2007). Rather than emphasizing conscious choices, psychoanalytic thinking posits the origin of meaning within the individual as well as in the external world and, as such, the individual must assume responsibility for the meaning given to any situation (Taubman, 2007). For teachers, the responses they have towards their students are interwoven with past histories and beliefs that are not easily accessible to them.

I have seen and experienced powerful transferential responses to students that have both helped and impeded their learning. What has been most striking about these responses is that the teachers—and I—typically feel that our defined role is undergoing some challenge or change at that moment. The feeling state, itself—whether positive or negative (cf., Freud, 1912) may not be clearly identified but there is a sense of heightened awareness about the need to adjust our role. Teachers will often speak with greater emotion about the student and, at the same time, become less explicit in reference to themselves when transference is in operation. An illustration of my own experience with transference might be helpful.

Recently, I was working with a fifth grade teacher of students who were second language learners of English in an attempt to have her consider that the content of her lessons could be more aligned with the curriculum of the school district for native speakers of English. She continued to insist—politely—that her students were more like students who were special needs/learning disabled and that they needed strategies that would teach basic reading skills. I felt every attempt I made to convey my point of view or to ask questions about her views of her students resulted in her creating roadblocks to our communication where she would talk about an issue that was tangential to what I was seeking to emphasize. I felt angry at her, threatened in my authority, and I had some vague, unformed notions of helplessness in the face of her hostile response to me.

I attempted to determine the source of my anger, which seemed two-fold: (1) that she was playing play a sort of "cat-and-mouse" game with me in my role as consultant, pretending to feel positive about our work together when she truly felt otherwise; and (2) that she was associating her second-language students more with children with special learning needs rather than with regular English-speaking students. During an observation in her classroom I had experienced her students as bright, engaging, and fluent in their reading skills. I felt that she had lowered her expectations of her students and inevitably she had lowerd her instructional approaches too. Both points needed deeper examination: what was causing such an emotional response on my part? What was the origin of my responses to her that might be reflecting my personal history and dynamics? Was I feeling anything else besides anger that might help explain my inhibited behavior with her?

The first point made above seemed more in line with what I would consider transference on my part as I have understood it as there was somewhat an irrational quality to it. I rather quickly identified it as feeling that my professional expertise was being attacked by this teacher and in a dishonest way. I felt a sense of outrage. I wanted to defend my abilities, but underneath I felt helpless in the face of her ostensibly polite but decidedly hostile rejection of my efforts. What was the source of my feeling? I began to grasp that my reaction to her response was related to earlier experiences in my life with criticism that was presented in a superficially pleasant manner, making me feel like I was flawed and a failure. This realization allowed me to put my interactions with her in some perspective.

The second point I made about treating second-language students as being more like students with special learning needs seemed initially to be more straightforward and more "understandable." It tapped into my moral outrage at her negative beliefs about the abilities of second-language learners, a form of prejudice which I have been combating for most of my professional life. What was important to pay attention to, as well, was the degree of passion in my response. Several psychoanalytic writers have noted that even "rational" beliefs can be examined for their transferential elements (Cohler and Galatzer-Levy, 2006; Weiner, 2006). Was my response to this teacher based on some personal experiences from my own childhood? Was I unconsciously struggling with my own prejudices? While I struggle for answers, the inquiry makes me think that I might, in the process, become more tolerant of the prejudices of others.

Mostly what these questions led to is not answers but a type of thinking that made myself the focus of inquiry. As a result, my communication and my relationship with this teacher began to change. A psychoanalytic "stance" has the capacity to engender a shift in role for a teacher. This thought has been a continuous one for me and has encouraged me to examine other views of learning and teaching in the hopes of deepening my understanding of the mechanisms of change that a psychoanalytic position can bring. In essence, this line of inquiry yields an interdisciplinarity or what Cole and Rogoff call "methodological pluralism" (Cole 1998; Rogoff, 2003).

TRANSFERENCE, PIAGET, AND VYGOTSKY

One of the fundamental ideas upon which Piaget's view of learning is based has to do with the construction of new knowledge based on prior history and experience. Through a process of adaptation, organized and meaningful schemata of knowledge are used to construct meaning of current experience. While Piaget ultimately rejected Freud's work as lacking empirical validity (Piaget, 1973), several writers have researched and speculated over the years about the potential connections between their views of learning.

Wachtel (1981), for example, argued that Piaget's notion of "evolving structures" mediating experience and behavior was compatible with transference in that individuals do not merely respond to external stimuli but selectively organize and make meaning of new input. In the case of Freud, these structures help to organize the self and are based on earlier experiences. Just as with Piagetian schemata, perceptions of current experiences can be absorbed into past experiences (assimilation) rather than accommodated to reflect more of present reality. This is transference and implies that it can occur in everyday situations.

Furth (1987) saw Freud's and Piaget's theories as overlapping in that both present a biological basis for the attempt to make meaning. Illeris (2007), maintains "that Piaget and Freud with their constructivist approaches . . . analyse(d) learning as the fundamentally life-maintaining, developing, qualifying and libidinal process it basically is..." (p. 78). Furth (1987) extended this argument suggesting that Freud recognized that there were affective components to knowing, and that Piaget speculated that there are cognitive structures apparent in the study of emotions (Piaget, 1980). This last position was the basis of Dorval's (2002) study of young children's speech (long considered part of children's cognitive development) for its "transferential substructure" and his own "countertransference reaction" as the researcher.

Vygotsky's (1978) work is typically viewed within a constructivist paradigm of learning, emphasizing the historical and social elements of making meaning Vygotsky (1929/1993) distanced himself from Freud's theory, as well, terming it "biological" and "characterological" in its approach to personality (p. 55). While Vygotsky acknowledged the methodological importance of psychoanalysis, in its rejection of a dichomotizing of psychological and physical processes, he was skeptical about psychic determinism (1930). Vygotsky did not deal with the unconscious in a systematic way but accepted it as a given (Angelini, 2008).

As with Piagetian theory, there has been an increasing interest in the potential integration of Vygotsky's work with psychoanalytic thought as a means of extending our understanding of the learning process. Many writers from within a Vygotskian framework have highlighted the close relationship between the environmental context, emotions and development (e.g., Bruner,

1990; Cole, 1990; Shweder, 1990; Valsiner, 1996). More directly related to my purpose here, Wertsch (1990) proposed connections between Vygotsky's theory and psychoanalysis, emphasizing the interaction and the exchange of meanings between the child and the adult as part of the environmental context and the emotions within learning.

Wilson and Weinstein (1992a, 1992b, 1996) investigated Vygotskian perspectives on the acquisition of language and the learning process and the potential interplay with psychoanalytic theory. They proposed that the "zone of proximal development" (ZPD—the space between what the learner can accomplish on a task independently and that which can be accomplished with teacher assistance) can help to elaborate the relationship between the intrapsychic and interpersonal. While transference involves a motivation to seek out repetition, the ZPD involves a motivation to learn within a "speech and internalization community." In analysis, when the transference and the ZPD combine, the potential outcome is insight in a broad sense (Wilson and Weinstein, 1996). It seems very conceivable that this would occur within classroom settings.

A PSYCHOANALYTIC UNDERSTANDING OF "SOCIAL-EMOTIONAL LEARNING"

A psychoanalytic understanding of teaching and learning can be used to integrate the emotional components of learning specifically, through what is often called "social-emotional learning." This movement has multiple origins but in part has been a backlash against the hegemony of testing and accountability movements in education in recent years. Advocates of social-emotional learning suggest that the push to raise standards and increase student achievement has caused educators to neglect the social and emotional supports that children need in order to reach their potential. The Collaborative for Academic, Social and Emotional Learning (CASEL), for example, states in its mission statement that " . . . children and adults are engaged life-long learners who are self-aware, caring and connected to others, and responsible in their decision-making. Children and adults achieve to their fullest potential, and participate constructively in a democratic society" (CASEL, http://casel.org/about-us/mission-vision/).

Yet, too often, the ways in which these efforts have proceeded over the past decade speaks to an individualistic, technocratic, and instrumentalist approach to social-emotional education. Through the prescription and implementation of curriculum, standards, and strategies that require teachers to be doing something to students to get them to behave, these approaches can actually be antithetical to the kind of social-emotional education that psychoanalysis would support. The social-emotional learning movement would suggest that this is most appropriately accomplished by having the student internalize a "neutral and universal" set of skills (Hoffman, 2009). As Hoffman (2009) noted in her critique of social-emotional learning, this "often devolves to a discourse about control, rules contracts, choices, activities, and organizational structures, [where] substance is replaced by structure [and] feeling is replaced by form" (pp. 545–46).

In keeping with an evidence-based and accountability ethos, what is valued is what can be measured. The language of research about student learning needs to be connected more to the language and experience of emotion in teaching and learning (Hoffman, 2009). Many initiatives in education involving social or emotional realms use vocabulary that is akin to psychoanalytic thought but are actually efforts to manipulate and control children. Empathy and self-awareness, for example, are connected to control and management. As Cifali Bega (2007) noted, ". . . our clinical approach has been taken over politically, and usually for the worse" (p. 17).

In order to connect to the emotional dimensions of teaching and learning, I believe that teachers can reflect on their own emotional histories and take responsibility for the meanings they bring to their relationships with students. I am proposing here that if we were to use a wider lens in the learning process, we can move from a perspective of teachers as disseminators of knowledge to one where teachers also facilitate learning through a more psychoanalytic stance about their own emotional lives. In doing so, teachers both impart knowledge and nurture student learning through their own reflective process.

SELF-REFLECTION AND THE TEACHER'S ROLE

I want to be certain not to imply a sharp ideological or practical contrast between an emphasis on teaching content and an emphasis on the emotional sphere of the teacher-student relationship. Such a dichotomy is simplistic (de Forest, 2007) and misses the idea that the content should be taught while students are simultaneously made aware of the dynamic of their students' and their own emotional responses to each other. In part, this is what Robertson (1996, 1998) considered a shift from teachers who "profess" their knowledge to students, to, instead, a vision of teachers who facilitate epistemological and developmental changes for their students.

This echoes the perspective of both Piaget (1972) and Vygotsky (1978) on the construction of the learner's knowledge through the teacher's action as a facilitator or "co-constructor" who models and guides the learner's accommodation of schemata and through engagement in the ZPD. While there may be vast differences between Piaget and Vygotsky in their interpretation of a teacher's intentions or understanding of the learning process, both describe a teacher who is a co-constructor of meaning.

A shift in understanding in the role of the teacher cannot occur without self-reflection. In exploring a psychoanalytic perspective, Taubman (2007) outlines the conventional instrumental notion of reflective practice as typically addressing the relative impact of a teachers on student learning—leading to objective-driven questions employed in state and national standards for teachers—or addressing self-reflection about cultural sensitivity, for example, or teacher attitudes or values. Taubman (2007) points out that neither of these approaches asks teachers to engage in any deeper reflective activity in terms of their intrapsychic or intersubjective lives. He extends this critique to the popular writings of Parker Palmer, author of *The Courage to Teach* (1998), Palmer (1997) is an advocate of self-understanding—"we teach who we are"—(p. 15). Taubman (2007) notes that this insight does not come with an encouragement for educators to reflect on their intrapsychic lives.

Lacan's work illuminates critical self-reflection and reflective practice. His work takes into account the importance of language and provides a way to think about ourselves without "reifying our identities or selves" (Taubman, 2007, p. 14). Ultimately, we most assume responsibility for our desires, fantasies that inform who we are and what we do.

This is at the heart of my line of inquiry, namely that teachers must take responsibility for their students' learning in a more authentic relationship that doesn't confuse what is taught with the relationship without which that knowledge can flourish. I am reminded of the more explicitly political vision of Paolo Freire (1993), who claimed that too many teachers view their task as "fill(ing) the students with the content of . . . narration—contents which are detached from reality . . . a sonority of words, rather than their transforming power" (p. 71). This view of learning assumes that there is no distinction between "being accessible to consciousness and entering consciousness" (Freire, 1993, p. 76). This distinction, which Freire sees as essential, would seem to parallel Freud's theoretical position that the analyst helps to bring to consciousness perceptions about the world that has been experienced.

As opposed to this "banking" notion of education—which mirrors the indoctrination process, adapting people to social oppression—Freire proposed a "problem-posing" process where teachers can also become students in an authentic dialogue with students, who can also assume the role of teachers (Freire, 1993). In this vision, that which is being thought about helps to shape the relationship between the teacher and student rather than "being the end of the cognitive act" (Freire, 1993, p. 79).

Freire (2008) described this method as having two modes, and an important distinction in classroom learning: the "pseudo-dialetic," which is the illusion of discovering knowledge with and from each other (as the teacher's questions involve solutions that are already in mind) and genuine dialectic, where the teacher poses questions with no intended single answer. The pseudo-dialectic position does not facilitate consciousness and does not result in a form of "liberation" for students.

Freire (2008) acknowledged the existence of school practices that represent a teacher's authority, but the classroom dialogue should be natural and not authoritative. As he wrote, " . . . the teacher-student and the students-teachers reflect simultaneously on themselves and the world without dichotomizing this reflection from action, and thus establish an authentic form of thought and action" (p. 252). Reality, to Freire, is in a continuous state of change and our actions are formed by our perceptions of that changing reality. Problem-posing allows teacher and student to contemplate their own realities and to work towards changing them.

While there are ways in which Freud's and Freire's visions of the human condition and education are irreconcilable, the notion of teachers and students reflecting on their realities and perceptions of them are central to processes of change for both. And the distinction that Freire makes between a pseudo-dialog and genuinely dialectic pedagogy is echoed in psychoanalytic literature, as well, when clinicians are cautioned against using reflections about transference as a form of manipulation of patients. In my work with educators to effect change in schools, there is a similar danger when I think I have the solutions while posing the questions.

CONCLUSION

With the efforts to understand the learning process that I have attempted to outline here—particularly in relation to transference and the importance of teachers' genuine reflections on their own motivations and experiences—the question remains as to what the role of the teacher might look like from a psychoanalytic perspective. I propose a series of elements that result from this psychoanalytically informed stance. It is not a return to a psychoanalytic pedagogy of previous decades, which sought to use clinical interventions with students to ensure their mental health but, rather, a call for educators to focus more on their own needs, biases, and perceptions within their relationships with students, engaging in an ongoing dialogue that is content-rich and that embodies powerful opportunities for individual change and growth.

The elements involved in a psychoanalytic stance towards learning include: (1) an open and receptive quality with students that reflects a willingness to learn from them; (2) a critical and reflective position with regard to oneself, exploring feelings, motivations, and wishes as they might arise; (3) an active monitoring for behavior on their students' or their own part that may represent unconscious transference; (4) a consistent approach to one's role through a clear vision of what being a teacher means to onself; and (5) a willingness to seek consultation, in confidence, with other teachers to explore possible areas of transference in teaching. This last element assumes that a teacher—or other professionals, including consultants—could benefit from an educational and supportive supervisory relationship (Pianta, 1999; Robertson, 1999).

I continue to learn about my impact on those who are engaged in educational change projects and I am working at having the courage to pay attention to the emotional level of human interaction. It is a humbling but empowering process that allows me to remain a learner while embracing the dynamics of change.

REFERENCES

Angelini, A. (2008). History of the unconscious in Soviet Russia. *International Journal of Psychoanalysis, 89*, 369–388.

Ascher, C. (2005). The force of ideas. *History of Education, 34, 3*, 277–293.

Boldt, G. & Salvio, P. (2006). *Love's return: Psychoanalytic essays on childhood, teaching and learning.* New York, NY: Taylor & Francis.

Britzman, D. (1998). *Lost subjects, contested objects: Toward a psychoanalytic inquiry of learning.* Albany, NY: State University of New York Press.

Britzman, D. & Pitt, A. (1996). Pedagogy and transference: Casting the past of learning into the presence of teaching. *Theory into Practice, 35, 2*, 117–123.

Bruner, J. (1990). *Acts of meaning.* Cambridge, MA: Harvard University Press.

Cifali Bega, M. (2007). *What is at stake when psychoanalysis and education come together? Some ethical and clinical issues.* Unpublished manuscript.

Cohen, S. (1979). In the name of the prevention of neurosis: The search for a psychoanalytic pedagogy in Europe 1905–1938. In B. Finkelstein, (Ed.), Regulated children/liberated children: Education in psychohistorical perspective (pp. 184–219). New York, NY: Psychohistory Press.

Cohler, B. (2006). Desire, teaching, and learning: An essay review on recent psychoanalytic contributions to education. *Schools: Studies in education, 3, 2*, 105–119.

Cohler B. & Galatzer-Levy, R. (2006). Love in the classroom: Desire and transference in teaching and learning. In G. Boldt and P. Salvo (Eds.) *Love's return: Psychoanalytic essays on teaching and learning* (pp. 243–26). New York: Routledge.

Cole, M. (1990). Cultural psychology: A once and future discipline? In J. Barman (Ed.) *Cross-cultural perspective: Nebraska symposium on motivation, Vol. 37*, pp. 279–376. Lincoln, NE: University of Nebraska Press.

Cole, M. (1998). *Cultural psychology: A once and future discipline.* Cambridge, MA: Harvard University Press.

Coles, R. (1970). *Erik H. Erikson: The growth of his work.* Boston, MA: Allyn & Bacon.

Daloz, L. (1986). *Effective teaching and mentoring: Realizing the transformative power of adult learning experiences.* San Francisco, CA: Jossev-Bass.

de Forest, J. (2007). Antecedents of dispositions testing: Lessons from the history of the good teacher. *Journal of Educational Controversy, 2*, 2, Retrieved from www.wce.wwu.edu/Resources/CEP/eJournal/v002n002/.

Dean, A. (2008). Psychodynamic theory in early childhood education: A look at the contributions of Anna Freud, Melanie Klein, Erik H. Erikson, Susan Isaacs, Bruno Bettelheim, E.C.M. Frijling-Schreuder and Margaret Ribble. *The International Journal of Bahamian Studies, 5.* Retrieved April 4, 2012 from journals.sfu.ca/cob/index.php/files/article/download/89/61.

Dorval, B. (2003). Reflective conception of internalization. *Psychoanalysis and Contemporary Thought, 26, 1*, 89–141.

Felman, S. (1987). *Jaques Lacan and the adventure of insightL Psychoanalysis in contemporary culture*. Cambridge, MA: Harvard University Press.
Finkelstein, B. (1979). *Regulated children/liberated children: Education in psychohistorical perspective*. New York: Psychohistory Press.
Freire, P. (2008). The "banking" concept of education. In D. Bartholomae & A. Petrosky (Eds.) *Ways of reading, 8*, 242–254. Boston, MA: Bedford/St. Martin's.
Freire, P. (1993). *Pedagogy of the oppressed: 20th anniversary*. New York, NY: Continuum Books.
Freud, A. (1929). On the theory of analysis of children. *International Journal of Psychoanalysis*, 10, 29-38.
Freud, A. (1946). *The psychoanalytical treatment of children*. London, UK: Imago Publishing Company.
Freud, S. (1953). Fragment of an analysis of a case of hysteria. In J. Strachey (Ed. and Trans.), *The standard edition of the complete psychological works of Sigmund Freud (Vol. 7*, pp. 1–122). London: Hogarth Press. (Original work published 1905).
Freud, S. (1955). The psychotherapy of hysteria. In J. Strachey (Ed. and Trans.), *The standard edition of the complete psychological works of Sigmund Freud (Vol. 2*, pp. 253–305). London: Hogarth Press. (Original work published 1895).
Freud, S. (1957). Five lectures on psycho-analysis. In J. Strachey (Ed. and Trans.), *The standard edition of the complete psychological works of Sigmund Freud (Vol. 11*, pp. 7–55). (London: Hogarth Press. (Original work published 1910).
Freud, S. (1957). The future prospects of psychoanalytic therapy. In J. Strachey (Ed. and Trans.), *The standard edition of the complete psychological works of Sigmund Freud (Vol. 11*, pp. 139–151). London: Hogarth Press. (Original work published 1910.
Freud, S. (1958) Observations on transference-love (further recommendations on the technique of psycho-analysis III). In J. Strachey (Ed. and Trans.), *The standard edition of the complete psychological works of Sigmund Freud (Vol. 12*, pp. 157–171). London: Hogarth Press. (Original work published 1915).
Freud, S. (1958). The dynamics of transference. In J. Strachey (Ed. and Trans.), *The standard edition of the complete psychological works of Sigmund Freud (Vol. 12*, pp. 97-108). London: Hogarth Press. (Original work published 1912).
Furth, H. (1987): *Knowledge as desire: An essay on Freud and Piaget*. New York: Columbia University Press.
Illeris, Knud (2007). *How we learn: Learning and non-learning in school and beyond*. London: Routledge.
Jung, C. (1966). The psychology of transference. In R. Hull (Trans.), *The practice of psychotherapy: Essays on the psychology of the transference and other subjects (2nd ed.*, pp. 163–338). Princeton, NJ: Princeton University Press. (Original work published 1946).
Kernberg, 0. (1965). Notes on countertransference. *Journal of the American Psychoanalytic Association, 13*, 38–56.
Lacan, J. (Ed.). (1977a). *Écrits: A selection*. (A. Sheridan, Trans.). New York: W. W. Norton. (Original work published 1966).
Lacan, J. (1977b). *The four fundamental concepts of psychoanalysis*. (J. Miller, Ed. & A. Sheridan, Trans.). New York: W. W. Norton. (Original work published 1973).
Lacan, J. (1988a). *The seminar of Jacques Lacan: Book I, Freud's papers on technique 1953–1954* (J. Miller, Ed., & J. Forrester, Trans.). New York: W. W. Norton. (Original work published 1975).
Lacan, J. (1988b). *The seminar of Jacques Lacan: Book 11, The ego in Freud's theory and in the technique of psychoanalysis 1954–1955* (J. Miller, Ed., & S. 'Ibmaselli, Trans.). New York: W. W. Norton. (Original work published 1978).
McLaughlin, J. (1981). Transference, psychic reality, and countertransference. *Psychoanalytic Quarterly, 50*, 639–664.
Milton, J., Polmear, C., & Fabricius, J. (2004). *A short introduction to psychoanalysis*. London: Sage.
Moi, T. (1992). Transference/countertransference. In E. Wright (Ed.), *Feminism and psychoanalysis: A critical dictionary* (pp. 431–435). Oxford, UK: Blackwell.

National Commission on Excellence in Education (1983). *A nation at risk: The imperative for educational reform*. Washington, D.C.

O'Loughlin, M. (2011). Commentary on Alcorn & Massé: Troubling pedagogy (Comentário sobre Alcorn & Massé: pedagogia problemática). *Educação Temática Digital, 13, 1*

Palmer, P. (1997). The heart of a teacher. *Change Magazine, 29(*6), 14–21.

Palmer, P. (1998). *The courage to teach: Exploring the inner landscape of a teacher's life*. San Francisco, CA: Jossey-Bass.

Piaget, J. (1972). *To understand is to invent*. New York: The Viking Press, Inc.

Piaget, J. (1973). The affective unconscious and the cognitive unconscious. *Journal of the American Psychoanalytic Association, 21*(2), 249–261.

Pianta, R. (1999). *Enhancing relationships between children and teachers*. Washington, D.C.: American Psychological Association.

Robertson, D. (1996). Facilitating transformative learning: Attending to the dynamics of the educational helping relationship. *Adult Education Quarterly, 47,* 41–53.

Robertson, D. (1998). *A teleological criterion for determining appropriate cross-professional applications among teaching, counseling, and psychotherapy*. Unpublished manuscript.

Robertson, D. (1999). Unconscious displacements in college teacher and student relationships: Conceptualizing, identifying, and managing transference. *Innovative Higher Education, 23* (3). 151-169.

Rogoff, B. (2003). *The cultural nature of human development*. New York, NY: Oxford University Press.

Rolnik, E. (2012). *Freud in Zion: Psychoanalysis and the making of modern Jewish identity*. London: Karnac Books.

Schmidt, V. (1924). *Psychoanalytic education in Soviet Russia*. London: International Psychoanalytic Press.

Shweder, R. (1990). Cultural psychology: what is it? In J. Stigler, R. Shweder & G. Herdt (Eds.), *Cultural psychology* (pp. 1–43). Cambridge, MA: Harvard University Press.

Stebbins, A. (2010). Freud, Lacan and erotic desire in education. *Atlantis*, *34*, *2*, 159–167.

Taubman, P. M. (2007). The beautiful soul of teaching: The contribution of psychoanalytic thought to critical self reflection and reflective practice. In M. Gordon & T. V. O'Brien (Eds.), *Bridging theory and practice in teacher education, Volume 12* (Series: Bold Visions in Educational Research, K. Tobin & J. Kincheloe, Eds.). Rotterdam/Taipei: Sense Publishers

Tiegs, E. & Katz, B. (1941). *Mental hygiene in education* . New York: Ronald Press Co.

Tobin, J. (2001). The missing discourse of sexuality in contemporary American early childhood education. *The Annual of Psychoanalysis, 23*.

Valsiner, J. (1996). Co-constructionism and development: A socio-historic tradition. *Anuario de Psicologia* , 69, 63–82.

Vygotsky, L. (1978). *Mind and society: The development of higher mental processes*. Cambridge, MA: Harvard University Press.

Vygotsky, L. (1993). The fundamental problems of defectology (abnormal psychology and learning disabilities). *Collected works of L. S. Vygotsky*. (*Volume 2)*. New York: Plenum Press.

Vygotsky, L. (1997). Problems of the theory and history of psychology, In R. Rieber & J. Wollock (Eds.), *The collected works of L.S. Vygotsky, (Volume 3)*. pp. 91–108. New York, NY: Plenum Press. (Original work published 1930.)

Wachtel, Paul L. (1981). Transference, schema, and assimilation: The relevance of Piaget to the psychoanalytic theory of transference. *The Annual of Psychoanalysis, 8,* 59–76. Madison, CT: International Universities Press.

Weiner, G. (2006). *More than a second hand emotion: Pedagogies of the heart and head*. Presented at the annual meeting of the American Educational Research Association. San Francisco, CA.

Wertsch, J. (1990). The voice of rationality in a sociocultural approach to mind. In L. C. Moll (ed.), *Vygotsky and education: Instructional implications and applications of sociohistorical psychology*. New York: Cambridge University Press.

Wilson, A. & Weinstein, L. (1992). An investigation into some implications of a Vygotskian perspective. *Journal of American Psychoanalytical Association, 40*, 349–379.
Wilson, A. & Weinstein, L. (1992). Language and the psychoanalytic process: Psychoanalysis and Vygotskian psychology, Part II. *Journal of the American Psychoanalytic Association, 40*, 725–759.
Wilson, A. & Weinstein, L. (1996). The transference and the zone of proximal development. *Journal of American Psychoanalytical Association, 44*, 167–200.

Chapter Fifteen

A Vision of the Psychodynamically Informed School (PIS)

Al Galves

I am going to describe my vision of what a psychodynamically-informed school (PIS) would look like and how it would operate. I want to give you some idea of the flavor of the school and what it would be like to teach and learn there. Before I do that I'll describe some of the psychodynamic principles which inform my vision of the school.

First, there is the principle that much of what drives the behavior of human beings is a part of the psyche which is deeper and more essential than the rational part of the psyche. People have given that part of the psyche many names. Freud referred to it as the unconscious. Others have called it deep structure, core material, schema, etc. In order for human beings to live good lives, they have to be able to manage themselves. In order to manage themselves they have to have access to that deeply embedded part of themselves. If they don't have access to that part of themselves, they will not understand themselves. They will be at a loss to know what makes them tick. And they will not have access to a part of themselves that is the source of much helpful insight, understanding, and awareness.

Second, there is the principle that human beings are born with powerful desires and, if they are unable to satisfy those desires, they can react in ways that are dangerous and harmful to themselves and others. Freud (2005) believed, on the basis of his work with many human beings, that the most powerful desire was the desire to be dominant, to be able to do what one wants to do, eat what one wants to eat, sleep where one wants to sleep, and mate with whom one wants to mate. Near the end of his life he was asked about the key to mental health. His answer was the capacity to work, the capacity to love, and the capacity to enjoy. So I would include the desire to love as one wants to love, to work as one wants to work, and to enjoy as one wants to enjoy. This means that the psychodynamically-informed school will help children learn how to satisfy these drives without hurting themselves or others.

Carl Jung (1993) believed that the main desire of human beings was to become whole, to fill in the undeveloped parts of the Self as one grew older. Other theorists have posited additional desires that drive human behavior. Abraham Maslow (1971) added the desires to belong and to develop one's faculties to the utmost degree. Alfred Adler (1998) added the desire for competence and mastery.

The purpose of education is to help people develop their knowledge and skill and to put them in the service of self-mastery and contribution to society. In order to do that students have to be aware of the desires that drive them and have to be helped to satisfy those desires in healthy ways.

The efforts of human beings to satisfy these drives can result in violence, aggression, and other kinds of harm to self and others. Thus it is vitally important that humans learn how to manage these drives in ways that are safe and life-enhancing. One of the key goals of the PIS is to help children learn how to do that.

A major part of the curriculum is activities designed to help children learn how to manage these drives in ways that enable them to live successfully in society. This includes the use of ritual and ceremony as well as skill in learning how to manage conflict with others in healthy ways.

The third principle of psychodynamics is that awareness is the key. This was the great contribution of Frederick Perls (1992). He came to believe that, if people could become aware of what they were actually doing and why, if they could be able to accept what was true about them and become aware of that truth, they would become healthier and more able to lead satisfying and creative lives. And he saw that an essential part of that process was becoming aware of the beliefs, attitudes, assumptions, and habits that lie beneath the surface of consciousness. So Perls developed a method of learning from dreams which involved playing the part of each of the images in the dream and using that process to become aware of the message from the dream.

Finally, there is the psychodynamic principle that early experience has great influence over later behavior. The work of the PIS is informed by the findings of Margaret Mahler (1975) and the Object Relations school. So children are helped to find the balance between autonomy and independence on the one hand and cooperation and connections with others on the other hand. Children are helped to become aware of the impact of their histories on their current behavior and helped to use that awareness in the service of becoming competent and comfortable in their skins. They learn that their history makes a difference but that it doesn't have to be overly constraining and that it can be a source of compassion for themselves.

In the PIS, the developmental needs of the whole child are addressed. What does that mean? It means that the school is designed to help children develop not only their logico-mathematical and verbal intelligences but all of the other kinds of intelligence identified by Howard Gardner in his book *Multiple Intelligences* (1993): musical, spatial, kinesthetic, linguistic, interpersonal, and intrapersonal. And some of the intelligences not mentioned in Gardner's book include political, intuitive, ecological, social, mechanical, and spiritual intelligence. They learn the value of curiosity and are given opportunities to develop it in ways that are unique to them. So the developmental domain of the school is very broad and far-reaching. And it is also deep.

Let's take intrapersonal intelligence as an example. What does it mean to help a child develop his or her intrapersonal intelligence? It means helping her learn how to manage her thoughts, feelings, perceptions, and intentions. But it goes much deeper than that. It also means helping her become aware of the beliefs, attitudes, fears, and desires that lie below the surface of consciousness but which nevertheless drive her behavior. It means helping her delve deeply into her relationship with her mother, father, and siblings, her role in the family, the inevitable feelings of jealousy, fear, anger, and shame that arise there. It means helping her learn to master that necessary task of finding the balance between her desire for domination and mastery and her desire to be part of the group and get along with others.

The way in which the psychodynamically-informed school is most unlike the typical public school is that it is committed to helping each child develop his or her will. It is designed to help children learn how to use their intentions and desires, especially their desire to learn what they want to learn, when they want to learn it, and how they want to learn it. Thus, it is designed to mobilize the most powerful educational force in the world: the desire of human beings to learn what they want to learn.

The typical public school pays virtually no attention to the will of students. It doesn't seem to care what students want to learn. From time to time it may offer students constrained choices but it never asks the student: what do you want to learn? It never even challenges students to wonder about that. Rather, the curriculum is pushed down the throats of students, whether they want it or not.

One of the key characteristics of the psychodynamically-informed school is that students have control over how they spend their time. Students are given the power to decide what they are going to focus on, what they are going to devote themselves to, what they are going to learn.

This is in keeping with what Erik Erikson (1994) learned about the stages of human development. He found that the master issue for humans at age 2 and 3 is initiative, learning how to take control over their behavior, move in the direction they want to move in, do what they want to do. And the master issue for children four to six years of age is autonomy, learning to be relatively free in what they pursue and devote themselves to. What a shame that as soon as they enter public school, those qualities are squashed.

In the PIS, students are exposed to various stimuli. They have an opportunity to look at and handle various kinds of toys, objects, dolls, machines, tools. They see pictures and models of animals, plants, machines, cars, trucks, and people. They are given the experience of listening to music, singing, dancing, playing musical instruments. But very quickly, as recently entered kindergartners, they are encouraged to decide what they want to do and how they want to do it. They are encouraged to exercise their wills. Immediately, the role of the teacher becomes helper, guide, resource, not the imparter of knowledge or learning.

The school makes liberal use of computers and teaching machines. Children can learn anything society wants them to learn on computers. Computers are wonderful tools for learning. The programs are designed to adjust to the learning level of the individual child. Children get immediate feedback on how they are doing. The learning process can be made interesting and enjoyable. Again, teachers become helpers and resources as children use computers to learn how to read and write and do mathematics.

One of the key skills of teachers in the PIS is the ability to reflect on what the child wants to learn, key off it, and use it to help the child develop skills in reading, writing, and mathematics. Let's suppose the child is interested in learning about cars and how they work. In the process of learning how the car works, the teacher can help the child learn how to read, do mathematics, write, use research tools such as manuals, dictionaries, and the Internet. Even a very young child can learn how gear ratios work, for instance, and, in the process, learn about mathematical ratios in general.

The same process can be used whether the child wants to learn about plants, people, or dinosaurs. In his book *Education and Ecstasy* (1987), George Leonard described a school like this. On the campus of Leonard's school there were centers for mathematics, science, language, social studies, history, performing arts, and athletics. In each center there were teachers, computers, experiments, models, equipment, books. Students could spend their time in any of the centers and could stay there as long as they wanted to.

In my vision, each student would have a relationship with at least one teacher that is trusting and close enough for the teacher to be able to challenge the child about playing it too safe, for example. Suppose a child was spending all of his time in the performing arts center. The teacher might engage the child in a conversation about the dangers of becoming too one-sided and unbalanced, the fear of pursuing something new, of trying something the child wasn't very good at. Through such a negotiating process, the child might broaden his experience and take some chances at trying something new. But if he didn't that would be fine with the school.

Society does have a legitimate interest in children learning certain skills and knowledge. For example, I do think that, in order to live a good life, a person must know how to read and write at a fundamental level and do simple mathematics. I also think students should learn something of the values on which our country is based and how our governments work. They should be helped to develop some social consciousness and wrestle with the basic issues of individual versus societal welfare. How do we reconcile this constraint with the kind of freedom envisaged in the PIS?

One way would be to condition the freedom of the child to do what s/he wants to do on demonstrating that s/he is being responsible about learning what society wants him or her to learn. So, for example, freedom could be contingent on the child demonstrating every three months that s/he is making adequate process in learning to read, write, do basic mathematics, and learn the basics of American civics. If s/he shows that s/he is being responsible, s/he continues to be free to use her time as s/he wants to. If she doesn't she is moved into a more controlled learning environment in which she loses some of her freedom.

Some might object that young children are unable to make good decisions about what they should be learning. Watching children from one year old on as they practice, experiment, explore, and develop leads me to reject that argument. My experience tells me that children have a natural ability to learn what they need to learn, when they need to learn it. They are learning machines. If we just let them continue to do that when they enter school, they will develop into healthy, intelligent children. And the teachers will be a whole lot happier than they are in today's public schools.

Our public schools can be changed to realize this vision. And this vision can be realized within the budgetary constraints of our public school systems. Yes, it will require major changes in how teachers see their roles and in the willingness of state legislatures to give public school systems more freedom in how they educate children. It will require a different set of standards of good performance. It won't require a major change in curricula but it will require a change in how the curricula are delivered. And it will require the addition of a major focus on the development of intra-personal skills and knowledge as one of the goals of public education. These are big changes. But they don't require the infusion of additional money into the public school system. They do require the people who run the public schools to base their programs on the natural motivations of human beings to learn what they want to learn, when they want to learn it, and how they want to learn it. That is a big change but it is doable.

These are not new ideas. There is a tradition of schools which operated this way. The earliest precursor was Summerhill, the school developed by A. S. Neill (1992). Ivan Illich (1970), John Holt (1982), John Taylor Gatto

(2005), and Alfie Kohn (1993) have described schools and educational programs that invoke these ideas.

And there are schools which operate this way today. The purest example is the Sudbury Valley School in Sudbury, Massachusetts (http://www.sudval.org/). In that school and others which are modeled after it, there is no pressure on any child to learn anything. Children spend the five hours a day of school doing what they want to do. Teachers, resources, computers, books, equipment are available to them but it is up to the individual child to decide how s/he uses her or his time.

I visited the Alpine Valley School in Wheat Ridge, Colorado (http://alpinevalleyschool.com). It is modeled after the Sudbury Valley School. I spent a morning there. When I arrived, three children were chasing the chickens that had escaped from the pen next door. Once they got them back in the pen, the children announced that they were going to the park and took off. There were two children playing pool. A child was reading on the couch. Another child was playing cards with one of the teachers. There were ten children working on computers. I met an older student who was working on a community project having to do with horses. There was another student playing on the playground.

I attended the daily meeting of the school court. Although there are no rules about what children have to learn or how they spend their time, there are rules about behavior such as taking care of property, cleaning up after oneself, being inconsiderate, fighting, sharing, and otherwise being good members of the community. The presiding judge was one of the students and the judging panel was comprised of students of various ages and a teacher. That morning, the court took up several issues and handled them with what appeared to me to be a fine sense of justice and practical wisdom. It occurred to me that one of the advantages of an environment that is so free is that it gives children an opportunity to exercise their moral sensibilities in a way not possible in the typical public school. Or they may choose not to exercise them and pay the consequences. Thus it is a much better environment for helping children learn how to manage their behavior in responsible ways and suffer the consequences of not doing so.

But what happens when these children want to go to college, you ask? Putting together transcripts that colleges will accept is a challenge but Sudbury schools have a very good record of helping their students get into college. In fact, I first learned about them through reading a book about how Sudbury students fared in college. It turned out that they tended to do very well in college, having been well schooled in using the kind of freedom that college students have. It turned out that a very high percentage of Sudbury students have gone on to outstanding careers in science, academia, and the arts. And it is instructive that no child has ever gone beyond twelve years old at the Sudbury School without learning how to read.

I've thought about the problem of the kinds of curriculum requirements that colleges and universities have for admission: three years of science, three years of mathematics, three years of foreign language, three years of language arts, etc. Aside from creative transcript development, how will this be addressed?

One way is for the school to tell eighth grade students that, if they are planning to go to college, they should contact two or three colleges to find out what course work they require for admission. Once they get the answer, the students can then design their own curriculum to meet the requirements. This assumes that the PIS will be able to accommodate students who want to learn the most conventional of college preparatory curricula. But the key difference here is that the student is asking the school to provide such courses rather than being the recipient of a top-down, system-derived curriculum.

What about the concern that, if we allow students to decide what they want to learn, we won't have enough scientists, mathematicians, and engineers to compete in the world market? First, that's an assumption that may not be warranted. Ergo, Steve Jobs and Bill Gates, neither of whom finished college and Benjamin Franklin, John D. Rockefeller, and Thomas Edison, none of whom went to college. Second, I have great faith in the ability of American entrepreneurs to build machines that can take over the work of human beings. Third, if that's what happens so be it. I believe our supreme societal value should be the freedom of each citizen to develop his or her skills and knowledge as s/he wants to. I understand the importance of the requirement that, in order to have a claim on the resources of other people (money), people have to be able to participate in the provision of goods or services that other people want, i.e., be viable participants in the economy but, beyond that, let the chips fall where they may.

What about the current concern with reading proficiency? This is a trumped up concern. Trumped up in the sense that the public school authorities have raised the bar for "reading proficiency" so that what was once expected of eighth graders is now expected of fourth graders. From reading popular newspaper accounts of the reading problems of American youth, you would think that large numbers of young people are unable to read. That is not the case. After all, if you couldn't read you wouldn't be able to play many of the video games which children spend hours playing. American children can read just fine. But they can't do the kind of "critical thinking" reading that is being demanded of them by the public schools. This is an example of the extent to which American public schools have been taken over by people who overvalue the importance of linear, logical, verbal thinking and undervalue all of the other possible uses of the human psyche—intuition, emotional intelligence, conscience, artistic practice, interpersonal connection, athletic intelligence, etc.

Here is some evidence. The test of reading proficiency for fourth graders in New Mexico asks students to read a passage on jaguars. The student is asked to answer the question: "Why does the author choose the word *burning* to describe the jaguar's eyes?" Two of the four multiple choice answers are: "To make the eyes appear hot" and "To show the eyes glow in the darkness." To me, there is not a significant difference between these answers. In order to get the right answer, the student needs to go back to the passage and find it. This is not a test of reading proficiency. This is a test of test-taking ability.

Another question on the test is: "What strategy would best help the reader understand the word *disappearance*? The multiple choices are:

Break the word into parts.
Use the word in a new sentence.
Sound out the first syllable of the word.
Say the word quickly.

This may be a test of knowledge of learning strategy but it isn't a test of reading proficiency.

And how will teachers fare in a school in which students have control over how they spend their time? They'll be a whole lot better off. They won't have to bear under the pressure of forcing children to pay attention to things they don't want to pay attention to. They won't have to continue playing in the charade that pretends that schools are helping children grow into healthy adults. They will be working with children who are doing what they want to do and who are being driven by the most powerful educational force in the world. Of course they will no longer be the basic imparters of knowledge and skill. But they will play the important roles of resource expert, mentor, coach, and confidante.

In the PIS children learn to honor and use the powerful drives which all of us carry inside—the drive to eat what we want to eat, sleep where we want to sleep, mate with whom we want to mate and, yes, to love who we want to love in the way that we want to love and to express ourselves in the way that we want to express ourselves. PIS students learn that the drive to be dominant is healthy. But, in order to live in society, one has to learn to manage those drives effectively. So aggression within the bounds of certain rules is encouraged. When aggression results in persons being seriously harmed, teachers intervene and help students learn from what has happened. Children learn that aggression is not a bad thing but that it has to be used in ways that don't result in bad outcomes, that are not overly disruptive or harmful. One tool for this kind of learning will be the kind of School Court that I witnessed at the Aspen Valley School in Denver. Such a Court will be useful for helping children learn to distinguish between aggression that is within bounds and aggression which is out of bounds. Over the years, children learn one of the most important lessons that can be learned: how to use aggression and anger in ways that work for themselves and for others.

Psychodynamically-informed schools will spend a great deal of attention and effort on helping students learn what makes them tick, why they do what they do and don't do what they don't do. This won't happen through didactic lectures by teachers. It will happen through therapy groups, individual therapy, and interventions in real-time events, events that occur on the playground, in classrooms and outside of the school.

At least five hours a week will be spent in therapy groups. These will be unstructured groups using the modern group techniques developed by Lou Ormont (1992) and his followers, or something like them or patterned after them. The purpose of the group is to help students become aware of what is really true about themselves, not what they wish were true or imagine to be true or make believe is true. The group will help them become aware of how their behavior is seen by others, how they affect others and some of the underlying fears, fantasies, dreams, wishes, concerns that drive their behavior. The adults who are leading the groups—teachers—will be adept at helping the students become co-therapists, helping them be willing to confront each other, be open and honest with each other. Groups will also focus on helping students learn how to use all of their feelings, even the so-called negative feelings of anger, jealousy, anxiety, guilt, and sadness to become more aware of what they want, what they are afraid of, what they don't want, and what they want to protect and nurture. And the groups will be designed to help students learn how to manage their interpersonal boundaries so they can learn to be appropriately free from constraints caused by concerns about how other people will react to their behavior and how not to be overly affected by the behavior of others towards them.

One of the crucial features of the PIS is the use of real-time incidents as opportunities for learning. Let's take bullying as an example. There is a lot of concern about bullying in our public schools. But my guess is that bullying incidents will not be used effectively to help students learn about themselves and how to manage their behavior. My guess—and I have some reason to believe this is true—is that bullying incidents in the typical public school will be met with a zero tolerance stance: "Stop that bullying. That won't go on here. You are suspended (or go immediately to the Principal's office)." Then some teacher will give a talk or lead a discussion on why bullying is bad and why it won't be tolerated.

In the PIS, a bullying incident is a trigger for an extended learning session. First, the teacher brings the perpetrator and the victim together and engages them in a therapeutic conversation about what has gone on. What was the motivation behind the bullying behavior? What was the bully trying to get out of it? What was the need that was being satisfied? Where did that need come from? What is its fundamental foundation? After all, many of us spend our Sunday afternoons watching National Football League games, cheering on a bunch of bullies and the bigger bullies they are the better we like it. During the past twenty years, our country has invaded a number of much weaker countries and pushed people around with relative impunity, behavior which could be called international bullying. My point here is that there is a fine line between appropriate aggression and bullying. It may be true that we know the difference when we see it. But the motivations behind both behaviors are very similar. One of the jobs of schools is to help children understand and live with such fine distinctions.

And some time will be spent helping the victim make some sense about his or her role in the incident? What was it that led him to be picked as the victim? How did she react? How did that work? What might have worked better?

And then back to the bully? Nothing wrong with wanting to be dominant and at the top of the pecking order. But not the way you're doing it here. What are some other ways in which you can be dominant and demonstrate your power and superiority . . . in the classroom; on the athletic field, in the art studio, in debate?

I can imagine the following kind of interchange taking place. A teacher has observed a child knocking the books out of another child's arms and laughing and taunting the victim:

> TEACHER: Hey guys, what's going on here? Come on over here with me so we can talk about it.
>
> TEACHER (TO BULLY): For the time being, let's not cast any blame here or mete out punishment. I'd like to spend some time understanding what happened and helping you understand it. So I have a question for you. It's a question that may be hard to answer but I'd like you to work at answering it and I want you to know that I will not judge your answer. Here's the question: What was the need that you were trying to satisfy by knocking the books out of Ethan's arms and then taunting him about it?
>
> BULLY: I don't know.
>
> TEACHER: Well, if you did know, what would it be?
>
> BULLY: I guess I was angry about something. I was mad.
>
> TEACHER: What were you mad about?

BULLY: I don't know.

TEACHER: Well, take some time to think about it. I think it will really be helpful if you can figure it out. It'll be worth your time.

TEACHER ALLOWS THE CHILD SOME TIME TO THINK ABOUT IT

TEACHER: What has happened to you that might be triggering that behavior?

BULLY: I don't know. Maybe it's that I'm feeling really frustrated at home. It's not just that I'm being pushed around and sat on but I'm not even allowed to complain. Whenever I do, I get "There'll be no back talk in this house young man."

TEACHER: So you're feeling pretty powerless and put down at home.

BULLY: Yeah, I guess so.

TEACHER: Well, that's pretty understandable. All of us want to be powerful and be able to do what we want to do. And it's very frustrating not to be able to even complain when we can't. But I don't want you knocking the books out of people's arms and then taunting them about it. So let's see if we can find some other ways in which you can feel powerful, move up in the pecking order and do what you want to do without hurting other people.

Note: I can think of the following possibilities which might come up here: playing sports, being in a play, excelling in other domains such as art, computer games, the classroom, etc.

TEACHER (TO VICTIM): So why do you think he picked on you?

VICTIM: I don't know, maybe because I'm small and I wear glasses?

TEACHER: Could be. What do you think you can do to keep this from happening again?

VICTIM: I don't know.

TEACHER: Here's one thing you can do. The next time he or anyone else does that to you, you go after him with everything you've got—legs, feet, fists, teeth, whatever you can to let him know that he's going to pay for doing that to you. I guarantee you that will be the last time that one does that to you. And other people will get the message not to mess around with you.

I understand that public school officials will be put off by this idea of how to handle bullying incidents, especially encouraging the victim to fight back physically. But this is an important lesson and learning opportunity for the victim. It is important to distinguish between violence for the purpose of defending oneself and violence for the purpose of dominating an innocent victim.

So physical fighting, fisticuffs is tolerated in the PIS. The PIS doesn't have a zero tolerance policy. It makes distinctions between legitimate defense and illegitimate bullying. Such distinctions are a key to being able to live in the real world. There's a difference between defending oneself and attacking innocent victims. The PIS recognizes that one of the dynamics that is always at play in the school is the pecking order and the attempts by all children to move up the pecking order and to eventually become comfortable wherever they end up. The school teaches children that there are many, many different domains, each with a pecking order. So you may be far down the list in one of the domains but near the top in another one. And the school helps each of its students find a pecking order in which s/he can be successful. This is one of the values of encouraging children to find the domain in which they want to develop their skills and excel and sending the message that all of the domains are valuable to society and provide opportunities for valued competence, mastery, and achievement.

And the PIS realizes that, just as with other animals, part of the process of growing up involves engaging in conflict with others, even physical conflict as long as it doesn't get out of hand. The school tries to limit this kind of developmental conflict to the sports field with its elaborate rules and rituals but realizes that it may go on in other places.

After meeting with the individuals involved in a bullying incident, the teacher may decide to take a couple of hours to go into the incident, study it, and learn from it with the entire class. The teacher will know that this kind of learning is just as important as learning to read, write, and do math, just as important as science, mathematics, and foreign languages.

Other kinds of interpersonal incidents will provide the fuel for similar learning experiences. Teachers will be on the lookout for opportunities in which such incidents can be the trigger for increasing emotional intelligence.

In his book *Emotional Intelligence* Daniel Goleman (1995) presents convincing evidence that interpersonal and intrapersonal intelligence are more closely associated with success in life than is intellectual intelligence. But you don't learn emotional intelligence through lectures and guided discussions. You learn it from dealing with real-life incidents in real time.

So all conflict in the school becomes an opportunity for learning. Students learn that conflict is inevitable when a bunch of highly motivated, energetic, talented human beings come together and start working on a common enterprise. Group projects in which students are working together are bound to create conflict. When the inevitable occurs, the teacher pounces on it and uses it to teach students how to listen to each other non-defensively, how to achieve a better balance between advocacy and inquiry in group discussions (Argyris, 1982). Students learn that, if they can become aware of how their behavior creates problems for other people in a non-defensive environment, they will automatically correct it. Students will learn the value of conflict management, not through lectures and stories but through real-time incidents of conflict between individuals and groups in the school.

Much time will be spent on helping children make sense of what is happening in their families. So children will be helped to reflect on their relationships with their mothers and fathers. With whom do they feel closest? Most comfortable? With whom are they allied? Who is the disciplinarian? In what ways do their mothers and fathers conform to the norms of the culture? In what ways are they deviant? What are they learning from their mothers and fathers and from the relationship between them?

Children are helped to become aware of how they are influenced by their mothers and fathers. They are informed of the natural tendency to live the unlived lives of their parents and to take on the wounds of their parents (Walkenstein, 2008). They learn how to manage those tendencies in ways that are helpful rather than hurtful.

Through the use of psychodrama, they are helped to replay important incidents from their family life so they can become aware of the reality of power relationships, degrees of freedom, alliances, and the influence of various emotions on the behavior of family members.

They are helped to see their parents as real people with unique strengths and weaknesses, motivations, dreams, desires, and lives to lead. They are helped to see the conflicts, jealousies, and resentments that occur in all families and the power of love and concern in addressing and resolving them.

Parents are involved in the entire fabric of the PIS. They are encouraged to be at the school as much as they can. They serve as a resource for all of the students, not only their own children. They serve as mentors for their own children as well as others. They have a special role in connecting the school and the students with the wider community, with the outside world. They are instrumental in providing children with opportunities to spend time out in the community, in workplaces, parks, civic spaces. They provide the school with a range of knowledge, skill, and experience that is not available to the typical public school.

Parents also participate with their children in family sessions designed to help family members become more aware of the dynamics in the family, more able to speak openly and honestly with each other and to hear what is being said without becoming overly defensive or wounded. At the same time children are learning of the influence that their parents have over them, parents are learning about how their words and behavior affect their children. The members of the family learn about the ever-present and necessary conflict that occurs in healthy families and how to use it to help each member adjust, find middle grounds, learn how to manage her boundary, adapt into a comfortable role and find a way to grow within the confines of the family system.

One of the options open to the school is to organize the curriculum around what Richard Hopkins (1994) calls the "root metaphor of narrative." In Hopkins' conception, students are encouraged to develop their individual stories and the curriculum is designed to help them move towards the realization of their stories, to begin to live their stories. Since stories include fantasy and reflect psychological dynamics, this approach helps students learn to manage their psyches as well as move in the developmental direction in which they want to go. Teachers can help students distinguish between fantasy and reality and become aware of how to use their thoughts, feelings, perceptions and intentions to negotiate the world. There is a focus on lived experience, learning from all parts of that experience and designing experiences that broaden and deepen learning. A major part of the curriculum is the design of experiences that will help students do that.

Hopkins says that the systemic change that is required to use narrative as the root metaphor of education will be easier to accomplish in the elementary school because "the boundaries between life and school are much more permeable in the earlier school years. . . . Children tend to start schooling with hope and enthusiasm. In their dependence and ingenuousness, they have less to hide." He notes that "the narratory principle . . . is firmly established in widely prevalent traditions of story-telling and story-writing among younger children" (p. 134).

But in the typical high school, Hopkins finds that "student energies and drives to autonomy are severely circumscribed by the priority of the disciplines and by hall passes and other demeaning restrictions, and the meaning of individual experience and its power to instruct are largely ignored" (p. 135).

So here are the characteristics of the secondary school that Hopkins envisions:

- The school is a "free movement" school. Compulsory attendance, hall passes, and arbitrary restrictions on moving about that do not serve the purpose of the school's program are limited.
- Student spend at least two hours a day in groups of 8 to 10. The groups are heterogeneous (no tracking) and ungraded. They are learning communities that are facilitated by teachers. The purpose of the group is to help each of its members construct his or her narrative. They are the places in which students present and try out their stories, through speaking, writing, painting, drama, photographs, videos, and other media. They are communities in which students and teachers help and challenge each other. They are also places in which students learn how to manage conflict and competition and find ways of cooperating and connecting with each other.
- Learning is organized around portfolios. Each student develops and maintains a portfolio in any and all media. "The learning group advises, assists, is the immediate audience for, evaluates and generally monitors portfolio development with the instructor helping out as a consultant."
- Courses are designed to help students develop their portfolios. The exact nature of the courses will depend on the needs of the students. They are going on all the time on an open-door basis but none is required.
- The teacher's role is that of consultant: helping students find resources, challenging students who are taking too safe a road, helping students make sense out of their experience, and take the risks that are necessary to learning and growth, listening, interpreting, cajoling, supporting, and challenging.

During their years in the psychodynamically-informed school, children learn various techniques they can use to understand themselves better and manage their lives. Examples are as follows:

- They learn techniques for quieting down, getting the internal noise down so that they can receive the messages from inside.
- They learn techniques for making difficult decisions, resolving dilemmas and finding middle grounds between the polarities of life. Included here would be the Chair Technique developed by Frederick Perls in which the person has a conversation between the two parts of herself that are wrestling with each other and the Four Square technique in which people can better see the pros and cons of the options that are available to them.
- They learn how to receive the important messages from their dreams.
- They learn techniques for accessing the Jungian archetypes, receiving messages from them and understanding their influence over motivation and behavior.

- They learn how to use the mistakes they make and unfortunate things that "happen" to them as a window into subconscious forces that drive their behavior.
- They learn about the different preferences explicated in the Meyers-Briggs Type Indicator and how to use them to better understand people who appear to be different, perverse, strange but who are just living out their preferences of how to use energy, get information, make decisions, and structure their lives.
- They learn how to manage their boundaries so that they are not overly affected by the behavior of others or concerns about the impact of their behavior on others.
- They learn how to get information from not only their thoughts and ideas but also from their emotions and bodily sensations.

With the kind of open environment that exists in the school, there is ample opportunity for learning how to use all of the emotions—anger, fear, anxiety, jealousy, sadness, and guilt. Teachers are adept at recognizing the presence of such emotions and engaging children in the practice of receiving the messages from those emotions and using the messages to become clear about what they want, what they don't want, what is precious to them, what they want and don't have, what they are afraid of, losing, what they are afraid of and why. One of the primary goals of the school is to help children develop the capacity to learn from all of their emotions and use the learning to live more the way they want to live.

Whenever children are participating in group projects, time is spent on helping them learn lessons from the experience: What kind of behavior was most helpful to the group? What was least helpful? How did each of you contribute to the group? Whose behavior was helpful? Whose was not helpful? Was an attempt made to make sure the introverts had an opportunity to be heard? Did the group make good use of the various types identified in the Meyers-Briggs Type Indicator? How do the members get feedback on their performance?

For those children past the age of puberty, much time is spent on sexual development and behavior. Children are helped to understand the power and naturalness of sexual drives, the importance of being clear about the options they have, and the consequences of sexual behavior. Special importance is given to such clarity so that children don't fall into the trap of doing something they don't want to do "in the heat of passion." Importance is also given to the fact that, given the availability of birth control measures, adolescents can make choices to be sexually active or not to be sexually active but will have to live with the consequences of those choices.

In the PIS all symptoms of mental disorders are seen as meaningful reactions to life situations and how they are being dealt with, as in some ways functional and potentially useful. So the symptoms of depression are used to help the child deal with loss or ruminate about life concerns that are troubling him or her. The symptoms of mania are used to help the child wonder about the pressures to be outstanding and very successful and to consider the difficulties of living day to day and making the difficult choices that we all have to make and living with the regret of not being able to do everything we want to do. The symptoms of anxiety disorders are used to help children become more comfortable with the fears they have and more understanding of where those fears come from. Children are taught to distinguish between rational fear and irrational fear and learn how to decide if they are going to walk with the fear or use it to stop themselves from doing something that is dangerous. When students experience psychotic symptoms—hallucinations and delusions—a special effort is made to provide them with a place in which they can be safe both physically and psychologically. An effort is made to help them see the symptoms as being somehow related to what has happened to them, as somehow functional and potentially useful in helping them become more comfortable in the world. The school uses the Open Dialogue approach (Seikkula and Trimble, 2005) to bring the important people in the child's life together for the purpose of finding a shared understanding of what has happened and what can be done to help.

As students become older, they spend more time outside of the school in the community. As younger students, they visit places of business and government offices as well as non-profit organizations. They get a feel for the length and breadth of the community, what goes on out there. As they reach middle and high school, they begin to do volunteer work and to serve as apprentices and trainees in places of their choosing. They come to see the community and everything in it as sources of learning and inspiration. And they learn the importance of contributing to the community, doing what they can to help out. This is a way of not only developing skills and knowledge but also developing a sense of community and the importance of contributing to the commonwealth.

The goal of the psychodynamically-informed school is to help students "fashion a self" in the words of John Taylor Gatto. In his speech upon receiving the Teacher of the Year award in New York City, Gatto decried the fact that our children spend all but a smidgen of their waking hours under the control of school and television, both of which "reduce the real world of wisdom, fortitude, temperance and justice to a never-ending, non-stop abstraction." (1990). "In centuries past," he explained, "the time of a child and adolescent would be occupied in real work, real charity, real adventure and the realistic search for mentors who might teach them what they really wanted to learn."

"My children attend school thirty hours a week, use about eight hours getting ready, going and coming home and spend an average of seven hours a week in homework—a total of 45 hours," Gatto said. "During that time, they are under constant surveillance, have no private time or private space, and are disciplined if they try to assert individuality in the use of time or space."

Answering his own question of what can be done, Gatto said:

> Right now we are taking all the time from our children that they need to develop self-knowledge. That has to stop. We have to invent school experiences that give a lot of that time back, we need to trust children from a very early age with independent study; perhaps arranged in school but which takes place *away* from the institutional setting. We need to invent curriculum where each kid has a chance to develop private uniqueness and self-reliance. (ms. 1990)

A major part of Gatto's prescription is to reinvoke the family as the main engine of education. "The curriculum of the family is at the heart of any good life, we've gotten away from that curriculum, time to return to it. The way of sanity in education is for our schools to take the lead in releasing the stranglehold of institutions on family, to promote during school time confluences of parent and child that will strengthen family bonds" (ms., 1990).

One way of describing the psychodynamically-informed school is to say it will work at realizing Gatto's vision.

What will it take for this kind of school to become available to large numbers of our children? We are no closer to it than we were in 1964 when George Leonard wrote *Education and Ecstasy*. And there aren't many signs on the horizon of movement in this direction. One move in the right direction is the charter school movement. Although charter schools are under the control of the public education authorities, they do provide an opportunity for experiments in alternative ways of educating children.

I think the best hope we have is a radical voucher system. By a "radical" voucher system I mean one in which the total amount of money spent on public education in a state is divided among the parents of children through the use of some rational formula. Parents are then free to spend that money as they wish. I understand the concerns that such a system would aggravate the already damaging inequalities between rich and poor families. But I think those concerns could be partially addressed through the distribution formula and through other equalization measures.

The great benefit of a voucher system is that it would create of real market in education. Eventually, some enterprising people would design a school much like the psychodynamically-informed school described here. Children who go to such a school will be healthier than children who go to more traditional schools. Eventually, people will take notice and PISs will attract more and more of the funds and become available to larger and larger numbers of children.

There is a legitimate concern that a voucher system would undermine some of the protections and benefits that teachers have earned through unions, tenure, etc. But this can be avoided by state legislatures which have been traditionally protective of teachers and public schools.

And public schools would be free to compete in a voucher system. I believe that need to compete would ultimately result in a much more effective and nourishing public school system.

REFERENCES

Adler, A. (1998). *Understanding Human Nature*. Center City, MN: Hazelden.

Argyris, C. (1982). *Reasoning, learning and action: Individual and organizational*. San Francisco: Jossey Bass.

Erikson, E. H. (1994). *Identity and the life cycle*. New York: W. W. Norton.

Freud, S. (2005). *Civilization and its discontents*. New York: W. W. Norton.

Gardner, H. (1993). *Multiple intelligences: The theory in practices, a reader*. New York: Basic Books.

Gatto, J. T. (2005). *Dumbing us down: The hidden curriculum of compulsory schooling*. Gabriola Island, British Columbia, Canada: New Society Publishers.

Gatto, J. T. (1990). Speech upon being awarded the 1990 Teacher of the Year Award by the New York City Public Schools.

Goleman, D. (1995). *Emotional intelligence*. New York: Bantam Books.

Holt, J. (1982). *How children fail*, Rev. ed. New York: Delta/Seymour Lawrence.

Hopkins, R. L. (1994). *Narrative schooling: Experiential learning and the transformation of American education*. New York: Teacher's College Press.

Illich, I. (1970). *Deschooling society*. Cuernavaca, Mexico: CIDOC.

Jung, C. G. (1993). *The basic writings of C.G. Jung*. New York: Random House.

Kohn, A. (1993). *Punished by rewards: The trouble with gold stars, incentive plans, A's, praise and other bribes*. New York: Houghton Mifflin

Leonard, G. B. (1987). *Education and ecstasy*. Berkeley, CA: North Atlantic Books

Mahler, M. S. (1975). *The psychological birth of the human infant*. New York: Basic Books.

Maslow, A. (1971). *The farther reaches of human nature*. New York: Viking

Neill, A. S. (1992). *Summerhill School: A new view of childhood*. Rev. Ed. New York: St. Martin's.

Ormont, L. R. (1992). *The group therapy experience: From theory to practice*. New York: St. Martins.

Perls, F. S. (1992). *Gestalt Therapy Verbatim*. Gouldsboro, ME: Gestalt Journal Press.

Seikkula, J. & Trimble, D. (2005). Healing elements of therapeutic conversation: Dialogue as an embodiment of love. *Family Process, Vol. 44* (4), pp. 461–475.

Walkenstein, E. (2008). *The imprinters: Surviving the unlived life of our parents*. Phoenix, AZ: Zieg, Tucker and Thiesen

Chapter Sixteen

Progressive Education and Psychoanalysis

Toward a Theory of the Subjective Experience of School Life

Daniel B. Frank

CITIZENSHIP AND THE PERSONAL AND PUBLIC MEANINGS OF SCHOOL EXPERIENCE

A parent drops his child off at school. A teachers stands in front of her class. A student sits next to a friend and both look toward the teacher. Normative moments in an average school day. But each moment is filled with meaning. Each is filled with meanings that are both shared and different for each individual and for the school.

Progressive education offers educators, students, and parents a philosophy of reflective practice that can inspire all members of the school community to understand the meaning of their own and other's school experiences. This approach also includes the importance of understanding the experiences students, teachers, and parents have when they are not in school. It is though personal and institutional commitment to these high standards and profound ideals that such reflection can allow all members of the school community to strive toward excellence, creativity, and citizenship.

Among the many traits that make up the mission of progressive schools is an understanding that the call to teach is more than the call to teach subjects. In progressive schools, the call to teach is more than the call to know each student well. The call to teach is to do both of these and more. The call to teach is to work with ideas and with people—children, adolescents, and adults—as individuals and in groups, in order to help them better understand the meaning of their experiences, and to provide them with a sense of inspiration to transform those understandings into meaningful actions that can provide learners and teachers with the capacity and commitment to make a difference in the world. This very effort requires the development of a school culture that supports the creation of trusted relationships among all constituent groups that comprise the school community.

All social organizations exist to create relationships between the individual and the community. Schools, as social organizations, are no different. But each social organization has its own local culture and, accordingly, each school has its own way of cultivating relationships and the meaning those relationships have for members of that school community. All cultures are organized within a structure of highly valued ideals, practices, and traditions, all of which carry important symbolic value and meaning within that culture. Each culture, too, is organized within a structure that has present a set of values and customs that are the exact opposite of those that are espoused by the culture as being so highly valued (Erikson 1976). And the culture of each school, too, is no different.

Each school has its own set of values and their opposites. This tension structures school life. A progressive school that claims that its mission is to cultivate in young people a sense of responsibility and cooperation also has present within it potentially regressive forces that pull toward irresponsible and competitive behavior. At times of strength, the school's idealized values will be visible and present in the life of the school. At times of vulnerability, feelings of emotional frustration, worry and hostility can emerge when the opposite of the school's central values take center stage, shifting the focus of the drama from idealization to disillusionment. A vulnerability of a progressive school with high ideals is the possibility that the higher the ideal, the longer the potential fall and the bigger the disappointment. Our strength, if we are not aware, can also be our weakness.

In this light, the primary task of the school is to conduct all of its activities in accord with its essential mission, which includes being committed to finding ways to repair ruptures, heal wounds, and sustain hope, even when the best developmental path for the person and the school may mean to help them come to terms with disappointment and struggle (Frank, 2005). The call to teach in a progressive school, in other words, requires all involved to be attuned to the shift in emotion and behavior that can occur in individuals and in groups when the spirit of high ideals devolves, sometimes inevitably, into disillusioning experiences (Dilg, 1999; Kaplan, 2004). This means that educators need to know themselves, and their students, well enough to be prepared to contain the anxieties generated within themselves, and in others, that can be evoked by the shifts from ideals to disappointments. It means that educators also need to find ways to work with others to create the necessary reparations and adjustments in order to allow the school, and the individuals involved, opportunities to acknowledge the transition and mourn the loss that disillusionment can engender so that a new balance leading to reparation, growth, and learning can be found. In this way, schools must move empathically with the rhythms of change and transition, whether generated from within the school, by the school, or in response to forces alive outside the school.

TEACHABLE MOMENTS: INSIGHTS INTO SELF AND SOCIETY

With an education that is based in processes of reflection and action that attempts to improve the quality of life through empathy, understanding, and acts of reparation, students then both learn how to create such growthful moments and, by doing so, internalize these values as citizens capable of making a difference in the world.

Progressive education has long called for hands-on, experiential, and learn-by-doing approaches to teaching. This approach requires that teachers plan curriculum and create such learning opportunities. In the experiential world, however, there are other moments, too, that are full of potential for learning. These are moments that crash into the classroom and the curriculum or float by with the softness of a feather in gentle flight, presenting themselves without announcement—either joyously or traumatically: sounds of children playing and laughing outside; the siren of a speeding fire truck; a student telling a personal story in response to a poem the class is reading; a teacher deciding to comment on an issue or behavior taking place in the classroom instead of ignoring it; news of schoolmates winning an athletic event; news of two airplanes exploding into the World Trade Center. These moments call for the teacher to be facile enough to respond quickly and openly to such external factors that impinge, perhaps unexpectedly, and maybe even delightfully, on the culture of the class. The possibilities for learning in such unanticipated moments are potential *teachable moments* (Garrison, 1997).

Teachable moments are, in essence, reflective moments. They are moments of encounter with possibility. They are moments in which teachers and students can learn, through individual and group reflection, from what they have done or experienced individually and in groups. But teachers have to be attuned to the presence of a teachable moment and its potential significance for reflection and learning.

Each person can have her or his own way of experiencing such learning, and, consequently, may learn something different from one another. Sometimes the lesson a teacher teaches in her response to the experience of encountering the unexpected is to stop and pay attention to it with the class in a guided and thoughtful way; and sometimes the lesson a teacher teaches is to acknowledge an awareness of the unexpected event, and then return with the class to the planned task in an effort to both work and contain any anxiety that may arise as a result of the class' brief encounter with the unexpected. There are times when such teachable moments are the sweetest opportunities for teaching and learning a teacher can imagine. There are other times when such moments offer more illusion than substance. These can be less desirable moments because either the teacher or the students, or both, can hide in the shadow of the unexpected event by either embracing the moment in an effort to distract the class, taking flight from anxieties that may be stimulated by the work at hand, or by ducking the moment altogether in order to avoid the anxiety of confronting the sudden expression of difficult emotion.

As human beings, what we learn from our experiences is personal. Outside events resonate in idiosyncratic ways with our own unique personal histories and personalities. Yet, as human beings, what we learn from experience is also public. The personal, emotional dramas that are alive within us also can find expression in our outward, public behavior. As members of a culture, we internalize values and systems of communication and meaning that structure the societies in which we live, and, in turn, we give expression to feelings, ideas, fears, hopes, and wishes that are valued, or not, by our communities. Sometimes such expressions are easy to identify, understand, and discuss with students, colleagues, and parents. But often the meanings contained in the words and actions, silences and hesitations of those with whom we work, regardless of age, are more disguised and hidden. And it is harder to learn from experience, to learn from what we do, if much of what needs to be understood and interpreted lies in the shadows of what we do and think and feel.

In other words, in order for progressive education to be interested in the development of a citizen's emerging public life, it must necessarily also be focused on the development of a person's character and sense of self. And at the same time, to see progressive education as an approach centered only on a vision of the child's development of character and self, as vital as this is, would be to miss the point, the need, and the great opportunity. The aim of progressive education is to nurture the development of character and self for the purpose of connecting personal interests, talents, and passions with social progress. Through detailed attention and knowledge of each student, teachers have the capacity to guide students toward a larger vision for themselves and others. In this way, intimacy creates expansiveness.

Personal life and public life, however, are not wholly opposites either. In the life of an individual, or in the life of a group, there can be, at any one moment, the simultaneous presence of both a core set of values and standards, wishes and desires, needs and wants, and their exact opposites. Both individuals and groups can contain simultaneously emotions of love and hate, compassion and aggression, collaboration and conflict, individual identity and group identity.

The drama of human experience occurs in the variety of enactments people experience, intentionally and unwittingly, as they struggle to find their way through these inherent life tensions. And there is no better place to study how human beings, of a wide variety of ages, experience the interplay of self and society than in the culture of a school.

Schools, especially ones that include people of a vast reach of ages, are compelling places to study. Through the study of school life one can come to appreciate and understand the complex, subtle, and intriguing relationship between the personal and the public in human experience. Given that schools, and even a single school, can have students, educators, staff, and parents of varying ages and backgrounds, there is hardly a better social organization to study than a school if we wish to understand, for example, the tensions in such broad areas of human experience as: narcissism and connectedness; resistance and openness; fear and flow; risk and freedom; regressive and optimal development.

A progressive school provides educators with a broad and imaginative agenda. Because progressive schools serve a mission that promotes the development of responsibility, character, understanding, and citizenship to make the world a better, more just, beautiful, and interesting place for all people, the potential for learning from experience is even greater because larger questions can be asked: *What is the relationship between narcissism and citizenship? How can connectedness, openness, and freedom develop in students a sense of self-confidence that can be applied to the task of forwarding creativity and social progress for all? How can reflective teaching and learning connect personal passions, interests, and talents with the ideals articulated in a progressive school's mission statement? How can reflection, in the here-and-now of school life, provide teachers and learners with insights into the meaning of their own and others' experiences, thereby creating the potential for appreciating how the everyday experiences of school life are themselves valued and compelling texts to be studied and appreciated?*

Progressive education, in other words, is committed to a dual process of teaching. One path helps students and teachers feel open enough to let ideas and people outside of their own immediate worlds influence their development and experience in meaningful ways. The second path aims to bring forward and out into the open aspects of the students' and the teachers' rich, full and complex inner worlds in order to influence the world around them. Getting the inside out, and the outside in is the creative arena in which progressive teaching and learning takes place. The aim of a progressive school is to provide a philosophy and worldview of profound ideals, safe structures, and open pathways that can invite and inspire students and teachers to feel a sense of freedom and progress in their experiences of teaching and learning.

FREEDOM: PERSONAL AND CIVIC

Colonel Francis Wayland Parker, the late nineteenth-century educator, writes: "The goal of humanity is freedom. The means of acquiring freedom may be summed up in one word—education. True education is the presentation of the conditions necessary for the evolution of personality into freedom" (Parker, 1894, p. 317). Freedom is both the means and the end of education: Freedom to inquire and respond; freedom to choose and be guided; freedom to speak authentically and be heard empathically; freedom to think critically and creatively and be challenged to think even more critically and creatively. John Dewey, the great American philosopher of education, believed that the concept of freedom was an important link between education and democracy: "Children in school must be allowed freedom so that they will know what its use means when they become the controlling body, and they must be allowed to develop active qualities of initiative, independence, and resourcefulness, before the abuses and failures of democracy will disappear" (1915, p. 304).

Having the freedom to practice progressive teaching in this way is a public issue. Most schools are not empowered by government to teach in this way. And for those schools that have the independence and freedom to pursue freedom on behalf of their students and teachers, it is important that each of those school communities assess and assure that the schools are supported by sound administrative and educational structures, processes, and policies. Feeling that one is free to be creative in such an educational culture, however, is both a public issue and personal matter that requires that teachers and administrators are encouraged and supported in the not-so-easy process of reflection in an effort to understand their own emotional subjectivity. It is important to know what inspires and what inhibits one to feel expansive or inhibited in one's collaborative work with teachers, and students. Sometimes the path toward freedom is clear and easy to identify. Other times, however, anxiety and uncertainty, in their various forms, can cloud clarity and foster illusions and other obstacles that can complicate and impede growth and learning for students, teachers and parents. Such impediments can lie in the educator's own past experience of being a student in school. It is important to appreciate how one's own "ghosts in the classroom," (Lawrence-Lightfoot, 2003; Tieman, 2007; O'Loughlin, 2010) can evoke feelings of threat and destruction regarding the loss of customary ways of seeing and being in the world, activating basic human conservative impulses and, when aware of the influence of one's past on the present, can also lead to having the freedom to stimulate both the joys of new, open possibilities as well (Marris, 1974.)

The path toward education for character, understanding, and citizenship requires that progressive educators pay close attention to issues of freedom. Freedom does not mean that students and teachers live in a world without boundaries and can do anything they want. Anarchy and chaos are social actions that have nothing to do with the practice of education in a progressive school. Freedom for the individual must be balanced with its impact on the quality of community life; and community life must aim to foster personal and collective freedom in the life of the school in ways that are in keeping with the school's core mission.

We must also be aware of the illusion of freedom. Francis Parker and John Dewey, who called Colonel Parker the father of progressive education, each warned us that none are really free unless all are free. The quest for freedom in education is not just an issue of liberty and license. It is an issue of justice and equality as well. A progressive school holds a high standard, aiming for what Colonel Parker termed, ". . . the highest degree of knowledge, skill, power and service." The school must strive to ensure the success of all. The success of some and not all is not good enough. The higher calling, the higher degree of responsibility is required to create a complete educational community, a place where school can be experienced as a model home, a place where, as Colonel Parker taught, each is responsible for all, and all are responsible for each.

Progressive schools are social organizations grounded in a moral social contract dedicated to provide a clear philosophy that is protected by identifiable and reliable structures that support, in breadth and in depth, in vision and in detail, the developmental needs of the students in accord with the fundamental ideals and mission of the school. To support the development of freedom in education—and all the responsibility that comes with cultivating and maintaining this special value in life and learning—schools, and all citizens who are associated with schooling, must attend to the objective obstacles that influence, for better or worse, the education of young people and the creativity of their teachers. These public issues include: politics and public policy, funding and poverty, curriculum and classmates, teachers and school culture, as well as enlightened and repressive understandings of what role schools should play in our society.

At the same time, and for the same reasons, school communities interested in supporting freedom and understanding must also attend carefully to the specific subjective experiences of how those external contexts give shape and meaning to the lives of students, teachers, administrators, staff, and parents. For in the inquiry of the subjective one will find detailed and compelling opportunities to observe, understand, and respond both to the fluid openings for learning and to the more densely complicated impediments to growth and freedom that challenge individuals and groups in the school. And, it is important to remember that when teachers and administrators are free to create a school culture that support fresh ideas, engaging teaching methods, and compelling curriculum and learning opportunities, students will come to know and appreciate who they are becoming as young people, what their interests, talents, and passions are as a result of having experienced inspiring and affirming relationships with teachers and classmates. Through the intimacy of supportive community life, flowers the expansiveness of the self and society.

PROGRESSIVE EDUCATION AND PSYCHOANALYSIS: INTEGRATING TWO EDUCATIONAL TRADITIONS

John Dewey said that for education to serve the developmental needs of students and the democratic needs of society, there needs to be a theory of human experience that can inform the standards and practices that exist in school life (Dewey, 1938). He advocated for the development of a theory of experience that can enable educators to inform their teaching with essential understandings of the human condition, both as individuals and as members of social and cultural groups and institutions.

A potential for the further development of a theory of school experience lies in the integration of ideas still being articulated in the two major fields of human inquiry: progressive education and psychoanalysis. In recent years, at Francis W. Parker School, Chicago, there is a growing body of work leading toward an emerging theoretical paradigm for developing a theory of experience that aims to foster an understanding of the variety of ways students, teachers, parents, and others experience school life. This paradigm focuses on the subjective experience of school life, a dimension of human experience that is informed by the interplay between the personal and the public, between self and citizen, between fantasy and reality, between teaching and learning. This emerging paradigm draws on the experience of school relationships—student to teacher, classmate to classmate, parent to student and school, writer to craft, reader to text, artist to media, scientist to experiment. This paradigm aims to support the professional practice of creating meaningful conversations based on a growing vocabulary, shared language, and integrated worldview in order to further develop reflective possibilities for thoughtful action, among teachers, administrators, staff, parents, board members and students.

Both progressive education and psychoanalysis are educational traditions now already beginning their second centuries of practice. Each has important conceptual connections to the fields of social systems and organizational studies. Since their respective origins more than 100 years ago, progressive education and psychoanalysis have each evolved in important ways, providing each with new ideas and new possibilities to influence the field of education and the overall welfare and benefit of students and their teachers.

Progressive education has its origins in the forward-thinking, socially progressive, and reflective approach to teaching and learning in schools influenced most notably by the ideas of Francis Wayland Parker and John Dewey. Psychoanalysis has its origins in the clinical and methodological insights inspired by Sigmund Freud and others, including Melanie Klein, Anna Freud, Donald Winnicott, Heinz Kohut, and Wilfred Bion, whose work, individually and collectively, have had an important influences on educators. But both traditions also have developed in valuable ways since their origins a century ago. In recent years, such educators as Deborah Meier, Howard Gardner, Sarah Lawrence-Lightfoot, Ted and Nancy Sizer, Dennis Littky, Vivian Paley, Bill Ayers, Michael Thompson, and Gordon Donaldson, among others, have made vital new contributions to the field of progressive education.

Psychoanalysis, although best known as a theory for individual clinical treatment, has also been developed as a method of inquiry into the meaning of human experience across the life course (Cohler and Galatzer-Levy, 1993). In addition, to the growing number of contemporary psychodynamically-oriented educators who have continued to develop a body of ideas related to teaching and learning (Barford, 2002; Boldt & Salvio, 2006; Britzman, 2009; Cohler, 2006; Cottle, 2007; Todd, 1997, 2003; Youell, 2006), there are also many applying psychoanalytic thinking to better understand the psychodynamic interplay of human experience in social systems, structures and organizations (Gould, Stapley & Stein, 2001; Frank, 2003; Huffington et al., 2004; Sievers, 2009).

Progressive education brings to the partnership a long tradition of being attuned to the dynamics of child development and the aim of fostering thoughtful, active citizens of character and integrity. In his 1895 essay, "What Psychology Can Do for the Teacher," John Dewey had this to say about the close intellectual relationship between education and psychology:

> Just as knowledge of mathematics and mechanics have wrought marvelous improvements in all the arts of construction; just as a knowledge of steam and electricity has made a revolution in modes of communication, travel, and transportation of commodities; just as a knowledge of anatomy, physiology, pathology has transformed medicine from empiricism to applied science, so a knowledge of the structure and functions of the human being can alone elevate the school from the position of a mere workshop, a more or less cumbrous, uncertain, and even baneful institution, to that of a vital, certain, and effective instrument is the greatest of all constructions—the building of a free and powerful character. (1964, p. 198)

As a psychological theory of what Dewey called, "the structure and function of the human being" (Dewey 1895/1964, p. 199), psychoanalysis offers educators a robust set of ideas and a method of inquiry into the challenges that confront the coherent development and education of the self in ways that bring important depth of meaning to the word "character" in the context of learning in schools. Paying attention to the emotions that students can feel toward their teachers, Freud offers this reflection on the occasion of the fiftieth anniversary of his own school:

> We courted them or we turned our backs on them, we imaged sympathies and antipathies in them which probably had no existence, we studied their characters and on theirs we formed or misinformed our own. They called up our fiercest opposition and forced us to complete submission; we peered into their little weaknesses, and took pride in their excellences; their knowledge and their justice. At bottom, we felt a great affection for them if they gave us any ground for it, though I cannot tell how many of them were aware of this. But it cannot be denied that our position in regard to them was a quite remarkable one. We were from the first equally inclined to love and hate them, to criticize and respect them. Psychoanalysis has given the name "ambivalence" to this readiness to contradictory attitudes, and it has no such difficulty in pointing to the source of ambivalent feelings of such kind. (Freud 1914, 242)

As a theory of experience about the human condition, psychoanalytic understandings about development, loss, change, and transitions in human relationships—both within an individual and within and between couples, groups, and organizations—can prove highly valuable to progressive educators who are striving to understand and develop the potential of their own personal lives, professional careers, educational institutions, and school communities (Salzberger-Wittenberg, Henry, and Osborne, 1983; Jersild,1955).

Both progressive education and psychoanalysis share these educational and developmental aims: To empower individuals and groups to be aware of themselves and their relationships with others; to develop personal and group responsibility leading toward freedom from inhibitions, prejudice, fear and ignorance; to foster a commitment to learning and understanding through thorough and empathic observation and developmentally attuned reflections and interventions; to cultivate through valued relationships with other people a sense of courage to be curious, inquisitive, honest, challenging, and respectful of the anxiety that ambiguity, ambivalence, and contradiction can evoke on the path toward clarity, focus, and direction.

Both of these intellectual traditions also share a tolerance and respect for trusting processes of learning and meaning formation that are often, by their very natures, unfolding, organic, messy, exploratory, uncertain, searching. And because these two traditions share this vision of who people can become and what they can do as a result of their learning experiences, both traditions demand clear and safe, well-conceived and well-managed boundaries that can help contain anxiety and that provide the necessary structures that optimal development requires.

The integration of these two humanitarian and educational traditions, in other words, offers educators, and others interested in issues of human and organizational development in schools, new possibilities for understanding the realities and fantasies of how young people experience the public act of going to school for an education and how adults experience the public act of going to school for work and adult professional development. Progressive education and psychoanalysis share a set of fundamental tenets about what it means to be human. Integrating various ideas, methods of inquiry and structures developed by these two traditions over the past 100 years can offer school educators the possibility of creating a compelling theory of school experience and related methods for inquiry, all grounded in reflective practice aided by responsible boundaries as the essential path toward the development of understanding, growth, and freedom.

Together, both traditions articulate the value of empathy as vital and necessary for appreciating the dynamic of transforming action into insight and insight into action. Together, both can lead schools toward identifying and managing those inevitable shadow forces, basic assumptions, and individual and social defenses that can frame the human condition, pulling it toward regressive behaviors that can arrest development, hinder understanding, and resist learning (Stokes, 1994). Together, both progressive education and psychoanalysis can lead us toward creating tangible and dependable structures for deep, developmentally attuned engagement in the culture of our schools in ways that will foster what Dewey understood as the highest standards and habits of mind a school can foster: open-mindedness, thoroughness, and wholeheartedness, all aimed at realizing the potential for the personal development of character to contribute to the formation of curiosity and creativity, citizenship and understanding, freedom and justice (Dewey 1938).

HIDDEN QUESTIONS AND THE SCHOOL ROMANCE: NARRATIVE CONTRIBUTIONS TO A THEORY OF THE SUBJECTIVE EXPERIENCE OF SCHOOL LIFE

Core clinical psychoanalytic concepts offer teachers and school administrators vital insights for their own observations, understandings, and interpretations of school life. Beginning with Sigmund Freud's concepts of transference and countertransference, and extending from Anna Freud's work to Melanie Klein's ideas about splitting and projective identification, to Donald Winnicott's understandings of holding environment, transitional objects, and potential space, to Heinz Kohut's focus on empathy as a mode of observation and the developing coherence of the self, these theoretical concepts, among others, can enlighten discussions about the subjective experience of school life.

In addition, other concepts, developed in relation to applied psychoanalytic studies of organizational structures, such as primary task and basic assumptions (Bion, 1961), social defense (Menzies Lyth, 1959), and the quality of negative capability (French, 2001/2009), and reparative leadership (Alford, 1989), to mention just a few, all contribute to the development of deeper understandings of the psychodynamics of teaching and learning in schools.

Developing a working theory of school experience is especially important today as the pressures on schools are as great as ever. As rapid and significant social changes have occurred, there is a growing perception that the family, the church, and the neighborhood community have weakened in their capacities to be stable social institutions capable of helping parents raise and educate their children. In this context, the public continues to turn to the school, wishing it to be that one stable, safe, and secure place where children can learn and grow. Feeling fragmented by the increasingly complex demands of adult life, parents and policy makers continue to embrace the school as the key institutional solution to manage both general and specific feelings of hope and disillusionment. When we idealize the school as a place in which we best anticipate and meet society's needs, we set the stage for both the inspired fulfillment of that ideal and the inevitable disappointment that will result when such ideals confront life's everyday realities. The more difficult the problem the school is expected to solve, the more powerful is the wish to idealize the school's capacity to save society, and each individual, as well. The more powerful the wish, the more likely and more painful is the inevitable disillusionment. The more powerful the disillusionment, the more important it becomes for the school to establish reliable structures for creating reparative processes.

This interpretive approach to inquiry into schooling and education provides an essential, experience-near (Geertz, 1983) understanding of the dynamics that structure the subjective experience of school life. Dennis McCaughan and I have called this dynamic the *school romance* (Frank and McCaughan, 1995).

Similar to Freud's notion of the *family romance* (Freud, 1908), the *school romance* is a concept that describes a significant and central process of emotional experience in school life. This is a process organized around feelings of idealization, disillusionment, and reparation—as educators, students, and parents work to maintain hope and sustain growth despite the inevitable disappointments that can happen in schools. Issues of ambivalence and identification join with feelings of conflict and love, aggression and creativity, fear and hope to inform the kinds of transference relationships and unconscious defensive strategies children and adults, individually and in groups, can have toward the school.

The school's promise as an institution dedicated to human development and learning lies in the abilities of those who work in our schools to sustain meaningful ideals and values through the essential structures of school culture, curriculum, and pedagogy and through the faculty's relationships with students, colleagues, and parents. Educators must attend to these dynamic relationships in ways that anticipate and manage the inevitable idealizations, wishes, disappointments, conflicts, joys, and resolutions that occur in the course of everyday school life. One way for educators to be aware of the presence of the powerful, if sometimes subtle, psychological forces we are describing as the school romance, is for educators to be attuned to the expression of questions that may be being asked by people in the school community in the most indirect, disguised, and hidden ways.

For more than twenty years, a group of educators at Francis W. Parker School in Chicago has been working explicitly to integrate aspects of these two traditions into the life of the school in order to develop a working theory of school experience that is grounded in the narratives that people tell about their experiences of school life. Stories of school are stories of the human condition, and many of the stories chosen for inclusion in a book entitled, *A Passion for Education* (Frank and Kaplan, 2005) were presented at one of two national roundtable conferences held at Francis W. Parker School: "The School Romance: Psychodynamic Approaches to the Subjective Experience of School Life" (1995) and "Hidden Questions: Listening to the Subjective Experience of School Life" (2000). These essays were later re-published in the early issues of *Schools: Studies in Education: A Journal for Inquiry Into the Subjective Experience of School Life*, a scholarly international education journal the Francis W. Parker School founded for pre-Kindergarten through twelfth grade public and independent school educators, and others interested in the psychology of school life, and that is now published by the University of Chicago Press (www.journals.uchicago.edu/Schools). Both of these conferences and the *Schools* journal are developmental links in an emerging educational and intellectual effort that I call *The School Romance Project*.

The School Romance Project aims to understand the subjective experience of school life in order to improve relationships and communication in the classroom and in the broader culture of the school. The insights developed from inquiry into the subjective experience of school life aim to help educators better understand the social and psychological themes that are alive in classroom teaching, curriculum development, and in faculty, administrative, parent, and board leadership. *The School Romance Project* intends to promote innovative and interdisciplinary conversations among local, national, and international educators, nursery through university, and with psychodynamically oriented clinicians and systems-psychodynamic organizational consultants who are interested in the human interplay between emotions and learning in the institutional context of school life (Gould, Stapley, & Stein, 2001; Frank, 2003; Sievers, 2009.)

The experience of the school dynamic, the *school romance*, is similar to what Freud describes in the *family romance* where a child's psychological growth, or resistance to growth, is shaped by how she or he experiences the pleasures and inevitable disappointments of family life. The task of growing up, he said, involves working through the early losses children can experience when they realize that their parents are not gods, and, in time, how they have to find ways to come to terms with the reality of who their parents are as mortal human beings, and, in addition, who one is oneself as a person, related to, but separate from one's parents.

In addition, Freud made us aware that as human beings we can unwittingly experience the present as a repetition of our own unique personal experiences of the past. This occurs in moments of return: when we unintentionally bring to the present the intrapsychic and socio-cultural systems paradigms of experience that have shaped our pasts. When we transfer aspects of our personal pasts onto the present in ways that we are not fully aware—especially our experience of our relationships with our own parents—can often compromise, and sometimes support, what we are trying to do and learn in our present relationships with friends and family, colleagues and associates, teachers and classmates, and with the parents of our students. If one can imagine that each student, teacher, and parent in the school has at least two or three major childhood transferences alive within them at any one time simply because we are all human beings, and then multiply that number by the number of students and teachers in the school, it is easy to see that schools can be very overcrowded psychological environments. And schools can be especially overwhelming environments as well, when teachers and school administrators are not aware and attuned to these issues as they arise in the lives of their students, colleagues, and parents, as well as within their own countertransference reactions to their own experience of their relationships with others in school life, when they are not prepared to manage the complicated and even fascinating dynamics that can come with these salient emotional dynamics within school experience.

Institutional memory can be a vital part of a school's culture, giving it a sense of history, legacy and meaning. But schools, like all organizations, can also suffer from social defenses in the form of institutional repetitions where aspects of the school's past are replayed unwittingly in the present, often playing out dramas, telling stories, and carrying meanings that have profound psychological significance but are not necessarily healthy, productive, or in keeping with the intended scripts currently promoted by the school (Douglas, 1986; Frank, 2004; Hirschhorn, 1988).

Stories told about school life are told in relationship to the search for questions and their meanings. To ask questions is to be human, even when we do not know we are asking questions of ourselves or others, even when we may be ambivalent about wanting others or ourselves to discover those questions or feelings that we have worked to conceal, whether wittingly or unwittingly. Such questions are present in the interrogative and in the declarative. Questions are expressed in words, silences, and gestures. There is, as good teachers and clinicians can attest, more to attending to the dynamics of hidden questions than the act of listening. Attending to hidden questions requires seeing, touching, smelling, tasting, and imagining. And in response to what we hear, see, touch, smell, taste, and imagine, we must determine how these experiences can evoke within us—as educators, as adults, as former adolescents and children—associations, memories, and feelings that still may be alive with questions buried somewhere in words, actions, and fantasies.

Forming questions, engaging in conversation, discovering answers, and forming more questions are activities that lie at the core of educational experience. Students and teachers ask questions about the world, themselves, their experiences, their relationships, the relevance and imagination of what they are teaching and learning, the meaning, enjoyment, and frustration of what they are studying, and the very nature of their schools. Parents, policy makers, and citizens at large also ask questions about the purpose and direction of schooling in contemporary American society.

Yet the experience of teaching and learning in schools is also shaped by questions that are not asked, or by those that are not quite fully formulated, but are instead lying in wait, cautiously, restlessly, at the edge of awareness. These questions are often revealed and concealed in the stories we both tell and do not tell about our experiences as teachers and as students. These are usually essential questions of trust, self-confidence, belonging, identity, justice, inclusion, relationships, and meaning. The potential for making meaningful connections—with people and with ideas—lies in the ability of educators to attend to and reflect on the essential questions being asked, whether in oral language or body language, no matter how implicitly disguised or explicitly revealed. These hidden questions express the underlying subtexts and textured contexts that permeate the subjective experience of teaching and learning in schools. Identifying and understanding the experiences that shape such questions can also raise issues about the broader context and culture of the school.

What, then, are hidden questions? How can we anticipate what they will be? How do we listen for them—those of our students and our own? How is our listening enhanced or hindered by the culture of the school as well as by our personal experiences and points of view? And, if identified, how do we make sense of these questions and respond to the person asking or resisting awareness of the questions? Through the curriculum we design? The modes of engagement we use in our teaching methods? Our manner of relating to students? Our shaping of school life and its culture? Our capacity to reflect and act on those hidden questions that stir within our own hearts?

Attending to the hidden questions that students, teachers, and parents may be pondering with all of our resourceful capacities—both personal and institutional—is a powerful way that schools can support the education and growth of students, teachers, and parents alike. There is a natural inclination for human beings to idealize others. It is just as natural that everyday encounters and relationships will reshape those idealizations. The real work of schools lies in the dedicated and creative labors of teachers, administrators, parents, and students to foster reparative moments and processes that can further learning and growth despite our encounters with frustration, crisis, and oppression.

We cannot attend to the hidden questions our students may ask, however, without encountering the hidden questions that may inform, and at times complicate, our own experience. In this way, the ideals and practice of education depend on our skills and courage to engage ourselves and our students in reflection, with all of its promise for pain and pleasure, risk and surprise, revelation and discovery, inquiry and resolution.

This approach to education assumes that there is more to observe and understand about human experience in general, and the experience of teaching and learning in particular, than that which is readily available at a quick or convenient glance. Through the study of the subjective experience of school life, reflective teachers will encounter a wide array of feelings, ideas, and meanings—familiar and unfamiliar—that students, teachers, and parents connect to their experiences of schooling. To be thorough and comprehensive in our exploration of both the hidden and the apparent, the shadowed and the illuminated questions and dimensions of school experience, we must be willing to explore fully the desired—and dreaded—world of emotions and fantasies that fill our schools every day (Erb, 2004; Boldt & Salvio, 2006). To be sure, this is an approach to education that, for both realistic and defensive reasons, all too easily can get lost in the noise of the day-to-day challenges of managing a classroom, running a school, and leading an adult life, with all of its complexities and preoccupations.

The commitment to understanding the hidden questions that underlie school life requires us to engage in an experience of conversation and inquiry about nothing more or less than a fundamental tension in human life. It is a tension between presence and absence; between what is revealed and concealed, manifest and latent, conscious and unconscious; between what we see or wish to see and what is hidden from easy sight; between what passes for truth and what passes as disguise.

The promise of this approach to education lies in our capacity to appreciate how teaching and learning—and the broader life of the school—are shaped, in many ways, by the complexities of the human heart, with all of its mysteries, shadows, and contradictions, with all of its potential for wonder, awe, and curiosity. The human heart has the capacity for using silence to communicate something vital and real, for using talk to cloud and confuse genuine communication, for using clouded talk to express genuine, ambivalent feelings about the deep longing and desire we each have for the rapture of connection and recognition. This desire is often contained in the powerful yet tender wish to be remembered, indeed loved, by another, and the simultaneous terror we have of really being discovered, known, heard, exposed. For as human beings, both younger and older, we are inclined to want to be both lost and found, hidden and visible, wanting to be noticed yet afraid of what others, or we ourselves, might find. It takes the art and craft, indeed the soul, of being a reflective teacher to be present enough in students' lives to be able to give what Freud called an "evenly hovering attention," to discover the subtle gestures of wondering, asking, and questioning that can make all the difference in both the emerging life of a young student and the organizational dynamics of the school.

Being attuned as an empathic and wise observer of students is not an easy thing to do. To a teacher, administrator, or staff member, it can sometimes feel as if one is being asked to read and interpret each individual student's gestures, expressions, or words as if they were highly coded and mysterious omens. It is even harder to try to comprehend the text of complicated, nonverbal communications being expressed by groups of students (Frank, 2004).

Omens can be signs of good or bad things to come. They are understood to be messages of meaning that are hidden, disguised, concealed. Parents and teachers know how children and adolescents constantly send such not-so-easy-to-read messages of meaning to adults, friends, and themselves in communication often complexly encoded in words, gestures, and silences. Hidden in these messages are essential questions children and adolescents may ask about themselves: *Who will be my friends this year? Will I like my teacher, and will my teacher like me? What am I good at, and will anybody—a teacher, a parent, or classmate—notice or care enough to help me improve my abilities and help me identify, appreciate, and organize my hopes and ambitions, or support me through my own anxieties as I discover own identity?*

And make no mistake: as adults we ask our own versions of those very questions ourselves: *Why do I work in a school? Am I connecting with my students and are they connecting with me? Will any administrator or teacher ever really know and appreciate who I am and what I do and with my students in ways that will help me grow as a person and as a professional?*

We also ask questions about the organizational dynamics of the school: *How do we balance tradition and innovation? Structure and flexibility? Diversity and unity? Role and biography? Transition and stability? Management and leadership? Change and continuity? Conflict and collaboration? Authority and freedom?*

These are questions of trust, self-confidence, belonging, justice, inclusion, relationships, identity, and meaning. When we, as parents and educators, can hear the essential questions we are asking and being asked, however implicit or disguised, and respond with empathy and clarity, we can help young people, and each other, interpret and understand what we and they are asking and saying about our lives and our relationships to others and to the world.

Hidden questions are the omens we must read. They may present themselves to us in a glance, a sigh, a laugh, an argument, a drawing, a poem, answers on a math sheet, a burst of hustle, or a disappointing play in an athletic competition, a beaming or shy smile, a sad, angry, or joyful tear. We cannot take such omens, such messages and communications for granted. We must be present enough in the lives of our students and our colleagues to be able to read the messages, the signs, the omens when they appear to us, however briefly, cautiously, ambivalently or mysteriously.

The aim, then, is to cultivate among educators and other professionals who work with children and adolescents a conversation that will explore in depth the visible and invisible, the tangible texture and the intangible shadows of school experience. By identifying and understanding the hidden, less evident questions that shape the lives of students, educators, and parents, as well as the school institution as a whole, we can strive to understand the hopes and concerns people bring to school, their diverse experiences of both delight and disappointment, and the ways their experiences of the school's culture, curriculum, pedagogy, and human relationships support processes of growth, learning, and reparation.

This interpretive method counts on the courage of educators to tell their stories and to listen to those of others. These reflective accounts of teaching and learning reveal aspects of experience that people feel sure about, as well as dimensions of emotional experience that are shaped by uncertainty, doubt, and the unknown. Despite anxiety, resistance, and regression—and the risk and vulnerability to the self that can result from genuine institutional and self-inquiry—teachers, students, and parents can guide us, through their stories, toward a sense of community and growth than can result from such shared intimacy. These accounts of everyday school life can guide us toward remaining open to exploring the light as well as the shadows of our experience, both personal and collective. By exploring the subjective experience of school life, in breadth and depth, aided by the integration of ideas emerging from current thinking in progressive education and psychoanalysis, the school community, as a whole community, can inspire a feeling of freedom and possibility to persevere in our capacity to identify, understand, and appreciate the deeper meanings and purpose of teaching children and adolescents in school.

OUR TURN

Long ago, Dewey told us in an essay entitled, "The Need for a Philosophy of Education" that there is a vital need to have a clear philosophy of education and a theory of school experience that can integrate issues of social and psychological freedom for all people. He said:

> Perhaps the greatest need of and for a philosophy of education at the present time is the urgent need that exists for making clear in idea and effective practice that its end is social, and that the criterion to be applied in estimating the value of the practices that exist in schools is also social. It is true that the aim of education is the development of individuals to the utmost of their potentialities. But this statement in isolation leaves unanswered the question as to what is the measure of the development. A society of free individuals is one in which all, through their own work, contribute to the liberation and enrichment of the lives of others, is the only environment in which any individual can really grow normally to his full stature. An environment in which some are practically enslaved, degraded, limited, will always react to create conditions that prevent the full development even of those who fancy they enjoy complete freedom for unhindered growth. (Dewey 1934, p. 12)

Francis Parker and John Dewey believed that schools were places of great hope, promising freedom from oppression and freedom for creativity and justice. Psychoanalysis, as a body of ideas about the meaning of being human and a method of inquiry into individual, group, and organizational experience, offers educators insights that can guide teachers toward understanding how students and parents, and how they themselves, experience school life in ways that can both foster and inhibit growth. Only with that self-awareness can teachers and administrators summon the attention and the mature shaping of conditions that will foster curiosity and freedom in each individual, in the school as a whole, and in the broader promise of democratic citizenship. The *school romance* and *hidden questions*, along with other core psychoanalytic concepts, give teachers a useful set of concepts for encountering and working with the idealizations as well as the inevitable disappointments of everyday school life in a helpful and reparative fashion. Within this conceptual framework, educators can create, alone and with others, the opportunities to recover and to repair from those moments of rift and rupture. It is here, in the practical knowledge that grows out of reflection and communication, that we discover the real gift of teaching in schools.

This emerging unity of thought, influenced by current thinking in progressive education and in contemporary relational and systems psychoanalysis, and organized in part around the concepts of the *school romance* and *hidden questions*, can guide educators in our aim to help students develop character, talent, confidence, and integrity in order to join with others as citizens empowered to make a creative difference in the world. To do so means that teachers and administrators in a school, individually and collectively, need to find ways to reflect on their philosophy, their standards, and their practice of teaching, learning, and leadership in order fully answer the call to teach.

Colonel Parker once said this to a group of teachers new to his school:

> Teachers often complain of their social position, their salaries, and the lack of sympathy in the public. "The fault," dear teachers, "is not in our stars, but in ourselves, that we are the underlings." Instead of stubbornly standing, and obstinately denying that there is no need of reform, and that all so-called new methods are worthless; let us honestly, earnestly, prayerfully study the great science of teaching. Let us learn, and courageously apply the truths that shall set us free; and the day will soon come when the teacher will lead society, and mould opinion. (Parker 1894, p. 348)

There is simply no higher standard, passionate vision or romantic embrace for the call to education than this.

ACKNOWLEDGMENTS

This paper is a revised and updated version of my 2006 paper, "Progressive education and the school romance: Toward a theory of the subjective experience of school life," published in *A Passion for Education*, edited by Daniel B. Frank and Andy Kaplan. Chicago: Francis W. Parker School. (pp. 31–54). Publishing permission has been granted by the Francis W. Parker School.

REFERENCES

Alford, C. F. (1989). *Melanie Klein and critical social theory: An account of politics, art and reason based on her psychoanalytic theory.* New Haven: Yale University Press.

Barford, D. (2002). . *The Ship of thought: Essays on psychoanalysis and learning.* London: Karnac Books.

Boldt, G. and Salvio, P. (eds). (2006). *Love's return: Psychoanalytic essays on childhood, teaching and learning.* New York: Routledge.

Bion, W. (1961). *Experiences in Groups.* London: Tavistock.

Britzman, D. (2009). *The very thought of education: Psychoanalysis and the impossible professions.* New York: SUNY Press.

Cohler, B. J. (2006). *Desire, teaching and learning: An essay review on recent psychoanalytic contributions to education.* Schools 3 (2): 105–119.

Cohler, B. J. and R. Galatzer-Levy. (1993). *The essential other: A developmental psychology of the self.* New York: Basic Books.

Cottle, T. (2007). *On stories and theories: In appreciation of miss freud.* Schools 4 (2): 91–100.

Dewey, J. (1895/1964). What psychology can co for the teacher. In *John Dewey on education: Selected writings.* Chicago: University of Chicago Press, 195–211.

Dewey, J. (1915). *Schools of tomorrow.* New York: E.P. Dutton and Company.

Dewey, J. (1933/1964). Why reflective thinking must be an educational aim. In *John Dewey on education: Selected writings.* Chicago: University of Chicago Press, 212–228.

Dewey, J. (1934/1964). The need for a philosophy of education. In *John Dewey on education: Selected writings.* Chicago: University of Chicago Press, 3–14.

Dewey, J. (1938). *Experience & education.* New York: Simon and Schuster.

Dilg, M. (1999). *Race and culture in the classroom: Teaching and learning through multicultural education.* New York: Teachers College Press.

Douglas, M. (1986). *How institutions think.* Syracuse, NY: Syracuse University Press.

Erb, P. (2004). Engaging desire: The role of erotic energy in the classroom. *Schools* 1 (1): 101–128.

Erikson, K. (1976). *Everything in its path: Destruction of community in the Buffalo Creek flood.* New York: Simon and Schuster.

Frank, D. B. (2003). *Book review of The systems psychodynamics of organizations: Integrating the group relations approach, psychoanalytic and open systems perspectives.* Edited by Gould, L., Stapley, L., Stein, M. New York/London: Karnac, 2001. Human Relations 56 (3) March, 2003 349–354.

Frank, D. B. (2004). Improvisations of the immature: Interpreting the drama of the senior year. *Schools* 1 (2): 117–140.

Frank, D. B. (2005). Everything to help and nothing to hinder: Grandiosity, ambivalence, and boundaries in the alliance between parents and the school. *Schools* II (1):194–213.

Frank, D. B. and D. McCaughan. (1995). The school romance: Approaches to the subjective experience of school life. In *When love is not enough: The management of covert dynamics in organizations that treat children and adolescents*, ed. D. Piazza. Binghamton, NY: The Haworth Press, 75–105.

French, R. (2001/2009). 'Negative capability': A contribution to the understanding of creative leadership. 197-216. In Sievers, B. (2009). *Psychoanalytic studies of organizations: Contributions from the International Society for the Psychoanalytic Studies of Organizations (ISPSO).*

Freud, S. (1908). Family Romances. In the standard edition. 9. London: Hogarth Press. 237–241

Freud, S. (1914/1955). *Some reflections on schoolboy psychology.* Vol. 13 of *The standard edition.* London: Hogarth Press, 241–244.

Garrison, J. (1997). *Dewey and eros: Wisdom and desire in the art of teaching.* New York: Teachers College Press.

Geertz, C. (1983). *Local knowledge: Further essays in interpretive anthropology.* New York: Basic Books.

Hirschhorn, L. (1988). *The workplace within: Psychodynamics of organizational life.* Cambridge: MIT Press.

Gould, L., Stapley, L., Stein, M. (2001). *The systems psychodynamics of organizations: Integrating the group relations approach, psychoanalytic and open systems perspectives.* New York/London: Karnac.

Huffington, C., D. Armstrong, W. Halton, L. Hoyle, and J. Pooley (eds). (2004). *Working below the surface: The emotional life of contemporary organizations.* London: Karnac.

Jersild, A. T. (1955). *When teachers face themselves.* New York: Teachers College Press.

Kaplan, A. (2004). Developing Character in and Educational Community. *Schools* 1 (2): 141–165.

Lawrence-Lightfoot, S. (2003). *The essential conversation: What parents and teachers can learn about each other.* New York: Random House.

Marris, P. (1974). *Loss and Change.* New York: Basic Books.

Menzies Lyth, Isabel. (1959). *The functions of social systems as a defence against anxiety: A report on a study of the nursing service of a general hospital.* Human Relations 13: 95-121.

O'Loughlin, M. (2010). Ghostly presences in children's lives: Towards a psychoanalysis of the social. In O'Loughlin, M. and Johnson, R. (eds). (2010). *Imagining Children Otherwise: Theoretical and cultural perspectives on childhood subjectivity.* New York: Peter Lang Publishing.

Parker, F. W. (1894/2001). *Talks on pedagogics: An outline of the theory of concentration and other writings,* ed. F. J. Cooke and E. A. Wygant. Chicago: Francis W. Parker School.

Salzberger-Wittenberg, I., G. Henry, and E. Osborne. (1983). *The emotional experience of learning and teaching.* London: Routledge.

Sievers, B. (ed) (2009). *Psychoanalytic studies of organizations: Contributions from the international society for the psychoanalytic studies of organizations (ISPSO).* London: Karnac.

Stokes, J. (1994). The unconscious at work in groups and teams: Contributions from the work of Wilfred Bion. In *The unconscious at work: Individual and organizational stress in the human services.* Ed. A. Obholzer and V. Z. Roberts. London: Routledge, 19–28.

Tieman, J. *The ghosts in the classroom: A primer in the lessons of shame.* Schools 4 (2): 39–55.

Todd, S. (ed) (1997). *Learning desire: Perspectives on pedagogy, culture and the unsaid.* New York: Routledge.

Todd, S. (2003). *Learning from the other: Levinas, psychoanalysis, and ethical possibilities in education.*

Youell, B. (2006). *The learning relationship: Psychoanalytic thinking in education.* London: Karnac.

Index

About the Contributors

Ana Archangelo is an associate professor at the Faculty of Education at UNICAMP (University of Campinas—Brazil) where she teaches undergraduate and post-graduate courses and supervises Master and PhD degrees. Her research interests focus on Social Exclusion, Psychoanalysis, and Education. She has investigated children who have shown what she has coined as "the capacity not to learn" for the last ten years. She was a Visiting Fellow at the Centre for Psycho-Social Studies (University of the West of England) and at the Centre for Psychoanalytic Studies (University of Essex), both in the UK. She has published chapters in books and articles in national and international journals. Her first book is "Love and Hate in Teachers' Lives" (O amor e o ódio no vida do professor), published in Brazil.

Derek Bunyard is currently the route manager for the Early Childhood Pathway in Education Studies at the University of Winchester, UK, having previously held various management positions in the university within a number of disciplines. His involvement with education has covered both the Arts and Sciences, while his specialist research area is centered on the philosophy of representation. His interest in psychoanalysis is wide-ranging, and in relation to early childhood studies this has been particularly influenced by the work of Melanie Klein and Donald Winnicott.

Carrie Catapano, LCSW, has over fourteen years experience providing psychodynamic psychotherapy to children and parents on a broad range of issues. Carrie serves as the Head of School and Clinical Director at West End Day School. Specifically at West End Day, Carrie and her staff of teachers and social workers, employ psychodynamic principles to help students tap into the emotions that are at the root of their distress. They ensure that every child's unique feelings are heard, addressed, and incorporated into overcoming any social or educational obstacle. This is the hallmark of the school. Carrie received her Masters degree from New York University and also completed her post Master's training at the New York Psychoanalytic Society and Institute. She maintains her private practice on the Upper West Side of Manhattan. The West End Day School is a small, independent special education private school, located on the Upper West Side of Manhattan, which caters to children with learning and social issues.

Carola B. Chase, LCSW, is a psychoanalyst and psychotherapist in private practice in New York City, working with children, adolescents, and adults. She is a member of The Contemporary Freudian Society, where she received her psychoanalytic training. Prior to this, Ms. Chase received an MS from the Bank Street College of Education in New York City and taught pre-school for several years. She was a consultant to a number of pre-schools, where she worked with staff, children, and parents. She presented a talk on "The Moral Development of Elementary School-Aged Children" at the law firm Cravath & Swain, and has spoken on other issues about childhood related issues (sibling rivalry, managing behavioral problems at home, etc.) to groups of parents. A paper on Anna Freud's Diagnostic Profile, "The Aging of the Anna Freud Diagnostic Profile: A Re-Examination and Re-application of the Psychoanalytic Assessment with Older Adults" won the 2009 Anna Freud Prize. This paper, in a different form, is published in Volume 65 of The Psychoanalytic Study of The Child. Ms. Chase is also a graduate of New Directions, a writing program connected with the Washington Center for Psychoanalysis.

Jonathan Cohen is an educator-clinician. He has worked with K-12 students, educators and parents since 1974 as a middle school special educator, school and clinical psychologist, practicing child and adult psychoanalyst, professional development facilitator, and school climate improvement leader/learner. He is also the co-founder and president of the National School Climate Center: Educating Minds and Hearts Because the Three R's Are Not Enough; Adjunct Professor in Psychology and Education, Teachers College, Columbia University; and Adjunct Professor in Education, School of Professional Studies, City University of New York. He has and does consult to the schools, districts, State Departments of Education, President Obama's Federal Bully Prevention Partnership, and the UN Children's fund on social, emotional, and civic learning, mental health/educational issues, bully prevention, student leadership and school climate improvement efforts. He is the author of many papers and books including the award winning *Educating Minds and Hearts: Social Emotional Learning and the Passage Into Adolescence* *and Caring Classrooms / Intelligent Schools: The Social Emotional Education of Young Children.*

Howard H. Covitz, PhD, ABPP, NCPsyA, is a later middle-aged psychoanalyst engaged in the private psychoanalytic treatment of personality disorders. He came to this role via a twisting and winding road that wound its way in and out of biblical studies, theoretical mathematics, teaching, and educational administration. He has taught high school, undergraduate, and graduate courses in diverse areas, including: Biblical Characterology, Theoretical Mathematics, Clinical Psychology, and Statistics. He was training analyst and—for many years—Director of the Institute for Psychoanalytic Psychotherapy in Bryn Mawr, PA. He lives with his wife in the Philadelphia suburbs from whence they travel to visit their grandchildren and their three grown children who have long-acted as able critics of his writings. His Oedipal Paradigms in Collision (1997) was nominated for the Gradiva Book of the Year Award.

Daniel B. Frank, PhD, is the principal of the Francis W. Parker School in Chicago, and Executive Editor of Schools: Studies in Education, an international education journal published by the University of Chicago Press that is dedicated to understanding the subjective experience of school life. Dan is a member of the School Liaison Committee of the American Psychoanalytic Association, and is the recent past-Executive Director of the International Society for the Psychoanalytic Study of Organizations. He speaks and writes about leadership in organizations and has been a Lecturer in Psychiatry at the University of Chicago and formerly taught in the Teacher Education Program at the Institute for Psychoanalysis in Chicago. Dan is a graduate of the University of Chicago, Amherst College, and the Francis W. Parker School.

Al Galves is a licensed psychologist in Colorado. He is the Executive Director of the International Society for Ethical Psychology and Psychiatry and a member of the Board of Directors of MindFreedom International. He is the author of *Harness Your Dark Side*. His website is www.algalves.com. He is retired and lives in Las Cruces, New Mexico.

Leon Hoffman, MD, chief psychiatrist at West Day School, has been a psychiatrist for four decades and a psychoanalyst for three decades. He is a Board Certified Adult, Adolescent, and Child Psychiatrist as well as Certified in Adult, Adolescent, and Child Psychoanalysis by the American Psychoanalytic Association. He has extensive experience with children with social and emotional difficulties, their parents, and the educators who work with them. He has been at the West End Day School for nearly two decades and has helped develop an interdisciplinary approach at West End Day School with psychodynamics as an umbrella feature of the educational and socio-emotional approach. He has published widely in a variety of areas both for the professional as well as general public.

Patrick Lewis is a storyteller-teacher-researcher working with children, undergraduate, and graduate students in Early Childhood & Elementary Education in the Faculty of Education at the University of Regina.

Karen L. Lombardi is professor at the Derner Institute of Advanced Psychological Studies, Adelphi University, Garden City, New York, and on the faculty of the Northwest Center for Psychoanalysis, Portland, Oregon, as well as on the faculty of the Postgraduate Programs for Psychotherapy and Psychoanalysis at Adelphi University. She is the author of numerous articles and book chapters as well as the author, with Naomi Rucker, of *Subject Relations: Unconscious Experience and Relational Psychoanalysis*, published by Routledge. She is currently working on a book concerning the psychic effects of internet culture on teenagers. She has a private practice in psychotherapy and psychoanalysis on Long Island, treating children and adults.

Robbie Lloyd is post-doctoral research fellow in Youth Health & Wellbeing at the Menzies School of Health Research, Darwin. Robbie has been working in and out of education for forty years focusing on child-centered learning and whole-school-cultures of well-being, and he has also combined community development and journalism with that focus on empowering local development, plus acceptance of difference as a gift among all humans. His latest work, *The All Fruits Theory* (Lloyd 2012, UndergowthInc, Darwin), argues for greater celebration of difference in consciousness as a strength, rather than pathologising and measuring by the psy-ed industries (psychology and education etc). Working as a Post-Doctoral Research Fellow in Youth Health & Wellbeing, based in Darwin, Robbie continues his twenty year work partnering with Indigenous friends on community empowerment and increased choice of life paths. Spirit-based, cross-cultural, cross-generational, and holistic in all approaches, Robbie sees creativity, imagination, conversation, relationships, discernment, mystery and wonder as the bases of healthy, hopeful nurturing development for children and young people.

Karen Lupe is a qualified counselor and psychotherapist- a graduate of the Psychosynthesis Institute of Transpersonal Psychology, Auckland, New Zealand. She has published several papers on the subjects of psychology, culture, and collective trauma. These include: "An Ocean with Many Shores: Indigenous Consciousness and the Thinking Heart" published in "PeninaUliuli: Contemporary Challenges for Pacific Peoples." Edited by Culbertson, Agee, and Makasiale 2007; "Being Afakasi" co-author- ibid; "Standing on the Threshold" published in "Su'esu'e Manogi- In Search of Fragrance" by Tui'atua Tupua Tamasese Ta'isi Efi et al. (editors) 2008. In 2007 Karen Lupe took on the role of cultural research consultant for the year long research project "The Afakasi Project." The project was conducted under the auspices of Auckland University to explore the self perceptions and experiences of Samoan mixed race adults and youth. No longer working in private practice as a psychotherapist, she is currently a student for the ministerial program of the Centre for Sacred Studies, California and continues to write part-time. Although in her client practice Karen worked primarily with adults, she, as a mother of four children, is passionately concerned about the welfare and well-being of this new generation of children. She believes that the very vulnerable, traumatized child carries an extra heavy psychic burden; already broken in spirit at a tender age, deserves the very best help that teachers, therapists, and other professionals can provide.

Katy Meyer, MS Ed., has worked in the educational field for more than fourteen years. She currently serves as the Education Head at West End Day School (WEDS), a school for children with special needs, where she supervises the educational program and develops curriculum. Before joining the WEDS staff, Katy worked in a private school, first as a classroom teacher for seven years and then as a learning specialist for four years. She obtained her Bachelor's Degree in Inclusive Elementary Education from Syracuse University and has two Master's Degrees—the first in Reading and Literacy from Bank Street College; and the second in Administration and Supervision from Fordham University. Katy is certified by New York State in Special Education, General Education and as a Reading Teacher and as a School Building Leader.

Michael O'Loughlin, PhD, is professor at Adelphi University, New York, is on the faculty of Derner Institute of Advanced Psychological Studies and in the School of Education. He is a clinical and research supervisor in the PhD program in Clinical Psychology and on the faculty of the Postgraduate Programs in Psychoanalysis and Psychotherapy at Adelphi. He published *The Subject of Childhood* in 2009 and edited *Imagining Children Otherwise: Theoretical and Critical Perspectives on Childhood Subjectivity* with Richard Johnson in 2010. He is co-editor with Glenys Lobban and Cora Smith of *Psychodynamic Psychotherapy in Contemporary South Africa: Theory, Practice, and Policy Perspectives*, to be published by University of Witwatersrand Press in Johannesburg in 2013. He is editor of the companion volume *The Uses of Psychoanalysis in Working with Children's Emotional Lives* also published by Jason Aronson. His interests include the working through of intergenerational and collective trauma, the social origins of psychosis and schizophrenia, and the emotional lives of children. He is currently Co-Chair of the Association for the Psychoanalysis of Culture and Society and he is treasurer of the Joint Psychoanalytic Conference. He is a research affiliate at Austen Riggs Center where he conducts research on psychosis in collaboration with Marilyn Charles.

Devin Thornburg is a professor of education at Adelphi University, specializing in learning and development of diverse populations and school reform. His doctorate in counseling psychology led to several years of clinical work and psychoanalytic training with children after he was a classroom teacher and before he was a university professor. His publications have spanned almost three decades, representing his scholarly and professional interests in work with children from culturally and linguistically diverse populations, their families and their teachers.

Norma Tracey is a member of the Australian Association of Social Work (MAASW) and has been a member of the New South Wales Institute of Psychoanalytic Psychotherapy (NSWIPP) for many years. Apart from her private practice of twenty-five years she has worked especially with Aboriginal mothers and infants for the last ten years. She is the author of two books, several booklets, and some thirty nationally and internationally published papers. She is co-founder of Gunawirra limited, a group of professionals who care for Aboriginal mothers and infants from pregnancy through to five years of age. They work in twenty-five pre-school centers throughout NSW.

Fabio Camargo Bandeira Villela is an assistant professor in the Department of Education at UNESP, Presidente Prudente campus. He graduated in Psychology at PUC-SP and in Law at Integrated Faculties "Antônio Eufrásio de Toledo" in Presidente Prudente. His Masters degree is in Education at PUC-SP and his PhD will be in Education (Psychology of Education) at UNICAMP. He has done research in psychoanalysis, as well as in Psychoanalysis and Education. He has developed projects involving playful activities for children with learning disabilities attributed to emotional factors and has written articles about Psychoanalysis and the classroom.

Donna Wolf-Palacio, LCSW, MFA, is a psychoanalyst and family therapist in Philadelphia. She is the Training and Education Coordinator for Hall Mercer Community Mental Health Center of Pennsylvania Hospital/UPHS/ She received her psychoanalytic training as a Fellow at the Postgraduate Center Institute in New York. She also has an MFA in Creative Writing from Columbia University and has taught a poetry workshop at the University of the Arts. A book of her poems, "What I Don't Know," was published by Finishing Line Press. She has received grants from the National Endowment for the Humanities and the Leeway Foundation and had a fellowship at the Psychoanalytic Center of Philadelphia.

www.ingramcontent.com/pod-product-compliance
Ingram Content Group UK Ltd.
Pitfield, Milton Keynes, MK11 3LW, UK
UKHW012035150926
475560UK00001B/23

9 780765 709219